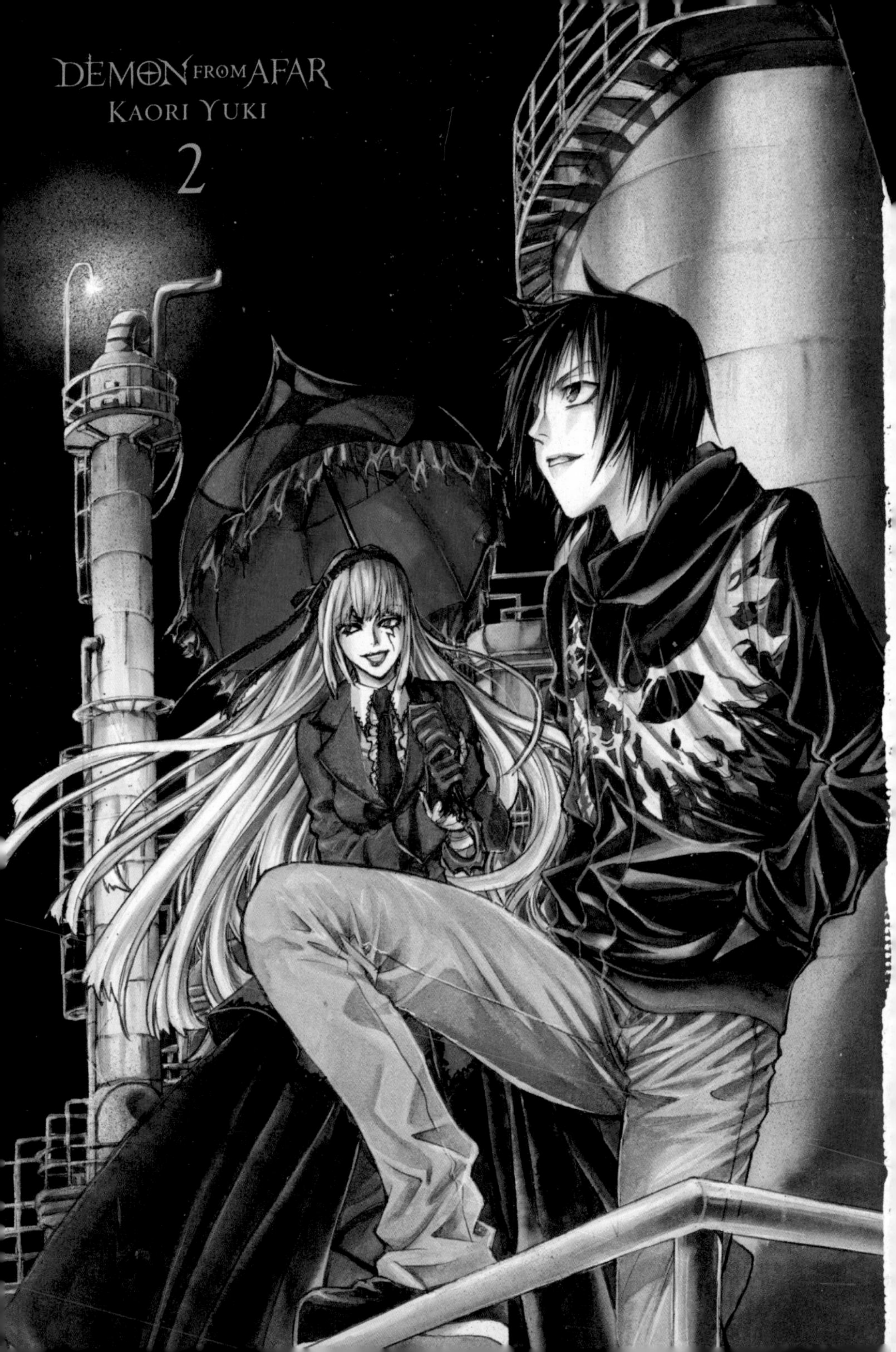
DEMON FROM AFAR
KAORI YUKI
2

DEMON FROM AFAR

Imperial Capital

Imperial Capital Arc
Chapter 5

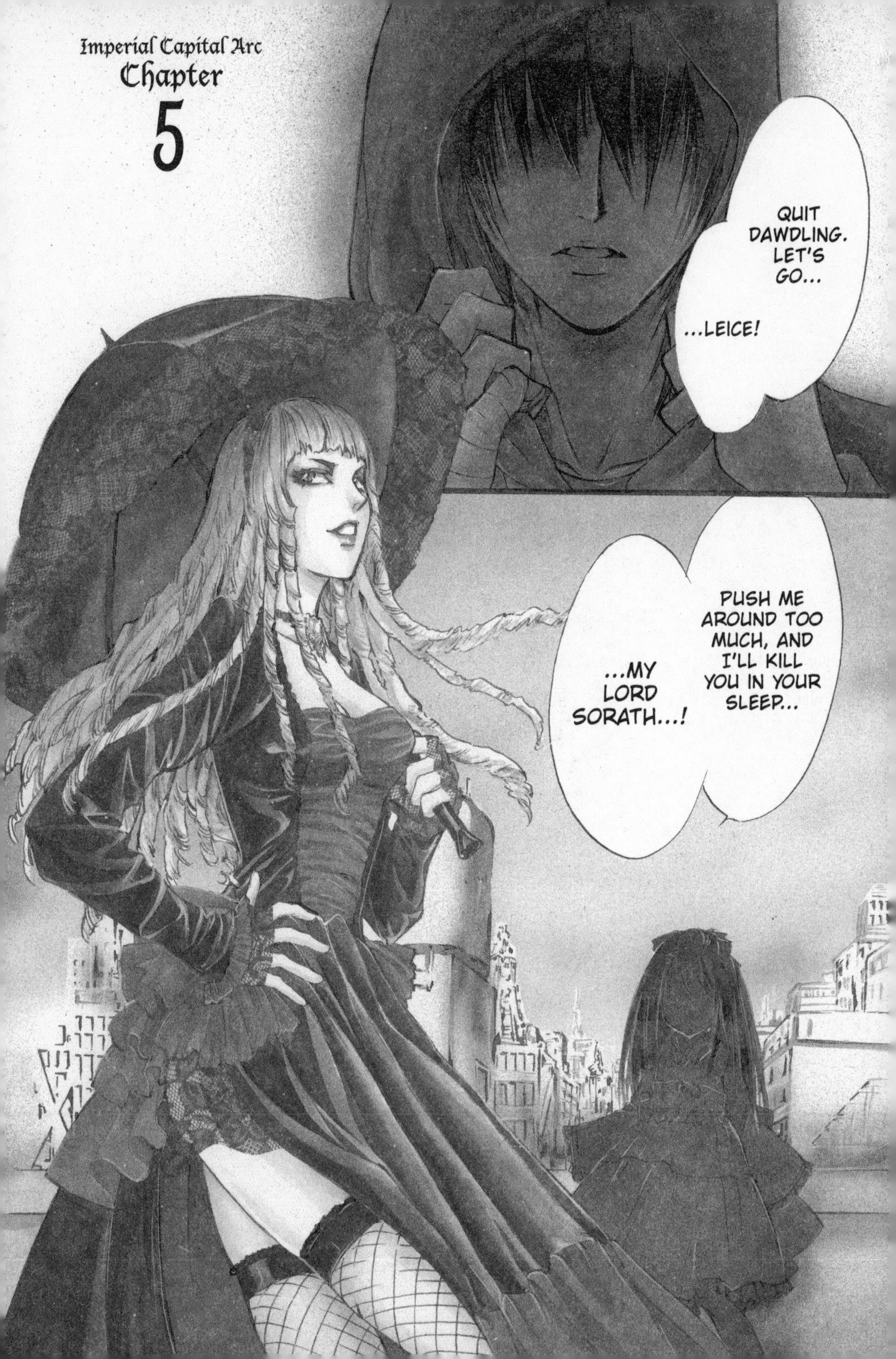
QUIT DAWDLING. LET'S GO...
...LEICE!
PUSH ME AROUND TOO MUCH, AND I'LL KILL YOU IN YOUR SLEEP...
...MY LORD SORATH...!

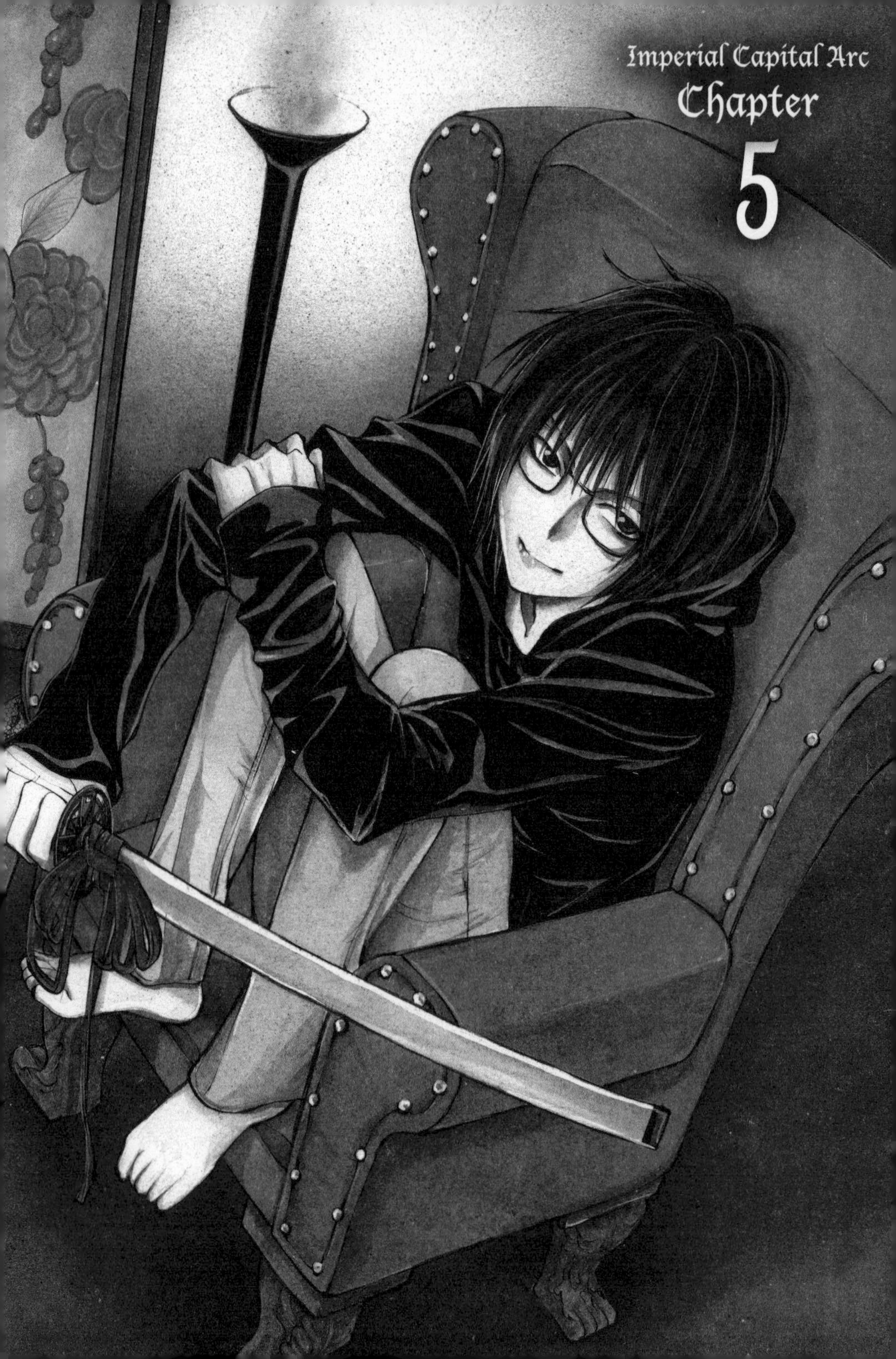
Imperial Capital Arc
Chapter
5

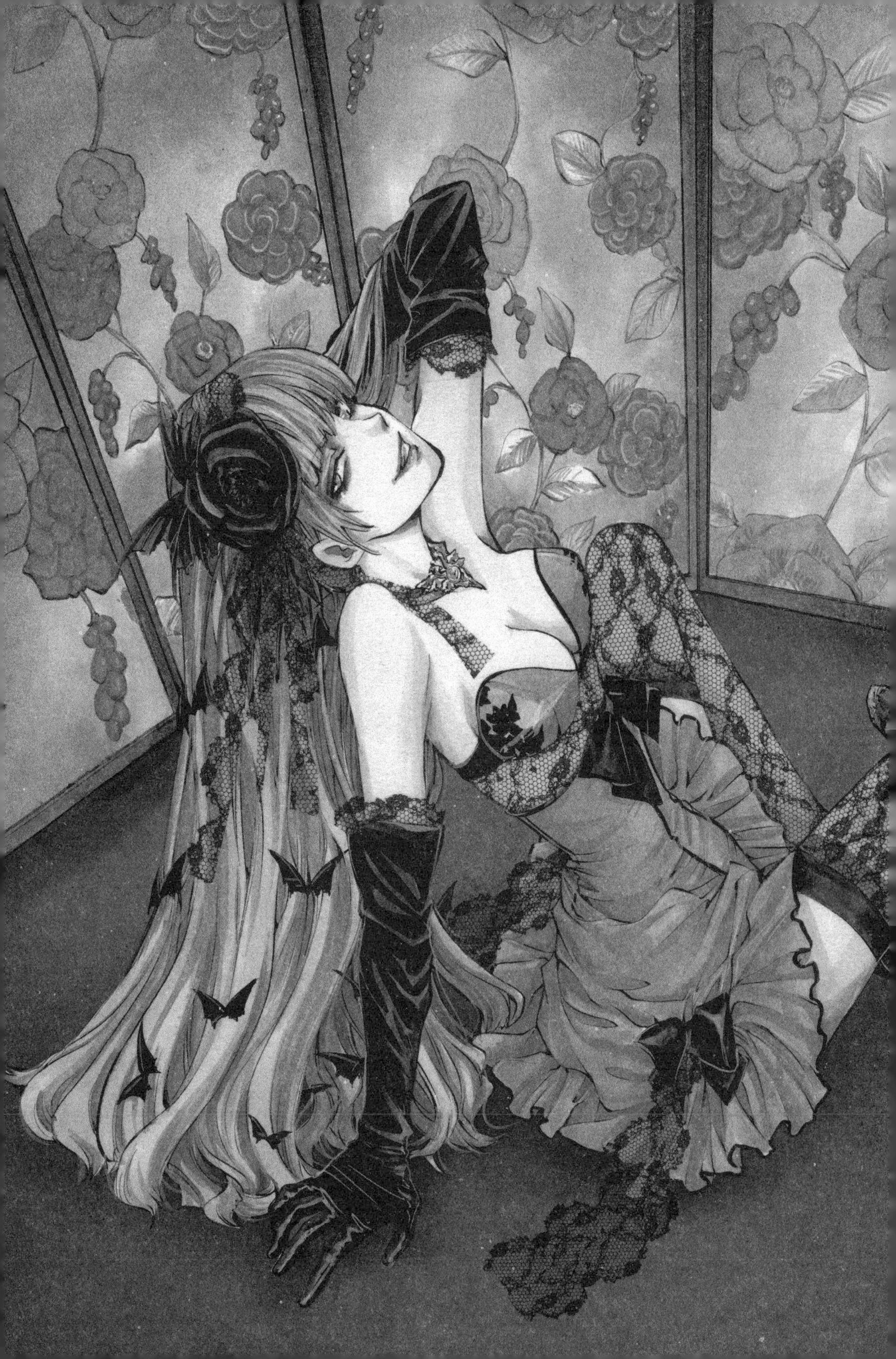

Characters

Garan

Baron Kamichika's son, and Sorath's cherished best friend. Truly loves Kiyora, his fiancée.

Kiyora

Garan's fiancée. Yin Miko used as a vessel for Noella. When Garan learns of her feelings for Sorath, it destroys their friendship.

Leice

The beautiful woman who serves as Baron Kamichika's closest accomplice. Her true identity is Mephistopheles, Duke of Hell. Targets Garan at his weakest and seduces him.

Sorath

Buried in rubble in the earthquake, Sorath was rescued by Garan. Bears a mysterious mark on his hand. Pledges eternal friendship with Garan and Kiyora, but their bond ruptures when Garan misreads Sorath's relationship with Kiyora.

Noella

The soul of the Yang Miko that enters Kiyora's body. She and Sorath are drawn to each other.

Sakaki

The mysterious acolyte who lives at the estate. Ostensibly in the Baron's service, but for some reason seems to be protecting Sorath.

Baron Kamichika

Summons the Lord of Great Terror, the root of all evil, in an attempt to attain eternal life and absolute power. High-handed and oppressive towards everyone.

An imperial Capital in an era of splendor and romanticism. The orphan Sorath is taken in as a servant at the dubiously nicknamed Blood Blossom Manor. As he probes into the secrets of the unsavory Baron, Sorath learns of an impending ceremony called Walpurgis Night. Spying on the ceremony, Sorath sees the Baron summon the Lord of Great Terror, only to have the demon go on a rampage thanks to the betrayal of the Baron's mysterious female companion Leice. What will become of the imperial Capital and Sorath!?

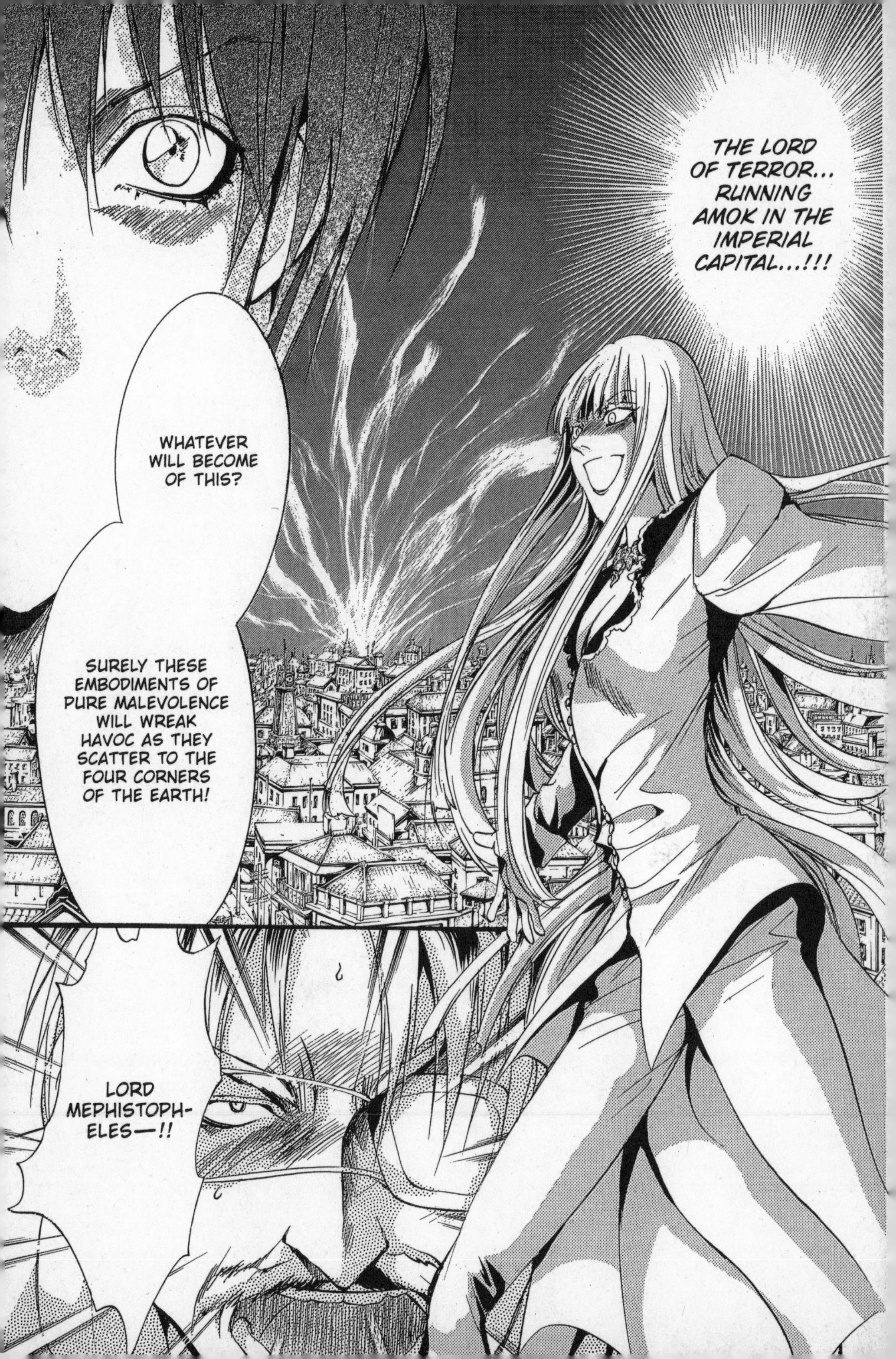
THE LORD OF TERROR... RUNNING AMOK IN THE IMPERIAL CAPITAL...!!!
WHATEVER WILL BECOME OF THIS?
SURELY THESE EMBODIMENTS OF PURE MALEVOLENCE WILL WREAK HAVOC AS THEY SCATTER TO THE FOUR CORNERS OF THE EARTH!
LORD MEPHISTOPH-ELES—!!

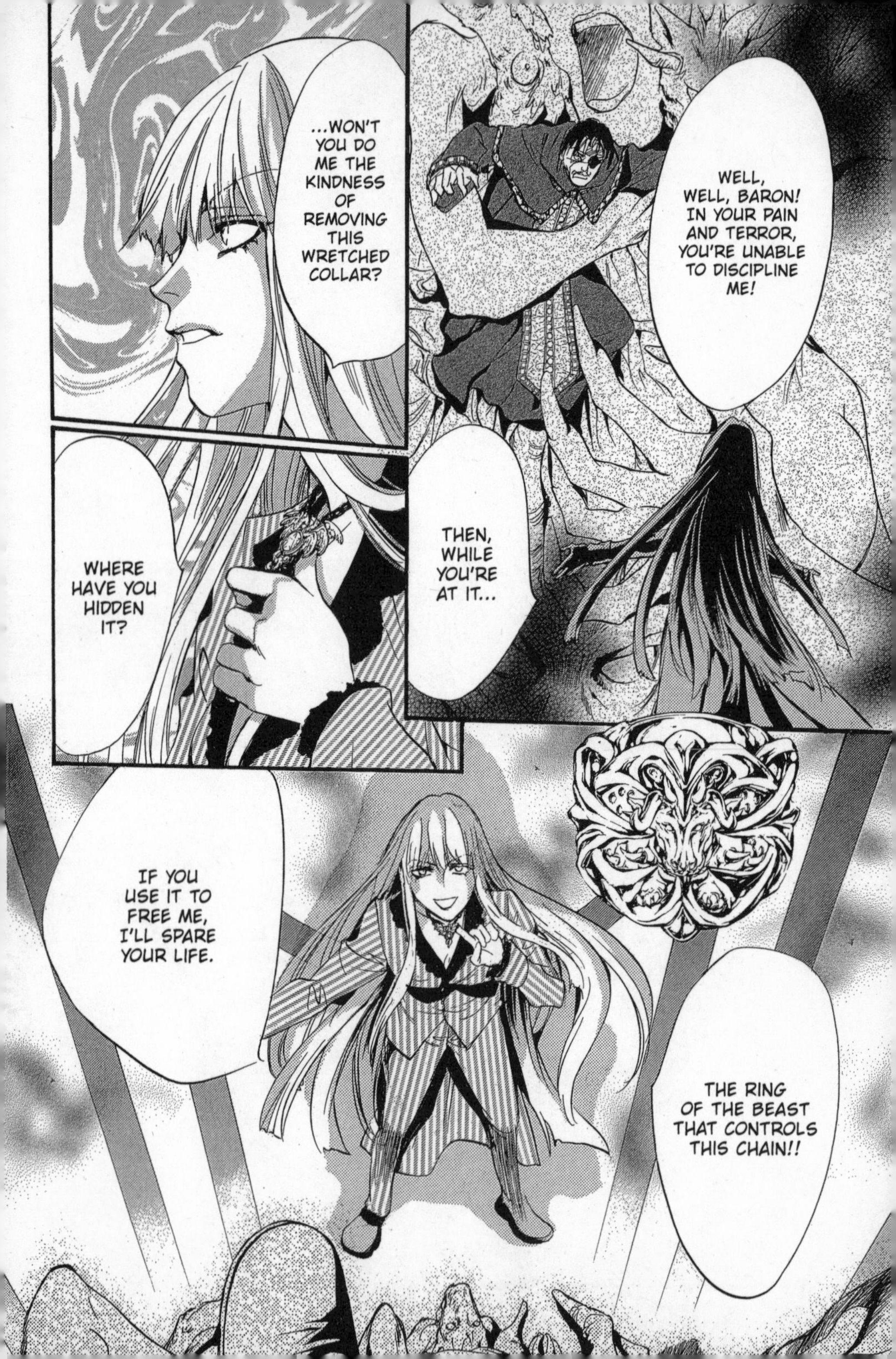
WELL, WELL, BARON! IN YOUR PAIN AND TERROR, YOU'RE UNABLE TO DISCIPLINE ME!
...WON'T YOU DO ME THE KINDNESS OF REMOVING THIS WRETCHED COLLAR?
THEN, WHILE YOU'RE AT IT...
WHERE HAVE YOU HIDDEN IT?
THE RING OF THE BEAST THAT CONTROLS THIS CHAIN!!
IF YOU USE IT TO FREE ME, I'LL SPARE YOUR LIFE.

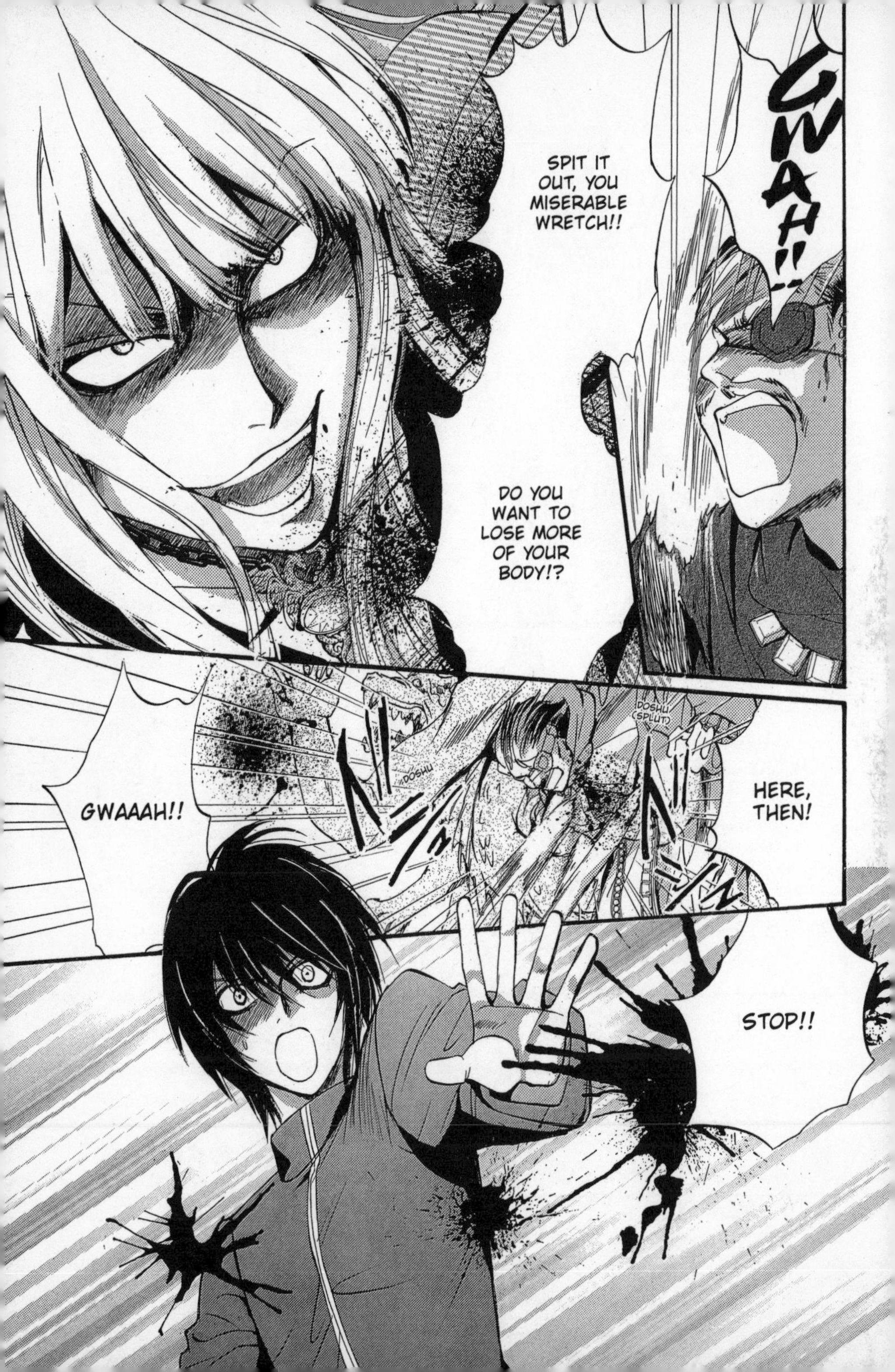
GWAH!!
SPIT IT OUT, YOU MISERABLE WRETCH!!
DO YOU WANT TO LOSE MORE OF YOUR BODY!?
HERE, THEN!
DOSHU (SPLUT)
DOSHU
GWAAAH!!
STOP!!

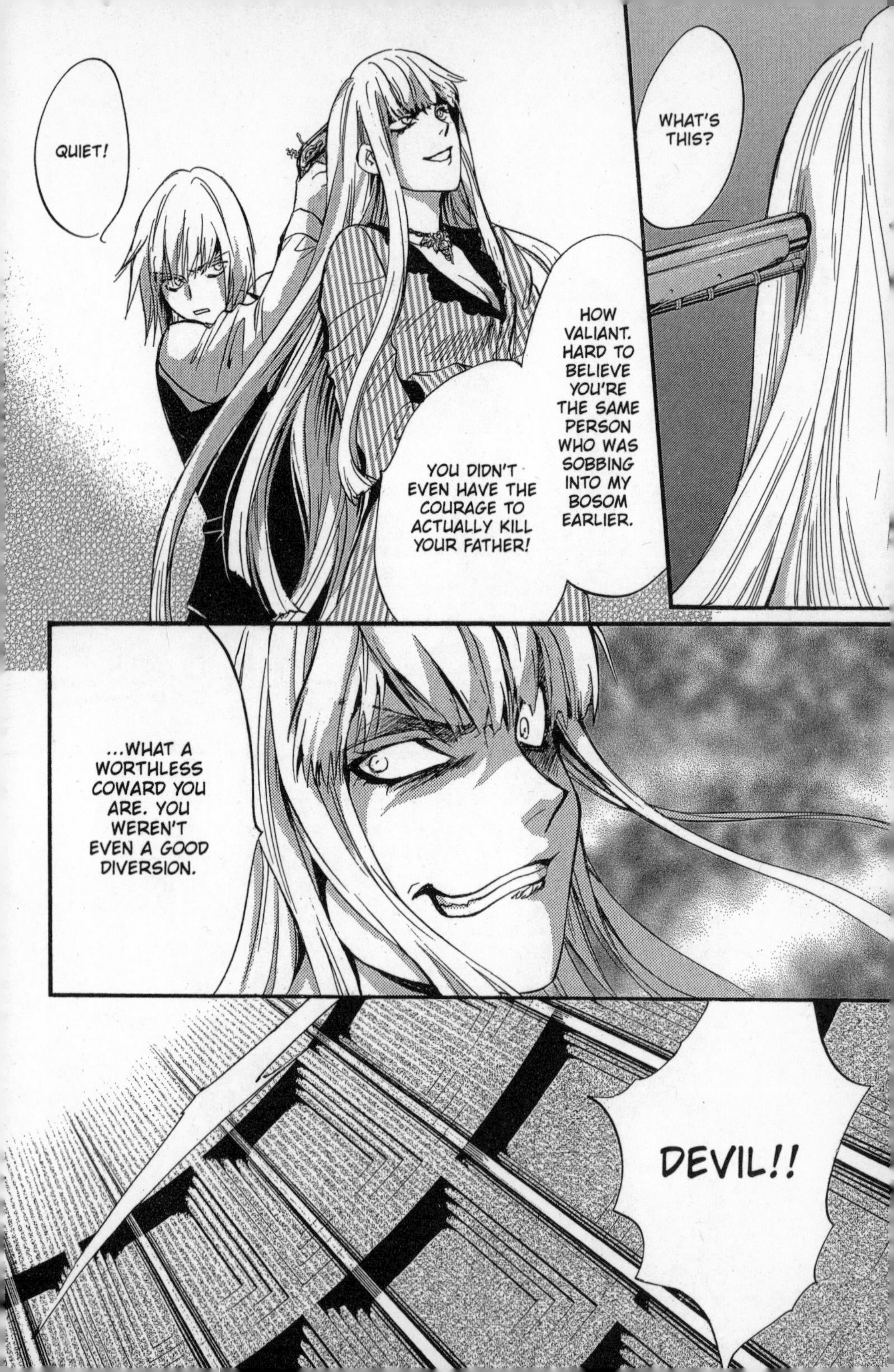
WHAT'S THIS?
HOW VALIANT. HARD TO BELIEVE YOU'RE THE SAME PERSON WHO WAS SOBBING INTO MY BOSOM EARLIER.
YOU DIDN'T EVEN HAVE THE COURAGE TO ACTUALLY KILL YOUR FATHER!
QUIET!
...WHAT A WORTHLESS COWARD YOU ARE. YOU WEREN'T EVEN A GOOD DIVERSION.
DEVIL!!

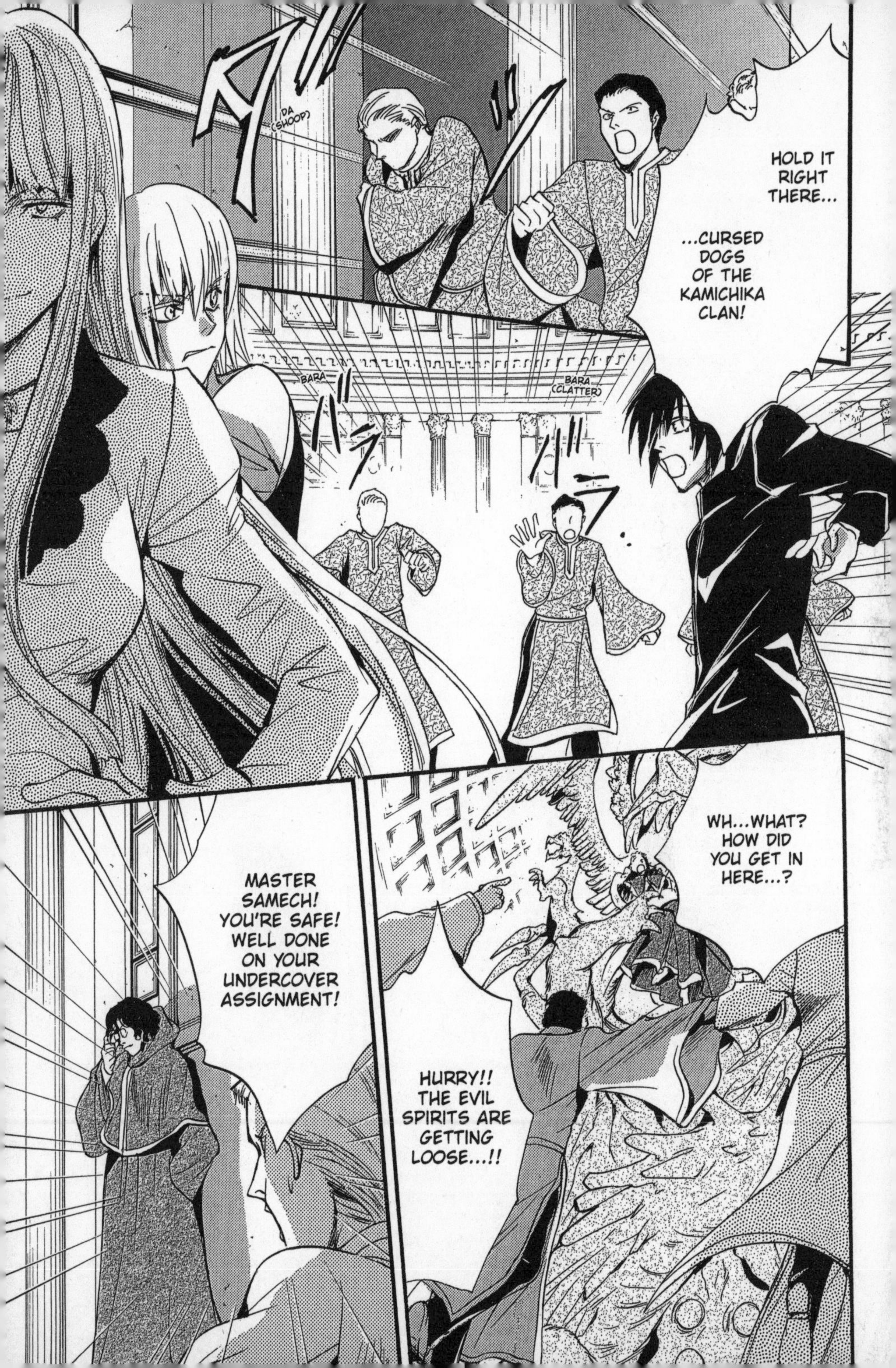
DA (SHOOP)
HOLD IT RIGHT THERE...
...CURSED DOGS OF THE KAMICHIKA CLAN!
BARA (CLATTER)
BARA
WH...WHAT? HOW DID YOU GET IN HERE...?
HURRY!! THE EVIL SPIRITS ARE GETTING LOOSE...!!
MASTER SAMECH! YOU'RE SAFE! WELL DONE ON YOUR UNDERCOVER ASSIGNMENT!

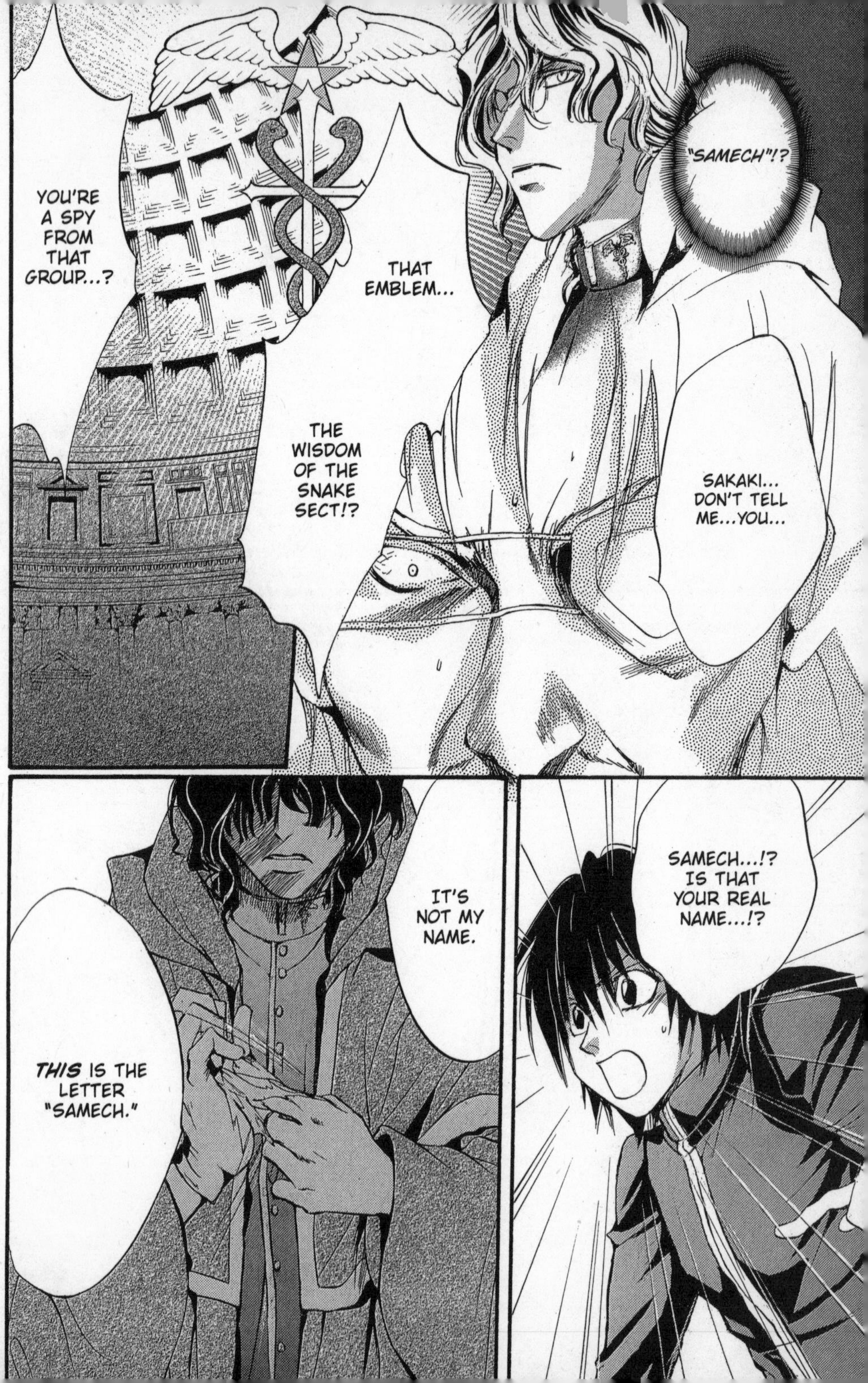
"SAMECH"!?
SAKAKI... DON'T TELL ME...YOU...
THAT EMBLEM...
THE WISDOM OF THE SNAKE SECT!?
YOU'RE A SPY FROM THAT GROUP...?
SAMECH...!? IS THAT YOUR REAL NAME...!?
IT'S NOT MY NAME.
THIS IS THE LETTER "SAMECH."

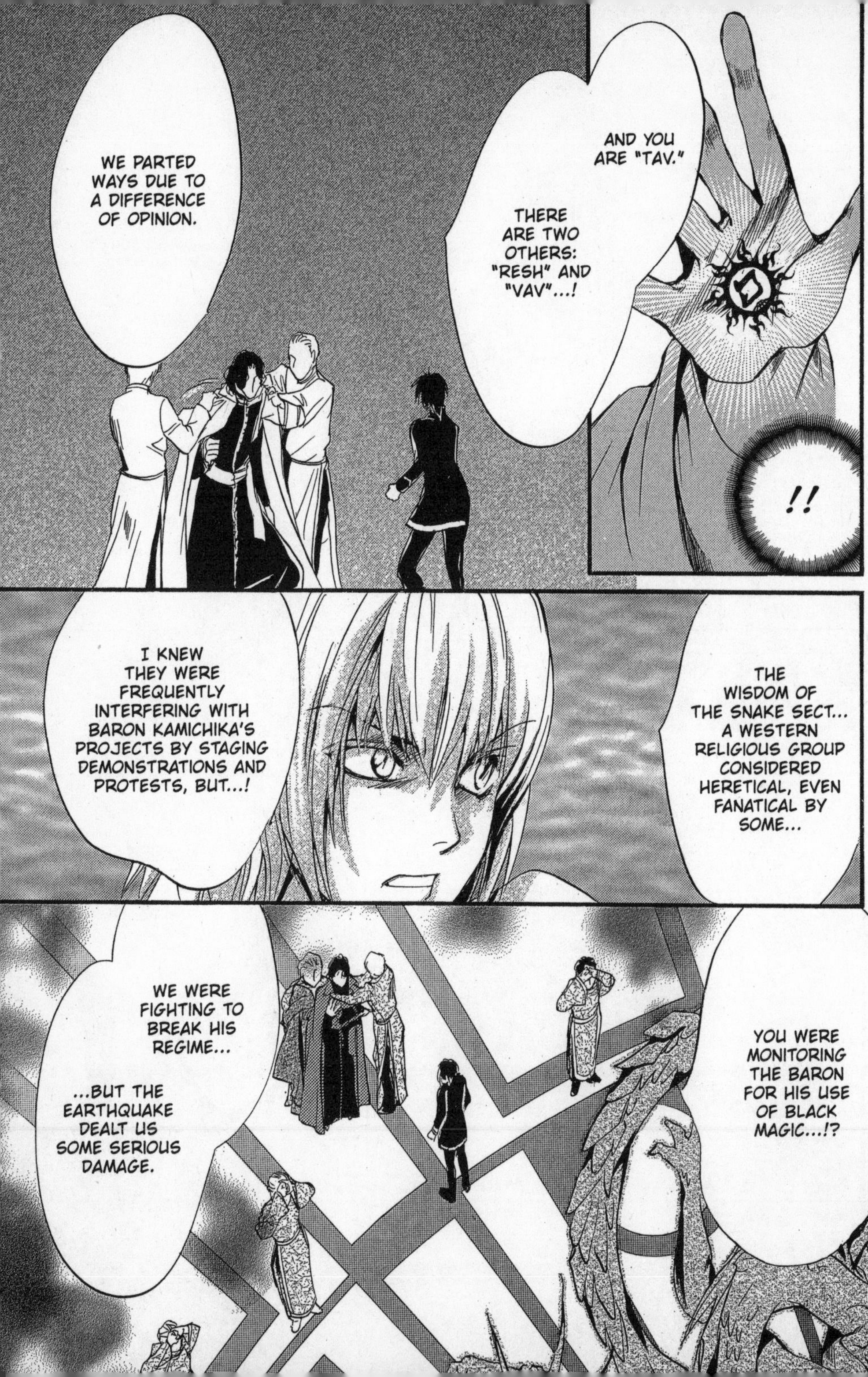
AND YOU ARE "TAV."
THERE ARE TWO OTHERS: "RESH" AND "VAV"...!
!!
WE PARTED WAYS DUE TO A DIFFERENCE OF OPINION.
THE WISDOM OF THE SNAKE SECT... A WESTERN RELIGIOUS GROUP CONSIDERED HERETICAL, EVEN FANATICAL BY SOME...
I KNEW THEY WERE FREQUENTLY INTERFERING WITH BARON KAMICHIKA'S PROJECTS BY STAGING DEMONSTRATIONS AND PROTESTS, BUT...!
YOU WERE MONITORING THE BARON FOR HIS USE OF BLACK MAGIC...!?
WE WERE FIGHTING TO BREAK HIS REGIME...
...BUT THE EARTHQUAKE DEALT US SOME SERIOUS DAMAGE.

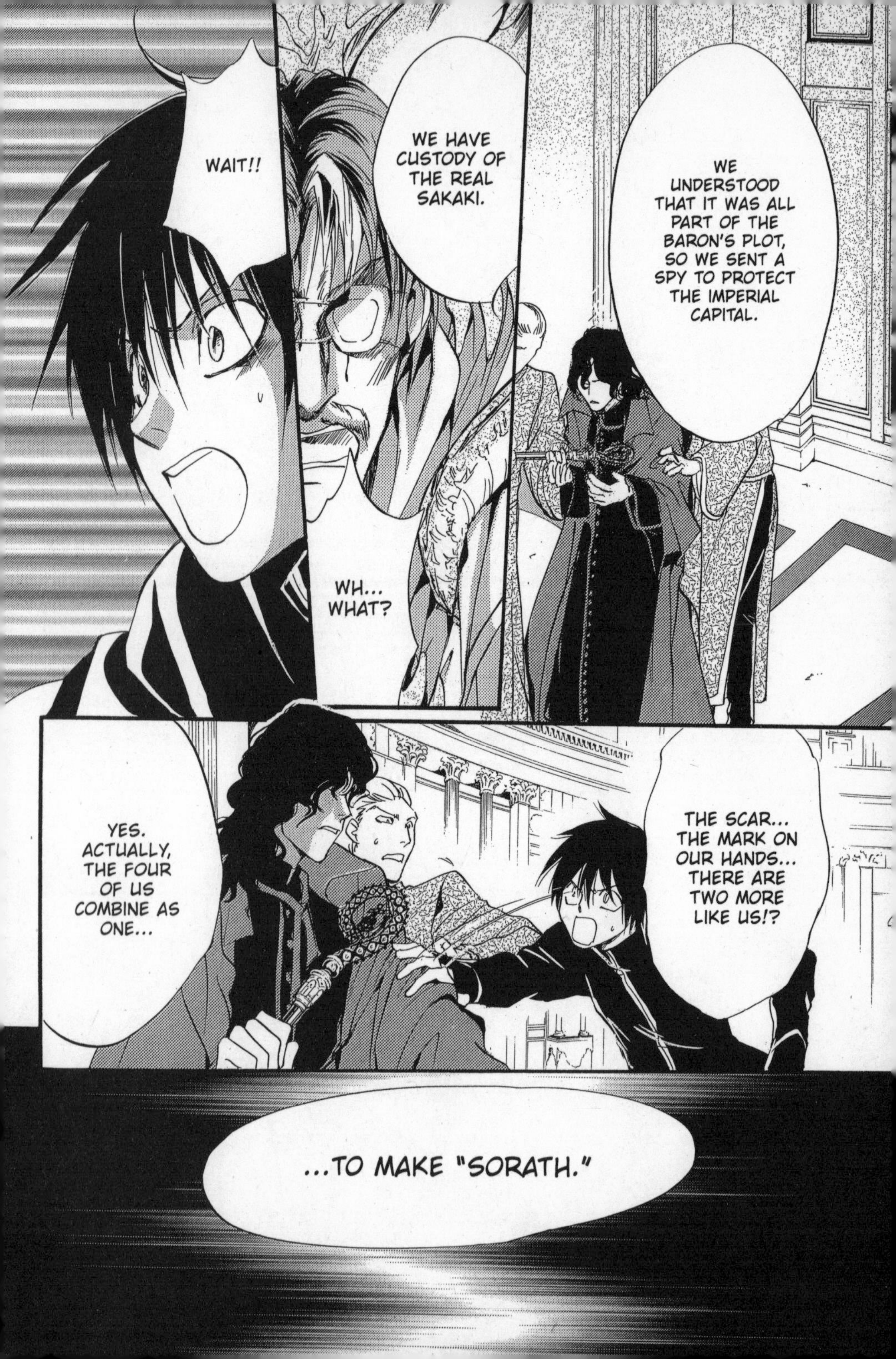
WE UNDERSTOOD THAT IT WAS ALL PART OF THE BARON'S PLOT, SO WE SENT A SPY TO PROTECT THE IMPERIAL CAPITAL.
WE HAVE CUSTODY OF THE REAL SAKAKI.
WH... WHAT?
WAIT!!
THE SCAR... THE MARK ON OUR HANDS... THERE ARE TWO MORE LIKE US!?
YES. ACTUALLY, THE FOUR OF US COMBINE AS ONE...
...TO MAKE "SORATH."

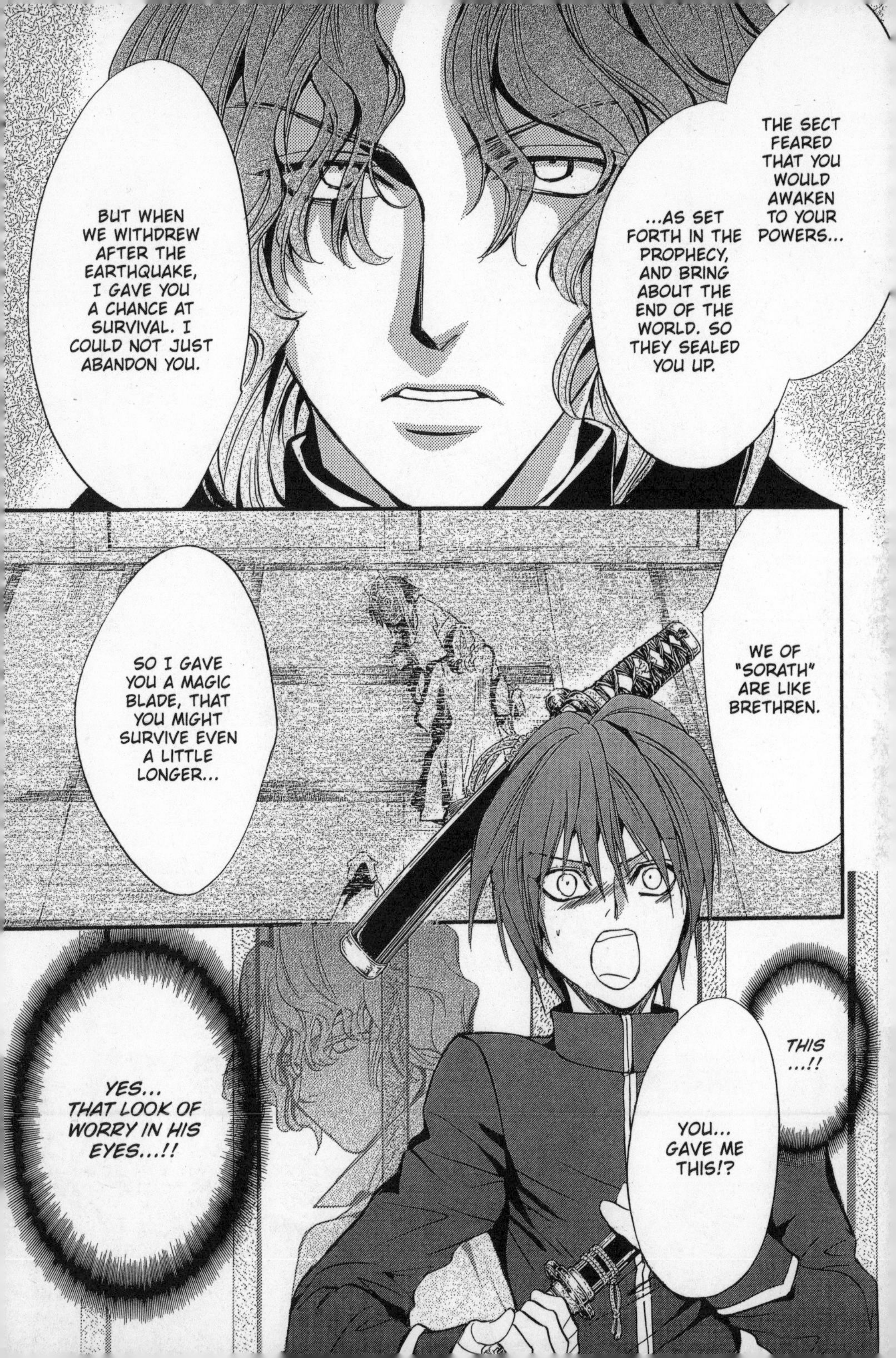
THE SECT FEARED THAT YOU WOULD AWAKEN TO YOUR POWERS...
...AS SET FORTH IN THE PROPHECY, AND BRING ABOUT THE END OF THE WORLD. SO THEY SEALED YOU UP.
BUT WHEN WE WITHDREW AFTER THE EARTHQUAKE, I GAVE YOU A CHANCE AT SURVIVAL. I COULD NOT JUST ABANDON YOU.
WE OF "SORATH" ARE LIKE BRETHREN.
SO I GAVE YOU A MAGIC BLADE, THAT YOU MIGHT SURVIVE EVEN A LITTLE LONGER...
THIS ...!!
YOU... GAVE ME THIS!?
YES... THAT LOOK OF WORRY IN HIS EYES...!!

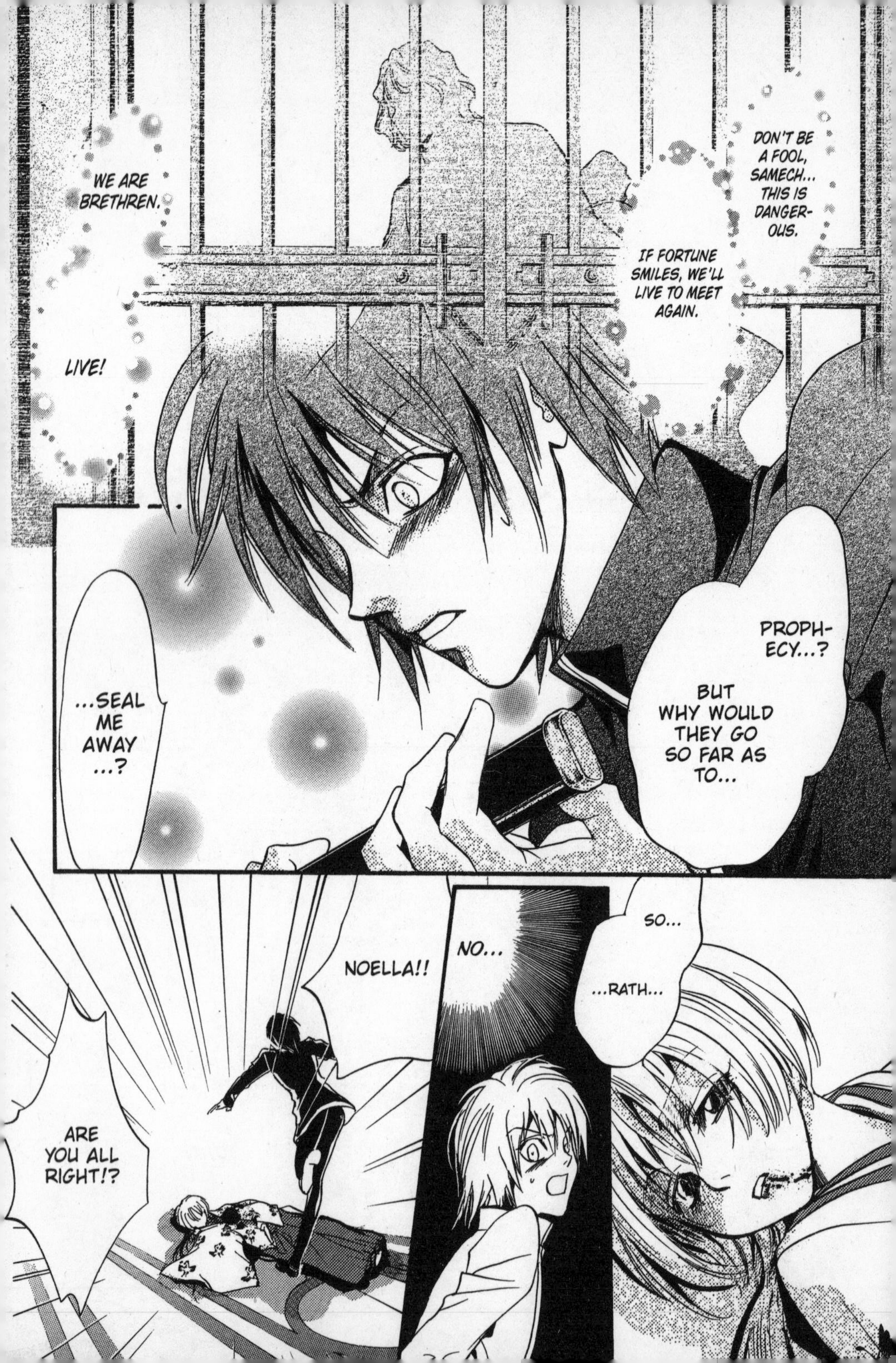
DON'T BE A FOOL, SAMECH... THIS IS DANGER-OUS.
IF FORTUNE SMILES, WE'LL LIVE TO MEET AGAIN.
WE ARE BRETHREN.
LIVE!
PROPH-ECY...?
BUT WHY WOULD THEY GO SO FAR AS TO...
...SEAL ME AWAY ...?
SO...
...RATH...
NO...
NOELLA!!
ARE YOU ALL RIGHT!?

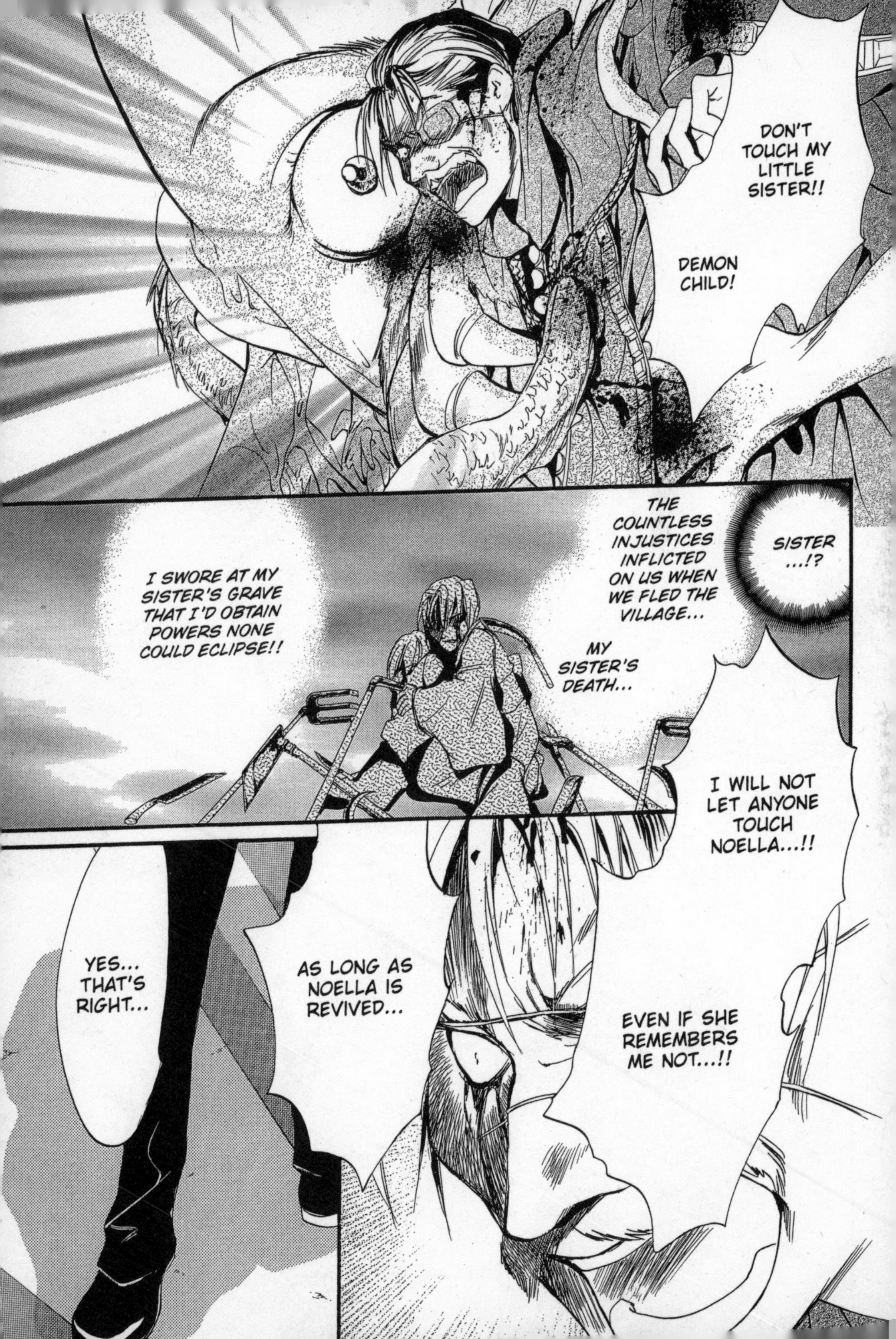
DON'T TOUCH MY LITTLE SISTER!!
DEMON CHILD!
SISTER ...!?
THE COUNTLESS INJUSTICES INFLICTED ON US WHEN WE FLED THE VILLAGE...
MY SISTER'S DEATH...
I SWORE AT MY SISTER'S GRAVE THAT I'D OBTAIN POWERS NONE COULD ECLIPSE!!
I WILL NOT LET ANYONE TOUCH NOELLA...!!
EVEN IF SHE REMEMBERS ME NOT...!!
AS LONG AS NOELLA IS REVIVED...
YES... THAT'S RIGHT...

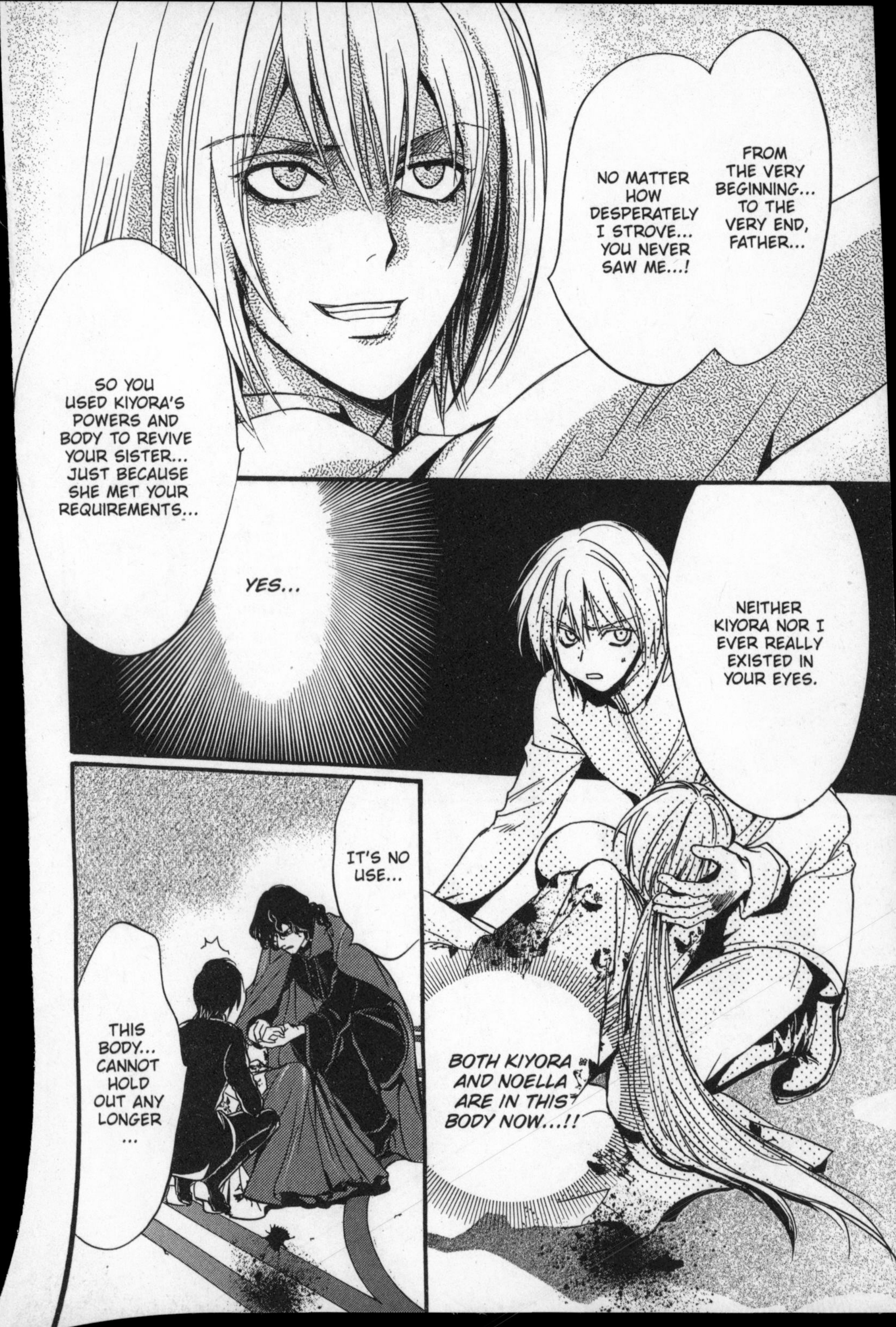
FROM THE VERY BEGINNING... TO THE VERY END, FATHER...
NO MATTER HOW DESPERATELY I STROVE... YOU NEVER SAW ME...!
SO YOU USED KIYORA'S POWERS AND BODY TO REVIVE YOUR SISTER... JUST BECAUSE SHE MET YOUR REQUIREMENTS...
NEITHER KIYORA NOR I EVER REALLY EXISTED IN YOUR EYES.
BOTH KIYORA AND NOELLA ARE IN THIS BODY NOW...!!
YES...
IT'S NO USE...
THIS BODY... CANNOT HOLD OUT ANY LONGER ...

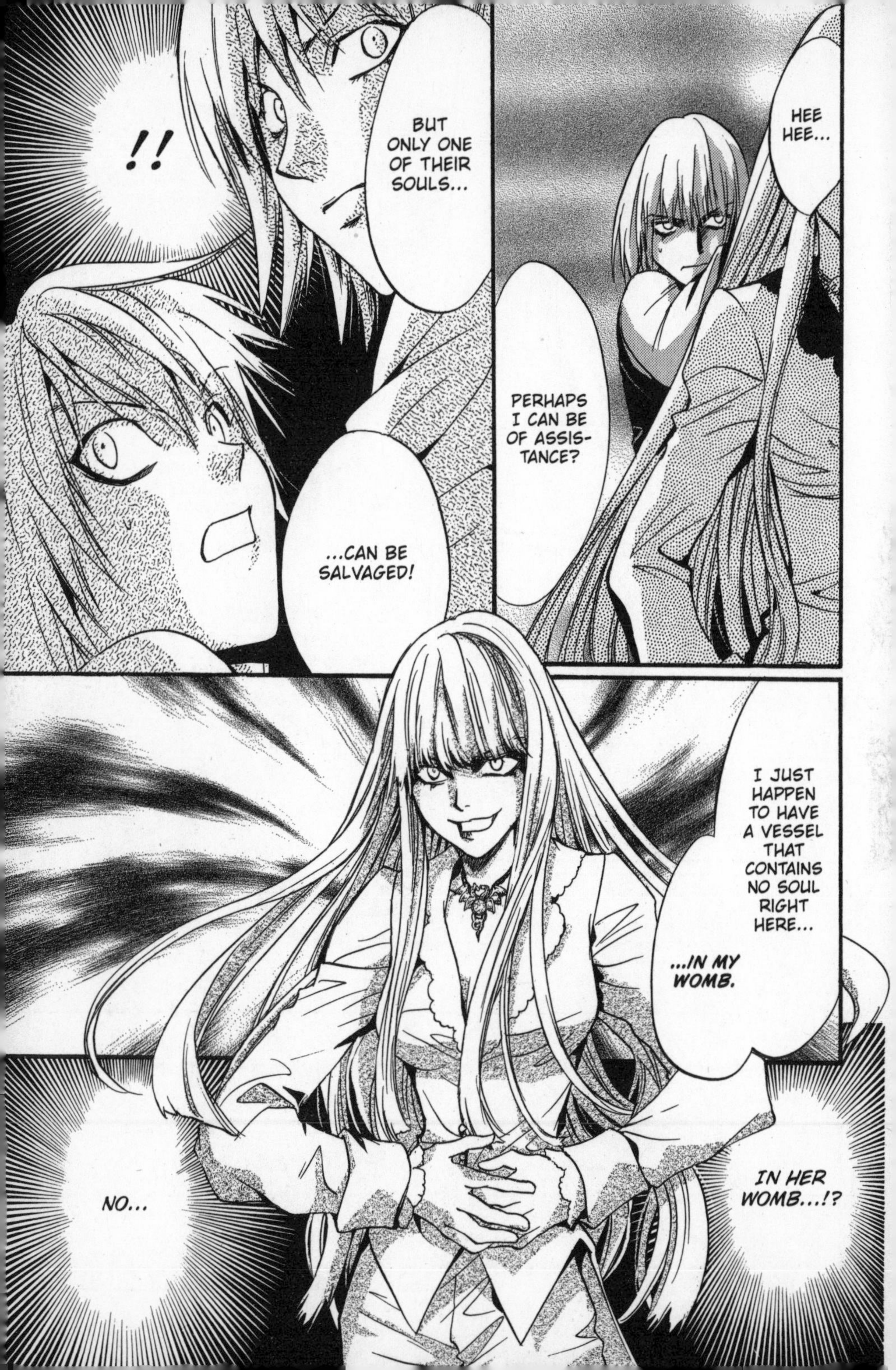
HEE HEE...
PERHAPS I CAN BE OF ASSISTANCE?
BUT ONLY ONE OF THEIR SOULS...
!!
...CAN BE SALVAGED!
I JUST HAPPEN TO HAVE A VESSEL THAT CONTAINS NO SOUL RIGHT HERE...
...IN MY WOMB.
IN HER WOMB...!?
NO...

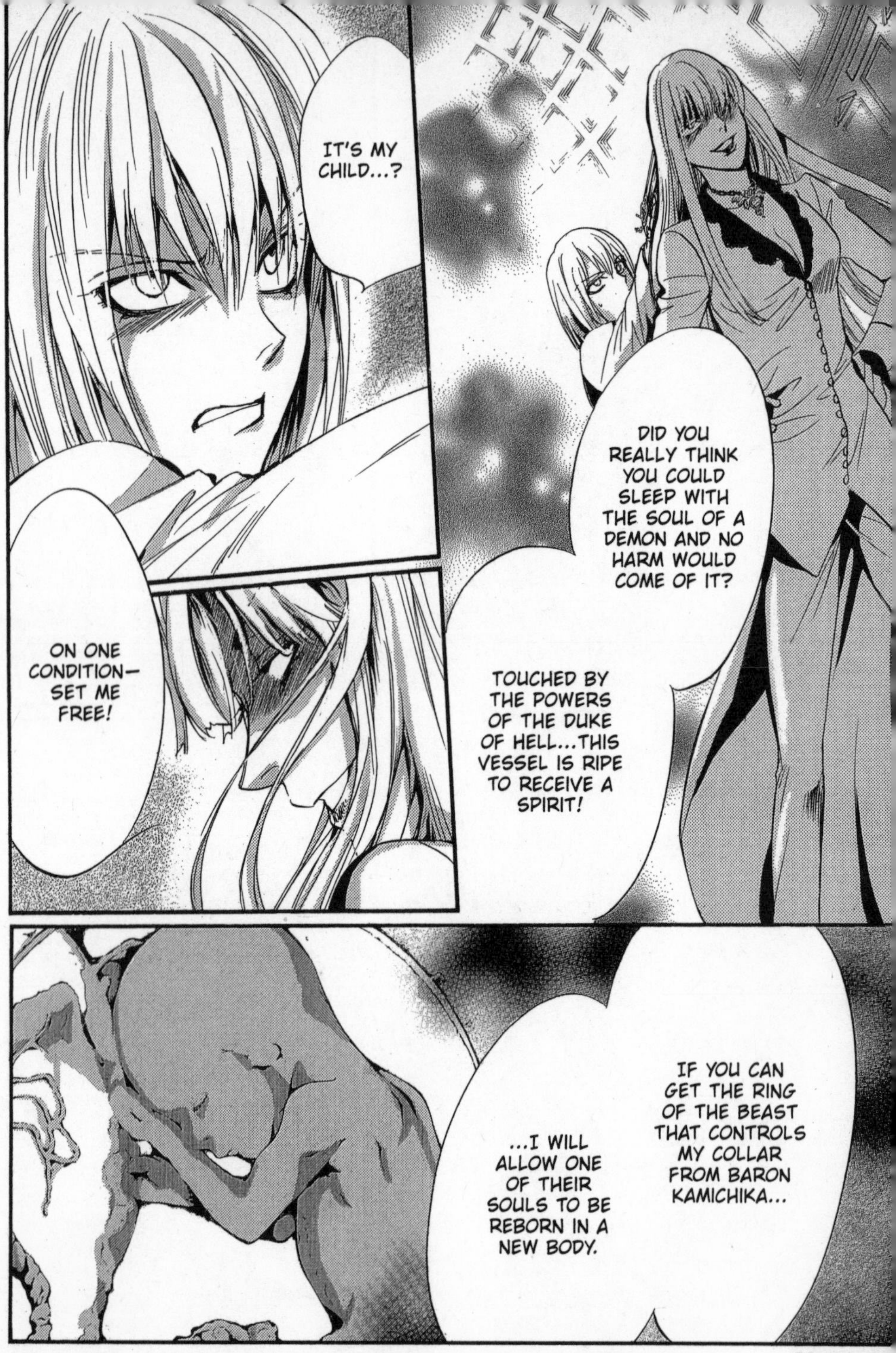
DID YOU REALLY THINK YOU COULD SLEEP WITH THE SOUL OF A DEMON AND NO HARM WOULD COME OF IT?
TOUCHED BY THE POWERS OF THE DUKE OF HELL...THIS VESSEL IS RIPE TO RECEIVE A SPIRIT!
IT'S MY CHILD...?
ON ONE CONDITION— SET ME FREE!
IF YOU CAN GET THE RING OF THE BEAST THAT CONTROLS MY COLLAR FROM BARON KAMICHIKA...
...I WILL ALLOW ONE OF THEIR SOULS TO BE REBORN IN A NEW BODY.

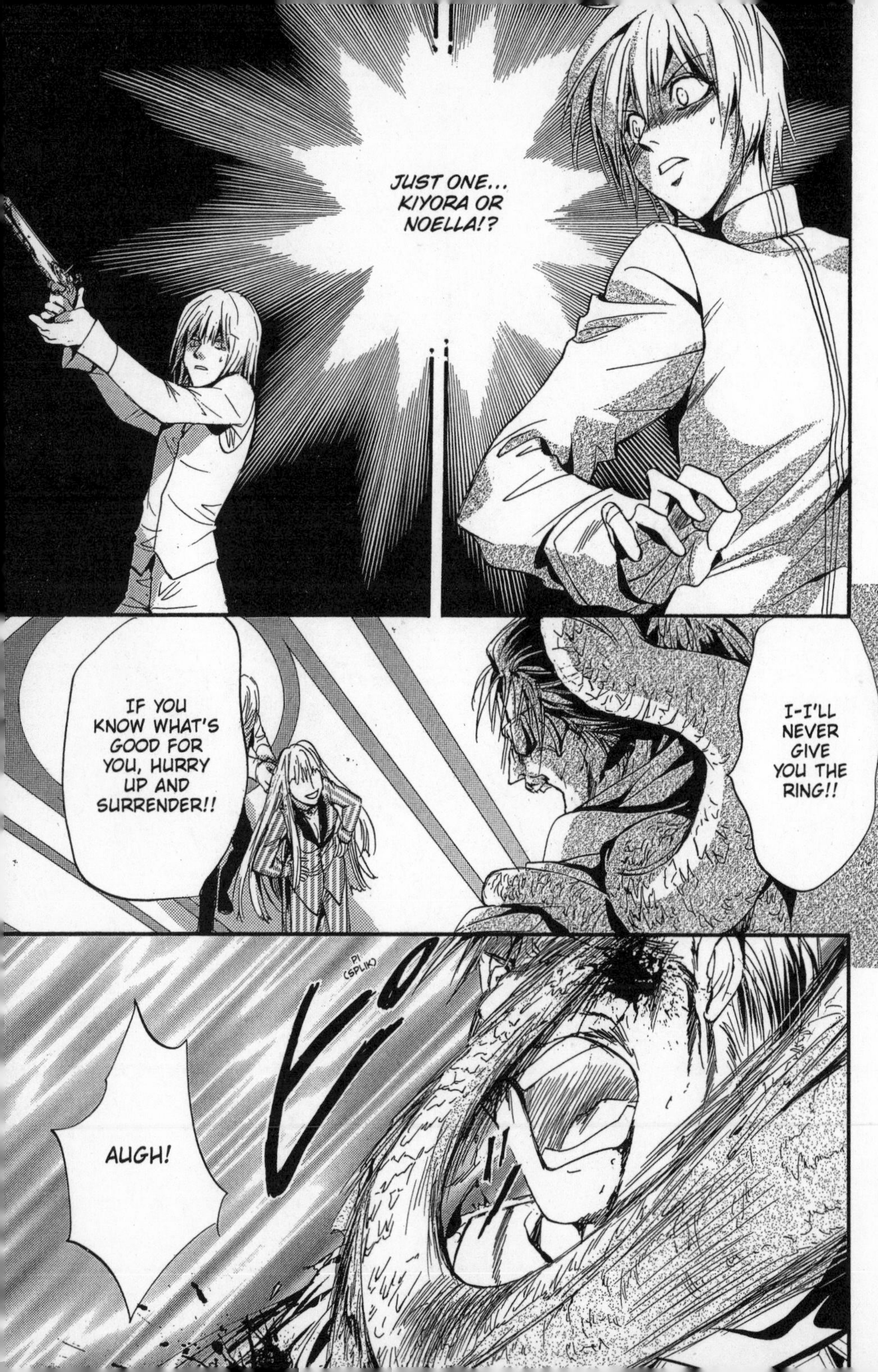
!!
JUST ONE... KIYORA OR NOELLA!?
I-I'LL NEVER GIVE YOU THE RING!!
IF YOU KNOW WHAT'S GOOD FOR YOU, HURRY UP AND SURRENDER!!
PI (SPLIK)
AUGH!

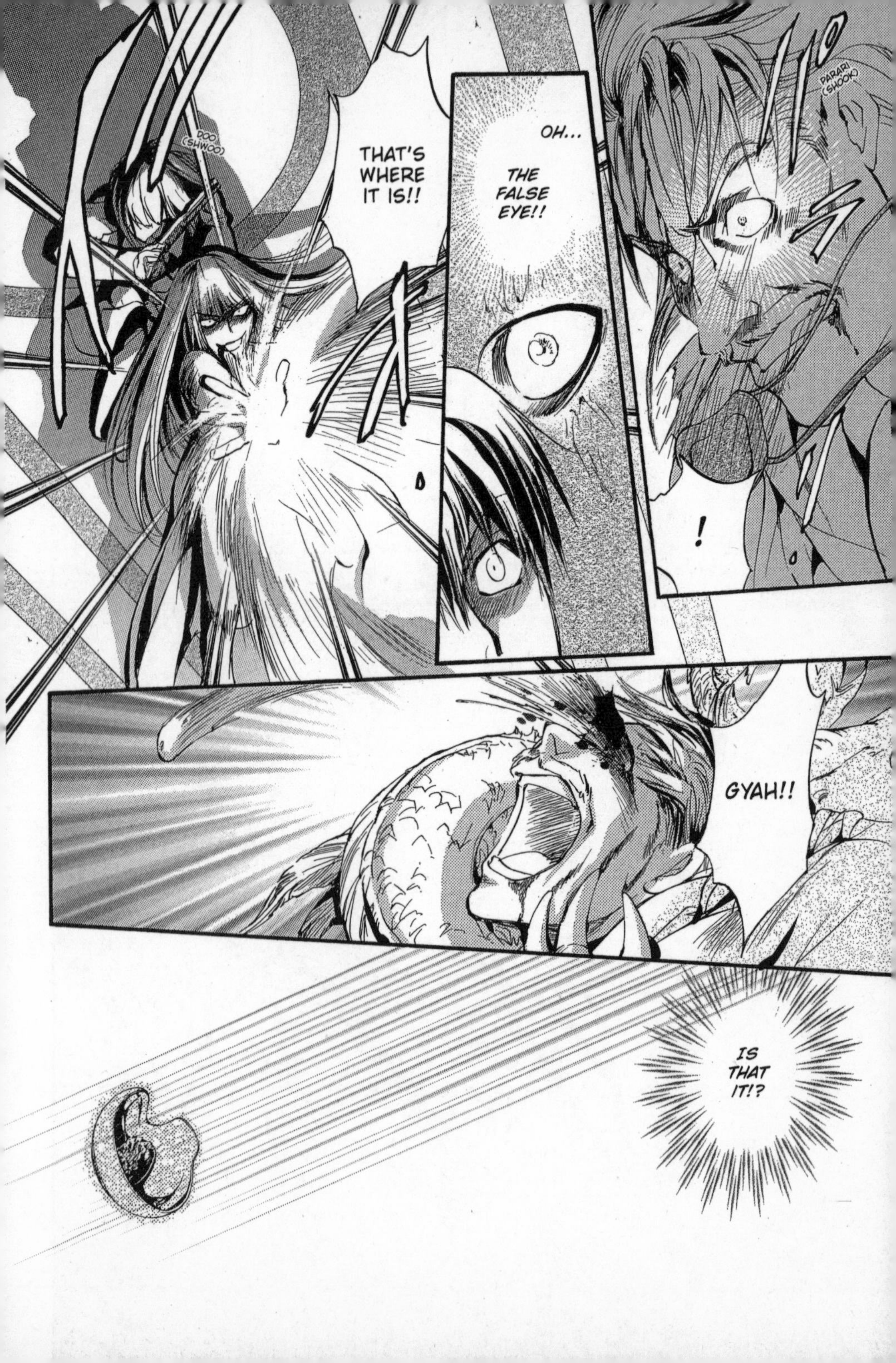
PARARI (SHOOK)
!
OH...
THE FALSE EYE!!
DOO (SHWOO)
THAT'S WHERE IT IS!!
GYAH!!
IS THAT IT!?

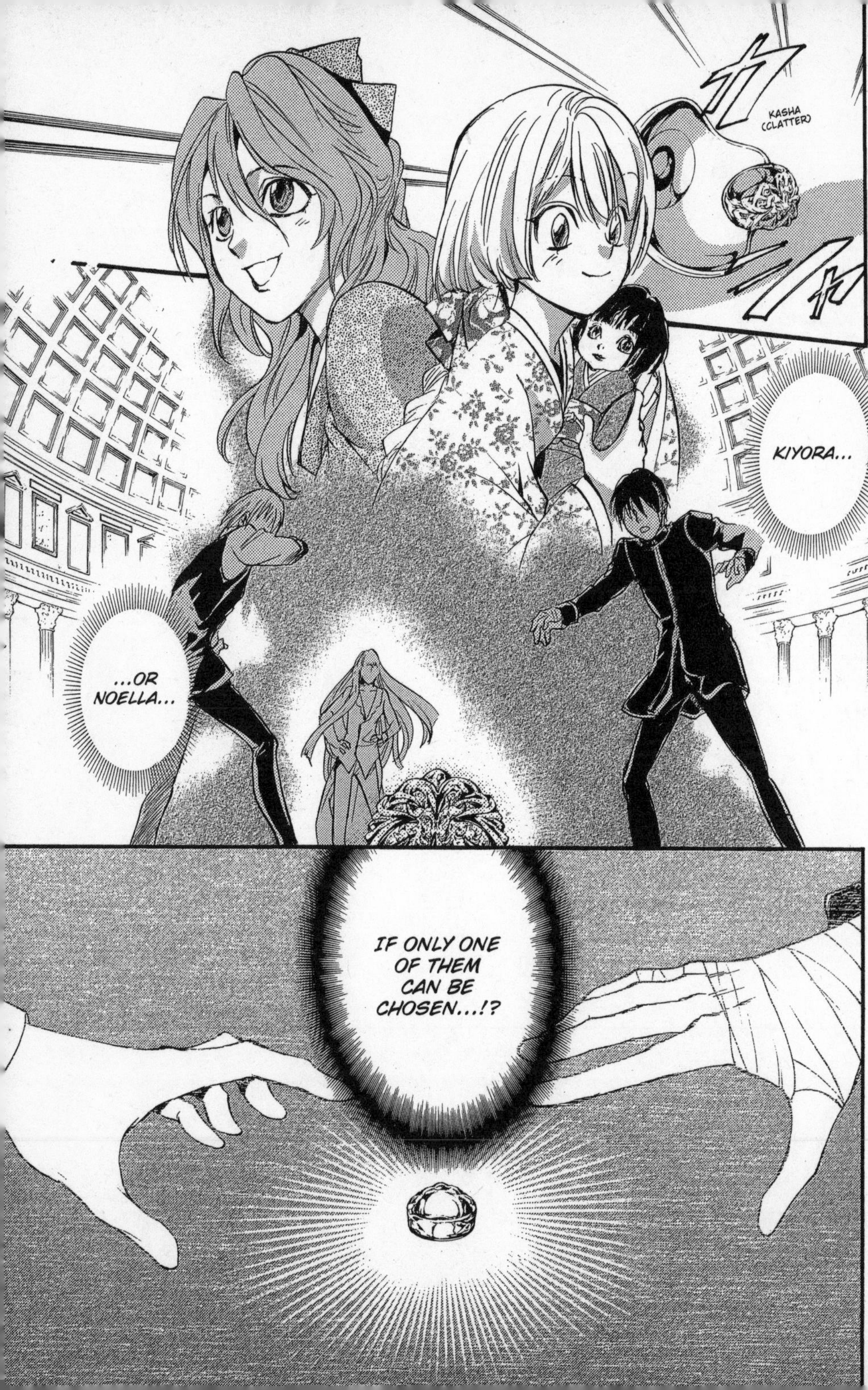
KASHA (CLATTER)
KIYORA...
...OR NOELLA...
IF ONLY ONE OF THEM CAN BE CHOSEN...!?

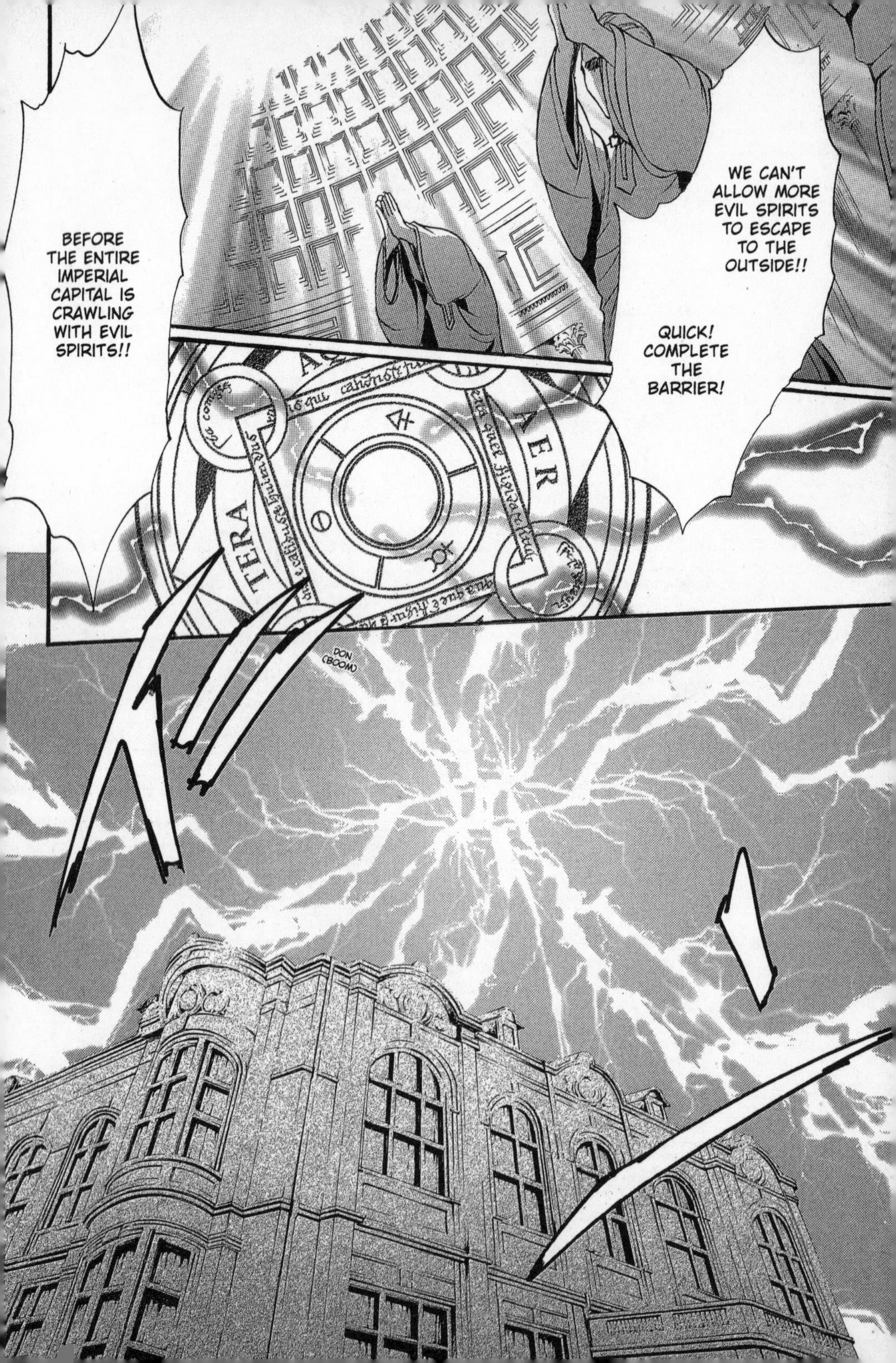
WE CAN'T ALLOW MORE EVIL SPIRITS TO ESCAPE TO THE OUTSIDE!!
QUICK! COMPLETE THE BARRIER!
BEFORE THE ENTIRE IMPERIAL CAPITAL IS CRAWLING WITH EVIL SPIRITS!!
TERA
AER
DON (BOOM)

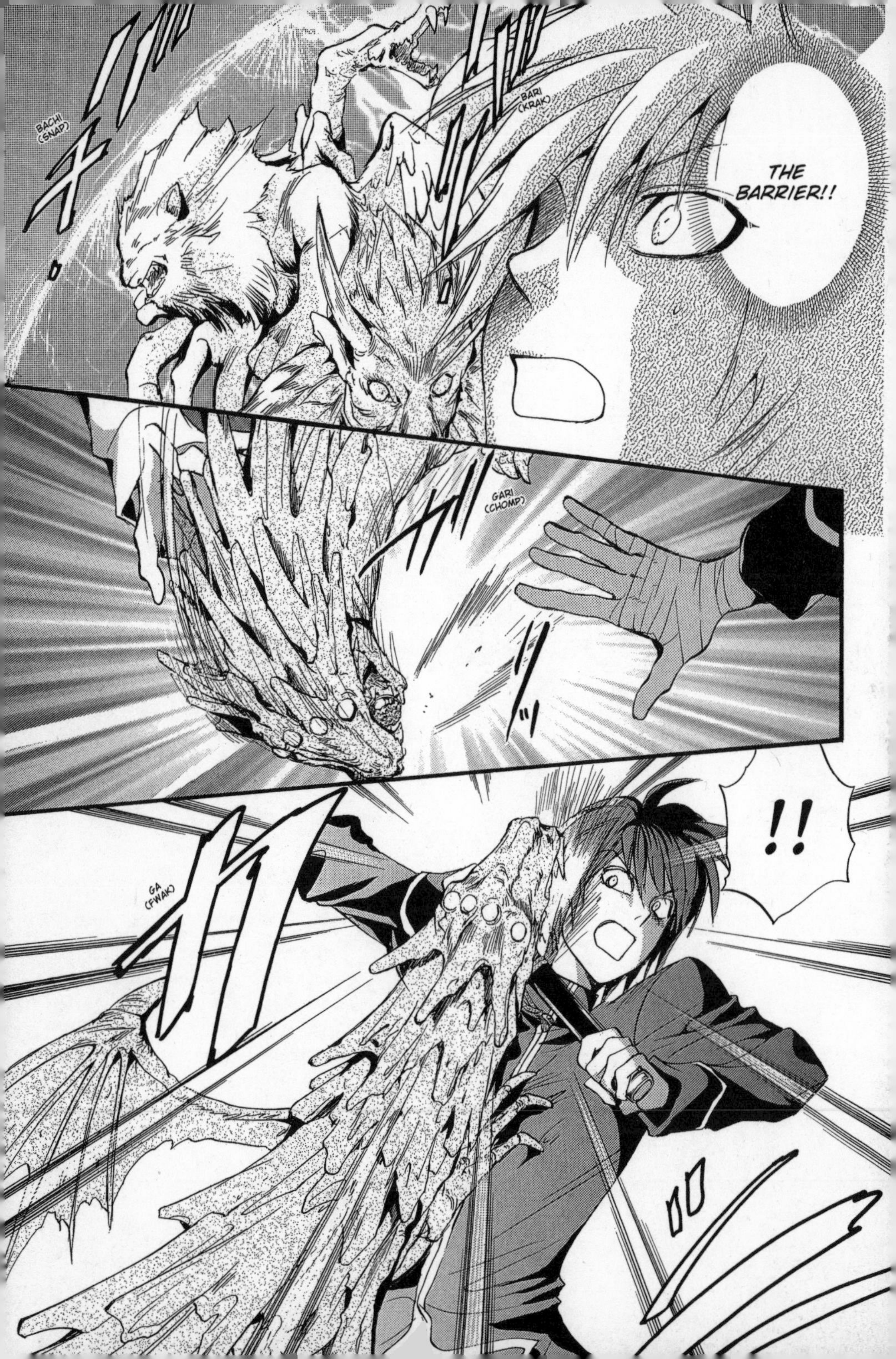
THE BARRIER!!
BARI (KRAK)
BACHI (SNAP)
GARI (CHOMP)
!!
GA (FWAK)

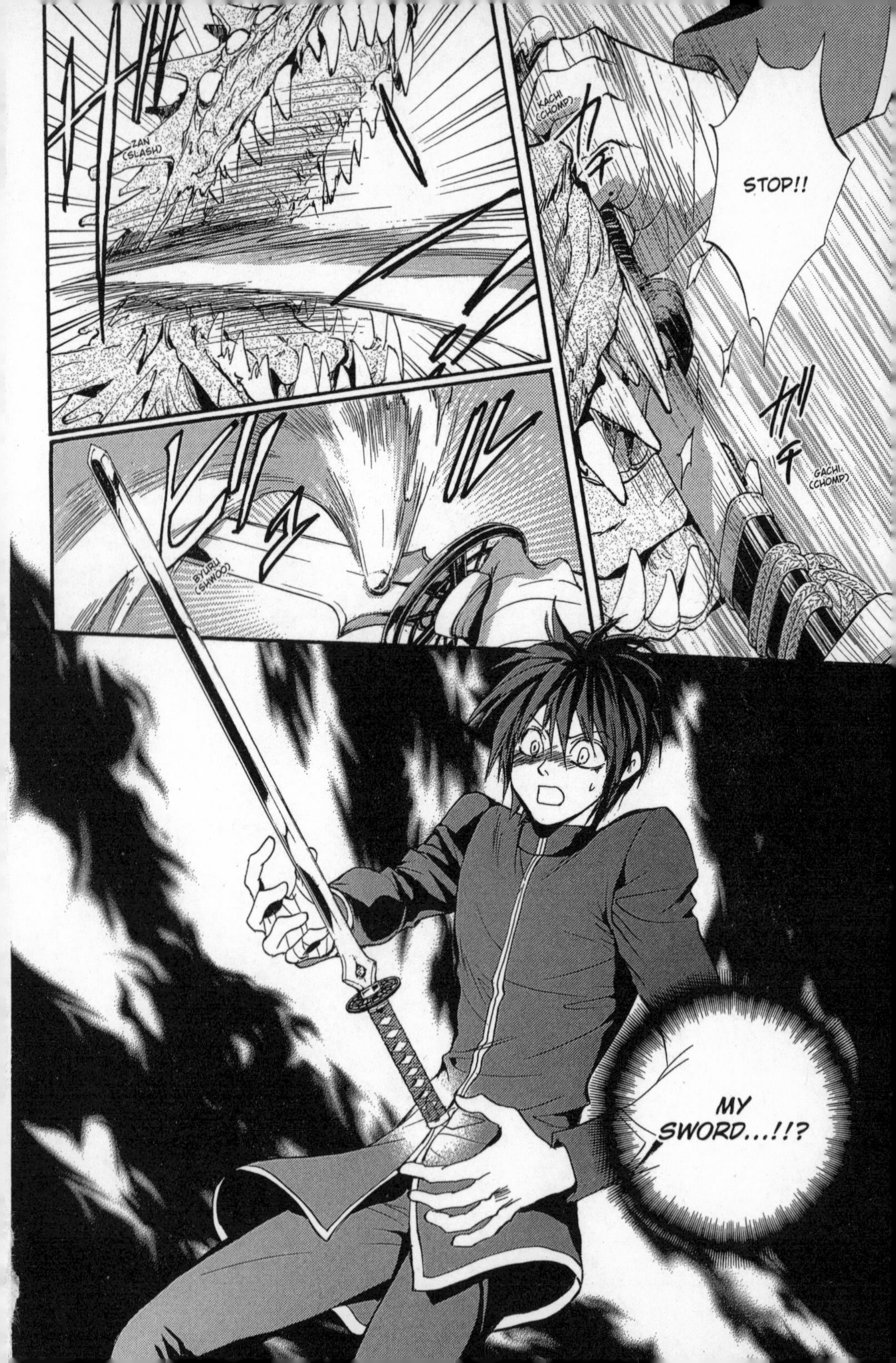

KACHI (CHOMP)
STOP!!
GACHI (CHOMP)
ZAN (SLASH)
BYURU (SHWOO)
MY SWORD...!!?

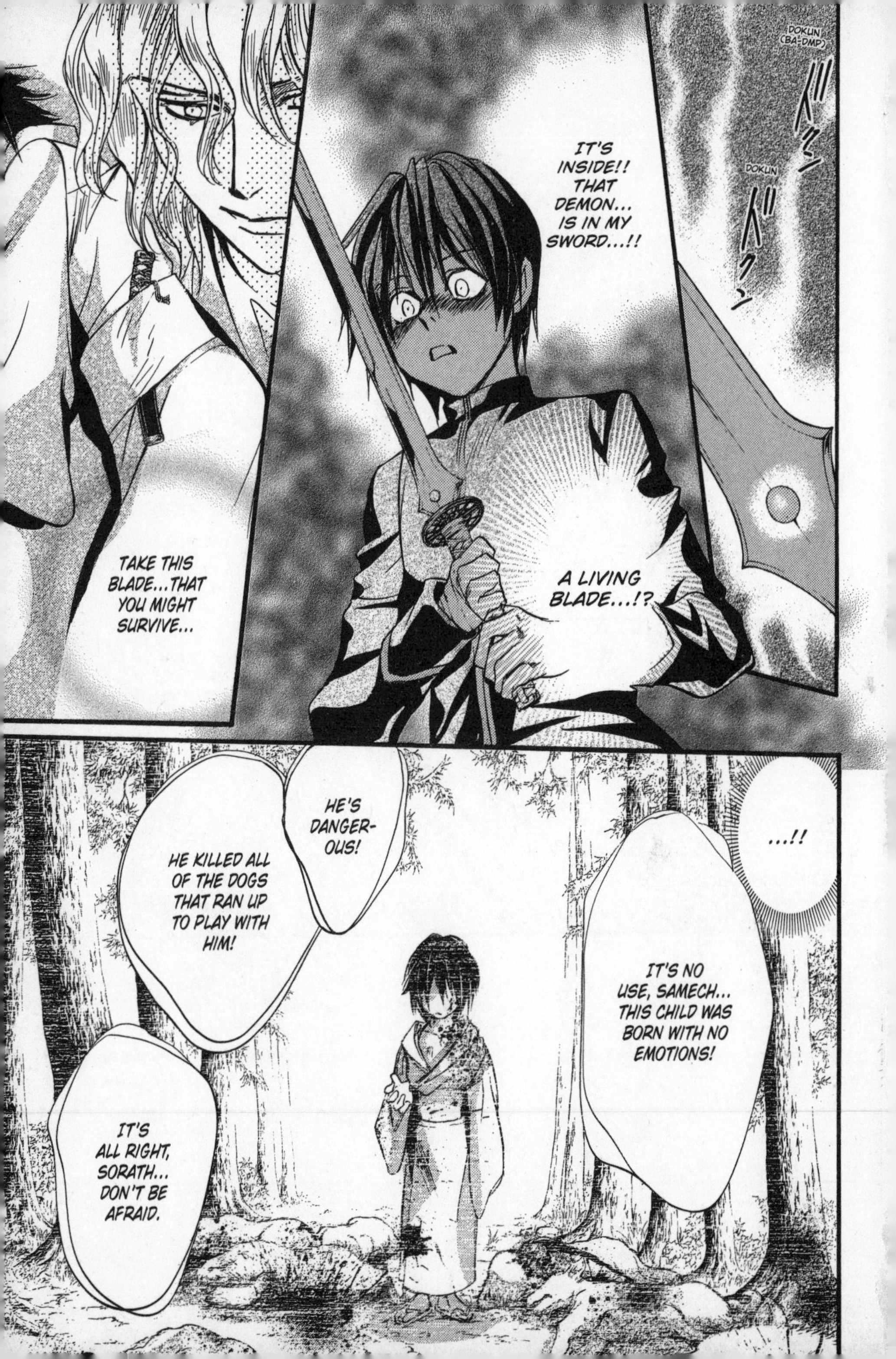
DOKUN (BA-DMP)
DOKUN
IT'S INSIDE!! THAT DEMON... IS IN MY SWORD...!!
A LIVING BLADE...!?
TAKE THIS BLADE...THAT YOU MIGHT SURVIVE...
...!!
HE'S DANGER-OUS!
HE KILLED ALL OF THE DOGS THAT RAN UP TO PLAY WITH HIM!
IT'S NO USE, SAMECH... THIS CHILD WAS BORN WITH NO EMOTIONS!
IT'S ALL RIGHT, SORATH... DON'T BE AFRAID.

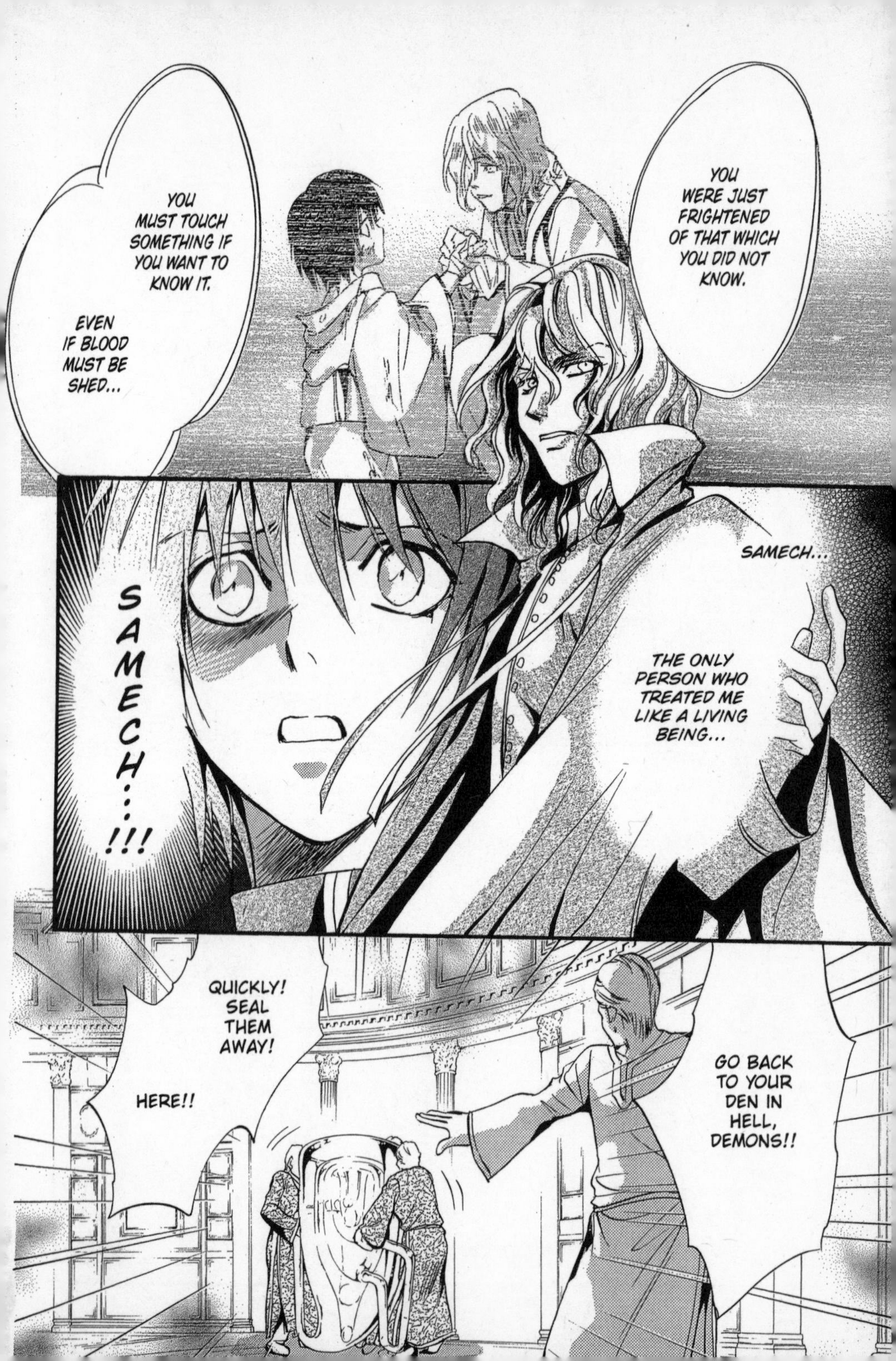
YOU WERE JUST FRIGHTENED OF THAT WHICH YOU DID NOT KNOW.
YOU MUST TOUCH SOMETHING IF YOU WANT TO KNOW IT.
EVEN IF BLOOD MUST BE SHED...
SAMECH...
THE ONLY PERSON WHO TREATED ME LIKE A LIVING BEING...
SAMECH...!!!
GO BACK TO YOUR DEN IN HELL, DEMONS!!
QUICKLY! SEAL THEM AWAY!
HERE!!

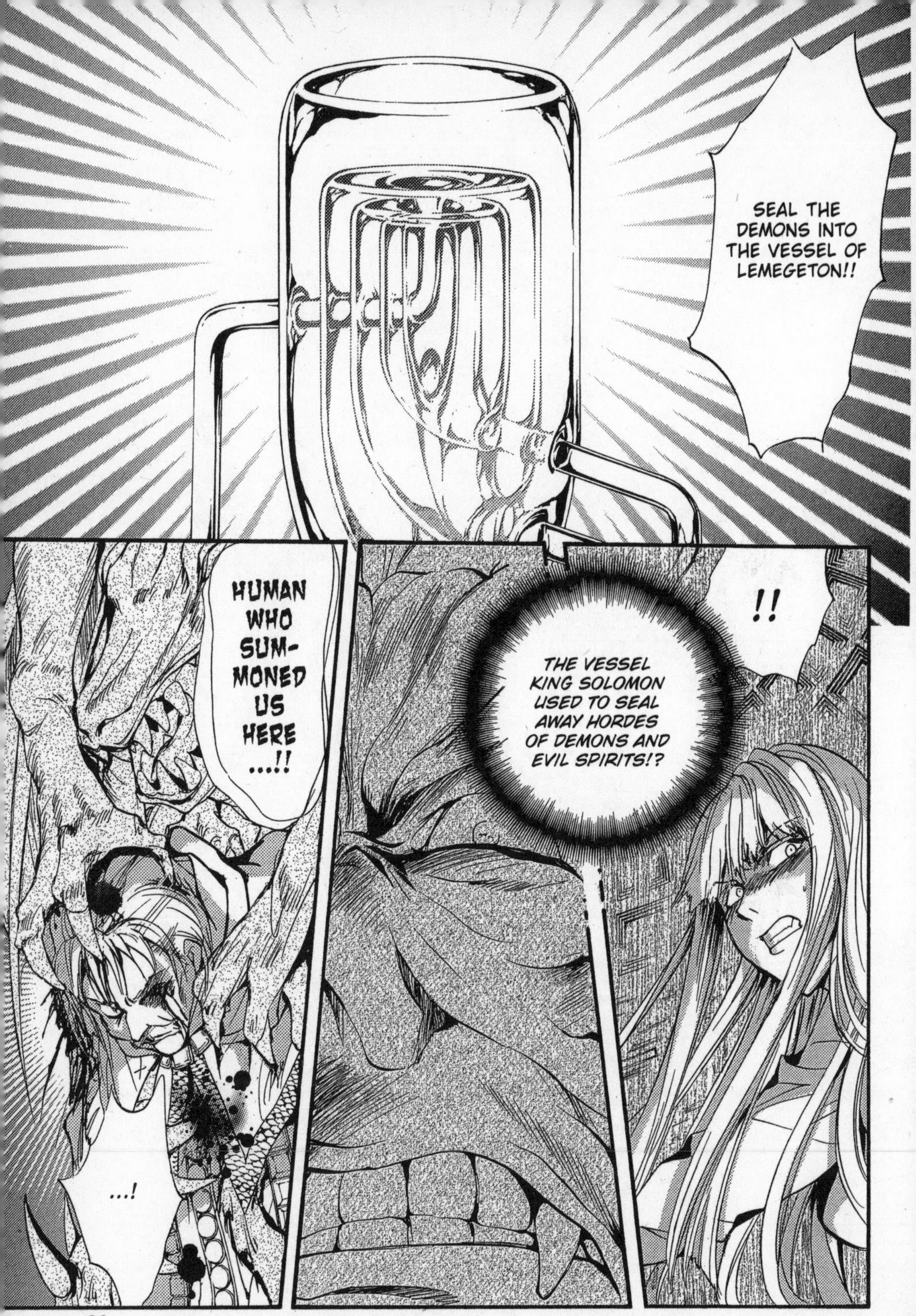
SEAL THE DEMONS INTO THE VESSEL OF LEMEGETON!!
!!
THE VESSEL KING SOLOMON USED TO SEAL AWAY HORDES OF DEMONS AND EVIL SPIRITS!?
HUMAN WHO SUM-MONED US HERE ...!!
...!

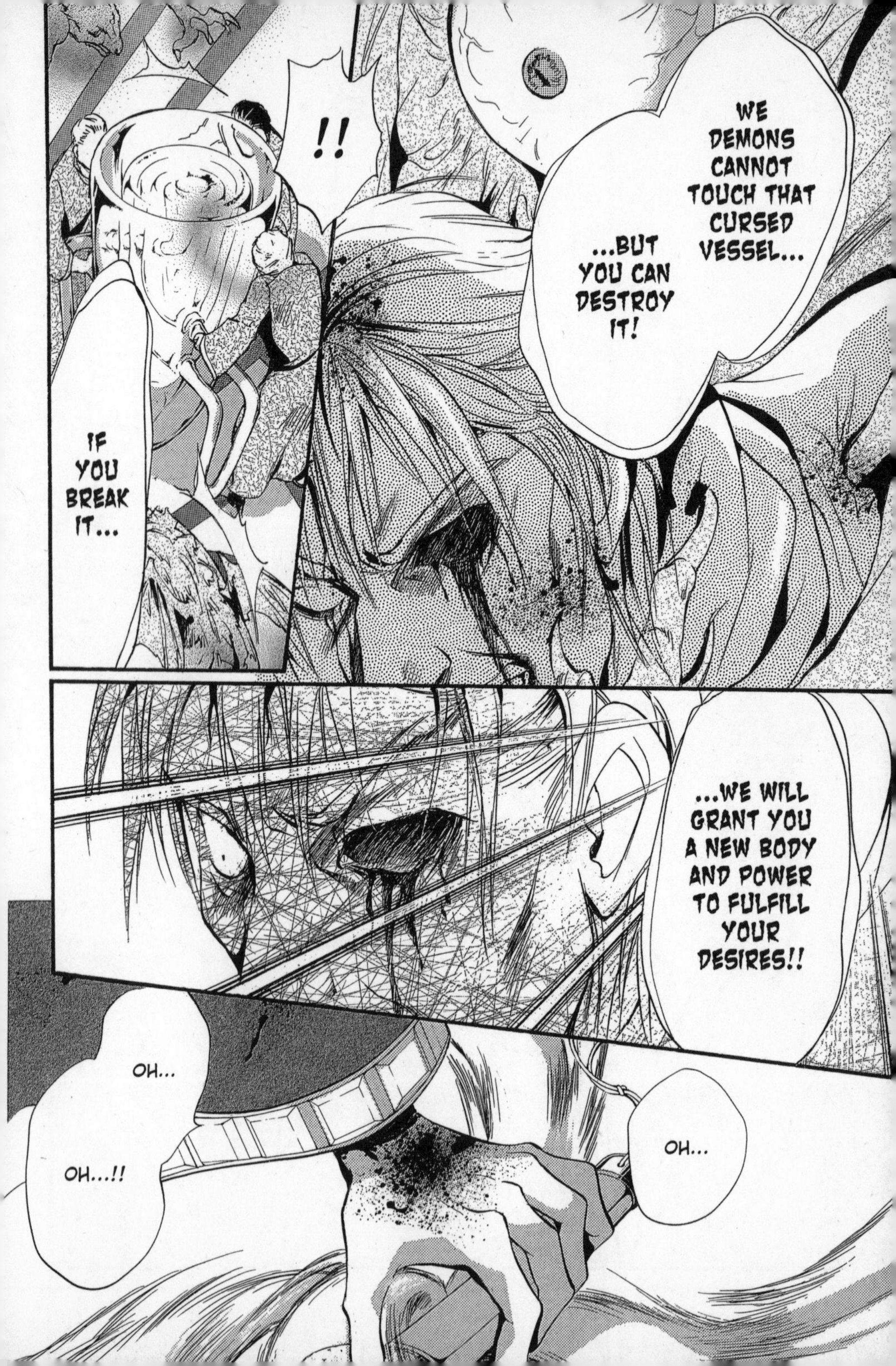
WE DEMONS CANNOT TOUCH THAT CURSED VESSEL...
...BUT YOU CAN DESTROY IT!
!!
IF YOU BREAK IT...
...WE WILL GRANT YOU A NEW BODY AND POWER TO FULFILL YOUR DESIRES!!
OH...
OH...
OH...!!

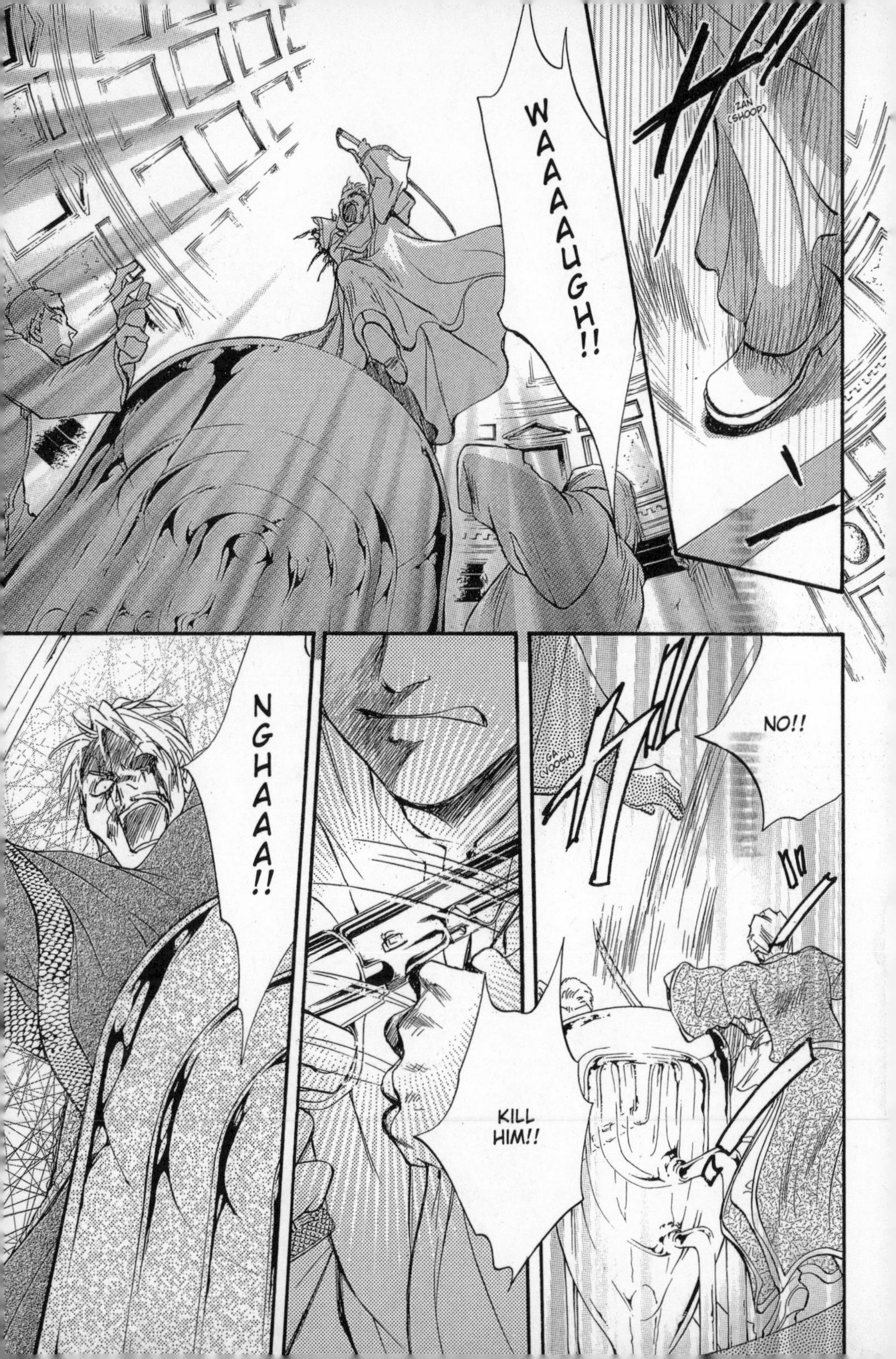
ZAN (SHOOP)
WAAAAAUGH!!
NO!!
GA (VOOSH)
KILL HIM!!
NGHAAAAA!!

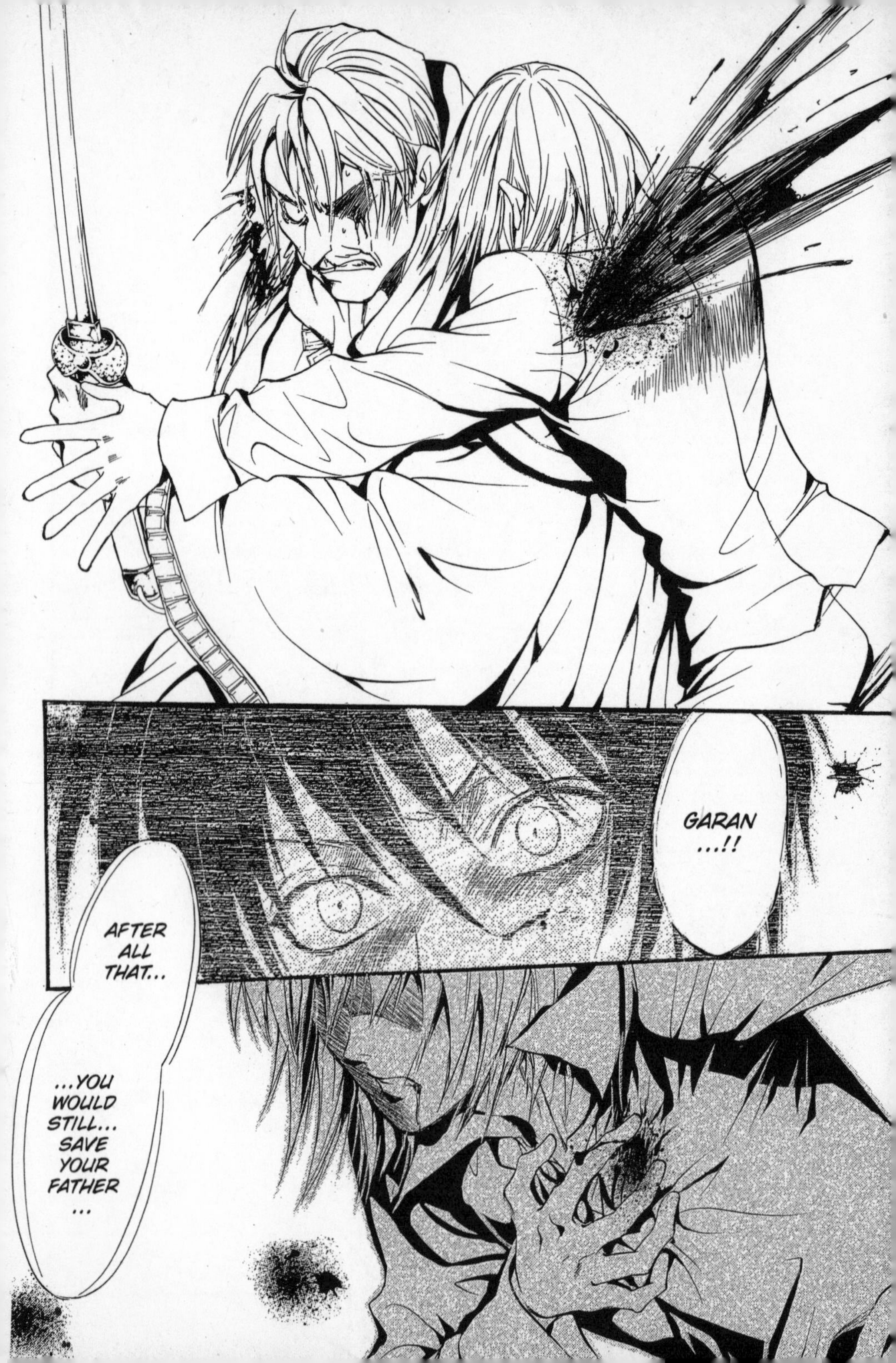
GARAN ...!!
AFTER ALL THAT...
...YOU WOULD STILL... SAVE YOUR FATHER ...

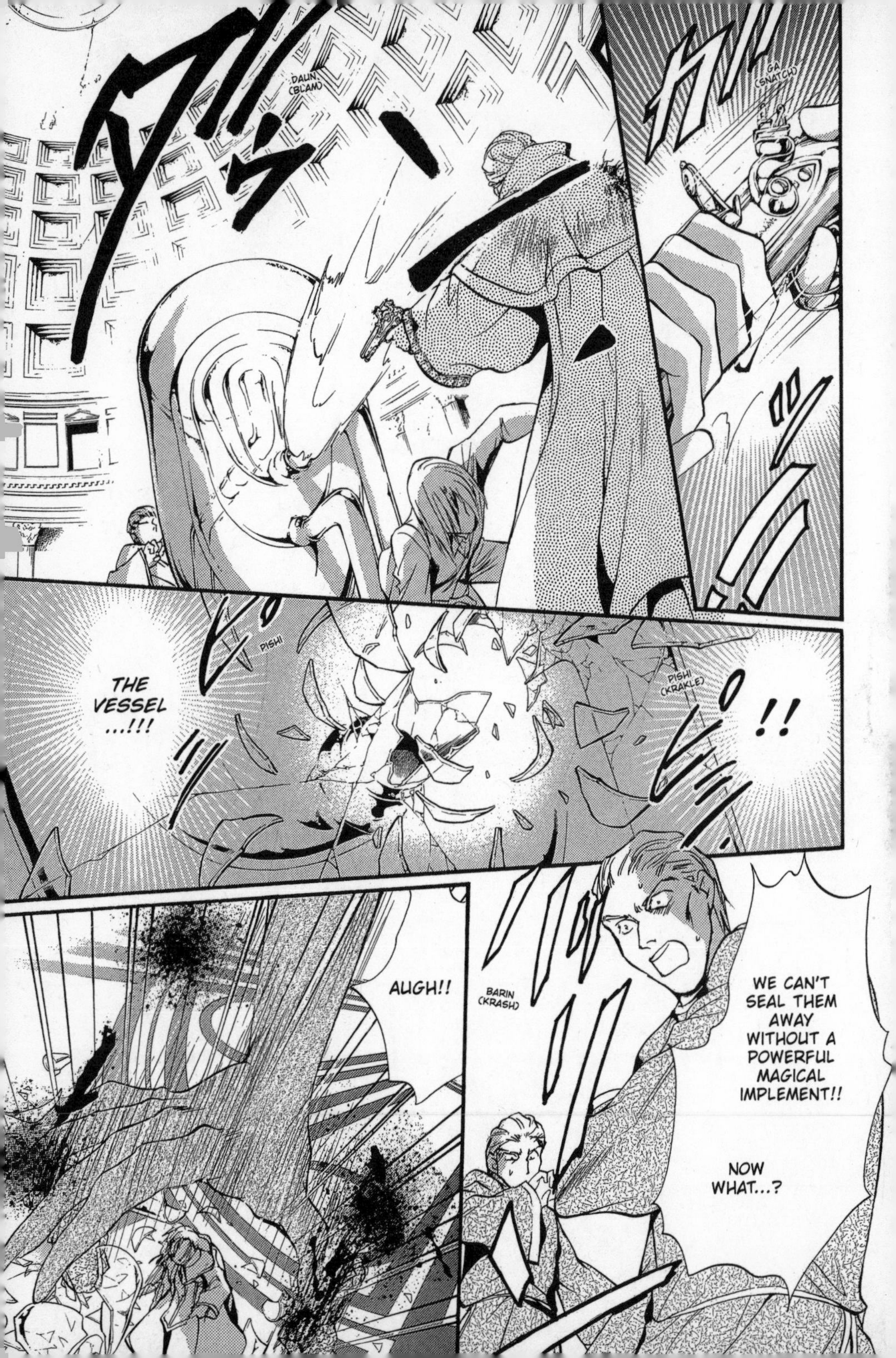
GA (SNATCH)
DAUN (BLAM)
!!
PISHI (KRAKLE)
PISHI
THE VESSEL ...!!!
WE CAN'T SEAL THEM AWAY WITHOUT A POWERFUL MAGICAL IMPLEMENT!!
BARIN (KRASH)
NOW WHAT...?
AUGH!!

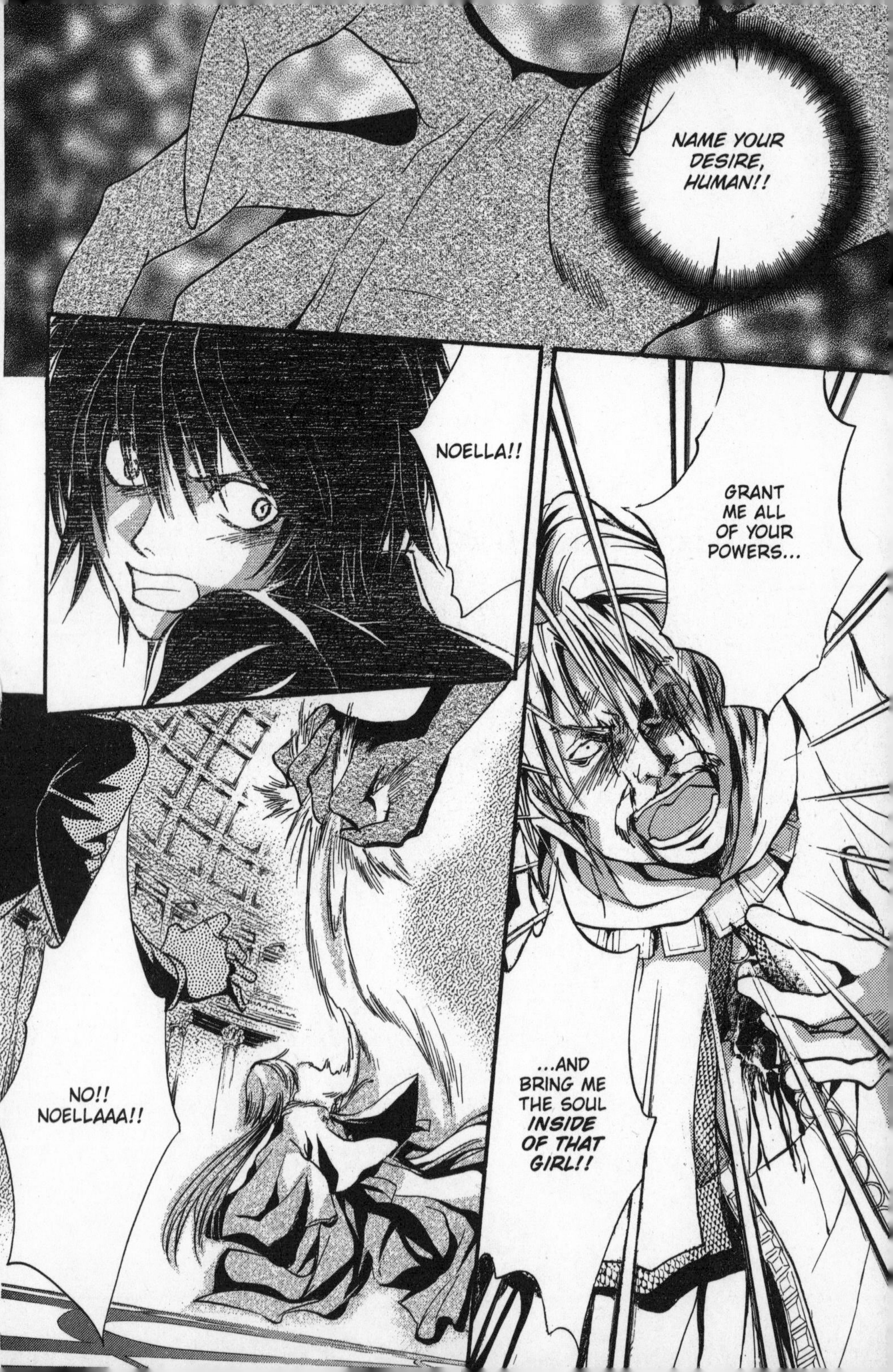
NAME YOUR DESIRE, HUMAN!!
GRANT ME ALL OF YOUR POWERS...
...AND BRING ME THE SOUL *INSIDE OF THAT GIRL!!*
NOELLA!!
NO!! NOELLAAA!!

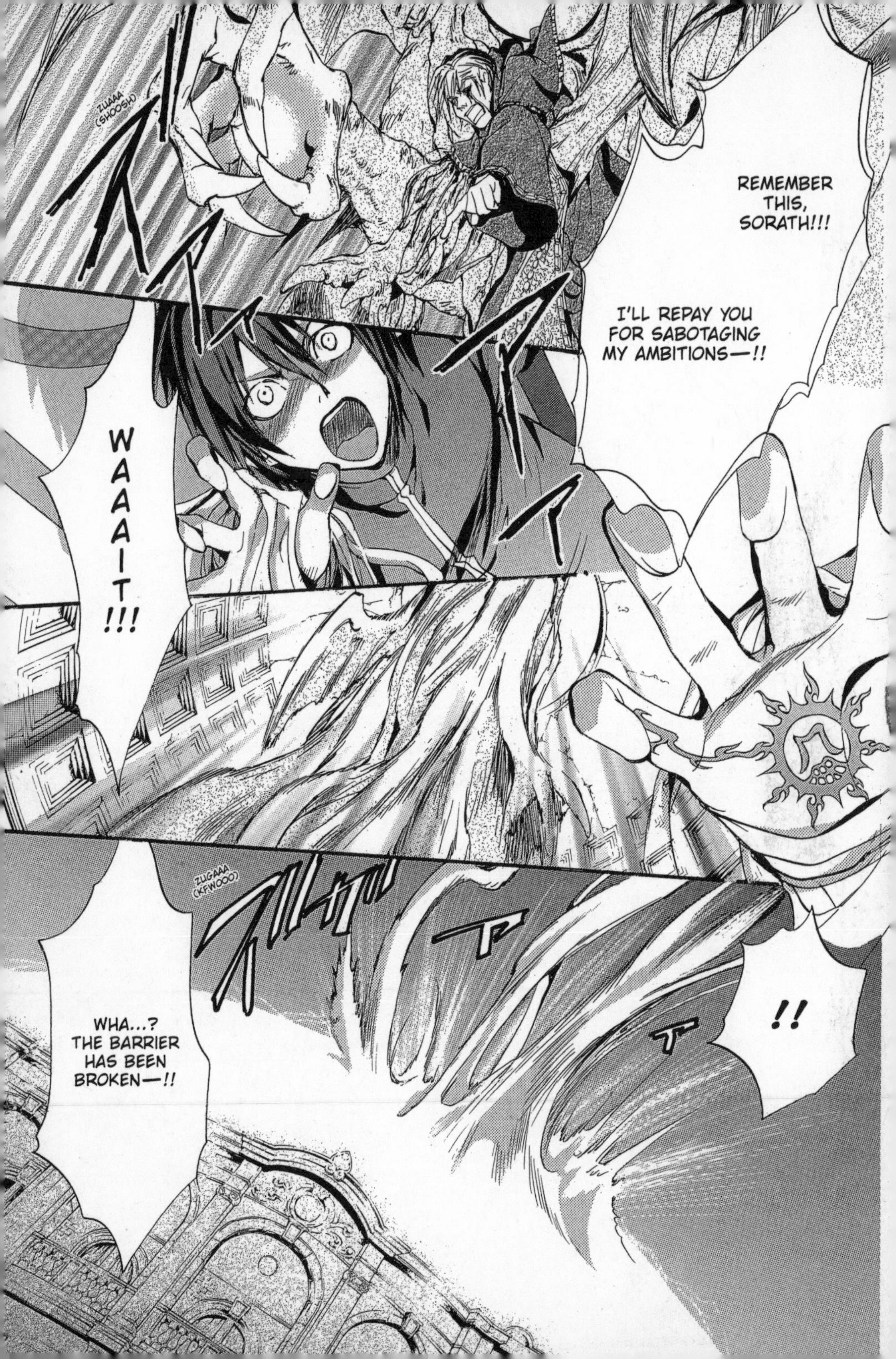
REMEMBER THIS, SORATH!!!
I'LL REPAY YOU FOR SABOTAGING MY AMBITIONS—!!
ZUAAA (SHOOSH)
WAAAAIT!!!
!!
ZUGAAA (KFWOOO)
WHA...? THE BARRIER HAS BEEN BROKEN—!!

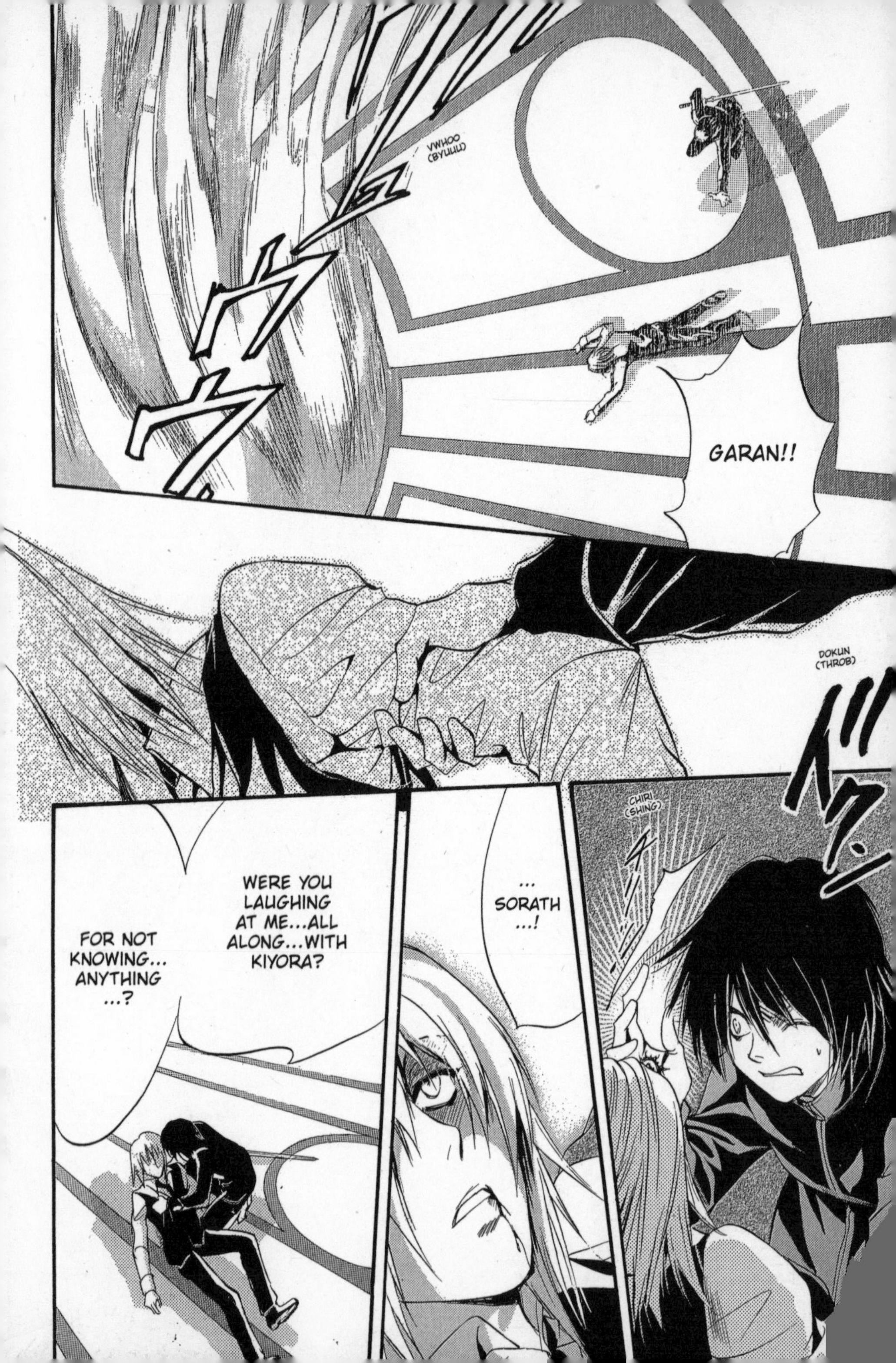
VWHOO
(BYUUU)
GARAN!!
DOKUN
(THROB)
CHIRI
(SHING)
...
SORATH
...!
WERE YOU LAUGHING AT ME...ALL ALONG...WITH KIYORA?
FOR NOT KNOWING... ANYTHING ...?

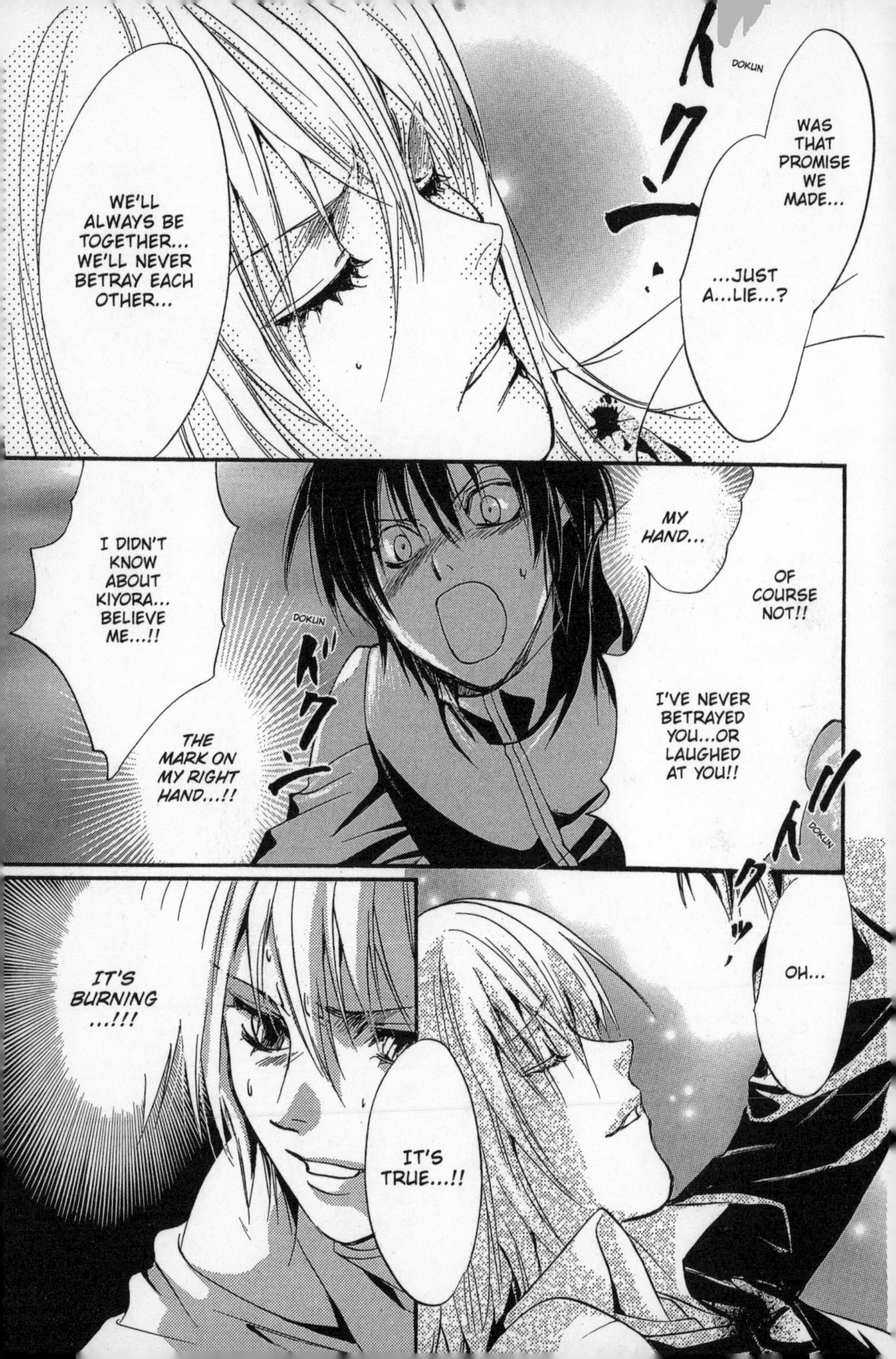
DOKUN
WAS THAT PROMISE WE MADE...
...JUST A...LIE...?
WE'LL ALWAYS BE TOGETHER... WE'LL NEVER BETRAY EACH OTHER...
MY HAND...
OF COURSE NOT!!
I'VE NEVER BETRAYED YOU...OR LAUGHED AT YOU!!
I DIDN'T KNOW ABOUT KIYORA... BELIEVE ME...!!
DOKUN
THE MARK ON MY RIGHT HAND...!!
DOKUN
OH...
IT'S BURNING ...!!!
IT'S TRUE...!!

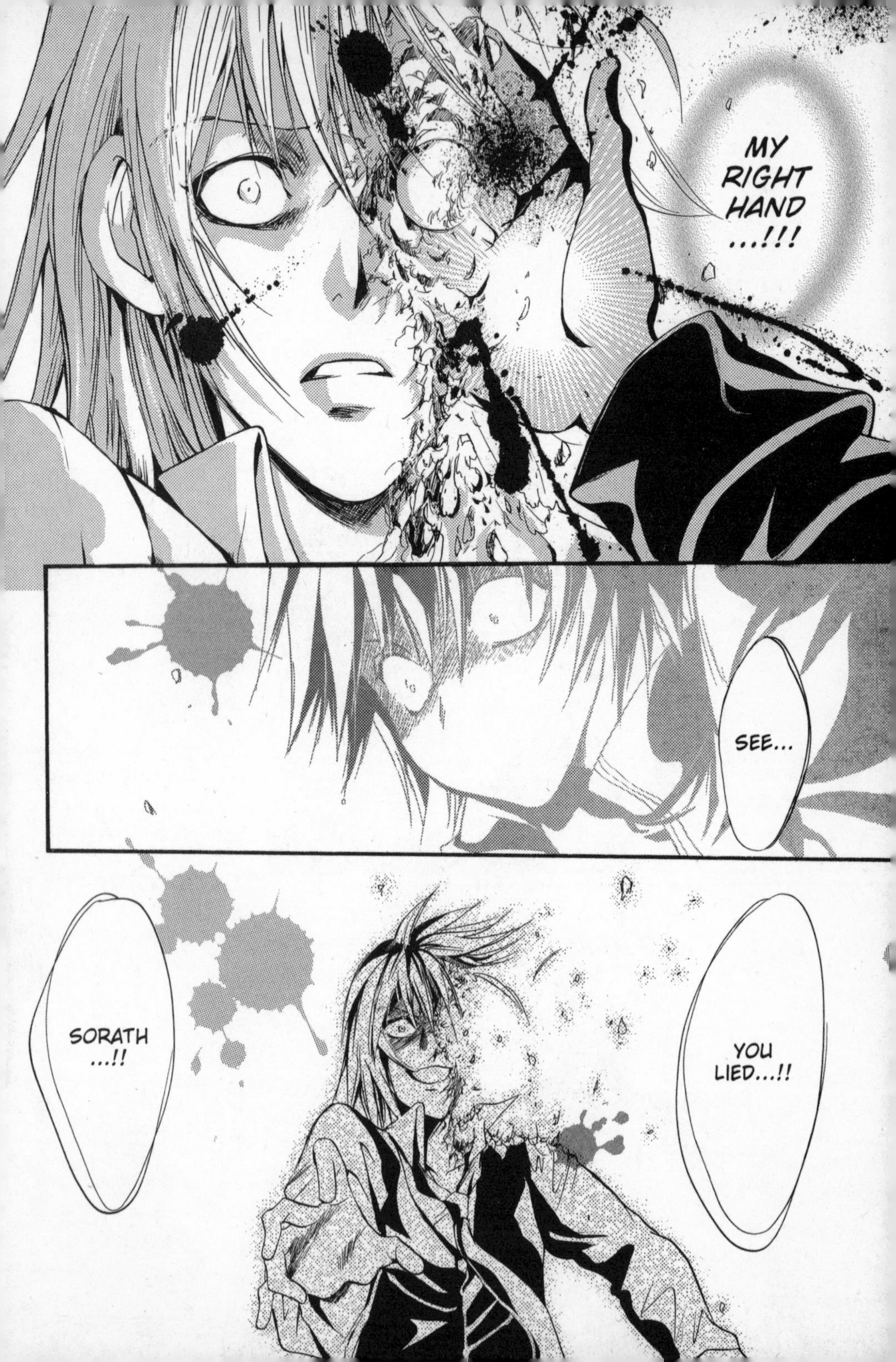
MY RIGHT HAND ...!!!
SEE...
YOU LIED...!!
SORATH ...!!

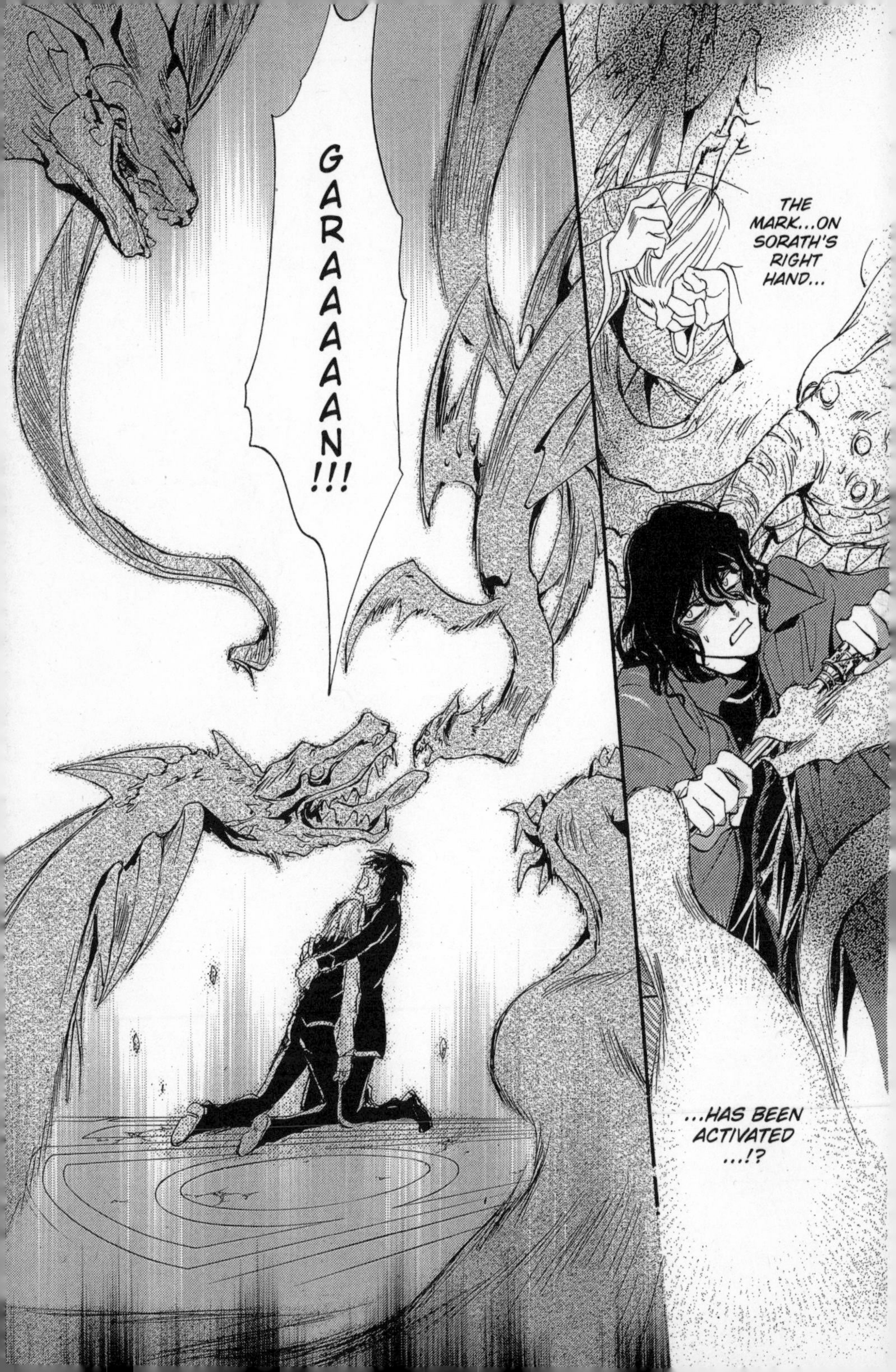
THE MARK...ON SORATH'S RIGHT HAND...
...HAS BEEN ACTIVATED...!?
GARAAAAAAN!!!

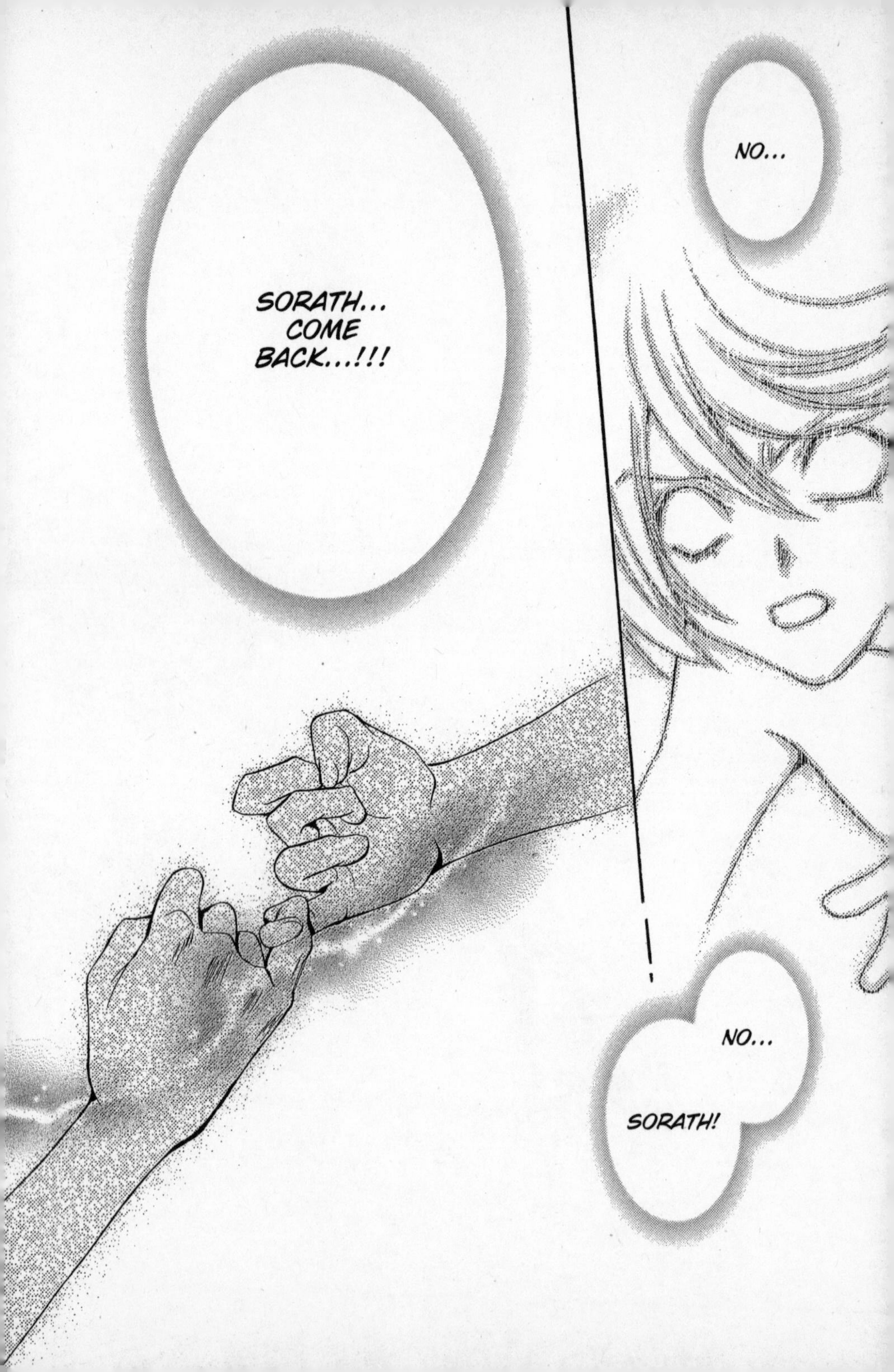
NO...
NO...
SORATH!
SORATH... COME BACK...!!!

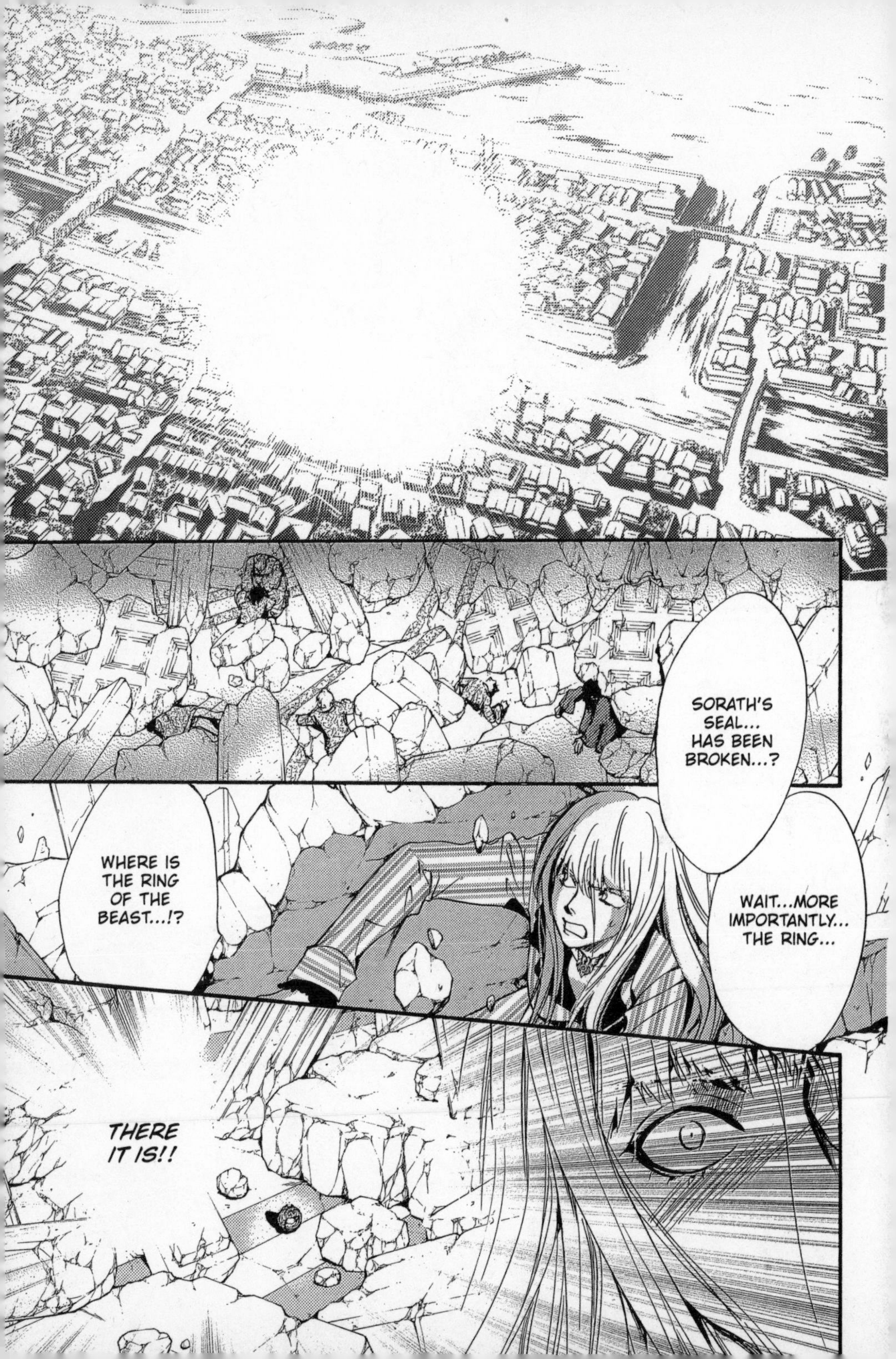
SORATH'S SEAL... HAS BEEN BROKEN...?
WAIT...MORE IMPORTANTLY... THE RING...
WHERE IS THE RING OF THE BEAST...!?
THERE IT IS!!

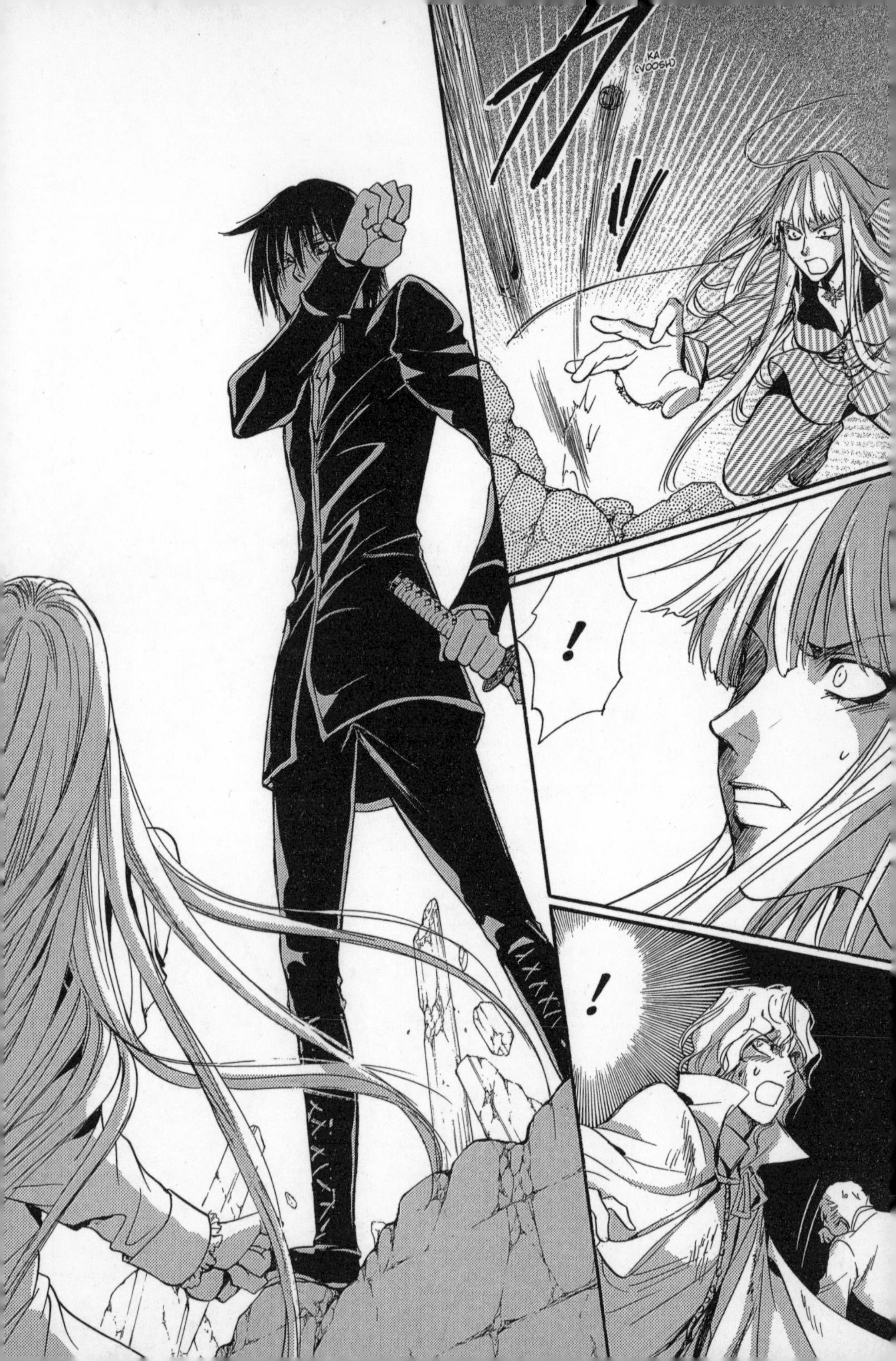
KA
(VOOSH)
!
!

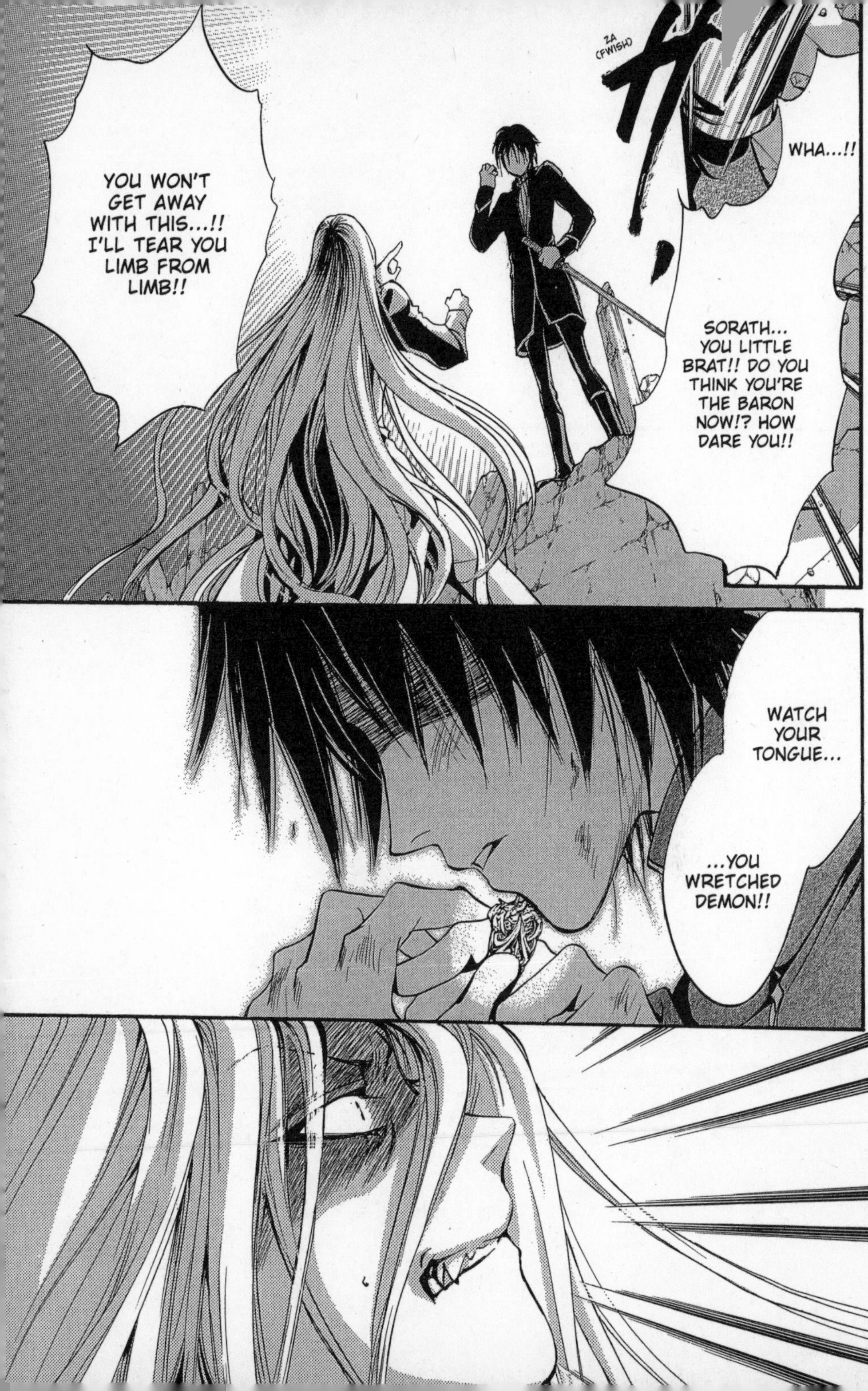
ZA (FWISH)
WHA...!!
SORATH... YOU LITTLE BRAT!! DO YOU THINK YOU'RE THE BARON NOW!? HOW DARE YOU!!
YOU WON'T GET AWAY WITH THIS...!! I'LL TEAR YOU LIMB FROM LIMB!!
WATCH YOUR TONGUE...
...YOU WRETCHED DEMON!!

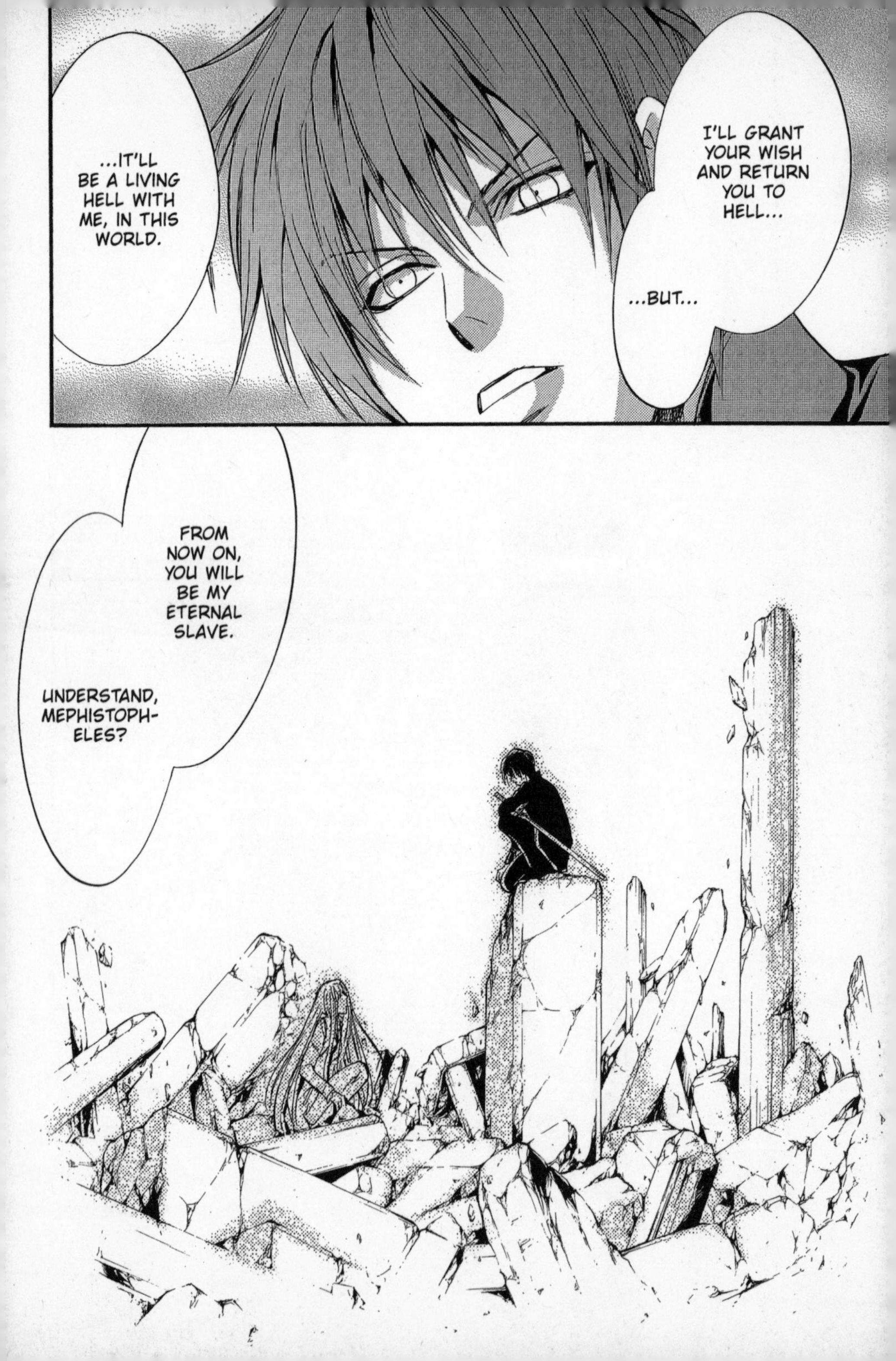
I'LL GRANT YOUR WISH AND RETURN YOU TO HELL...
...BUT...
...IT'LL BE A LIVING HELL WITH ME, IN THIS WORLD.
FROM NOW ON, YOU WILL BE MY ETERNAL SLAVE.
UNDERSTAND, MEPHISTOPHELES?

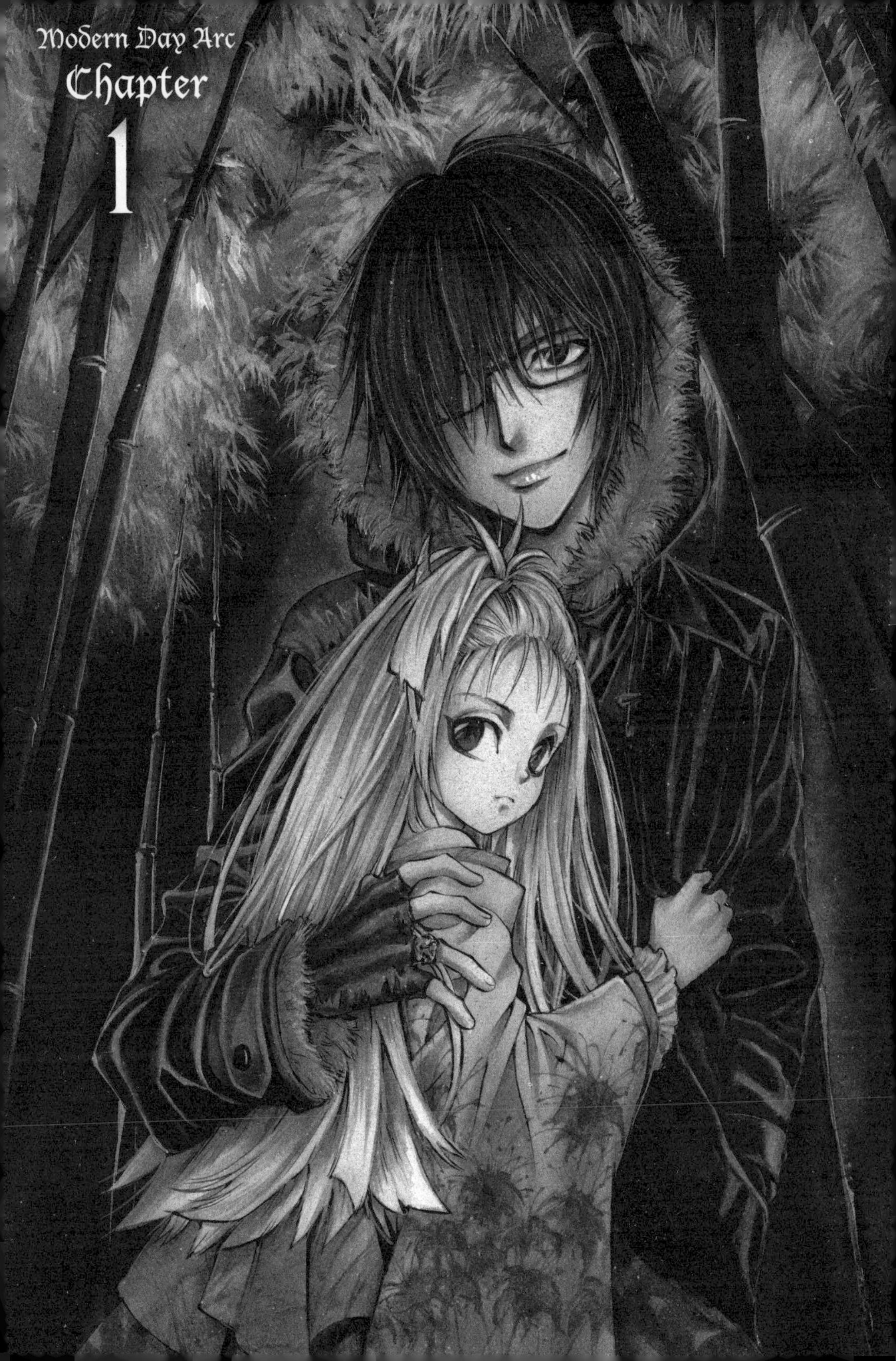
Modern Day Arc
Chapter
1

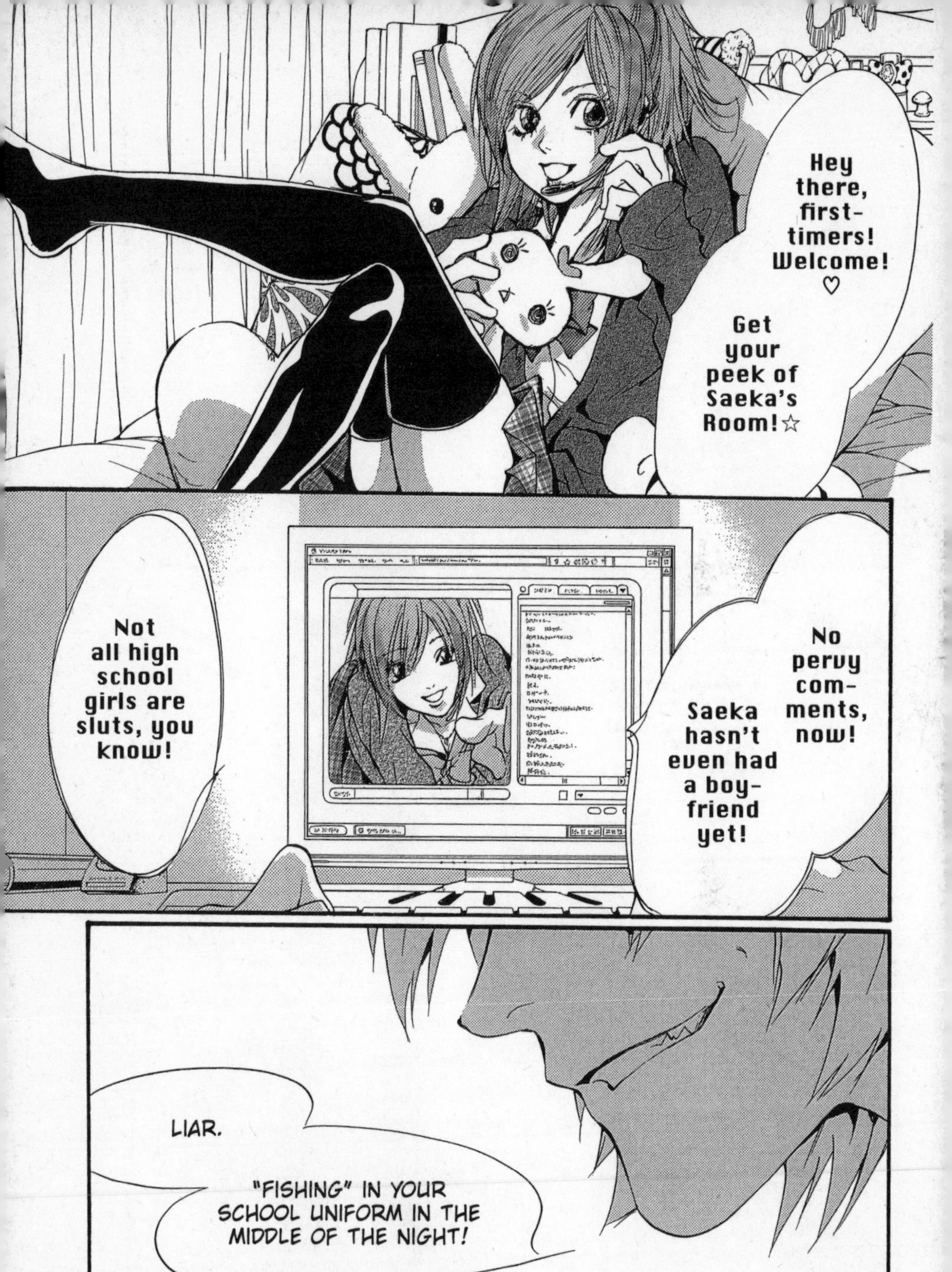
Hey there, first-timers! Welcome! ♡
Get your peek of Saeka's Room!☆
No pervy com-ments, now!
Saeka hasn't even had a boy-friend yet!
Not all high school girls are sluts, you know!
LIAR.
"FISHING" IN YOUR SCHOOL UNIFORM IN THE MIDDLE OF THE NIGHT!

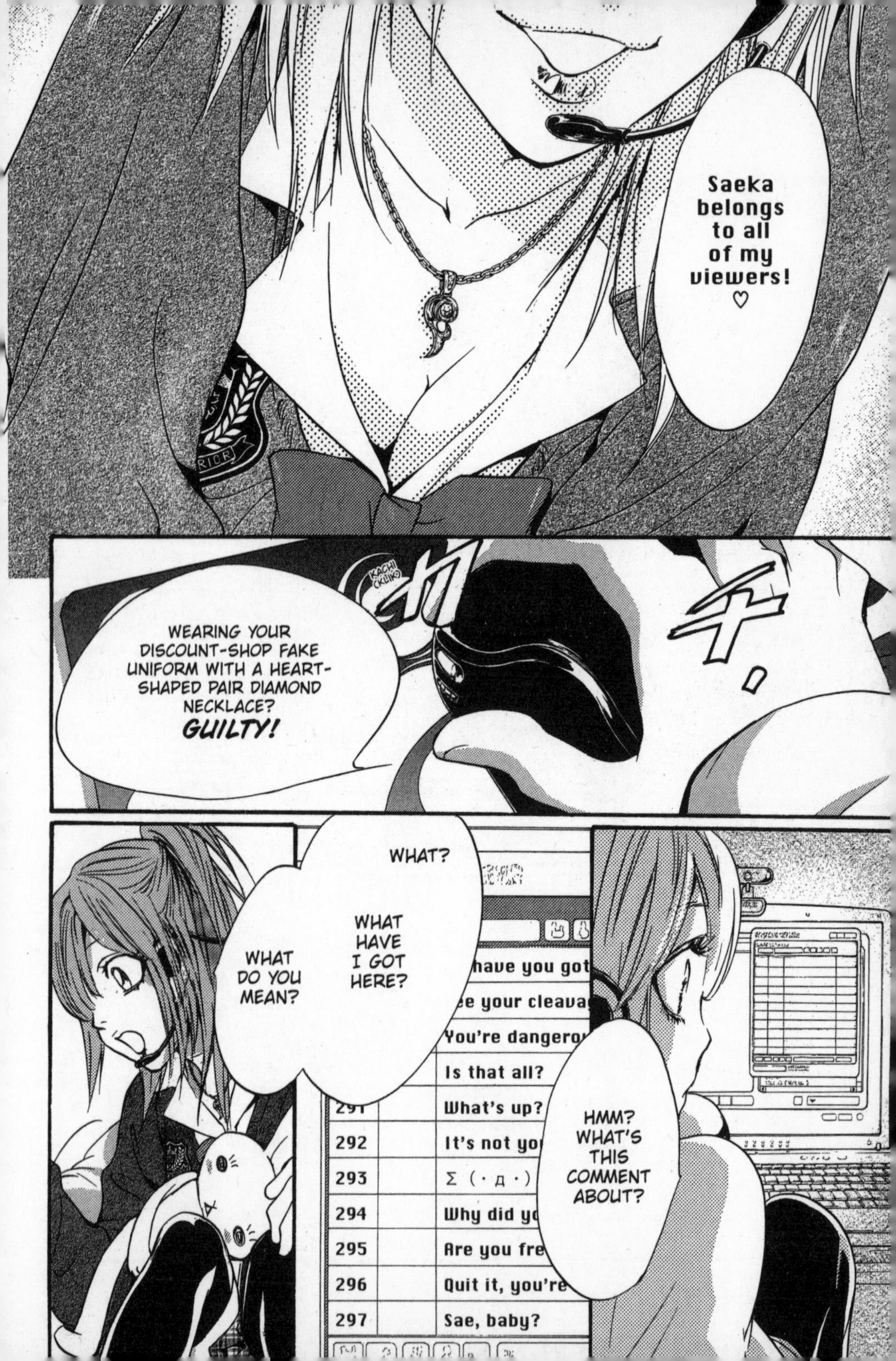
Saeka belongs to all of my viewers! ♡
KACHI (KLIK)
WEARING YOUR DISCOUNT-SHOP FAKE UNIFORM WITH A HEART-SHAPED PAIR DIAMOND NECKLACE? GUILTY!
HMM? WHAT'S THIS COMMENT ABOUT?
have you got
ee your cleavag
You're dangero
Is that all?
291 What's up?
292 It's not yo
293 Σ(・д・)
294 Why did yo
295 Are you fre
296 Quit it, you're
297 Sae, baby?
WHAT?
WHAT HAVE I GOT HERE?
WHAT DO YOU MEAN?

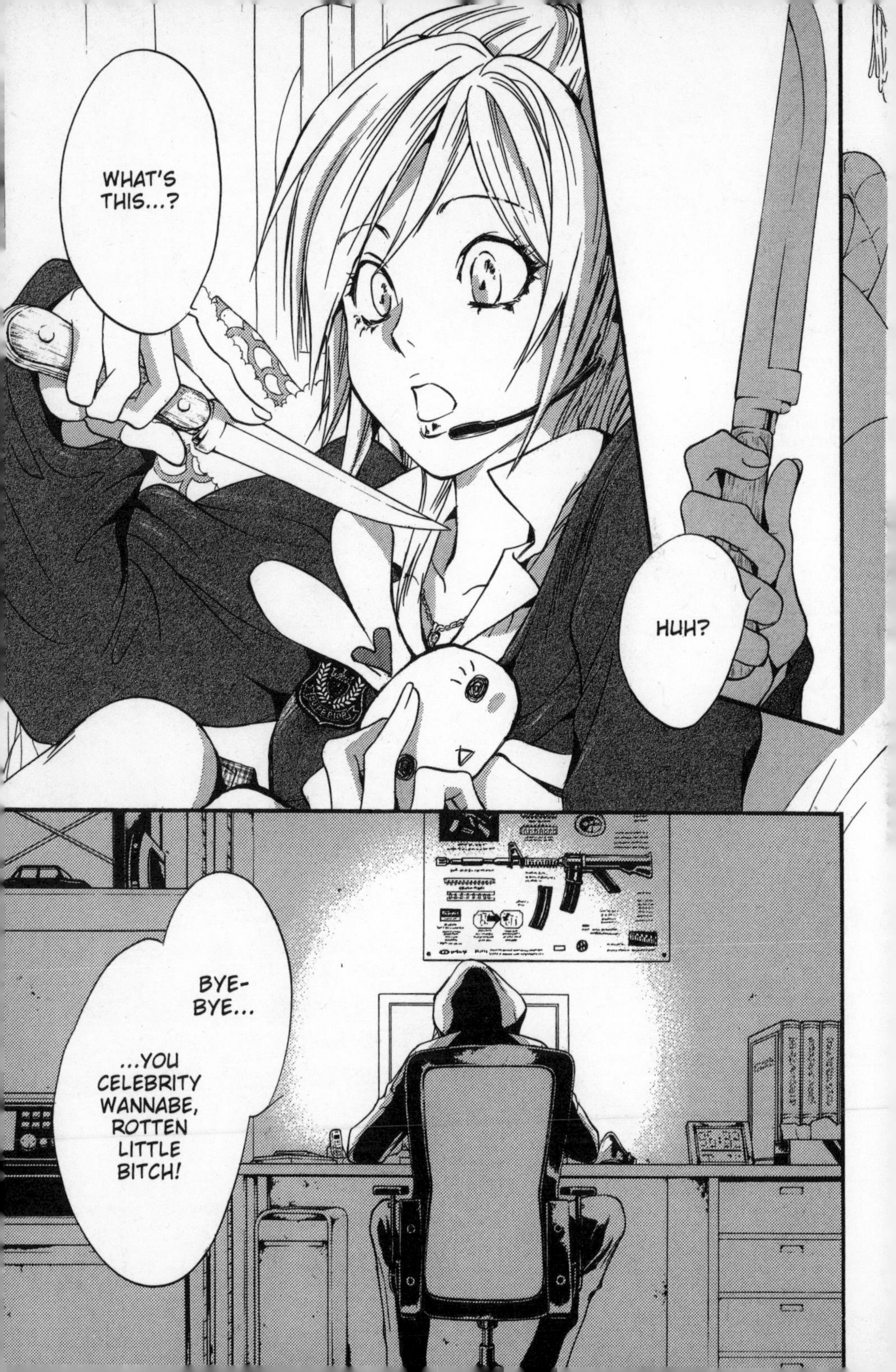
WHAT'S THIS...?
HUH?
BYE-BYE...
...YOU CELEBRITY WANNABE, ROTTEN LITTLE BITCH!

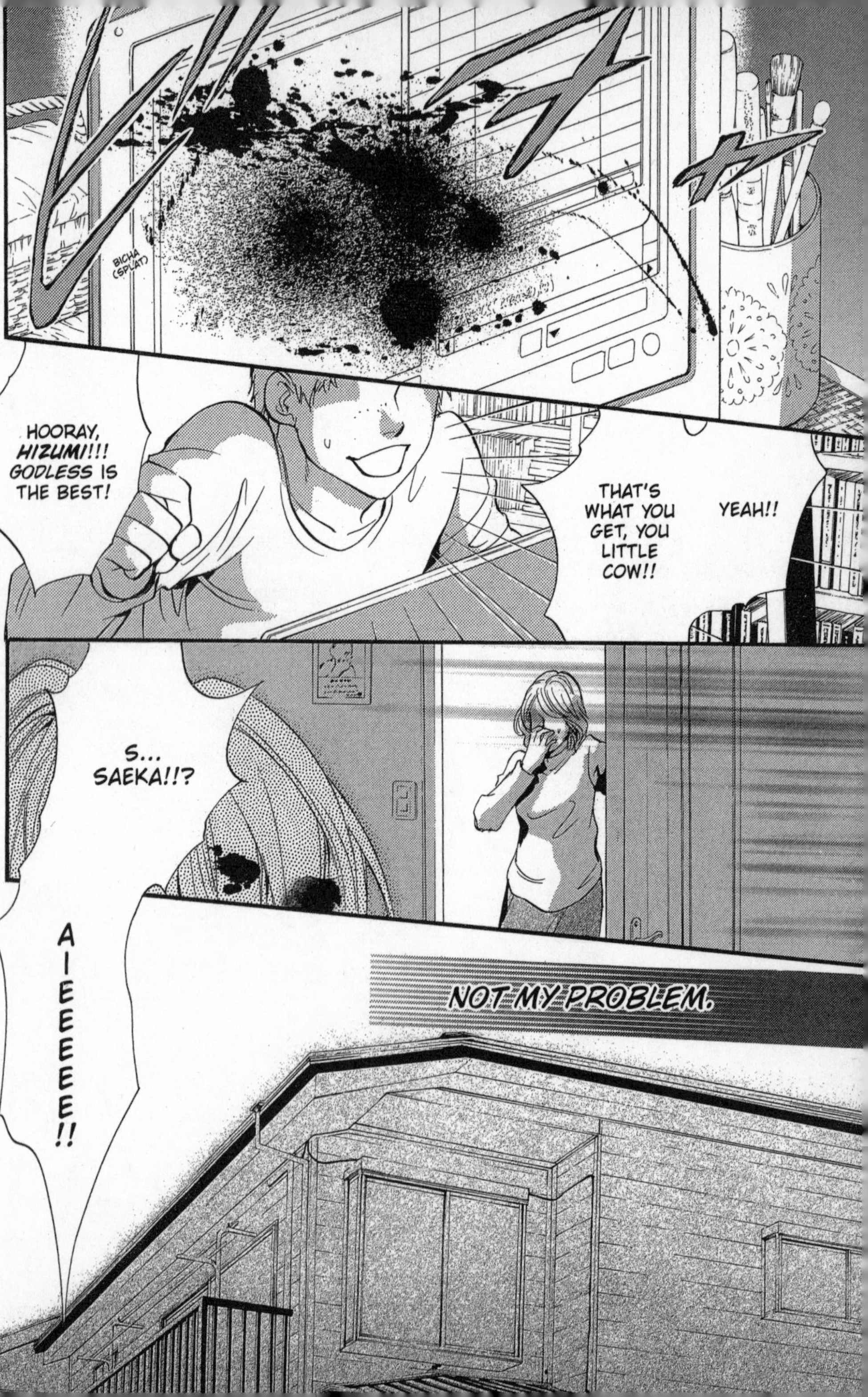
BICHA (SPLAT)
YEAH!!
THAT'S WHAT YOU GET, YOU LITTLE COW!!
HOORAY, HIZUMI!!!! GODLESS IS THE BEST!
S... SAEKA!!?
NOT MY PROBLEM.
AIEEEEE!!

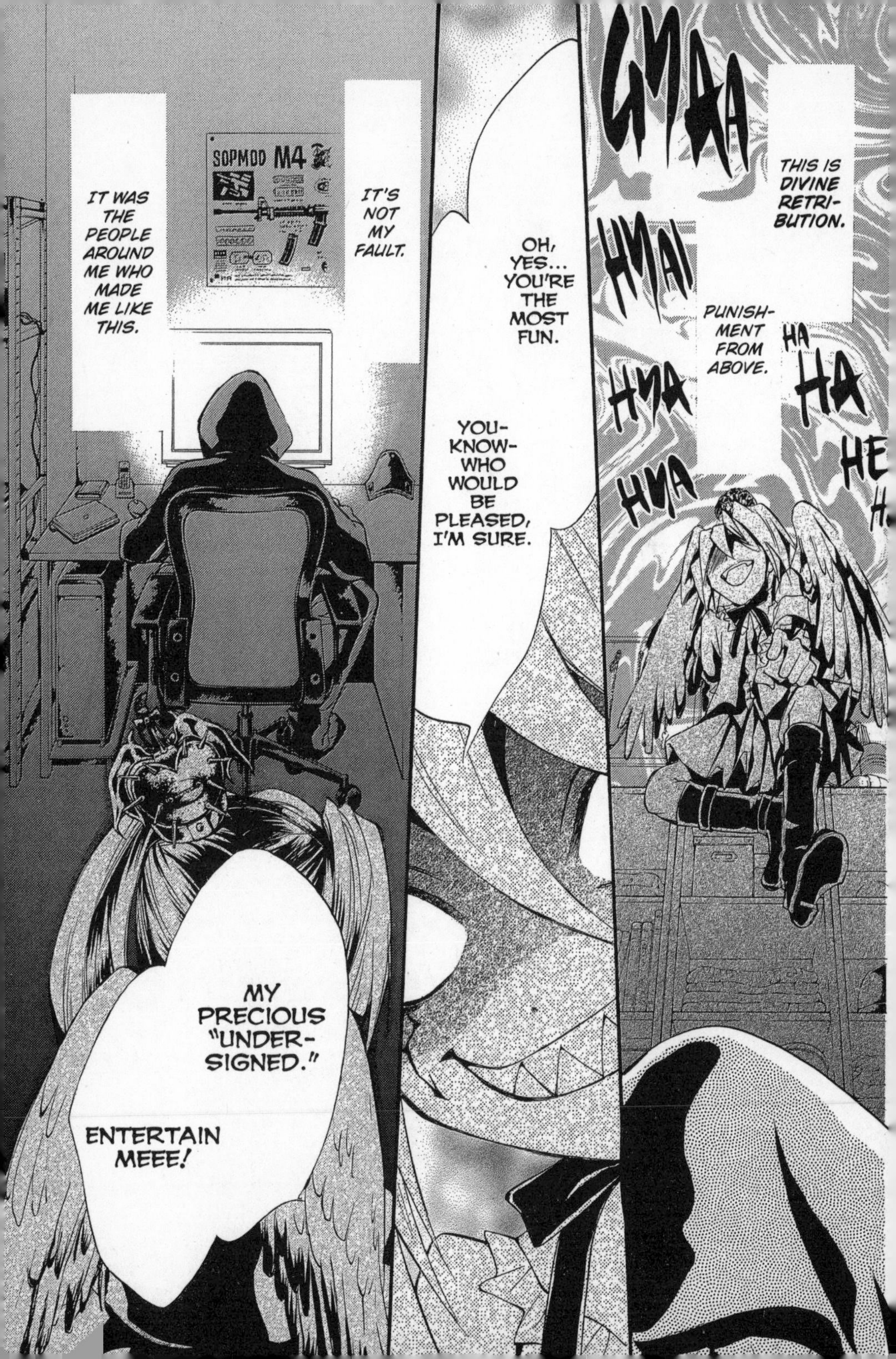
GYAA
THIS IS DIVINE RETRIBUTION.
HYAI
PUNISHMENT FROM ABOVE.
HA HA
HYA
HE
HYA
OH, YES... YOU'RE THE MOST FUN.
YOU-KNOW-WHO WOULD BE PLEASED, I'M SURE.
IT'S NOT MY FAULT.
IT WAS THE PEOPLE AROUND ME WHO MADE ME LIKE THIS.
SOPMOD M4
MY PRECIOUS "UNDERSIGNED."
ENTERTAIN MEEE!

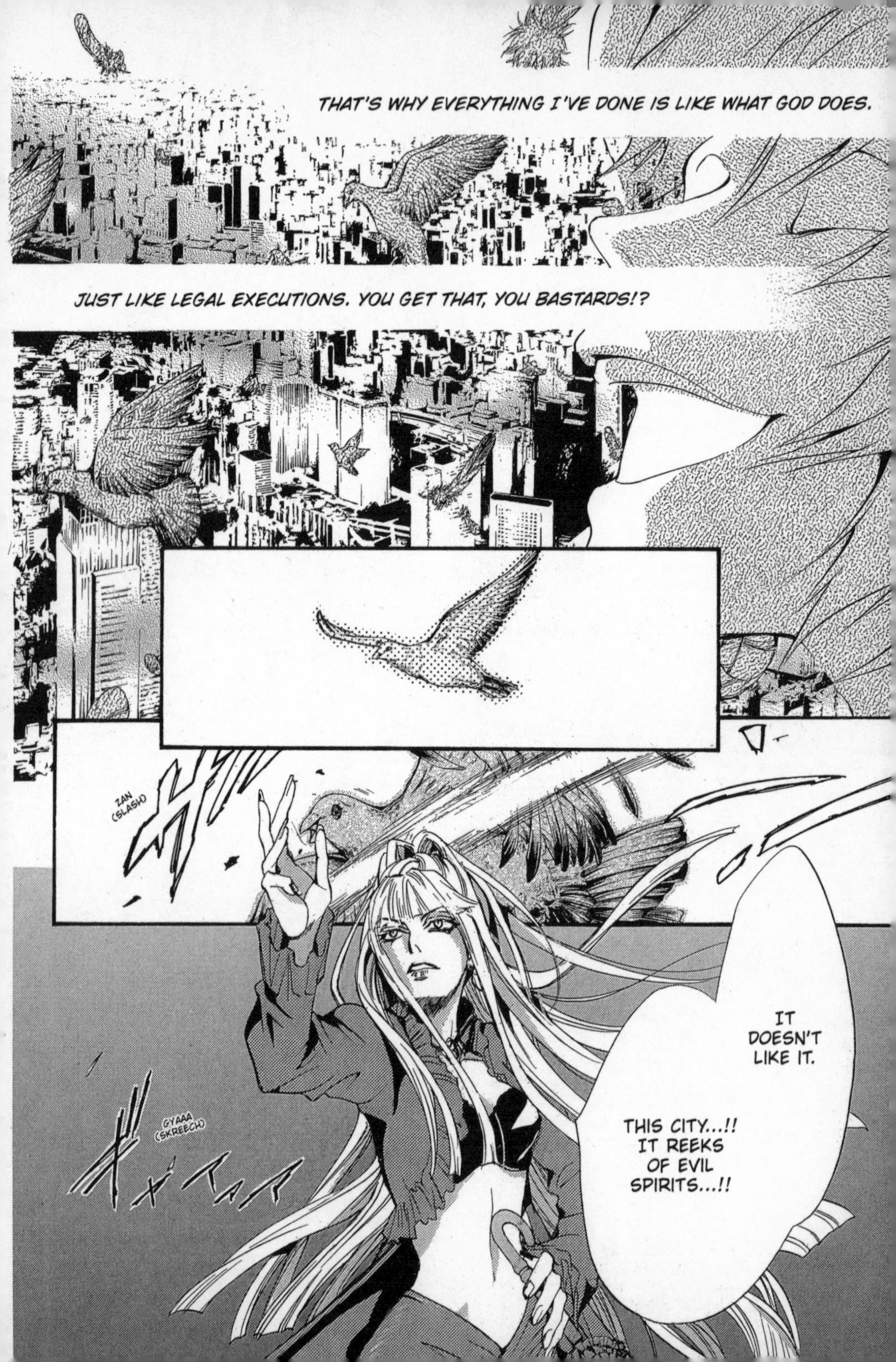
THAT'S WHY EVERYTHING I'VE DONE IS LIKE WHAT GOD DOES.
JUST LIKE LEGAL EXECUTIONS. YOU GET THAT, YOU BASTARDS!?
ZAN (SLASH)
IT DOESN'T LIKE IT.
THIS CITY...!! IT REEKS OF EVIL SPIRITS...!!
GYAAA (SKREECH)

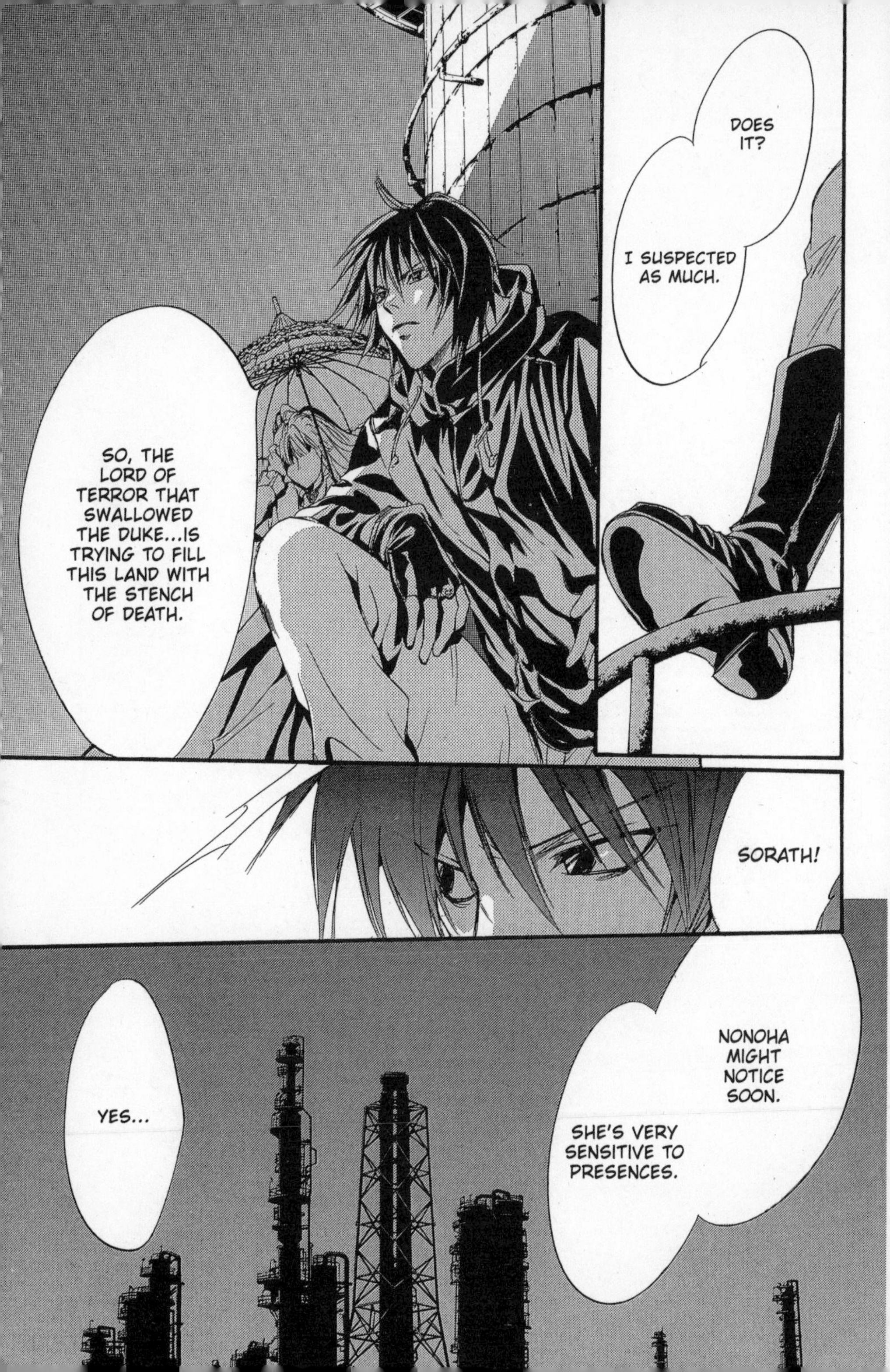
DOES IT?
I SUSPECTED AS MUCH.
SO, THE LORD OF TERROR THAT SWALLOWED THE DUKE...IS TRYING TO FILL THIS LAND WITH THE STENCH OF DEATH.
SORATH!
NONOHA MIGHT NOTICE SOON.
SHE'S VERY SENSITIVE TO PRESENCES.
YES...

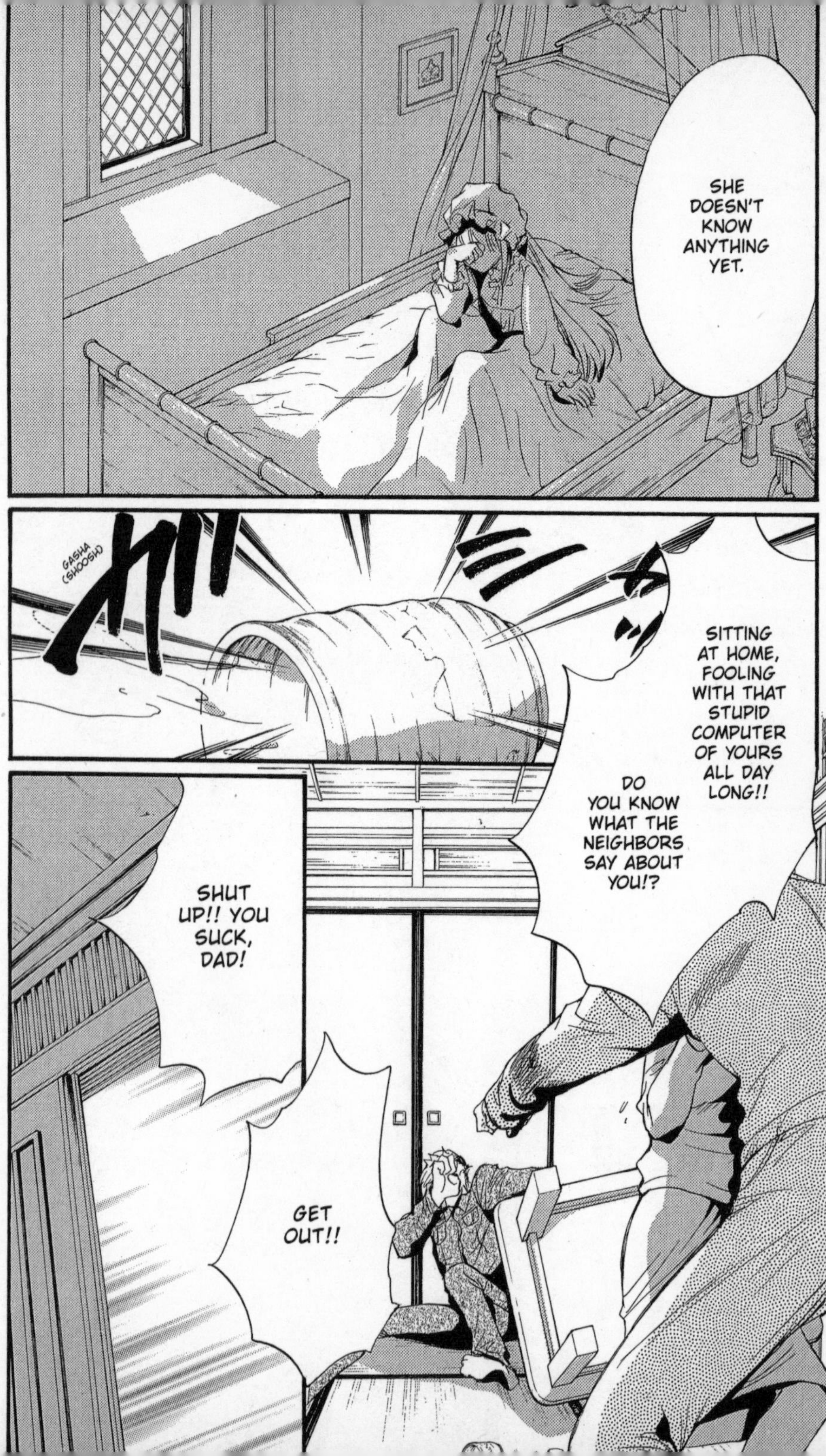
SHE DOESN'T KNOW ANYTHING YET.
GASHA (SHOOSH)
SITTING AT HOME, FOOLING WITH THAT STUPID COMPUTER OF YOURS ALL DAY LONG!!
DO YOU KNOW WHAT THE NEIGHBORS SAY ABOUT YOU!?
SHUT UP!! YOU SUCK, DAD!
GET OUT!!

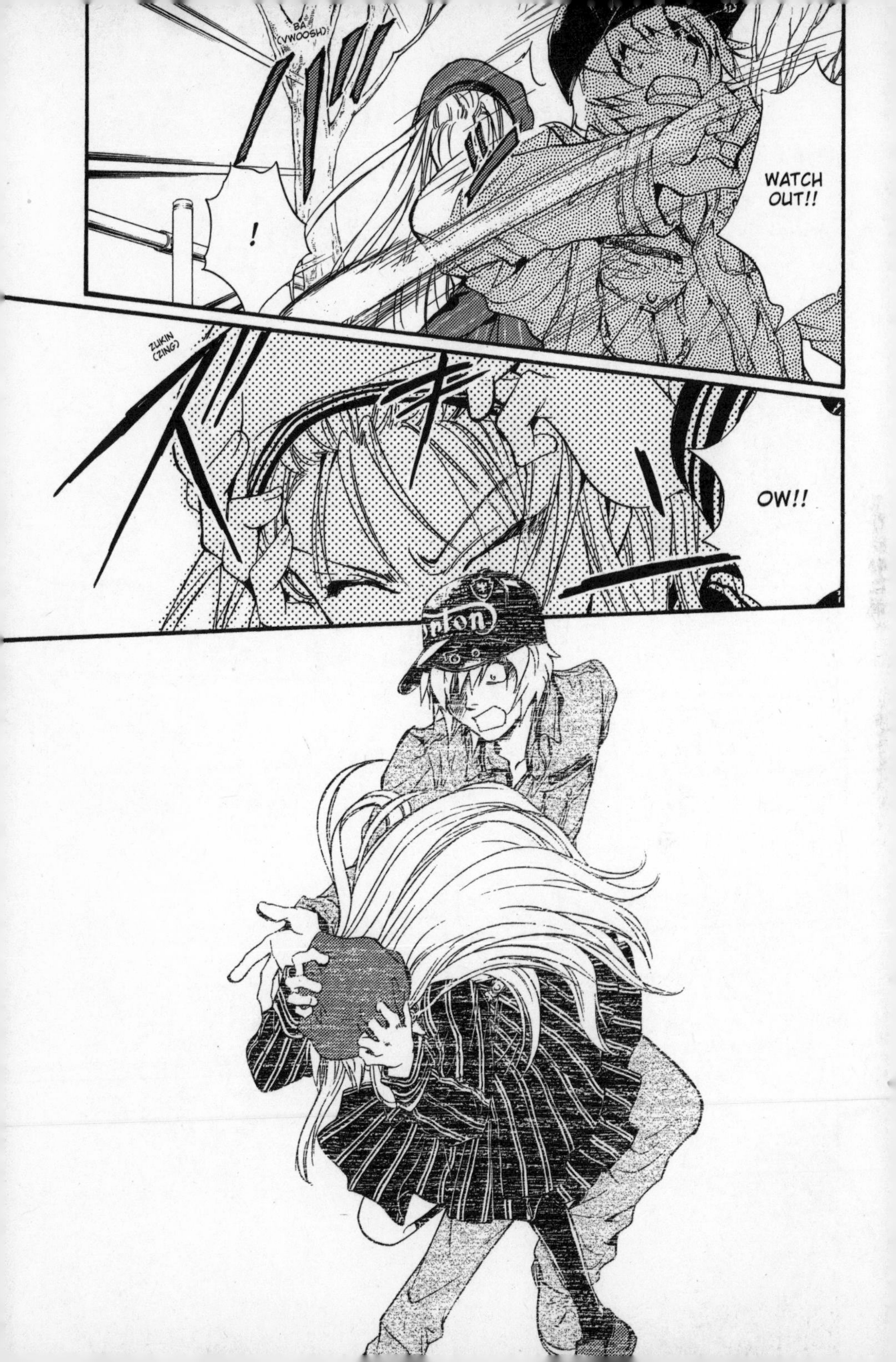
WATCH OUT!!
BA (VWOOSH)
!
OW!!
ZUKIN (ZING)

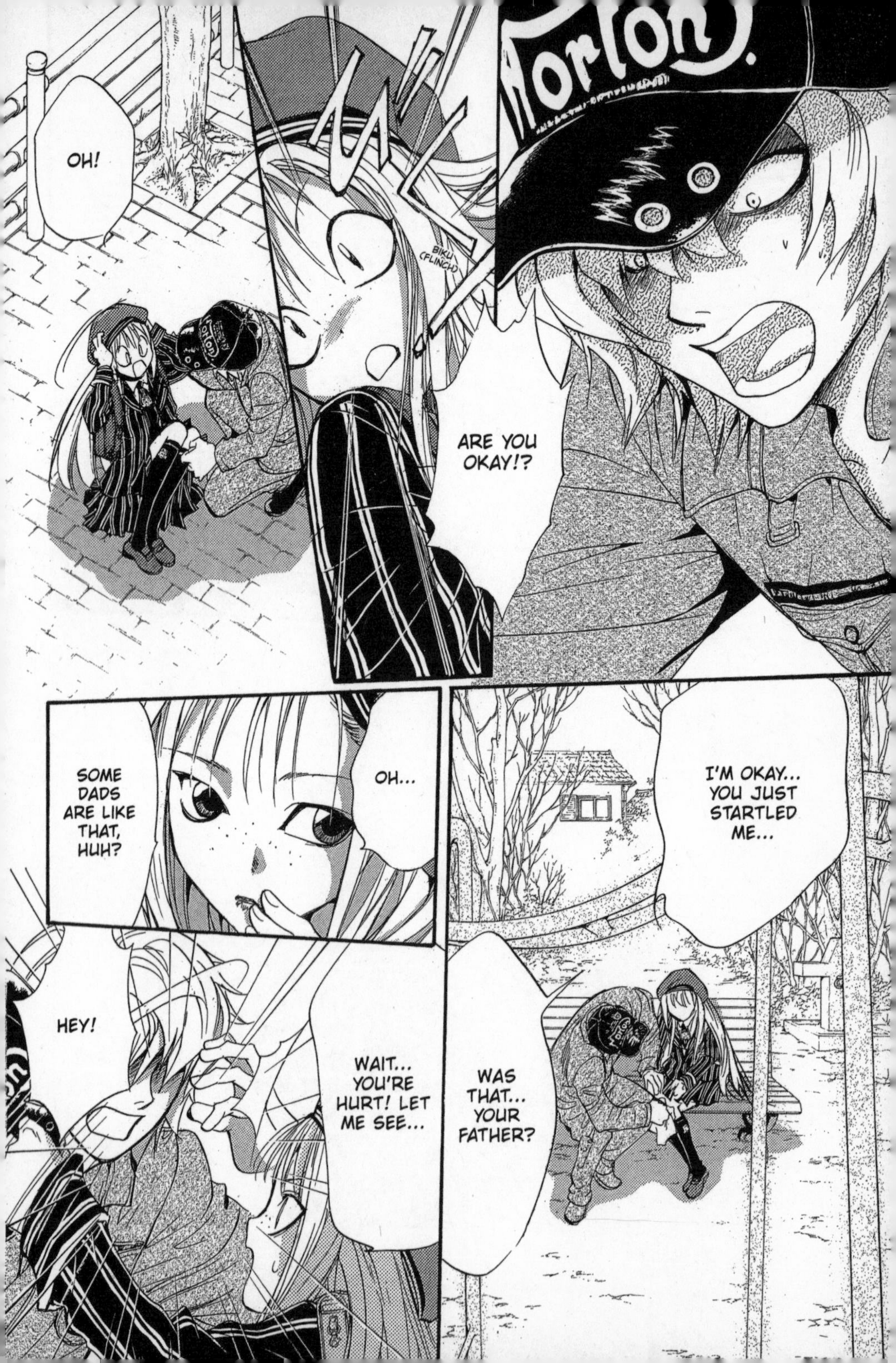
ARE YOU OKAY!?
BIKU (FLINCH)
OH!
I'M OKAY... YOU JUST STARTLED ME...
WAS THAT... YOUR FATHER?
OH...
SOME DADS ARE LIKE THAT, HUH?
WAIT... YOU'RE HURT! LET ME SEE...
HEY!

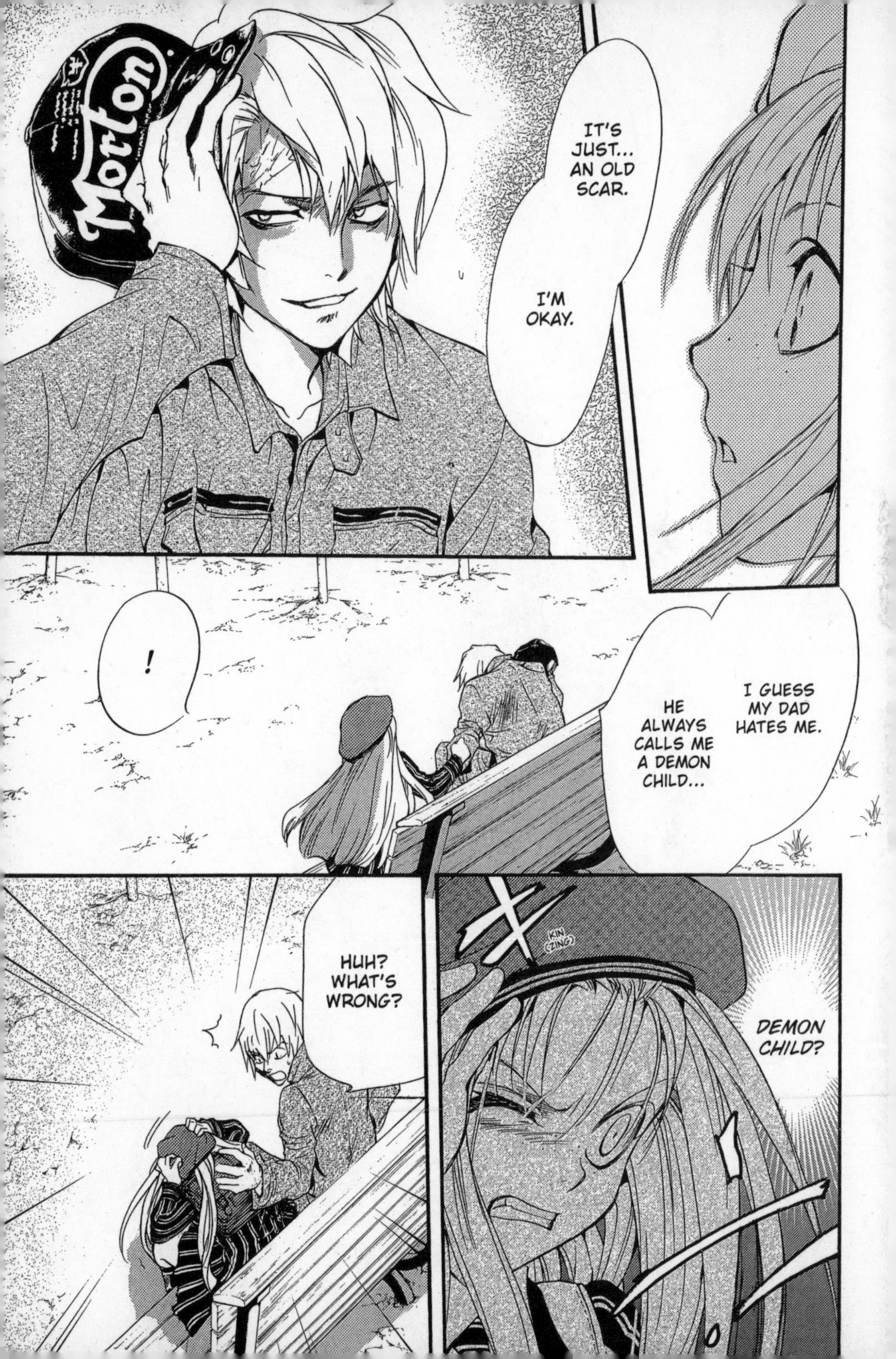
Morton
IT'S JUST... AN OLD SCAR.
I'M OKAY.
I GUESS MY DAD HATES ME.
HE ALWAYS CALLS ME A DEMON CHILD...
!
KIN (ZING)
DEMON CHILD?
HUH? WHAT'S WRONG?

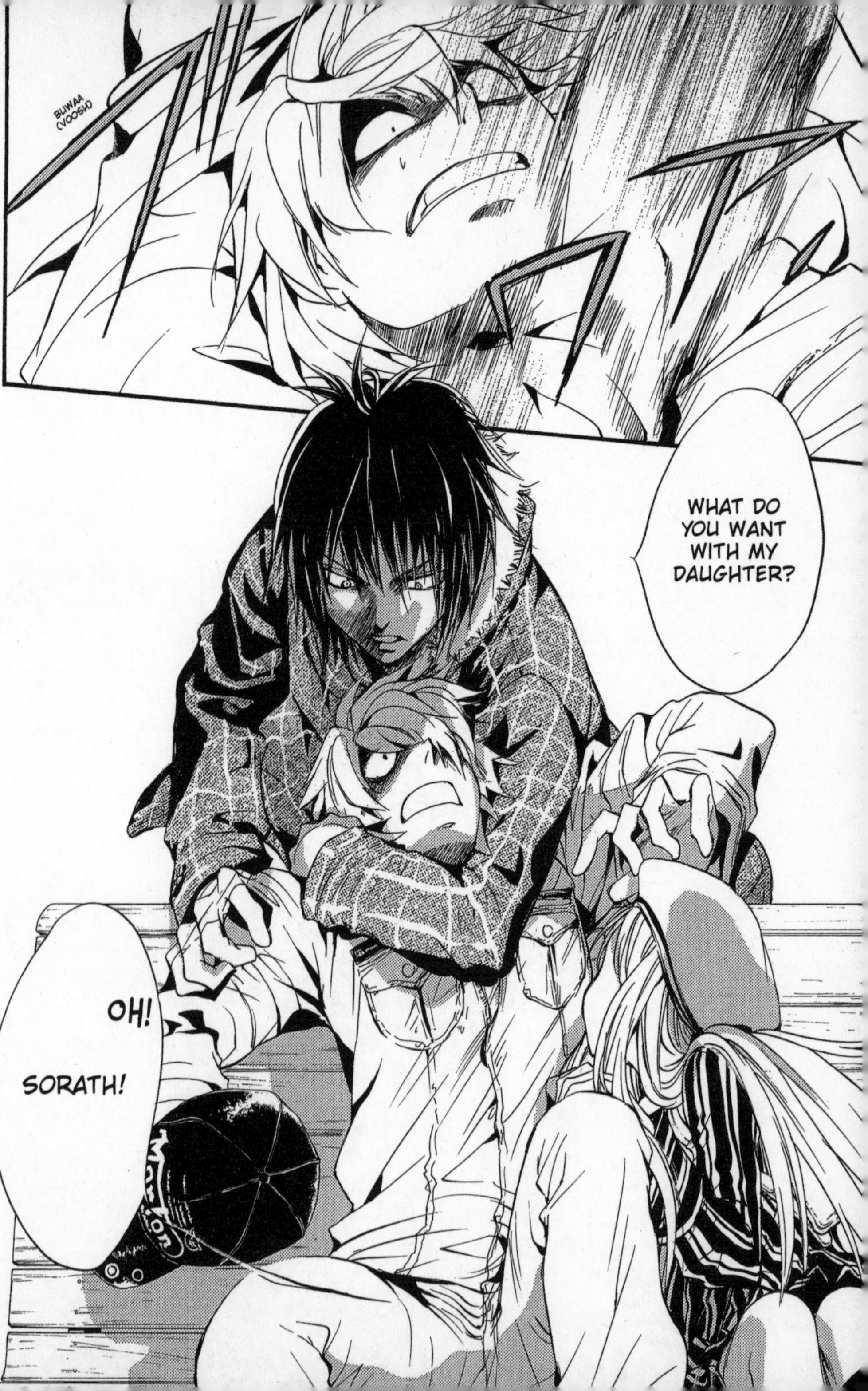
BUWAA (VOOSH)
WHAT DO YOU WANT WITH MY DAUGHTER?
OH!
SORATH!

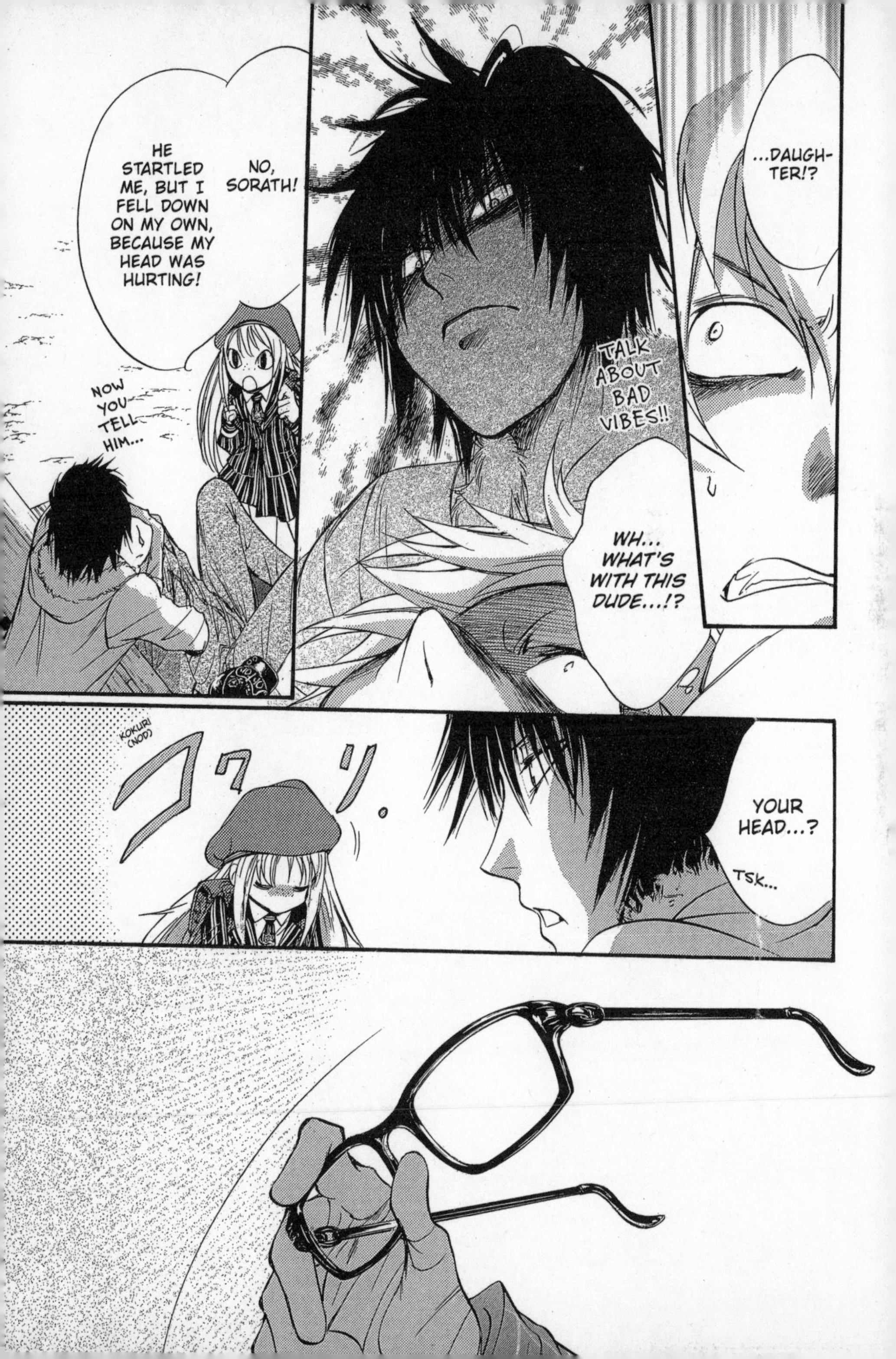
...DAUGHTER!?
TALK ABOUT BAD VIBES!!
WH... WHAT'S WITH THIS DUDE...!?
NO, SORATH!
HE STARTLED ME, BUT I FELL DOWN ON MY OWN, BECAUSE MY HEAD WAS HURTING!
NOW YOU TELL HIM...
YOUR HEAD...?
TSK...
KOKURI (NOD)

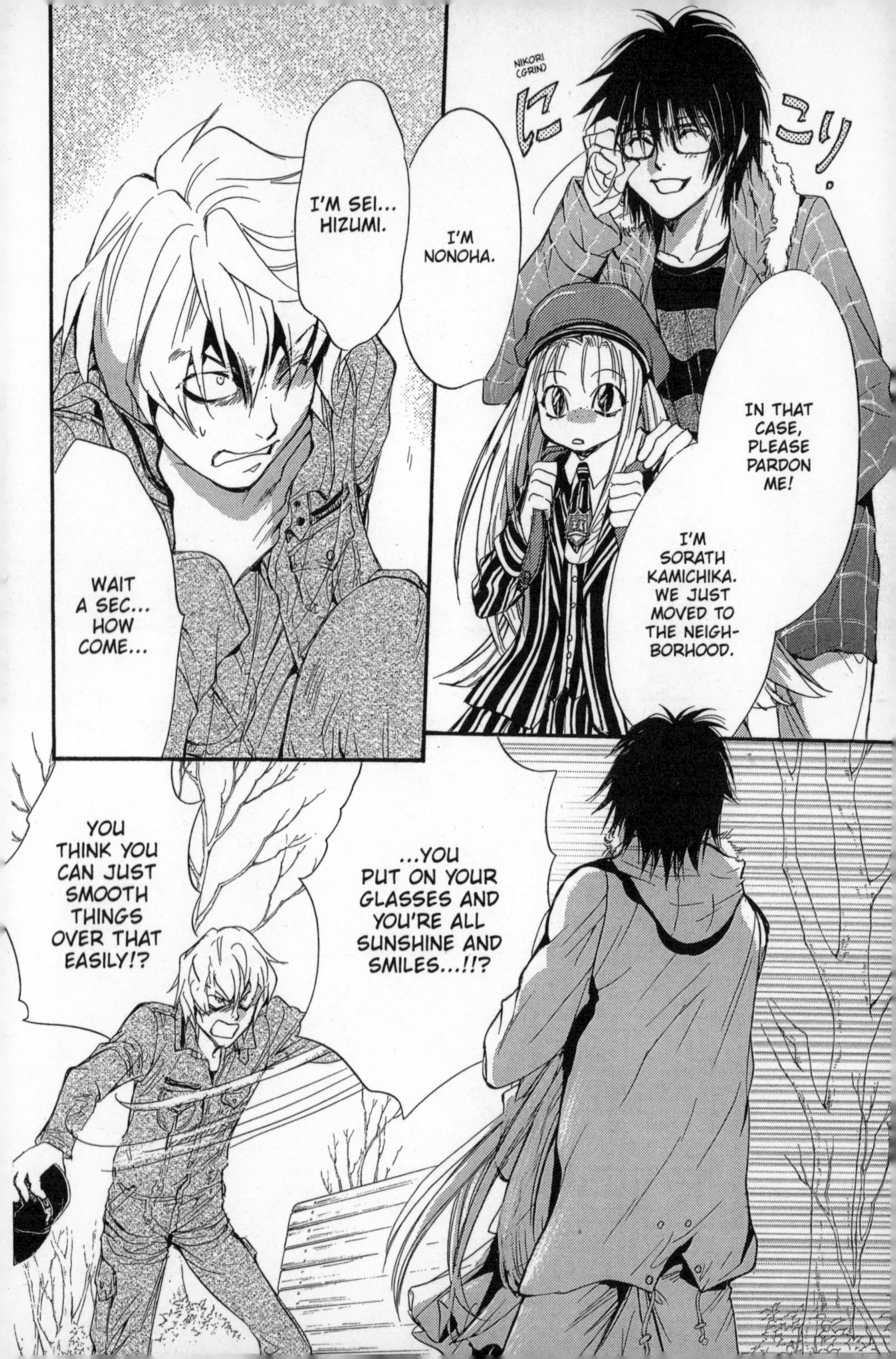
NIKORI (GRIN)
にこり。
IN THAT CASE, PLEASE PARDON ME!
I'M SORATH KAMICHIKA. WE JUST MOVED TO THE NEIGH-BORHOOD.
I'M NONOHA.
I'M SEI... HIZUMI.
WAIT A SEC... HOW COME...
...YOU PUT ON YOUR GLASSES AND YOU'RE ALL SUNSHINE AND SMILES...!!?
YOU THINK YOU CAN JUST SMOOTH THINGS OVER THAT EASILY!?

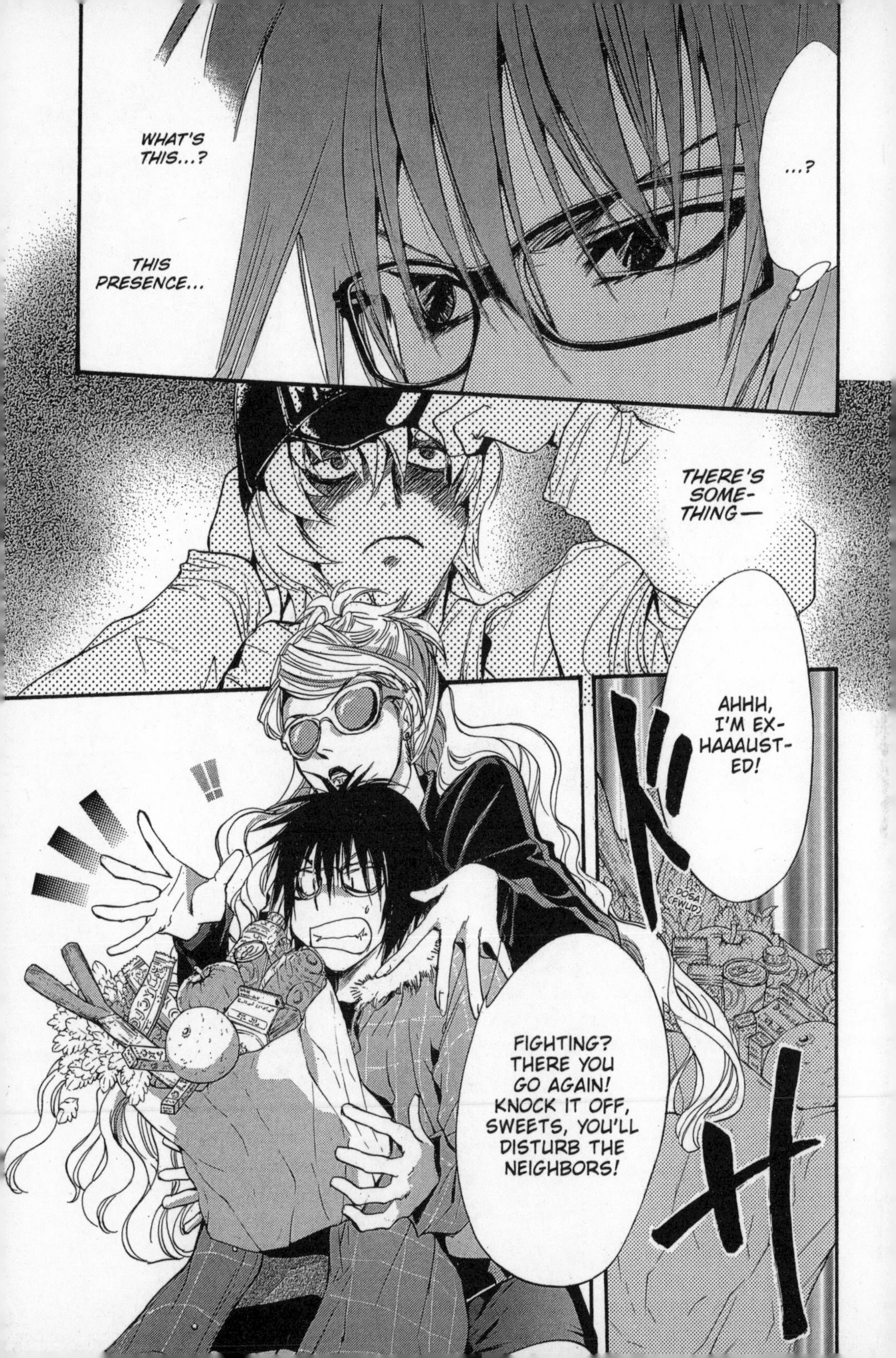

...?
WHAT'S THIS...?
THIS PRESENCE...
THERE'S SOMETHING—
AHHH, I'M EXHAAAUSTED!
DOSA (FWUD)
FIGHTING? THERE YOU GO AGAIN! KNOCK IT OFF, SWEETS, YOU'LL DISTURB THE NEIGHBORS!

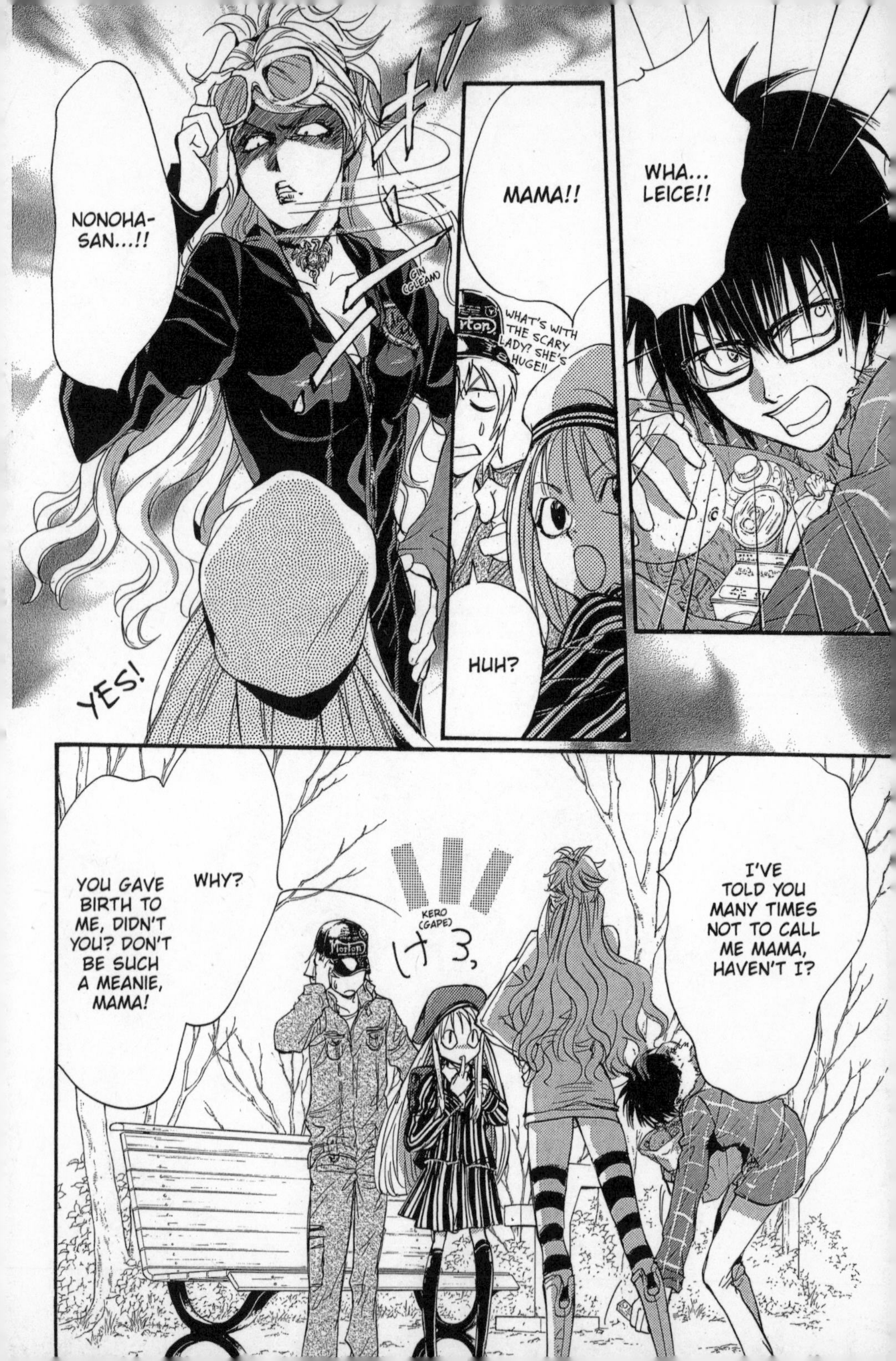
WHA... LEICE!!
MAMA!!
WHAT'S WITH THE SCARY LADY? SHE'S HUGE!!
HUH?
NONOHA-SAN...!!
GIN (GLEAM)
YES!
I'VE TOLD YOU MANY TIMES NOT TO CALL ME MAMA, HAVEN'T I?
KERO (GAPE)
WHY?
YOU GAVE BIRTH TO ME, DIDN'T YOU? DON'T BE SUCH A MEANIE, MAMA!

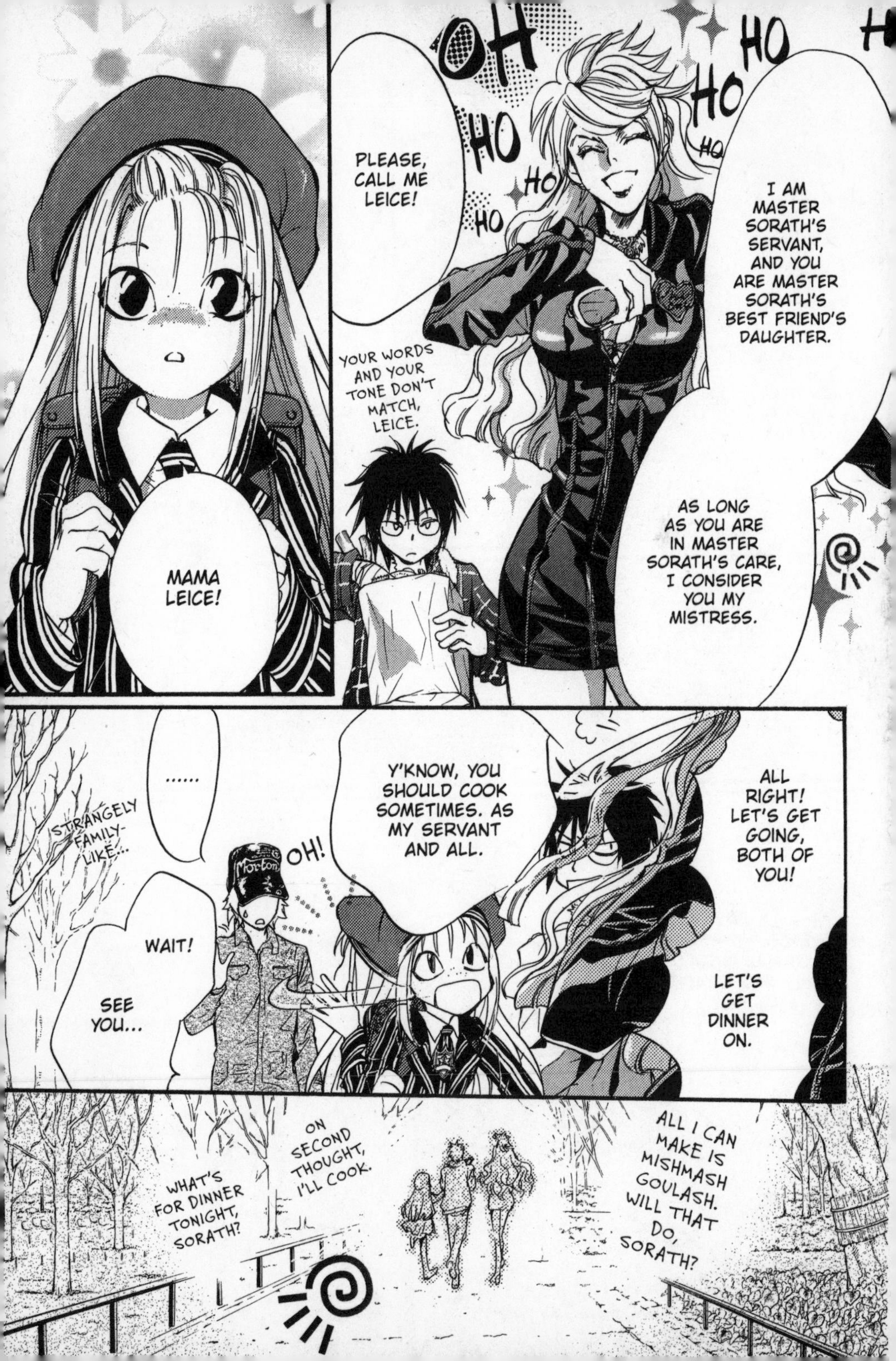

OH HO HO HO HO HO HO
I AM MASTER SORATH'S SERVANT, AND YOU ARE MASTER SORATH'S BEST FRIEND'S DAUGHTER.
AS LONG AS YOU ARE IN MASTER SORATH'S CARE, I CONSIDER YOU MY MISTRESS.
PLEASE, CALL ME LEICE!
YOUR WORDS AND YOUR TONE DON'T MATCH, LEICE.
MAMA LEICE!
ALL RIGHT! LET'S GET GOING, BOTH OF YOU!
LET'S GET DINNER ON.
Y'KNOW, YOU SHOULD COOK SOMETIMES. AS MY SERVANT AND ALL.
OH!
Morton
......
STRANGELY FAMILY-LIKE...
WAIT!
SEE YOU...
ALL I CAN MAKE IS MISHMASH GOULASH. WILL THAT DO, SORATH?
ON SECOND THOUGHT, I'LL COOK.
WHAT'S FOR DINNER TONIGHT, SORATH?

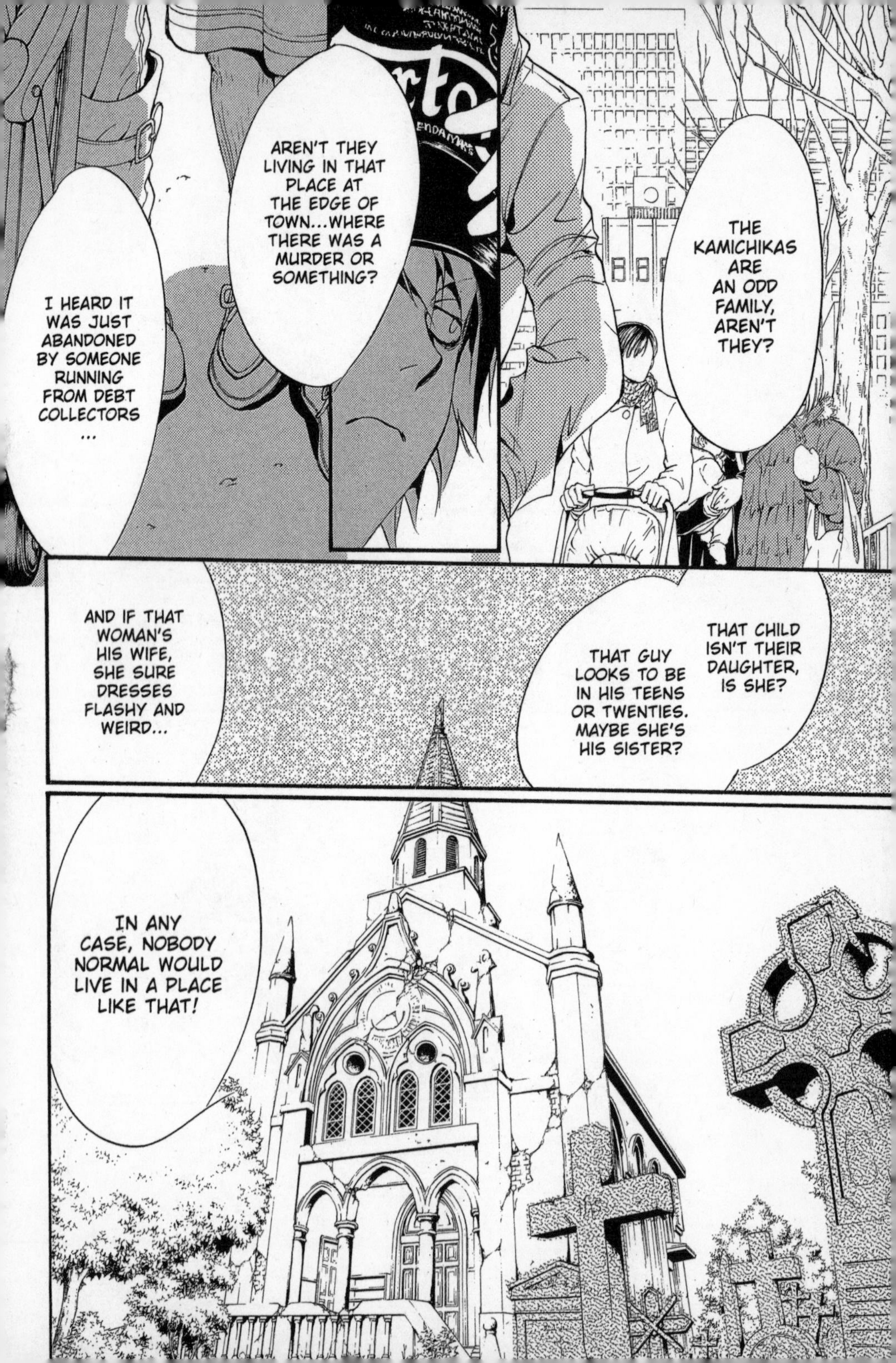
THE KAMICHIKAS ARE AN ODD FAMILY, AREN'T THEY?
AREN'T THEY LIVING IN THAT PLACE AT THE EDGE OF TOWN...WHERE THERE WAS A MURDER OR SOMETHING?
I HEARD IT WAS JUST ABANDONED BY SOMEONE RUNNING FROM DEBT COLLECTORS...
THAT CHILD ISN'T THEIR DAUGHTER, IS SHE?
THAT GUY LOOKS TO BE IN HIS TEENS OR TWENTIES. MAYBE SHE'S HIS SISTER?
AND IF THAT WOMAN'S HIS WIFE, SHE SURE DRESSES FLASHY AND WEIRD...
IN ANY CASE, NOBODY NORMAL WOULD LIVE IN A PLACE LIKE THAT!

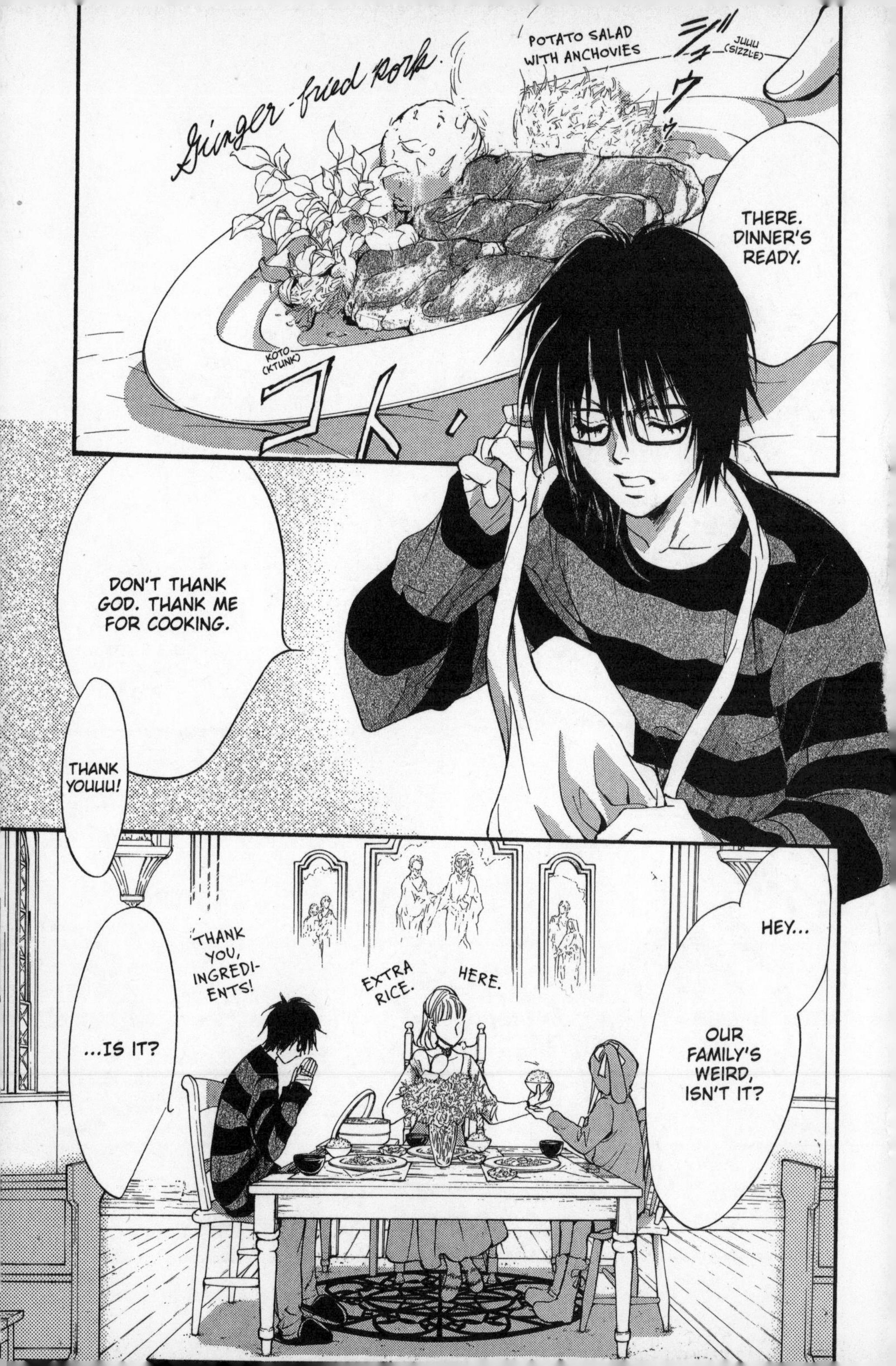
JUUU (SIZZLE)
THERE. DINNER'S READY.
POTATO SALAD WITH ANCHOVIES
Ginger-fried pork.
KOTO (KTUNK)
DON'T THANK GOD. THANK ME FOR COOKING.
THANK YOUUU!
HEY...
OUR FAMILY'S WEIRD, ISN'T IT?
HERE.
EXTRA RICE.
THANK YOU, INGREDI-ENTS!
...IS IT?

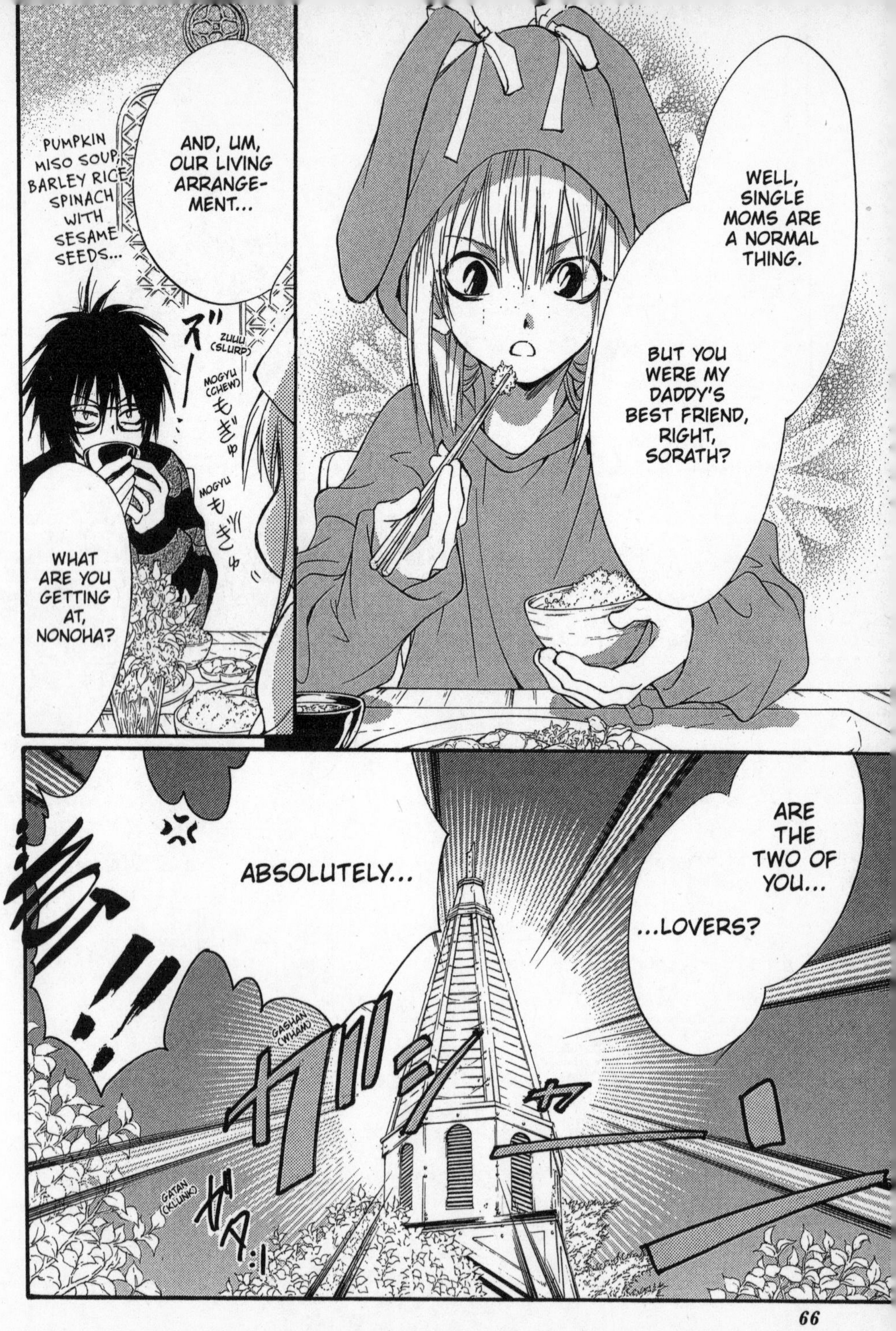
WELL, SINGLE MOMS ARE A NORMAL THING.
BUT YOU WERE MY DADDY'S BEST FRIEND, RIGHT, SORATH?
AND, UM, OUR LIVING ARRANGEMENT...
PUMPKIN MISO SOUP, BARLEY RICE, SPINACH WITH SESAME SEEDS...
ZUUU (SLURP)
MOGYU (CHEW)
MOGYU
WHAT ARE YOU GETTING AT, NONOHA?
ARE THE TWO OF YOU...
...LOVERS?
ABSOLUTELY...
GASHAN (WHAM)
GATAN (KLUNK)

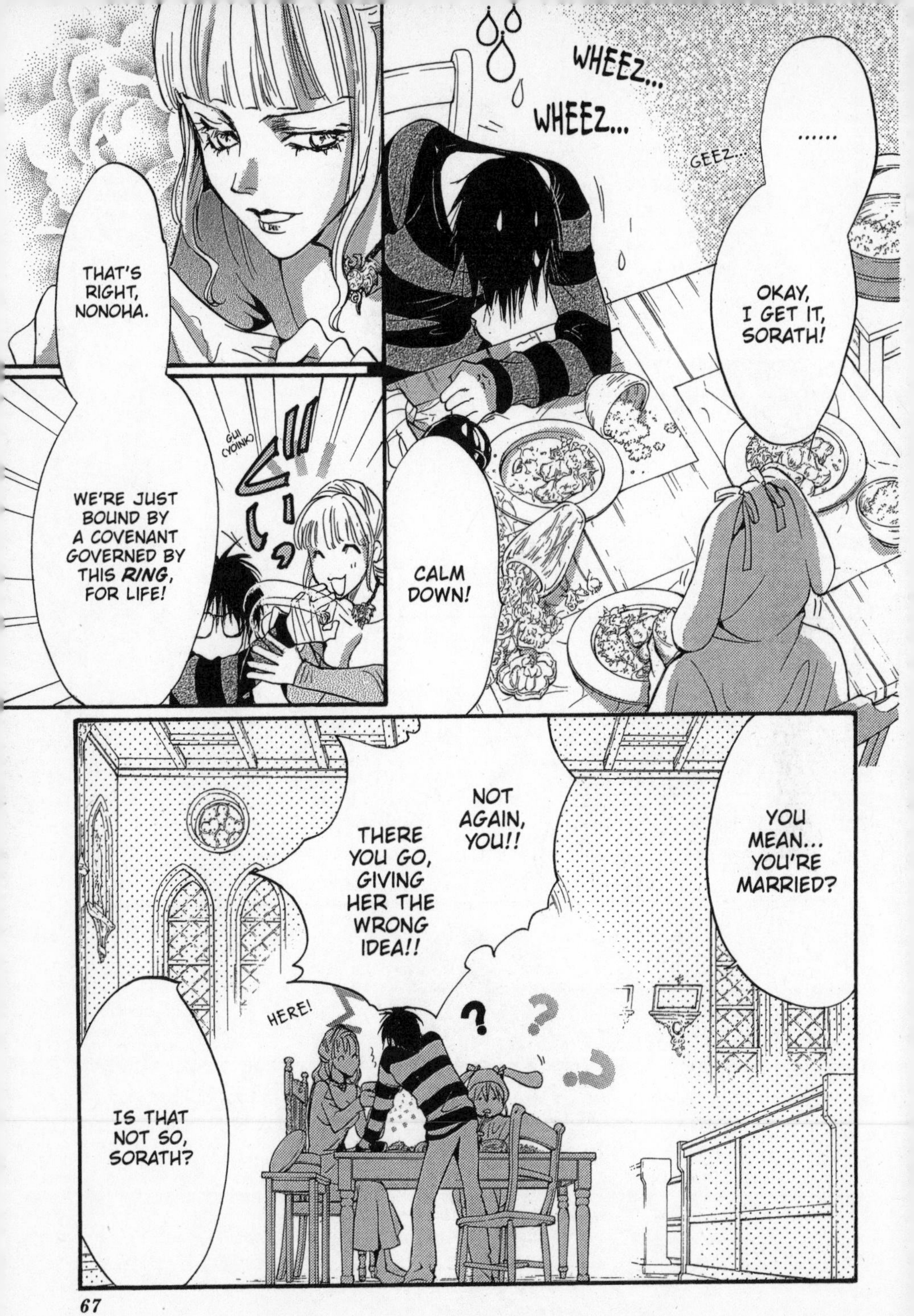
......
GEEZ...
WHEEZ...
WHEEZ...
OKAY, I GET IT, SORATH!
CALM DOWN!
THAT'S RIGHT, NONOHA.
GUI (YOINK)
WE'RE JUST BOUND BY A COVENANT GOVERNED BY THIS *RING*, FOR LIFE!
YOU MEAN... YOU'RE MARRIED?
NOT AGAIN, YOU!!
THERE YOU GO, GIVING HER THE WRONG IDEA!!
HERE!
IS THAT NOT SO, SORATH?

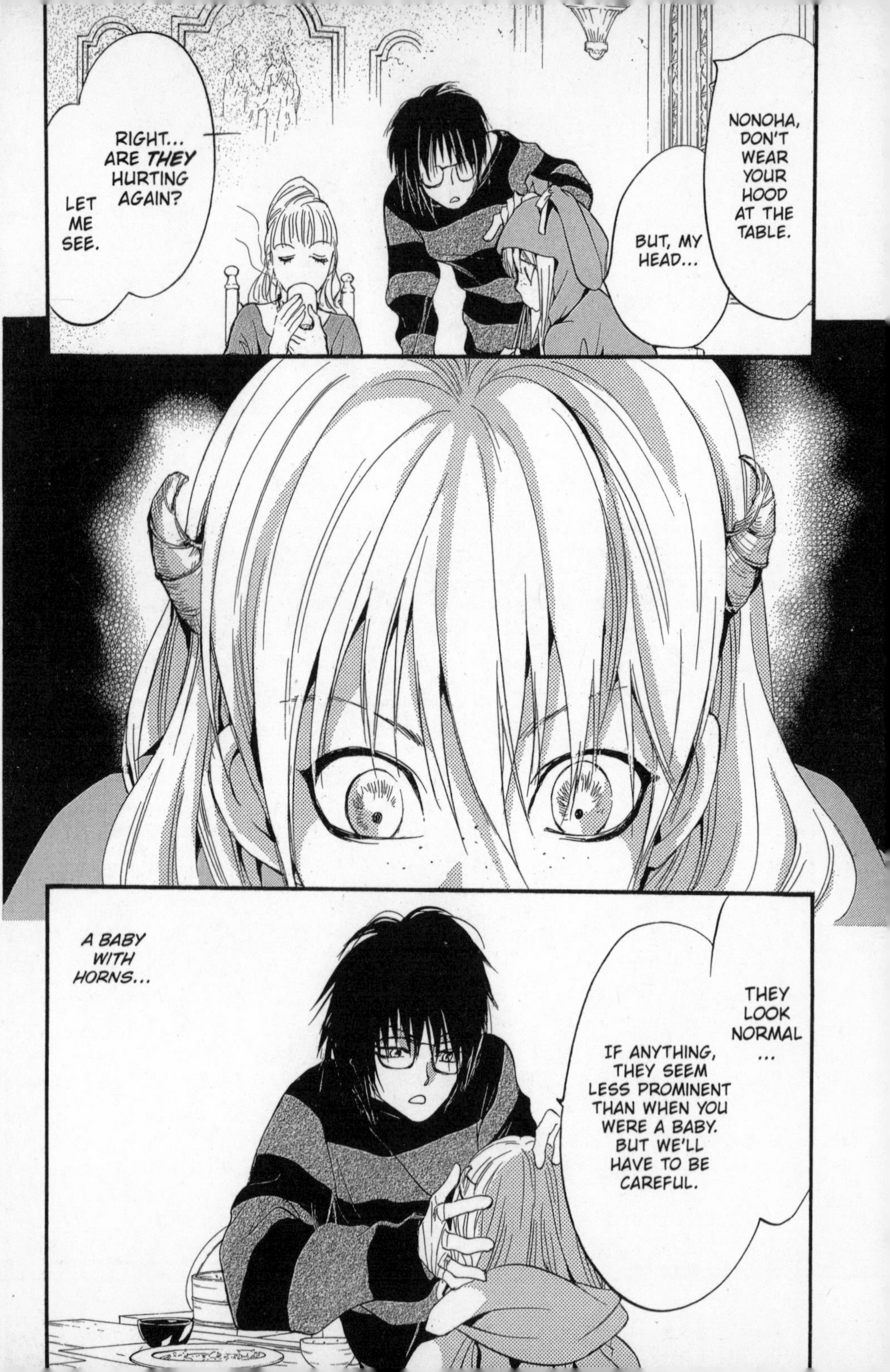
NONOHA, DON'T WEAR YOUR HOOD AT THE TABLE.
BUT, MY HEAD...
RIGHT... ARE *THEY* HURTING AGAIN?
LET ME SEE.
THEY LOOK NORMAL...
IF ANYTHING, THEY SEEM LESS PROMINENT THAN WHEN YOU WERE A BABY. BUT WE'LL HAVE TO BE CAREFUL.
A BABY WITH HORNS...

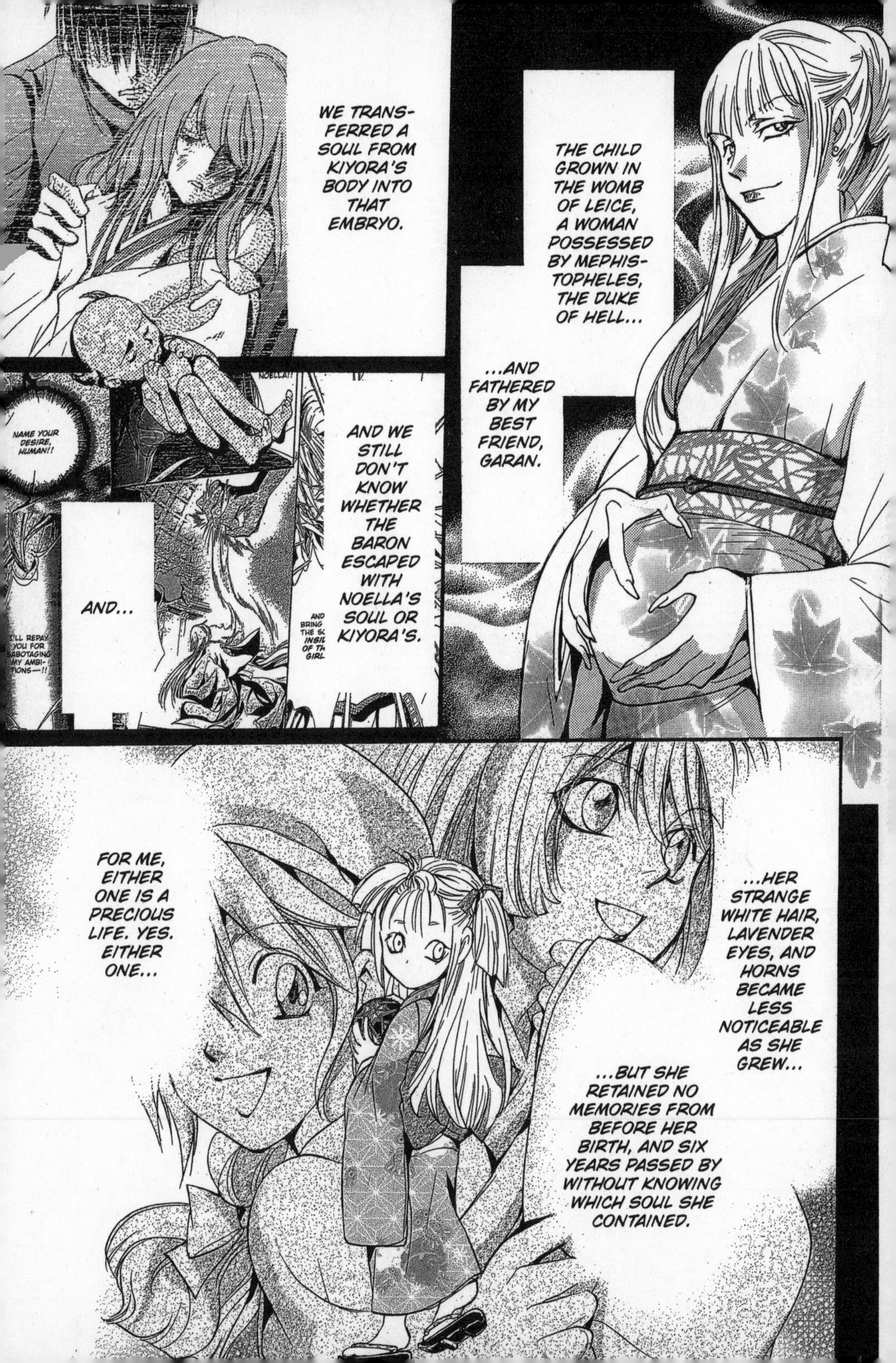
THE CHILD GROWN IN THE WOMB OF LEICE, A WOMAN POSSESSED BY MEPHISTOPHELES, THE DUKE OF HELL...
...AND FATHERED BY MY BEST FRIEND, GARAN.
WE TRANSFERRED A SOUL FROM KIYORA'S BODY INTO THAT EMBRYO.
NOELLA!!
AND WE STILL DON'T KNOW WHETHER THE BARON ESCAPED WITH NOELLA'S SOUL OR KIYORA'S.
NAME YOUR DESIRE, HUMAN!!
AND...
'LL REPAY YOU FOR SABOTAGING MY AMBITIONS—!!
...HER STRANGE WHITE HAIR, LAVENDER EYES, AND HORNS BECAME LESS NOTICEABLE AS SHE GREW...
...BUT SHE RETAINED NO MEMORIES FROM BEFORE HER BIRTH, AND SIX YEARS PASSED BY WITHOUT KNOWING WHICH SOUL SHE CONTAINED.
FOR ME, EITHER ONE IS A PRECIOUS LIFE. YES. EITHER ONE...

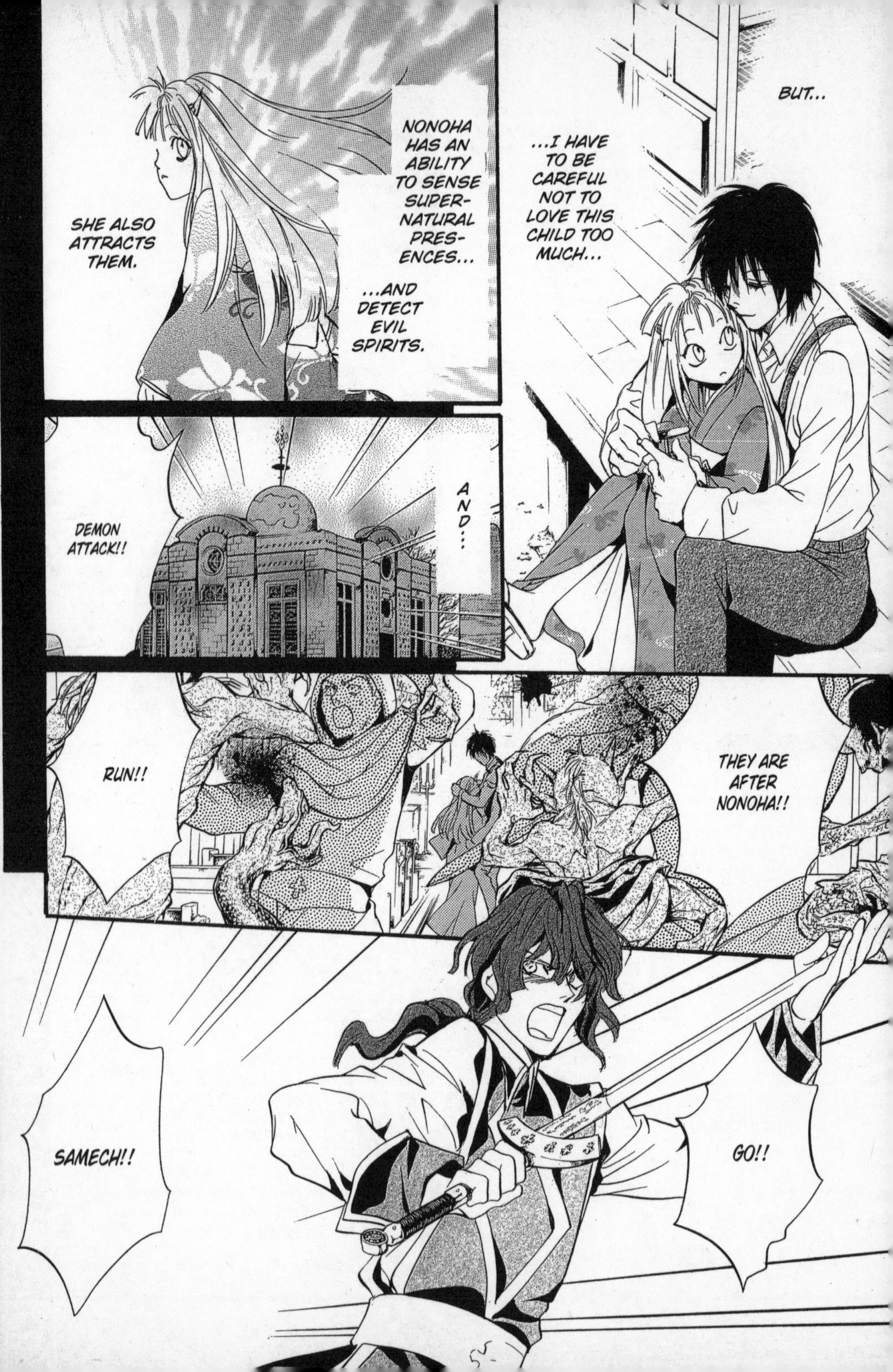
BUT...
...I HAVE TO BE CAREFUL NOT TO LOVE THIS CHILD TOO MUCH...
NONOHA HAS AN ABILITY TO SENSE SUPER-NATURAL PRES-ENCES...
...AND DETECT EVIL SPIRITS.
SHE ALSO ATTRACTS THEM.
AND...
DEMON ATTACK!!
THEY ARE AFTER NONOHA!!
RUN!!
GO!!
SAMECH!!

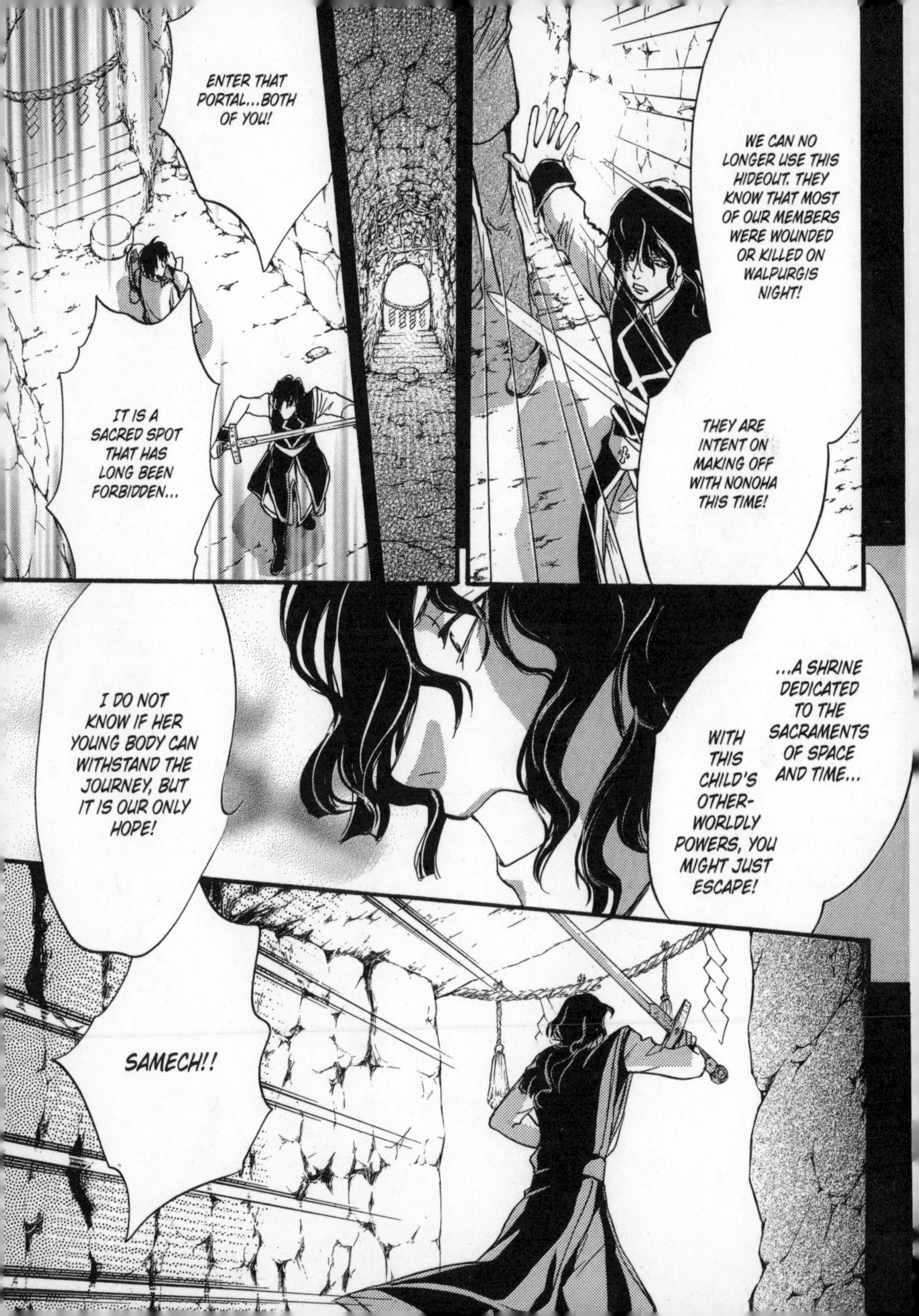
WE CAN NO LONGER USE THIS HIDEOUT. THEY KNOW THAT MOST OF OUR MEMBERS WERE WOUNDED OR KILLED ON WALPURGIS NIGHT!
THEY ARE INTENT ON MAKING OFF WITH NONOHA THIS TIME!
ENTER THAT PORTAL...BOTH OF YOU!
IT IS A SACRED SPOT THAT HAS LONG BEEN FORBIDDEN...
...A SHRINE DEDICATED TO THE SACRAMENTS OF SPACE AND TIME...
WITH THIS CHILD'S OTHER-WORLDLY POWERS, YOU MIGHT JUST ESCAPE!
I DO NOT KNOW IF HER YOUNG BODY CAN WITHSTAND THE JOURNEY, BUT IT IS OUR ONLY HOPE!
SAMECH!!

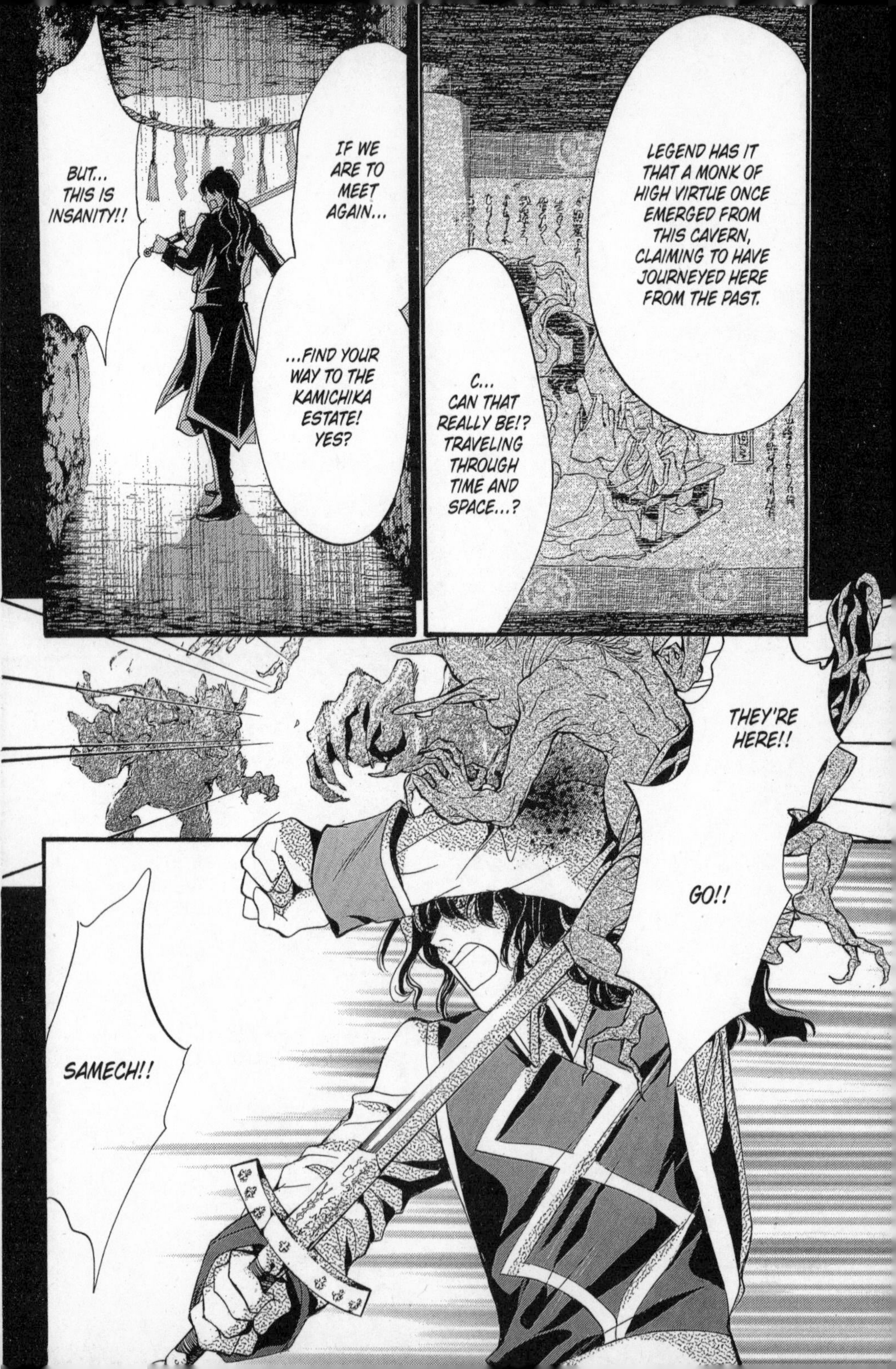
LEGEND HAS IT THAT A MONK OF HIGH VIRTUE ONCE EMERGED FROM THIS CAVERN, CLAIMING TO HAVE JOURNEYED HERE FROM THE PAST.
C... CAN THAT REALLY BE!? TRAVELING THROUGH TIME AND SPACE...?
IF WE ARE TO MEET AGAIN...
...FIND YOUR WAY TO THE KAMICHIKA ESTATE! YES?
BUT... THIS IS INSANITY!!
THEY'RE HERE!!
GO!!
SAMECH!!

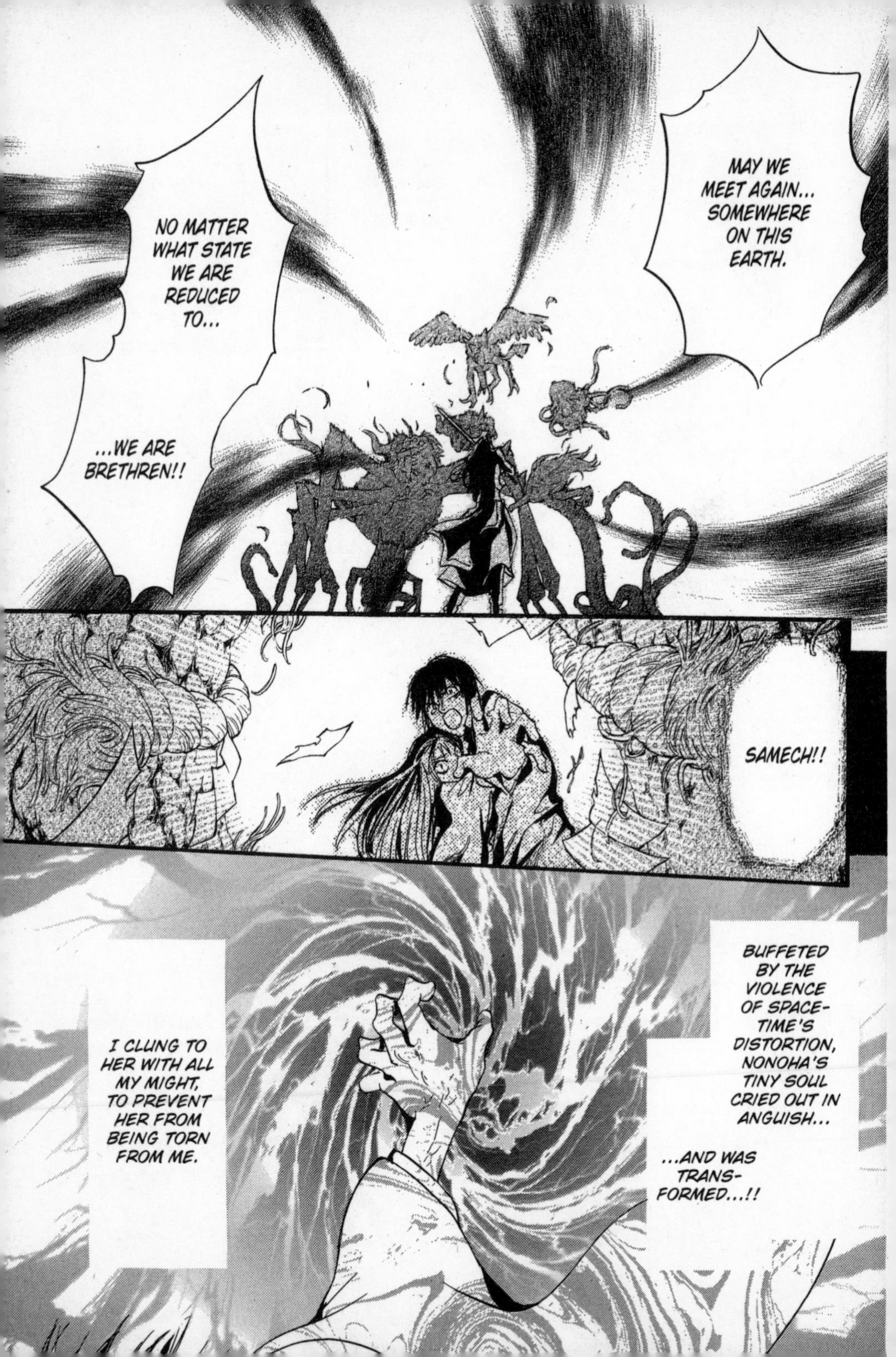
MAY WE MEET AGAIN... SOMEWHERE ON THIS EARTH.
NO MATTER WHAT STATE WE ARE REDUCED TO...
...WE ARE BRETHREN!!
SAMECH!!
BUFFETED BY THE VIOLENCE OF SPACE-TIME'S DISTORTION, NONOHA'S TINY SOUL CRIED OUT IN ANGUISH...
I CLUNG TO HER WITH ALL MY MIGHT, TO PREVENT HER FROM BEING TORN FROM ME.
...AND WAS TRANS-FORMED...!!

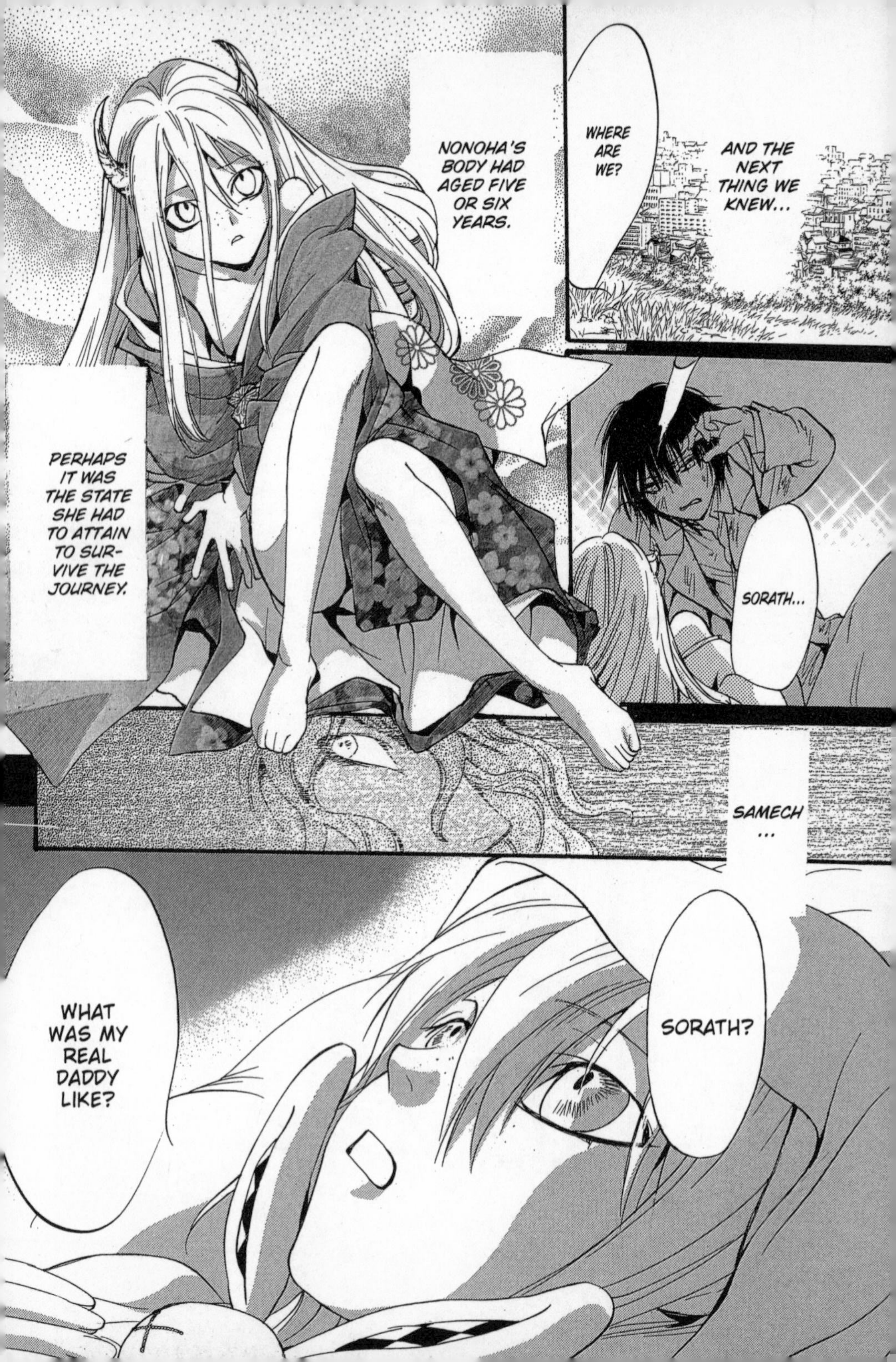
AND THE NEXT THING WE KNEW...
WHERE ARE WE?
SORATH...
NONOHA'S BODY HAD AGED FIVE OR SIX YEARS.
PERHAPS IT WAS THE STATE SHE HAD TO ATTAIN TO SURVIVE THE JOURNEY.
SAMECH...
SORATH?
WHAT WAS MY REAL DADDY LIKE?

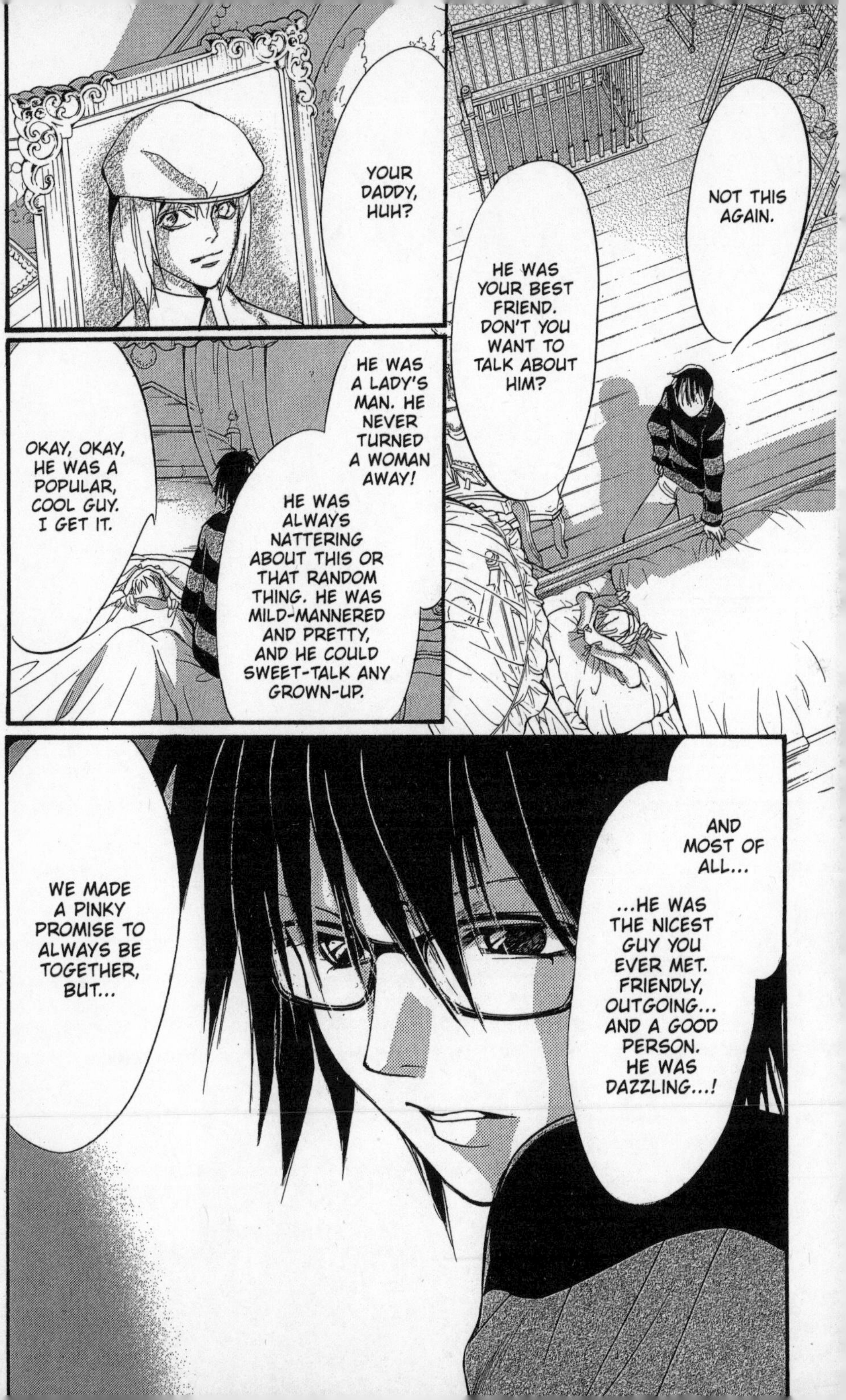
NOT THIS AGAIN.
HE WAS YOUR BEST FRIEND. DON'T YOU WANT TO TALK ABOUT HIM?
YOUR DADDY, HUH?
HE WAS A LADY'S MAN. HE NEVER TURNED A WOMAN AWAY!
HE WAS ALWAYS NATTERING ABOUT THIS OR THAT RANDOM THING. HE WAS MILD-MANNERED AND PRETTY, AND HE COULD SWEET-TALK ANY GROWN-UP.
OKAY, OKAY, HE WAS A POPULAR, COOL GUY. I GET IT.
AND MOST OF ALL...
...HE WAS THE NICEST GUY YOU EVER MET. FRIENDLY, OUTGOING... AND A GOOD PERSON. HE WAS DAZZLING...!
WE MADE A PINKY PROMISE TO ALWAYS BE TOGETHER, BUT...

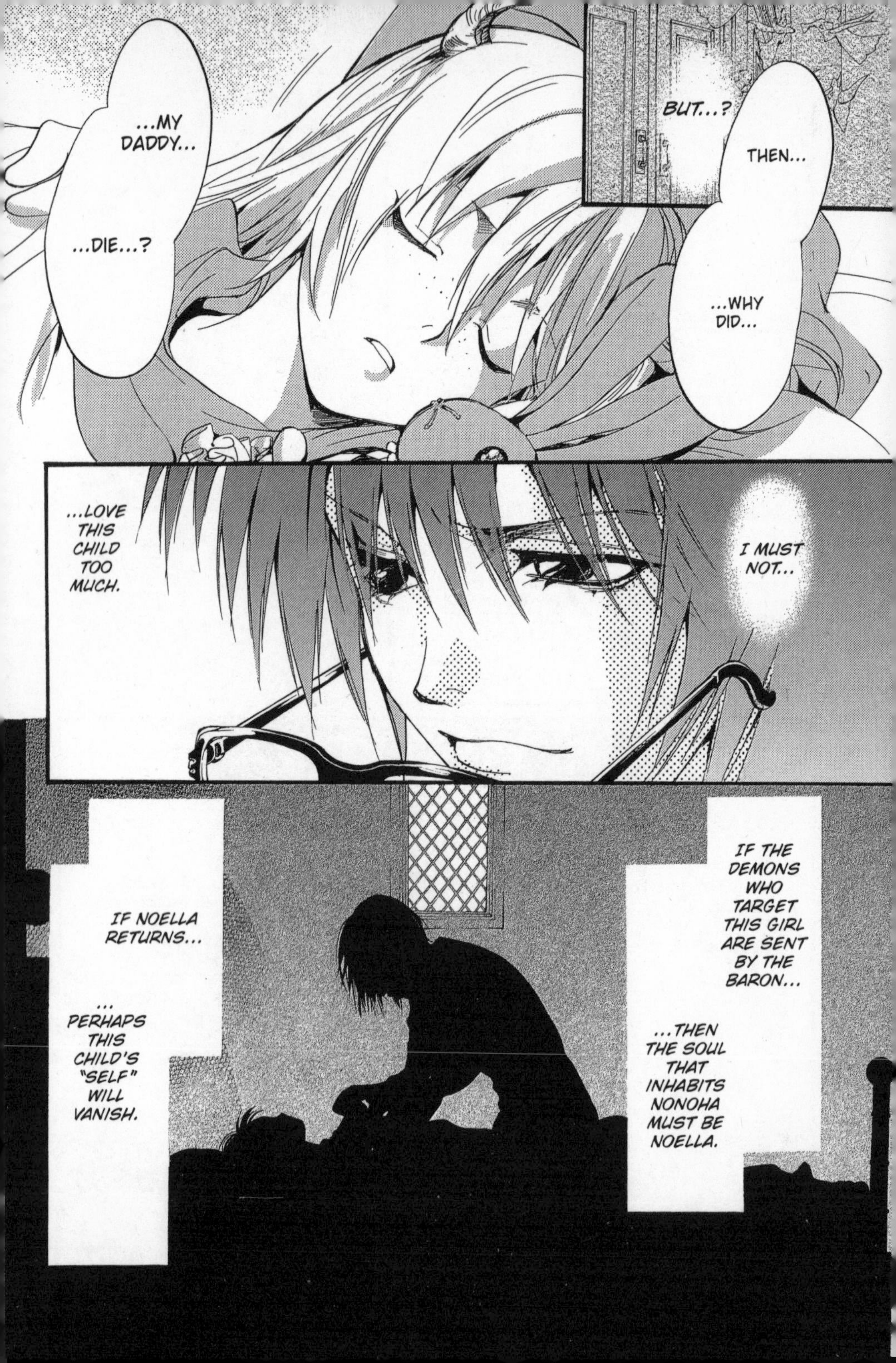
BUT...?
THEN...
...WHY DID...
...MY DADDY...
...DIE...?
I MUST NOT...
...LOVE THIS CHILD TOO MUCH.
IF THE DEMONS WHO TARGET THIS GIRL ARE SENT BY THE BARON...
...THEN THE SOUL THAT INHABITS NONOHA MUST BE NOELLA.
IF NOELLA RETURNS...
...PERHAPS THIS CHILD'S "SELF" WILL VANISH.

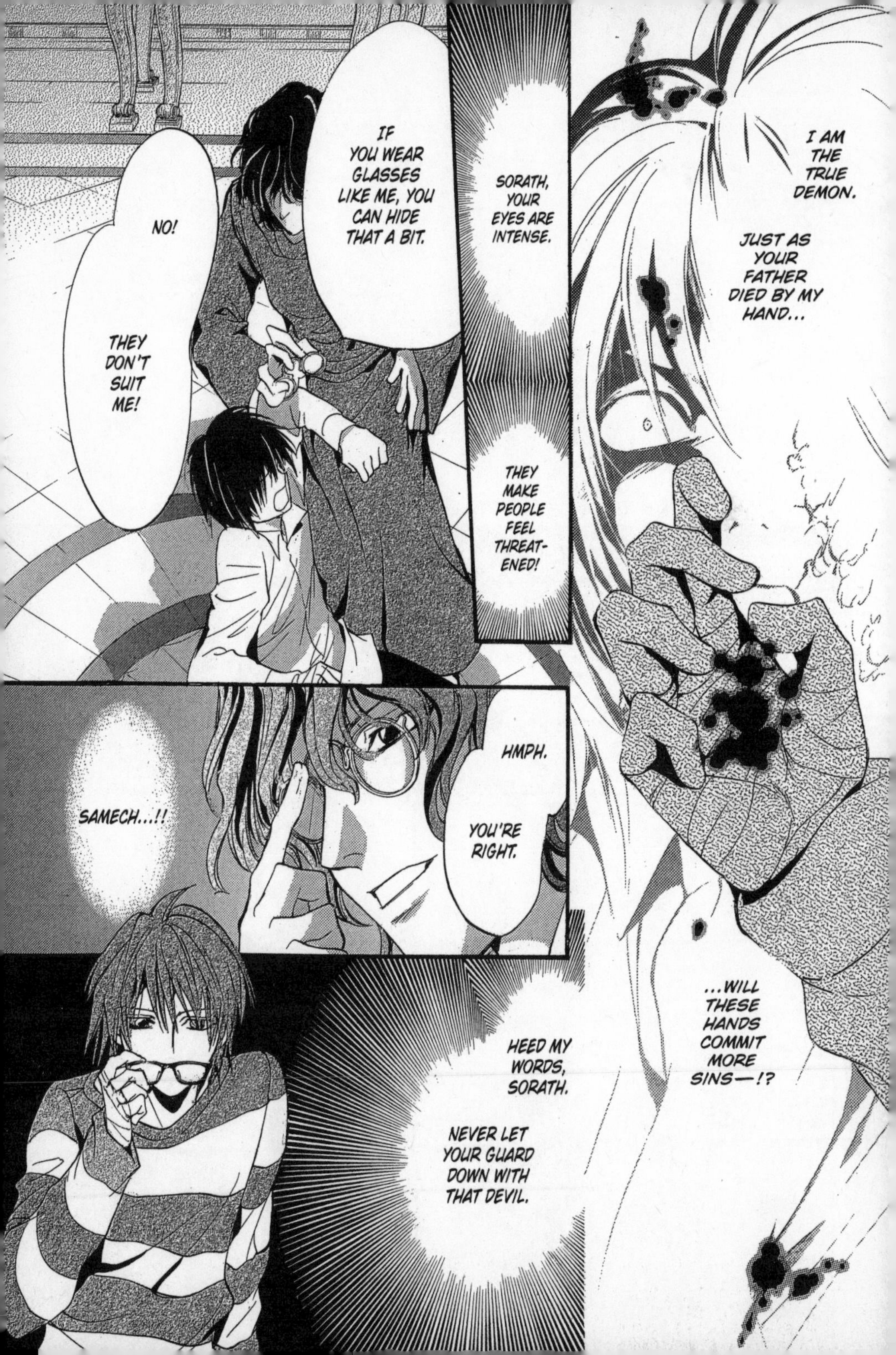
I AM THE TRUE DEMON.
JUST AS YOUR FATHER DIED BY MY HAND...
...WILL THESE HANDS COMMIT MORE SINS—!?
SORATH, YOUR EYES ARE INTENSE.
THEY MAKE PEOPLE FEEL THREAT-ENED!
IF YOU WEAR GLASSES LIKE ME, YOU CAN HIDE THAT A BIT.
NO!
THEY DON'T SUIT ME!
HMPH.
YOU'RE RIGHT.
SAMECH...!!
HEED MY WORDS, SORATH.
NEVER LET YOUR GUARD DOWN WITH THAT DEVIL.

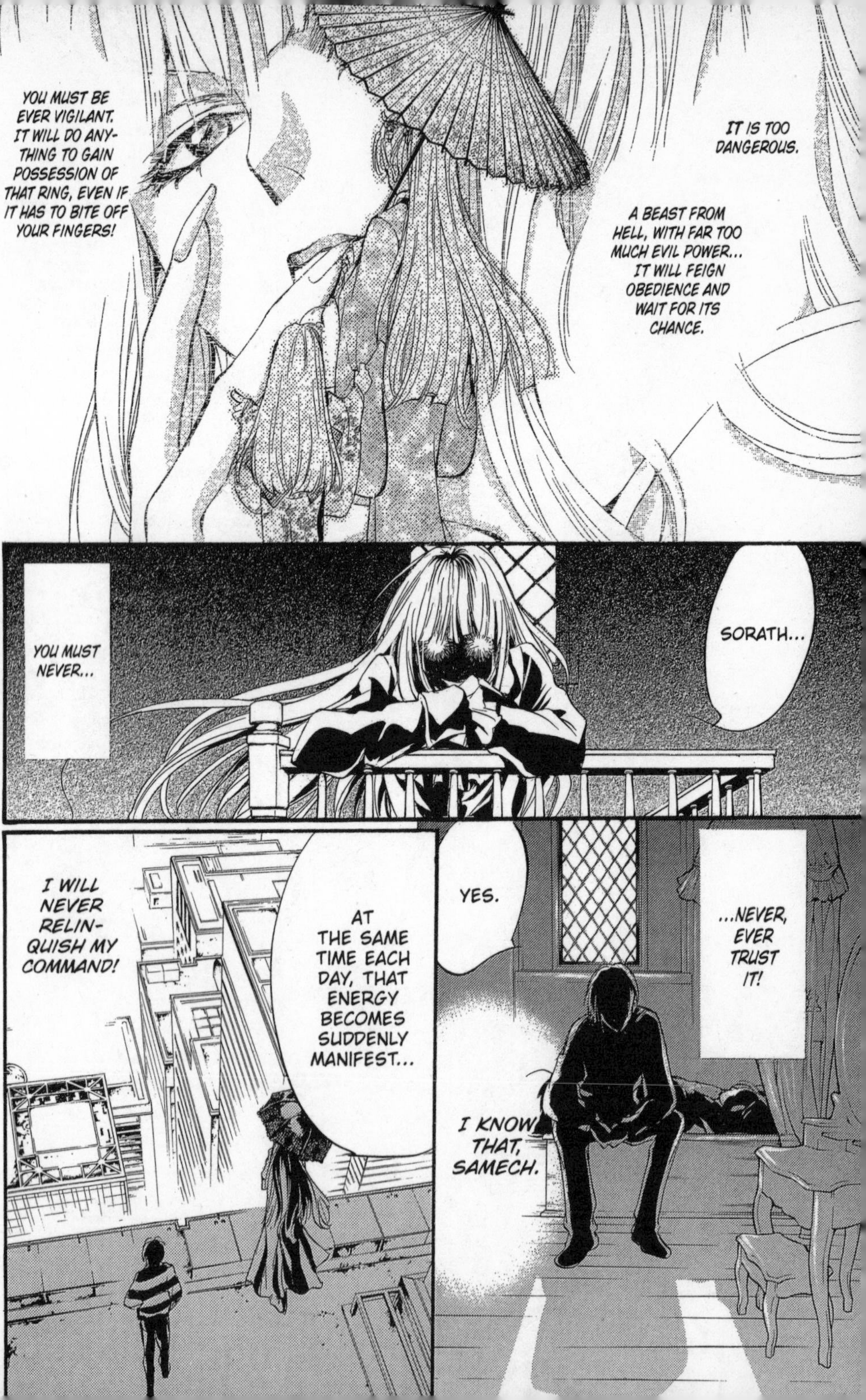
IT IS TOO DANGEROUS.
A BEAST FROM HELL, WITH FAR TOO MUCH EVIL POWER... IT WILL FEIGN OBEDIENCE AND WAIT FOR ITS CHANCE.
YOU MUST BE EVER VIGILANT. IT WILL DO ANY-THING TO GAIN POSSESSION OF THAT RING, EVEN IF IT HAS TO BITE OFF YOUR FINGERS!
SORATH...
YOU MUST NEVER...
...NEVER, EVER TRUST IT!
YES.
I KNOW THAT, SAMECH.
AT THE SAME TIME EACH DAY, THAT ENERGY BECOMES SUDDENLY MANIFEST...
I WILL NEVER RELIN-QUISH MY COMMAND!

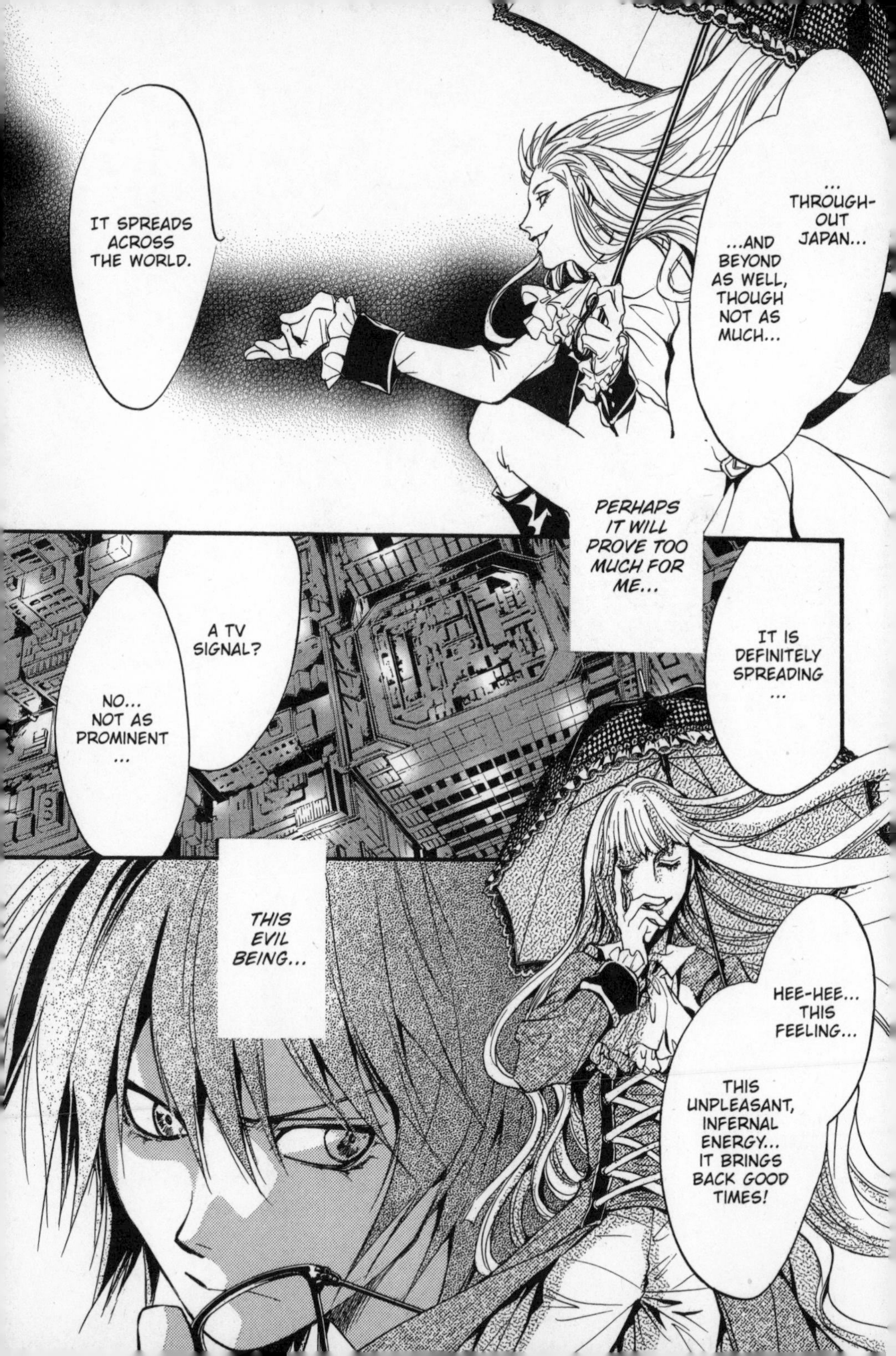

... THROUGH-OUT JAPAN...
...AND BEYOND AS WELL, THOUGH NOT AS MUCH...
IT SPREADS ACROSS THE WORLD.
PERHAPS IT WILL PROVE TOO MUCH FOR ME...
IT IS DEFINITELY SPREADING...
A TV SIGNAL?
NO... NOT AS PROMINENT...
HEE-HEE... THIS FEELING...
THIS UNPLEASANT, INFERNAL ENERGY... IT BRINGS BACK GOOD TIMES!
THIS EVIL BEING...

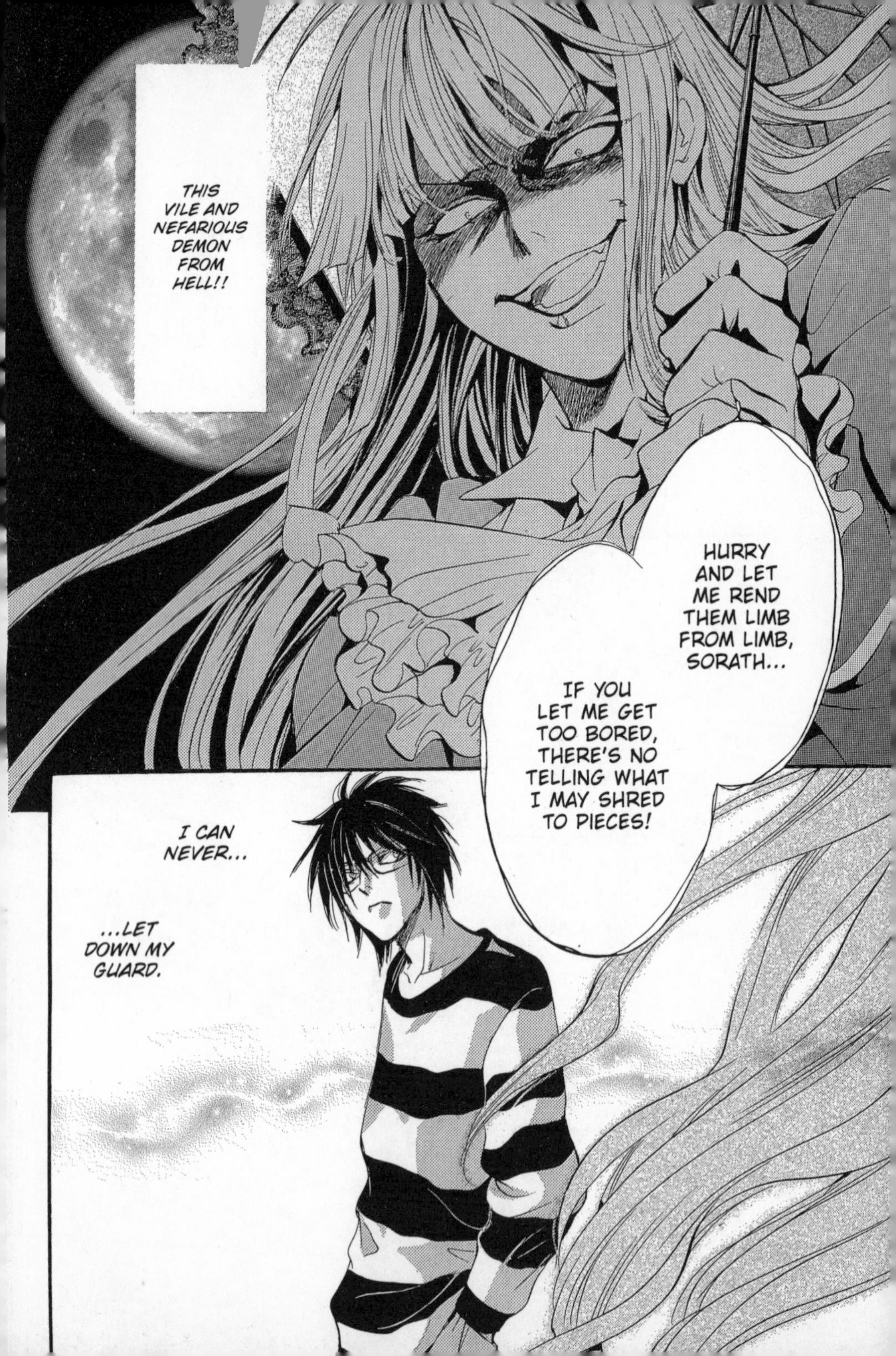
THIS VILE AND NEFARIOUS DEMON FROM HELL!!
HURRY AND LET ME REND THEM LIMB FROM LIMB, SORATH...
IF YOU LET ME GET TOO BORED, THERE'S NO TELLING WHAT I MAY SHRED TO PIECES!
I CAN NEVER...
...LET DOWN MY GUARD.

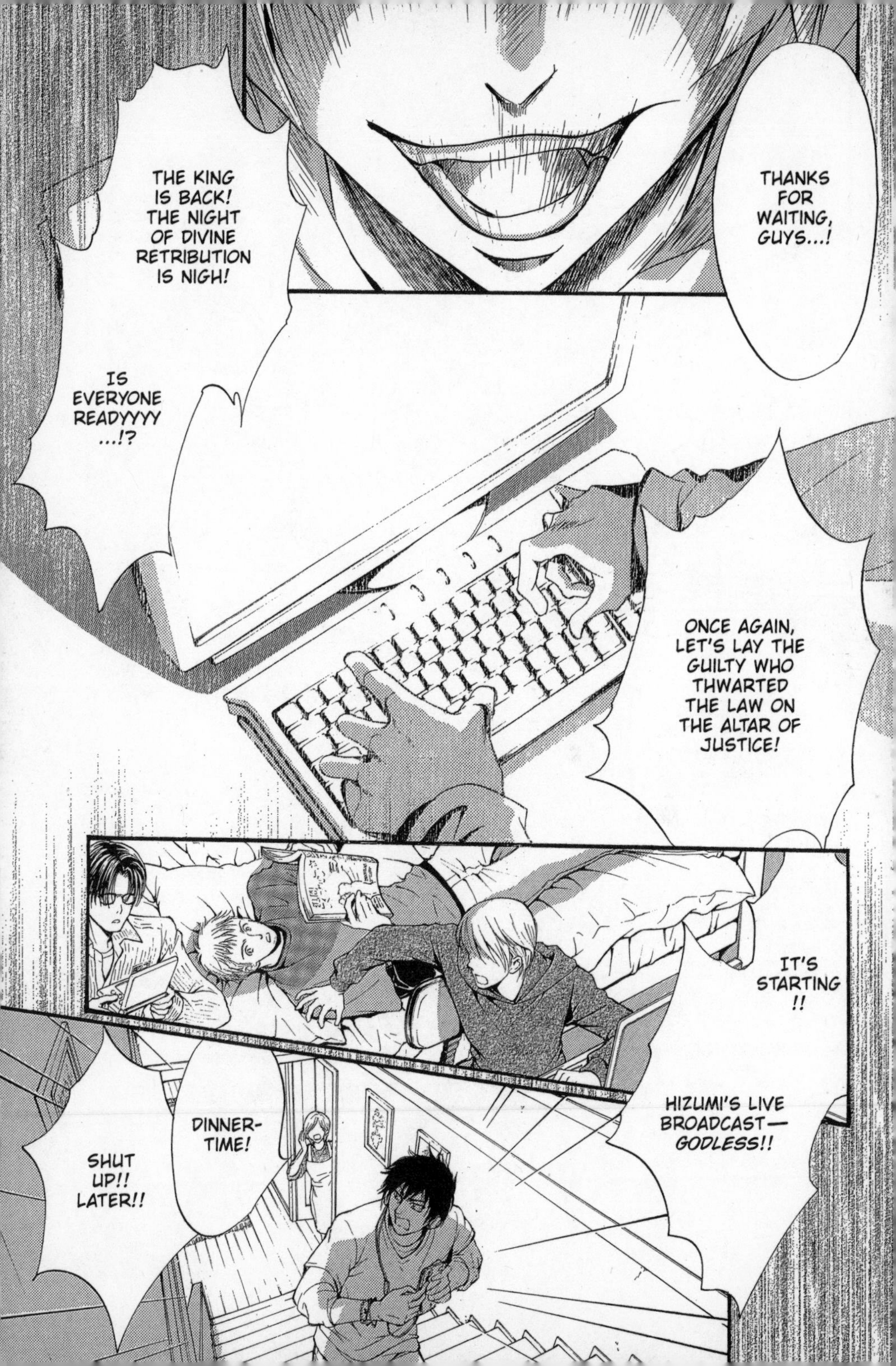
THANKS FOR WAITING, GUYS...!
THE KING IS BACK! THE NIGHT OF DIVINE RETRIBUTION IS NIGH!
IS EVERYONE READYYYY ...!?
ONCE AGAIN, LET'S LAY THE GUILTY WHO THWARTED THE LAW ON THE ALTAR OF JUSTICE!
IT'S STARTING !!
HIZUMI'S LIVE BROADCAST— GODLESS!!
DINNER-TIME!
SHUT UP!! LATER!!

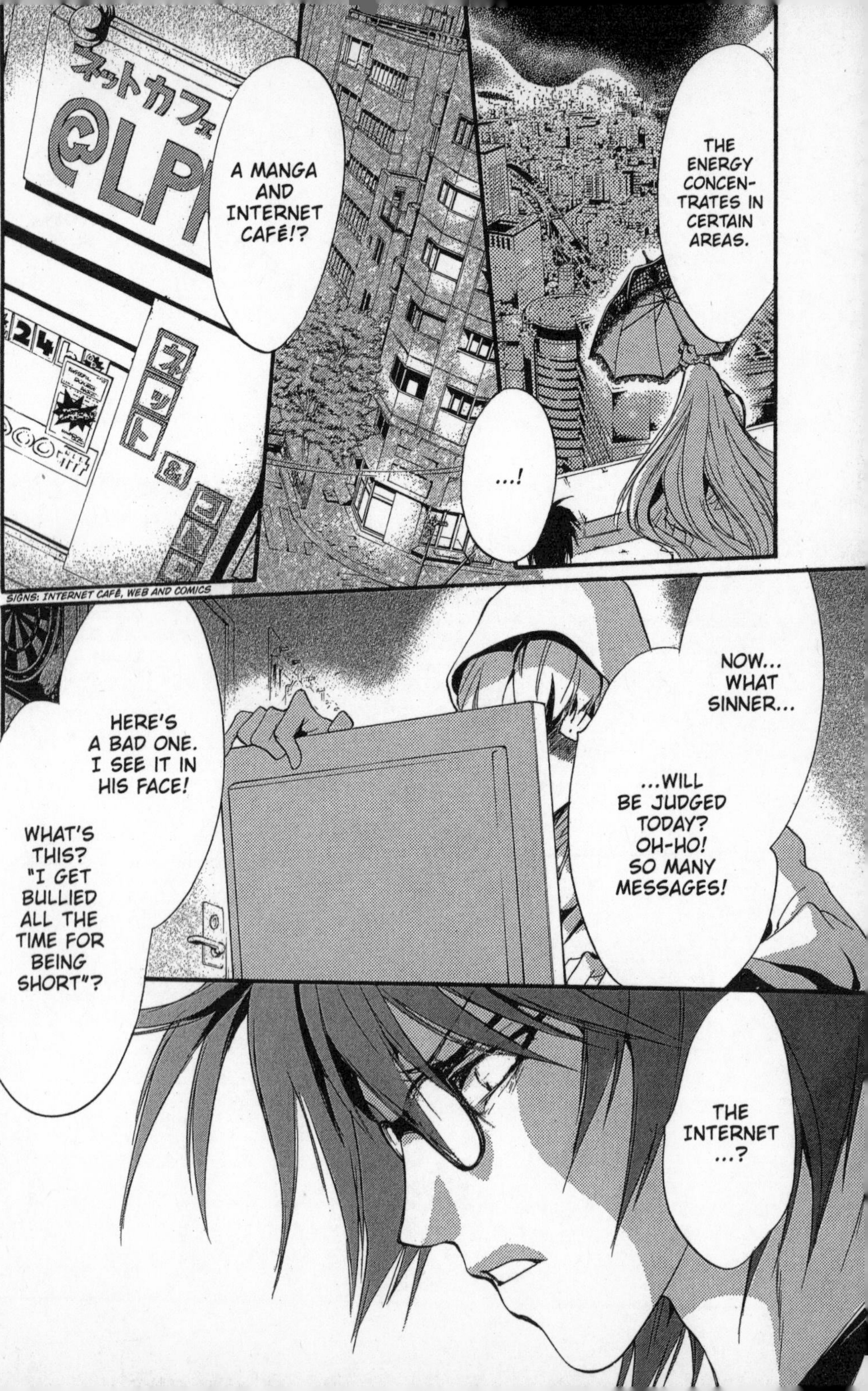
THE ENERGY CONCENTRATES IN CERTAIN AREAS.
...!
A MANGA AND INTERNET CAFÉ!?
SIGNS: INTERNET CAFÉ, WEB AND COMICS
NOW... WHAT SINNER...
...WILL BE JUDGED TODAY? OH-HO! SO MANY MESSAGES!
HERE'S A BAD ONE. I SEE IT IN HIS FACE!
WHAT'S THIS? "I GET BULLIED ALL THE TIME FOR BEING SHORT"?
THE INTERNET ...?

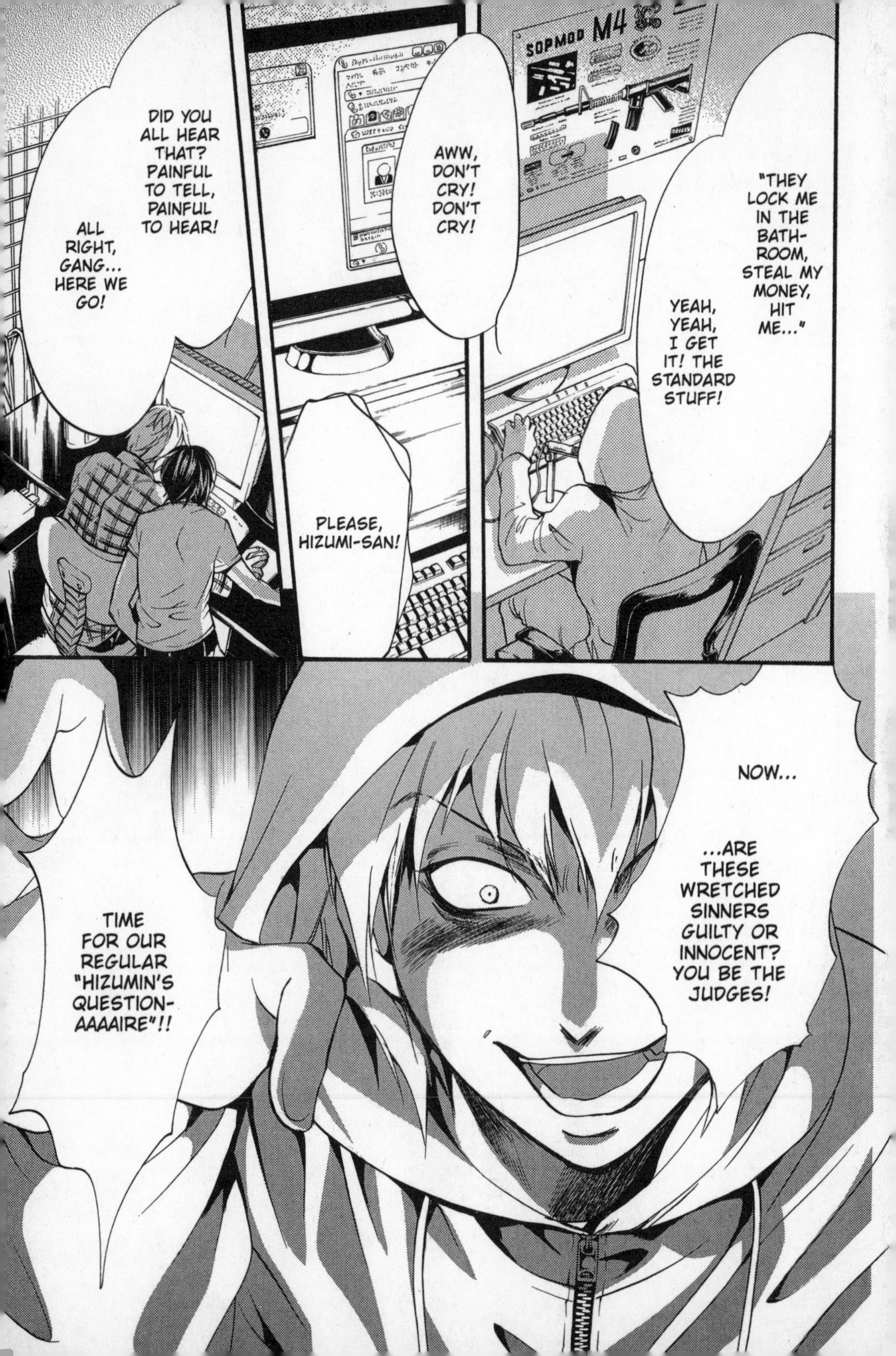
SOPMOD M4
"THEY LOCK ME IN THE BATH-ROOM, STEAL MY MONEY, HIT ME..."
YEAH, YEAH, I GET IT! THE STANDARD STUFF!
AWW, DON'T CRY! DON'T CRY!
PLEASE, HIZUMI-SAN!
DID YOU ALL HEAR THAT? PAINFUL TO TELL, PAINFUL TO HEAR!
ALL RIGHT, GANG... HERE WE GO!
NOW...
...ARE THESE WRETCHED SINNERS GUILTY OR INNOCENT? YOU BE THE JUDGES!
TIME FOR OUR REGULAR "HIZUMIN'S QUESTION-AAAAIRE"!!

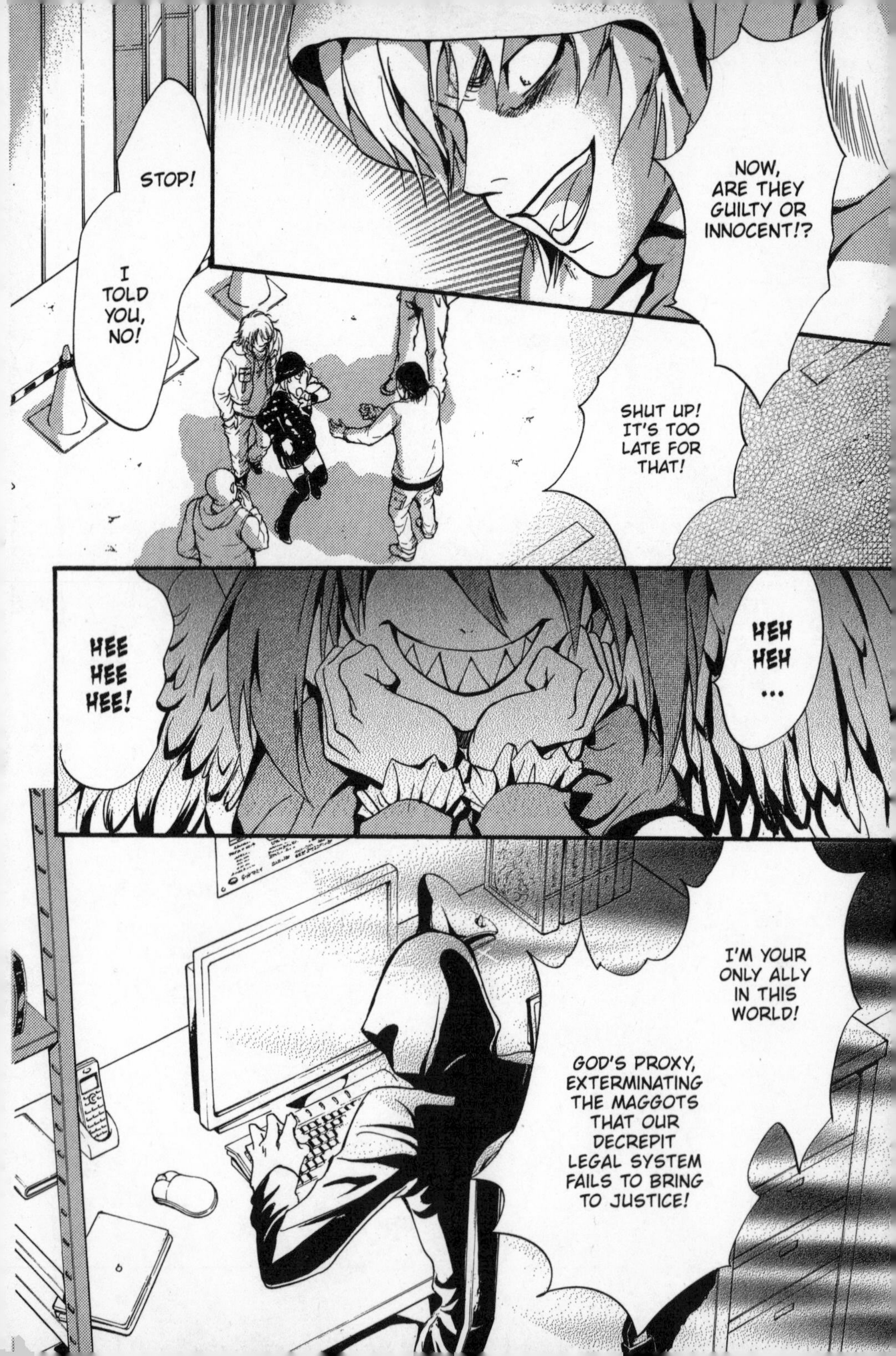
NOW, ARE THEY GUILTY OR INNOCENT!?
STOP!
I TOLD YOU, NO!
SHUT UP! IT'S TOO LATE FOR THAT!
HEH HEH ...
HEE HEE HEE!
I'M YOUR ONLY ALLY IN THIS WORLD!
GOD'S PROXY, EXTERMINATING THE MAGGOTS THAT OUR DECREPIT LEGAL SYSTEM FAILS TO BRING TO JUSTICE!

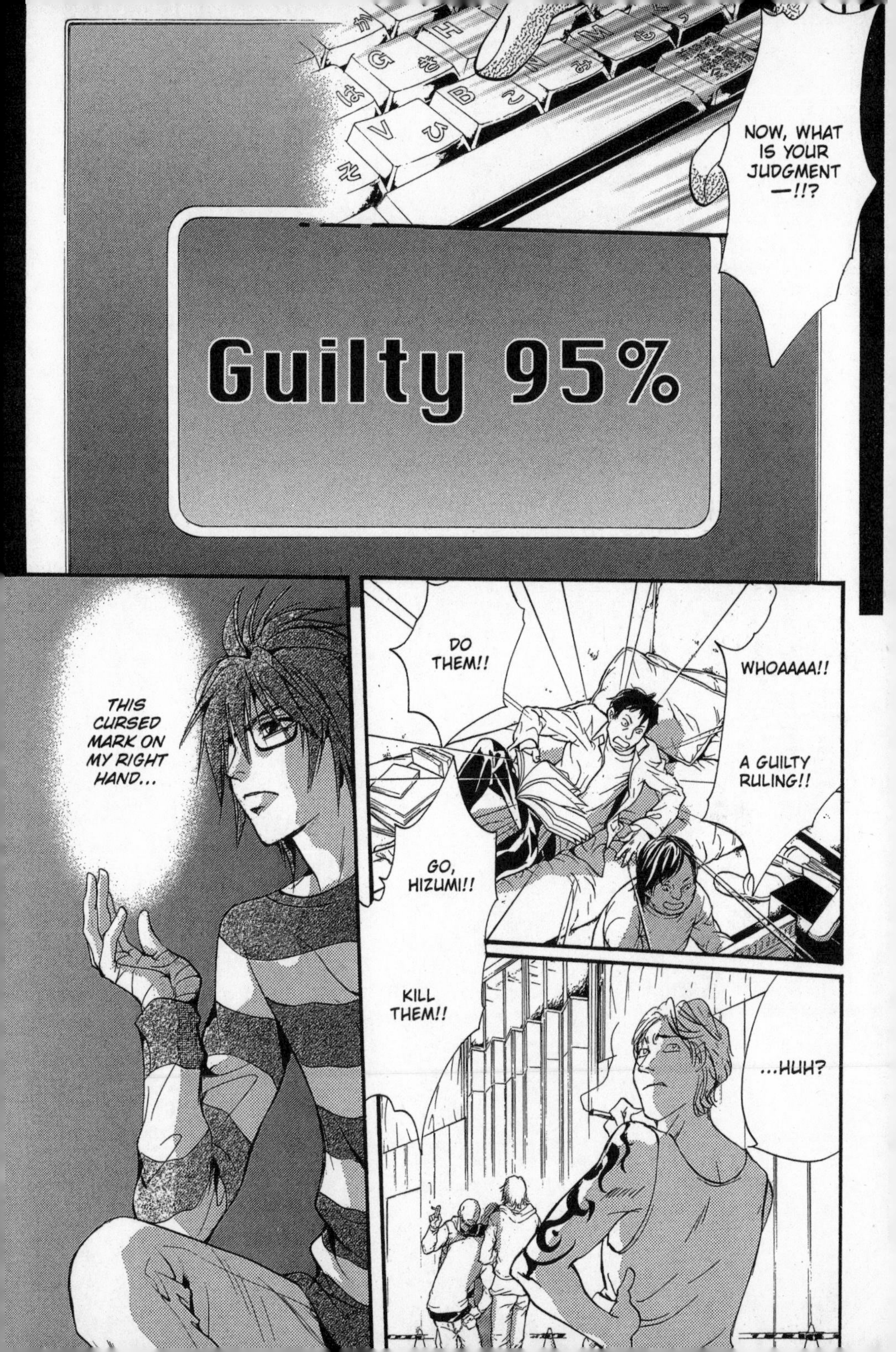
NOW, WHAT IS YOUR JUDGMENT—!!?
Guilty 95%
WHOAAAA!!
DO THEM!!
A GUILTY RULING!!
GO, HIZUMI!!
KILL THEM!!
...HUH?
THIS CURSED MARK ON MY RIGHT HAND...

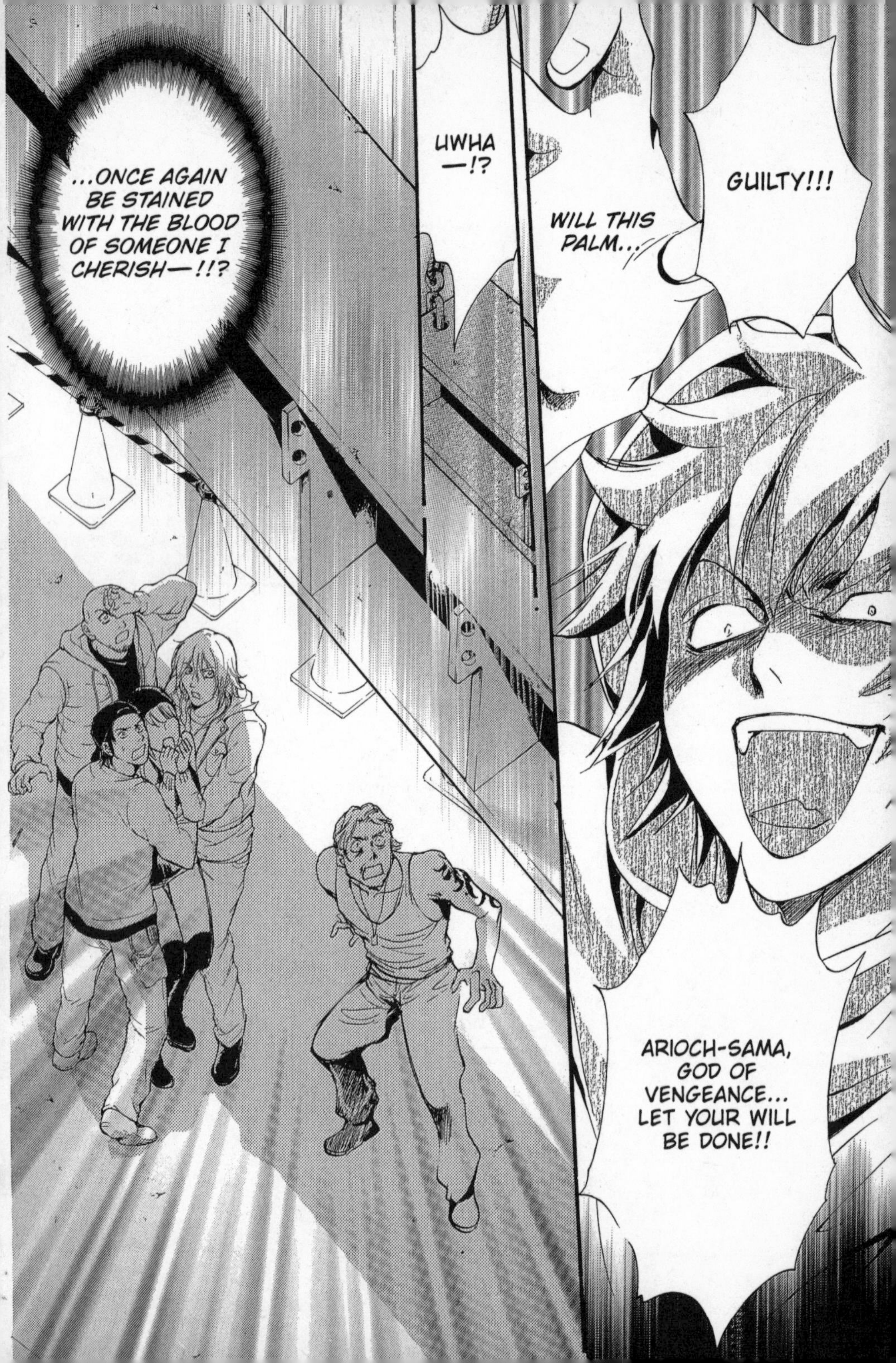
GUILTY!!!
WILL THIS PALM...
ARIOCH-SAMA, GOD OF VENGEANCE... LET YOUR WILL BE DONE!!
UWHA—!?
...ONCE AGAIN BE STAINED WITH THE BLOOD OF SOMEONE I CHERISH—!!?

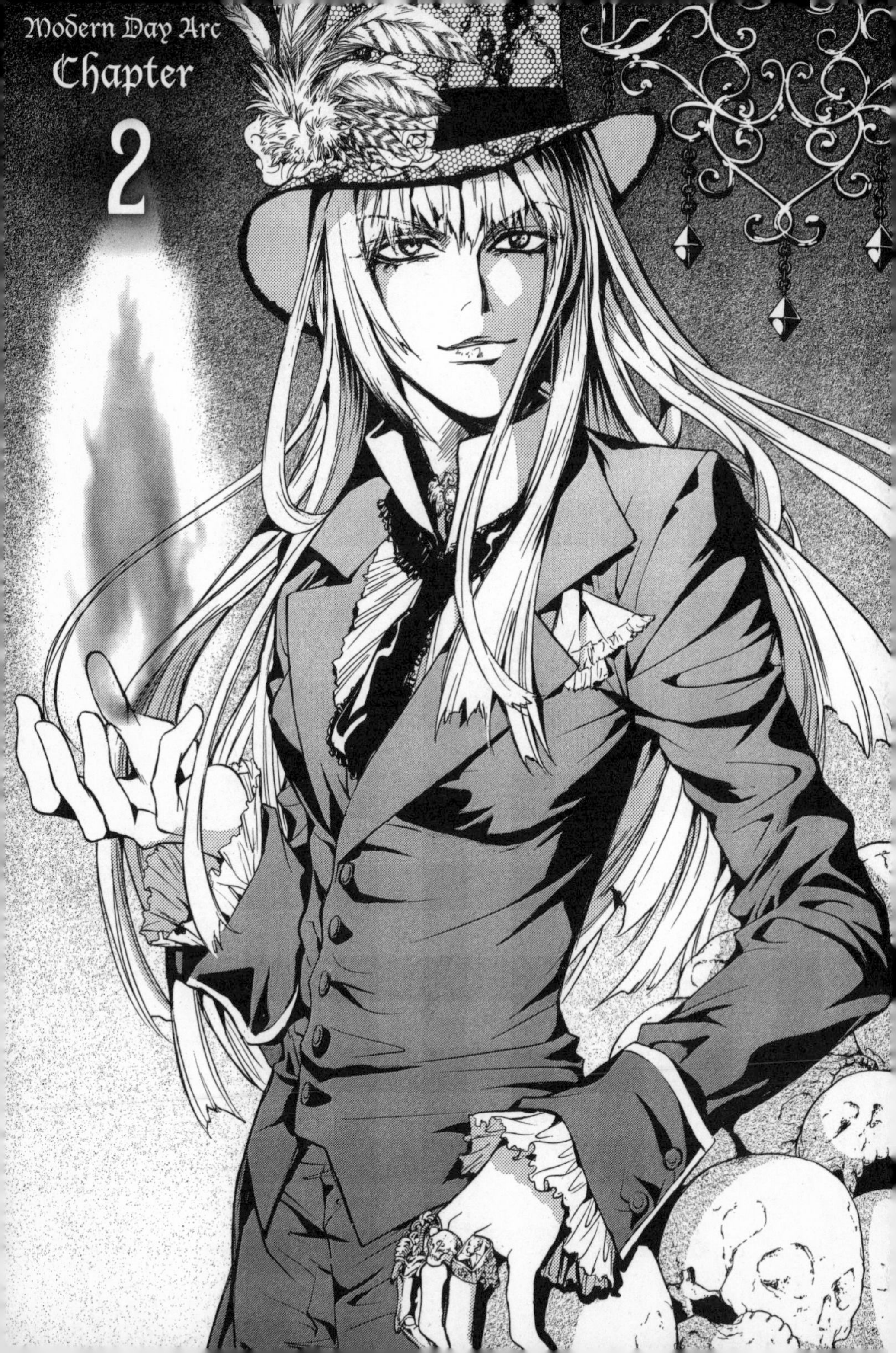
Modern Day Arc
Chapter
2

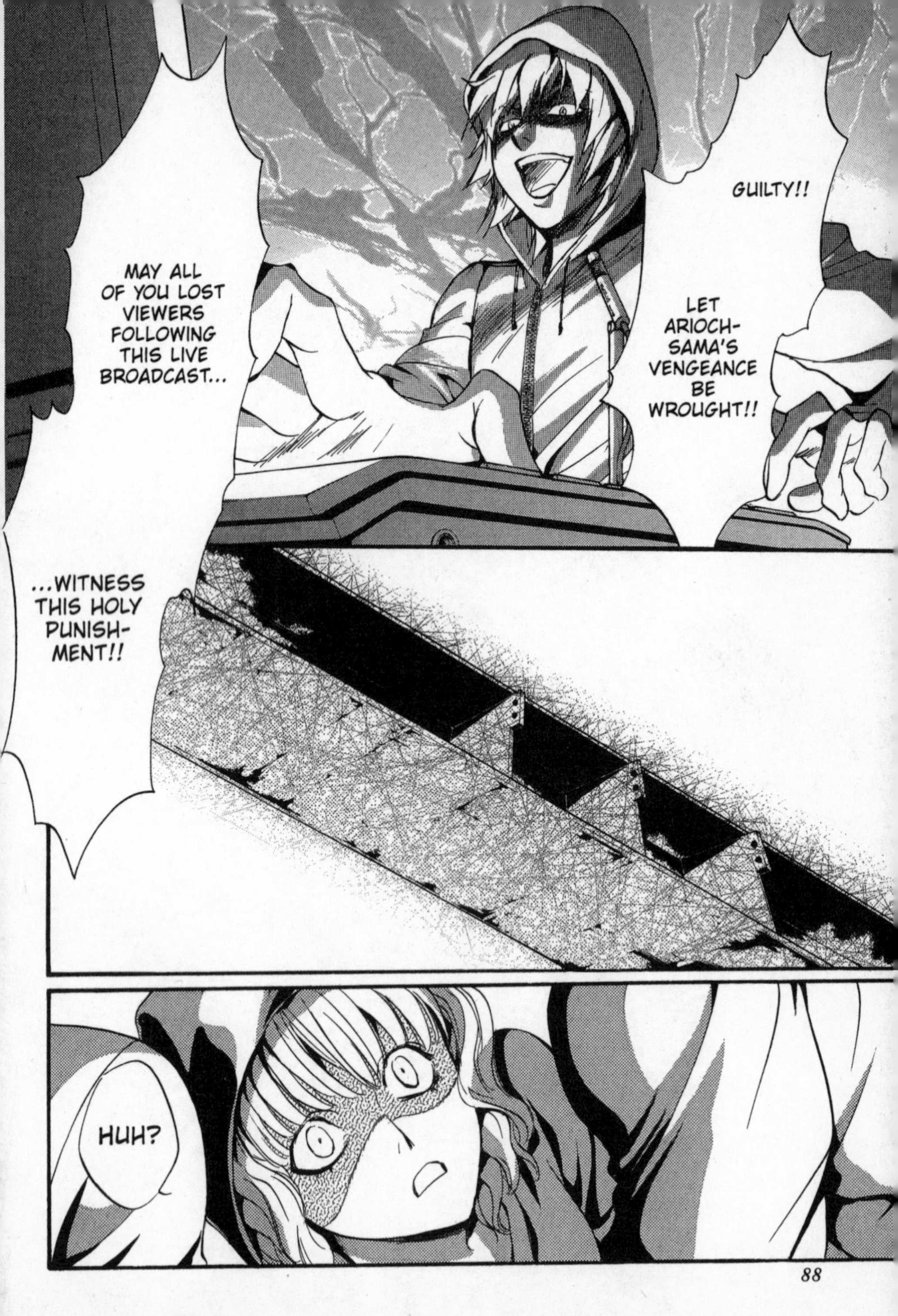
GUILTY!!
LET ARIOCH-SAMA'S VENGEANCE BE WROUGHT!!
MAY ALL OF YOU LOST VIEWERS FOLLOWING THIS LIVE BROADCAST...
...WITNESS THIS HOLY PUNISHMENT!!
HUH?

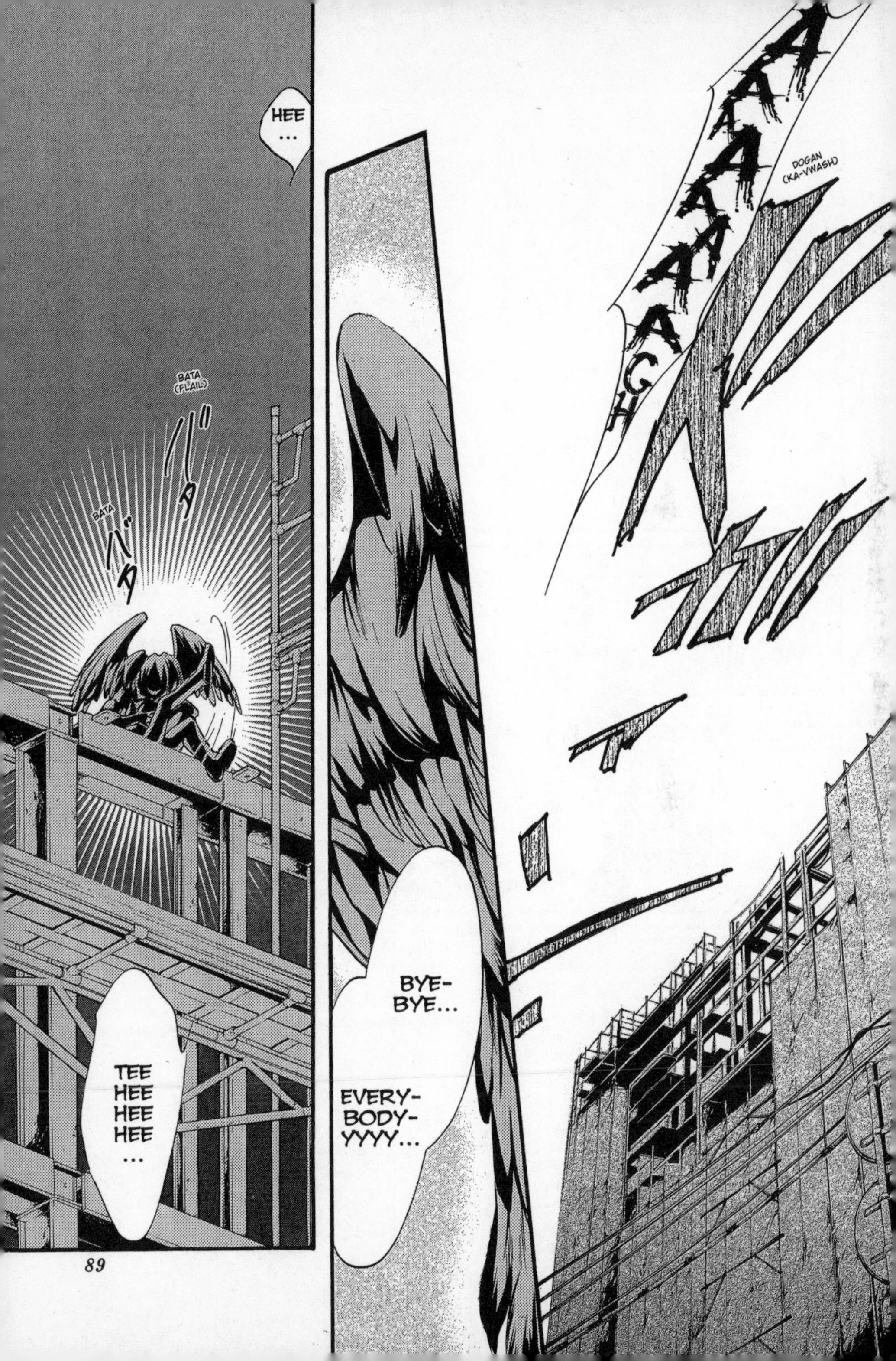
AAAAAAAGH
DOGAN (KA-VWASH)
BYE-BYE...
EVERYBODY-YYYY...
HEE ...
BATA (FLAIL)
BATA
TEE HEE HEE HEE ...

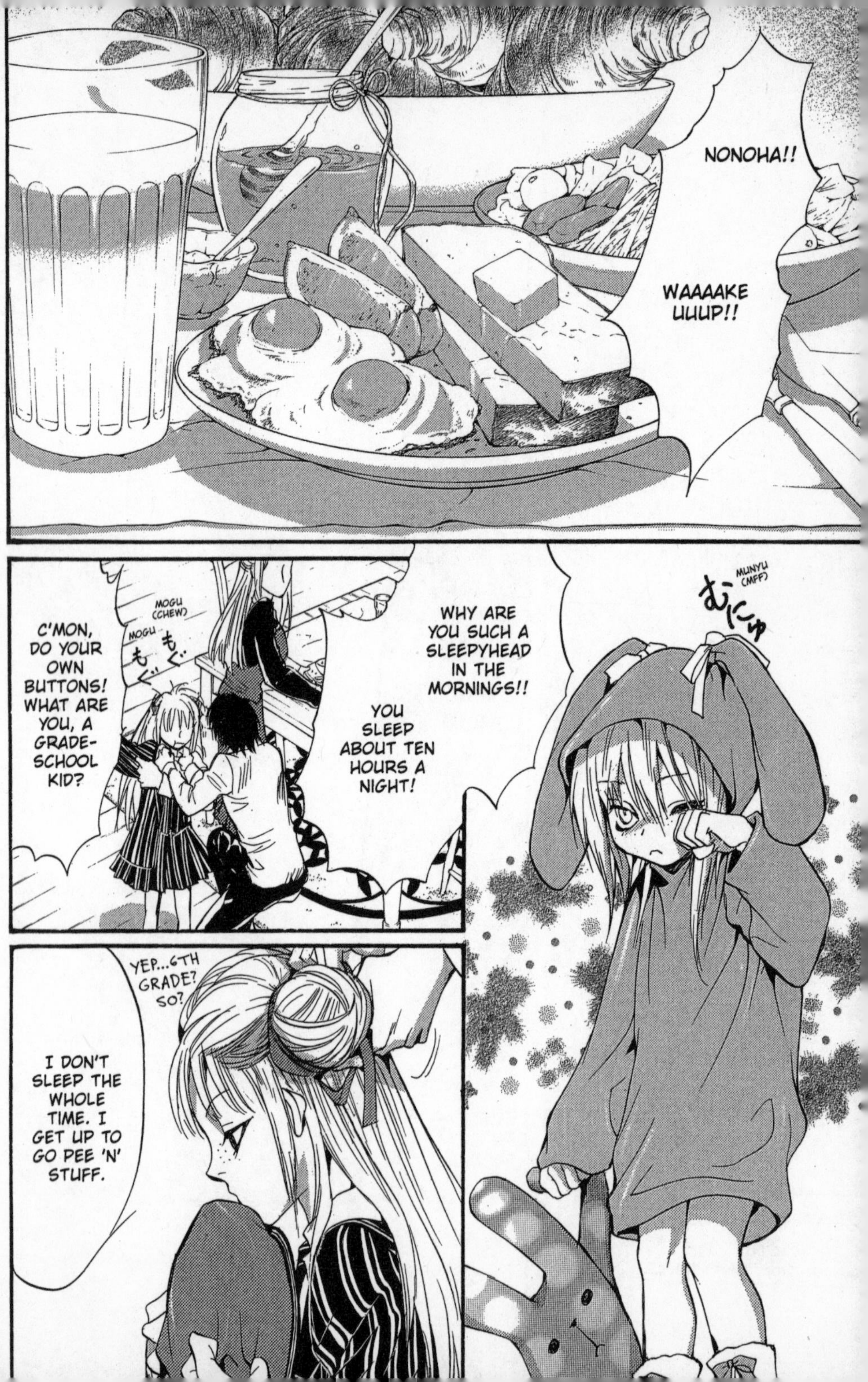
NONOHA!!
WAAAKE UUUP!!
むにゅ
MUNYU (MFF)
WHY ARE YOU SUCH A SLEEPYHEAD IN THE MORNINGS!!
YOU SLEEP ABOUT TEN HOURS A NIGHT!
もぐ もぐ
MOGU (CHEW) MOGU
C'MON, DO YOUR OWN BUTTONS! WHAT ARE YOU, A GRADE-SCHOOL KID?
YEP...6TH GRADE? SO?
I DON'T SLEEP THE WHOLE TIME. I GET UP TO GO PEE 'N' STUFF.

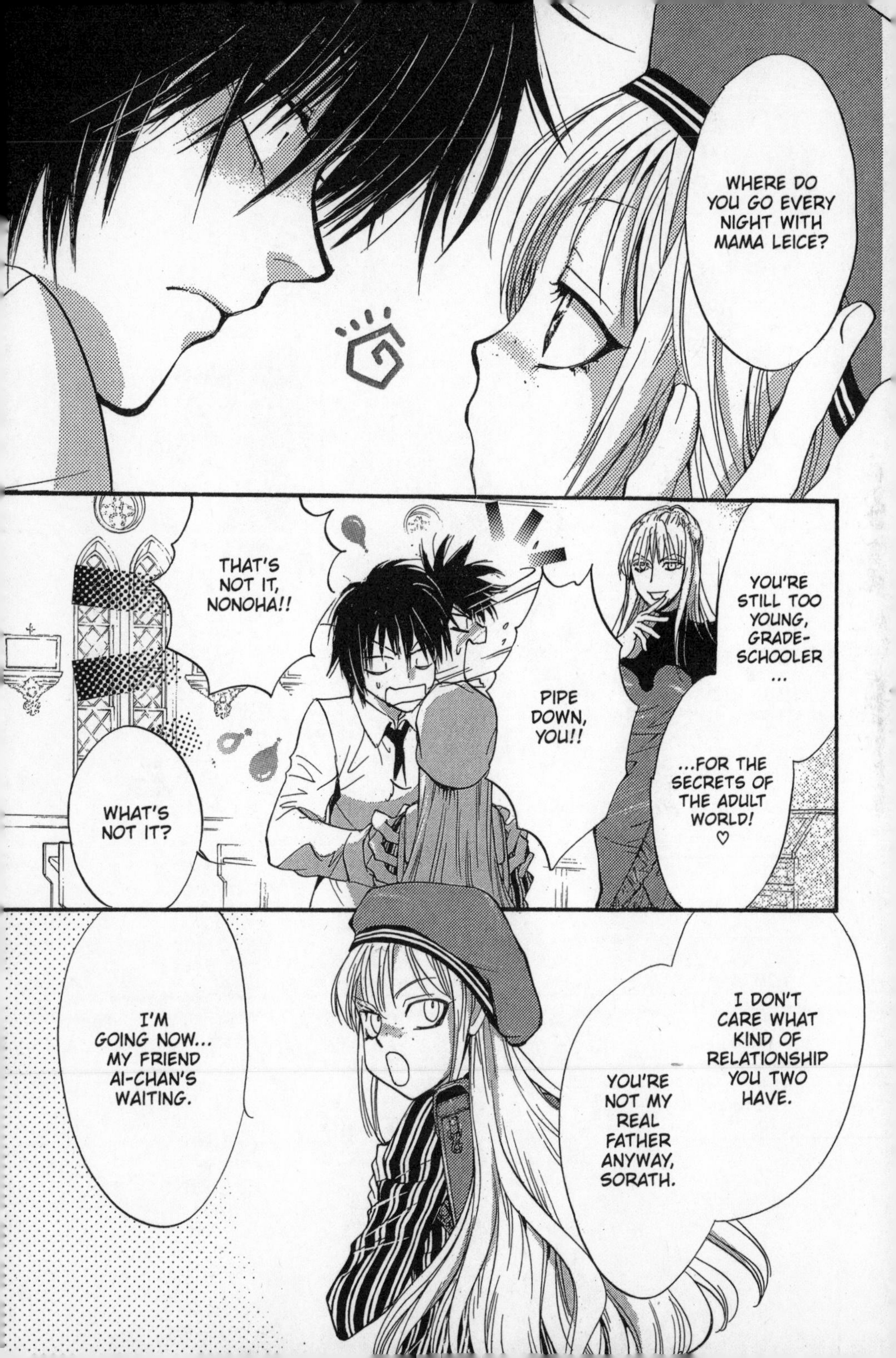
WHERE DO YOU GO EVERY NIGHT WITH MAMA LEICE?
YOU'RE STILL TOO YOUNG, GRADE-SCHOOLER...
...FOR THE SECRETS OF THE ADULT WORLD! ♡
PIPE DOWN, YOU!!
THAT'S NOT IT, NONOHA!!
WHAT'S NOT IT?
I DON'T CARE WHAT KIND OF RELATIONSHIP YOU TWO HAVE.
YOU'RE NOT MY REAL FATHER ANYWAY, SORATH.
I'M GOING NOW... MY FRIEND AI-CHAN'S WAITING.

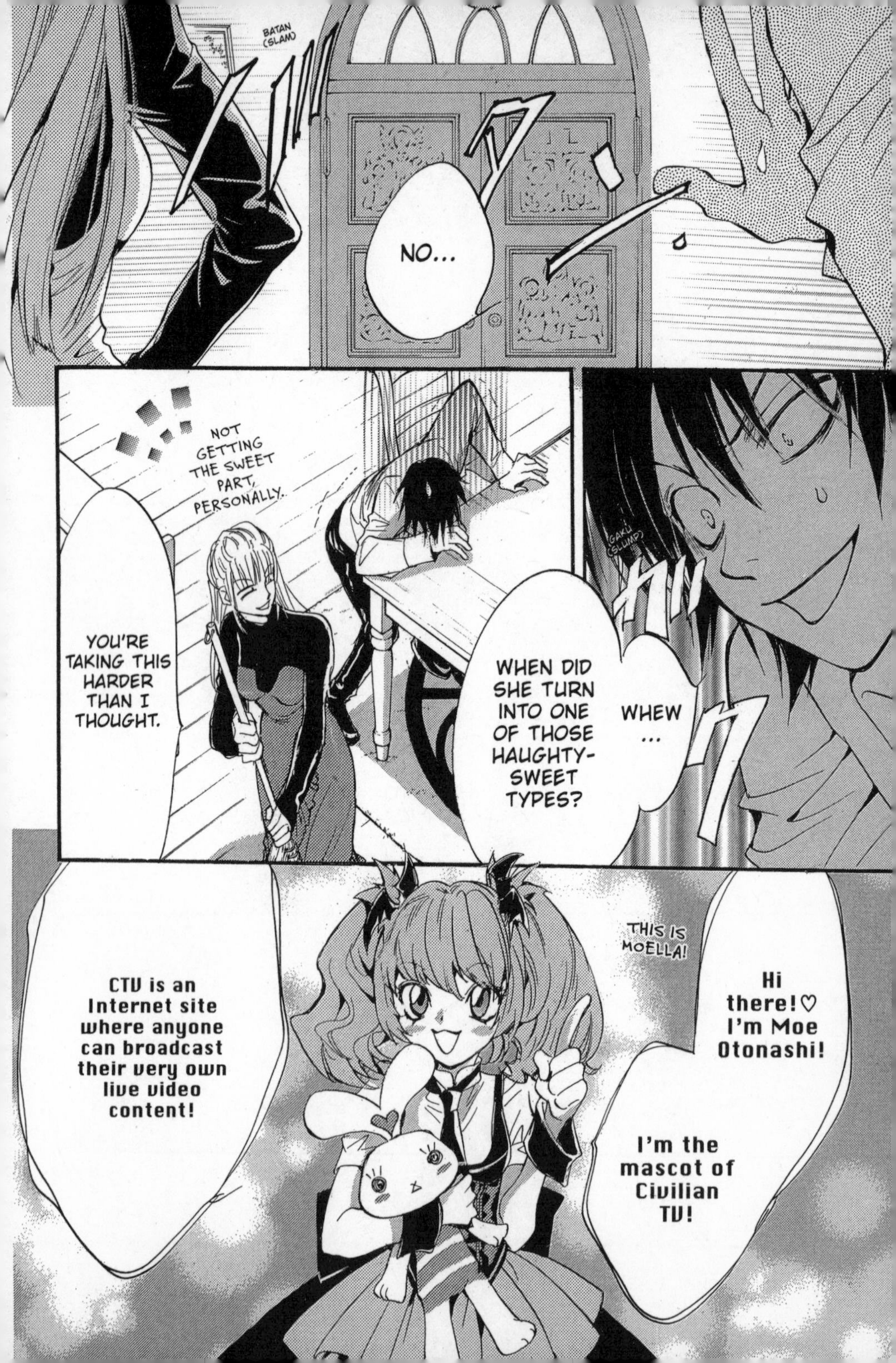
BATAN (SLAM)
NO...
GAKU (SLUMP)
WHEW ...
WHEN DID SHE TURN INTO ONE OF THOSE HAUGHTY-SWEET TYPES?
NOT GETTING THE SWEET PART, PERSONALLY.
YOU'RE TAKING THIS HARDER THAN I THOUGHT.
Hi there!♡ I'm Moe Otonashi!
THIS IS MOELLA!
I'm the mascot of Civilian TV!
CTV is an Internet site where anyone can broadcast their very own live video content!

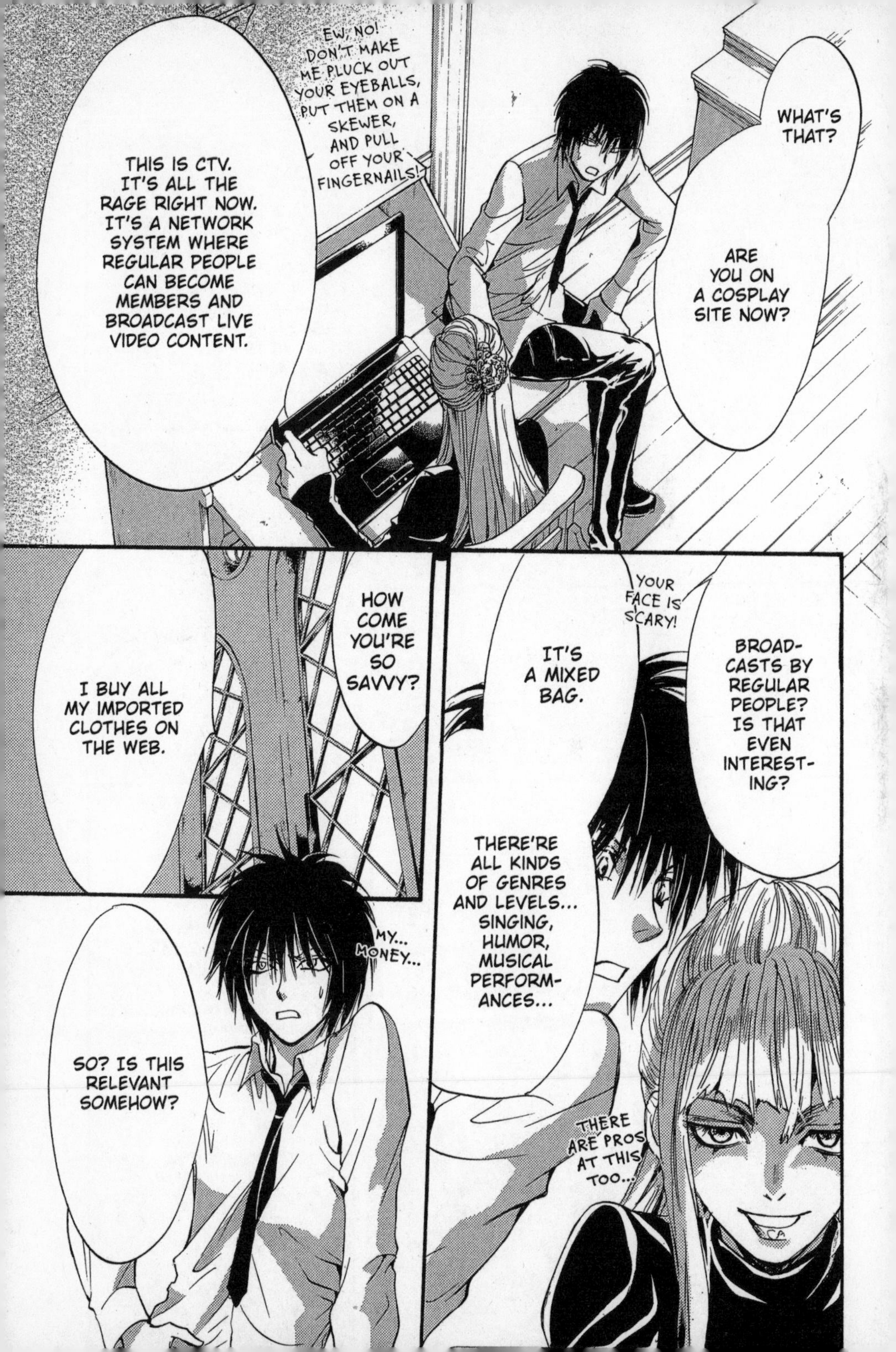
WHAT'S THAT?
ARE YOU ON A COSPLAY SITE NOW?
EW, NO! DON'T MAKE ME PLUCK OUT YOUR EYEBALLS, PUT THEM ON A SKEWER, AND PULL OFF YOUR FINGERNAILS!
THIS IS CTV. IT'S ALL THE RAGE RIGHT NOW. IT'S A NETWORK SYSTEM WHERE REGULAR PEOPLE CAN BECOME MEMBERS AND BROADCAST LIVE VIDEO CONTENT.
BROAD-CASTS BY REGULAR PEOPLE? IS THAT EVEN INTEREST-ING?
YOUR FACE IS SCARY!
IT'S A MIXED BAG.
THERE'RE ALL KINDS OF GENRES AND LEVELS... SINGING, HUMOR, MUSICAL PERFORM-ANCES...
THERE ARE PROS AT THIS TOO...
HOW COME YOU'RE SO SAVVY?
I BUY ALL MY IMPORTED CLOTHES ON THE WEB.
MY... MONEY...
SO? IS THIS RELEVANT SOMEHOW?

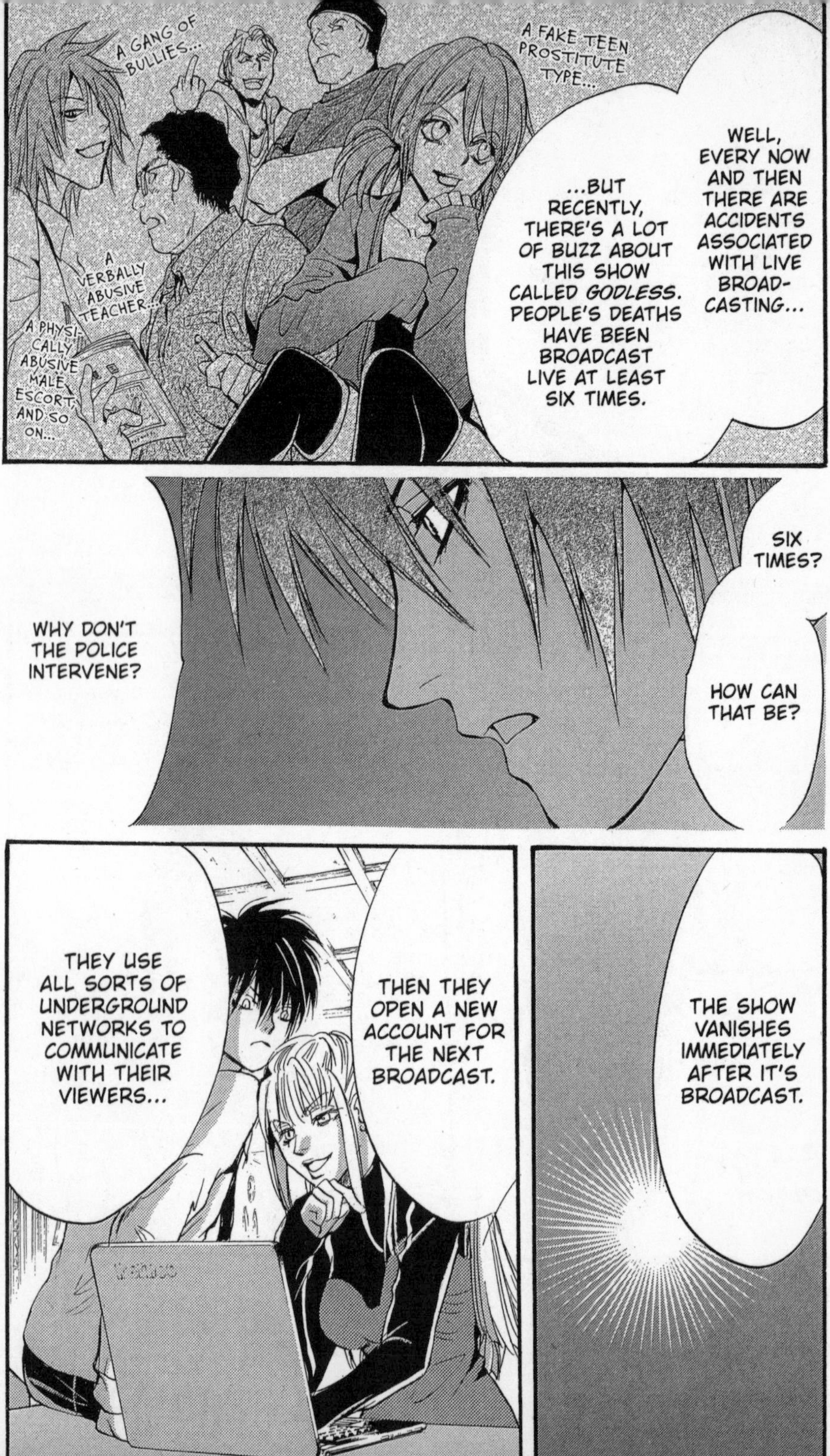
WELL, EVERY NOW AND THEN THERE ARE ACCIDENTS ASSOCIATED WITH LIVE BROAD-CASTING...
...BUT RECENTLY, THERE'S A LOT OF BUZZ ABOUT THIS SHOW CALLED *GODLESS*. PEOPLE'S DEATHS HAVE BEEN BROADCAST LIVE AT LEAST SIX TIMES.
A FAKE TEEN PROSTITUTE TYPE...
A GANG OF BULLIES...
A VERBALLY ABUSIVE TEACHER...
A PHYSI-CALLY ABUSIVE MALE ESCORT, AND SO ON...
SIX TIMES?
HOW CAN THAT BE?
WHY DON'T THE POLICE INTERVENE?
THE SHOW VANISHES IMMEDIATELY AFTER IT'S BROADCAST.
THEN THEY OPEN A NEW ACCOUNT FOR THE NEXT BROADCAST.
THEY USE ALL SORTS OF UNDERGROUND NETWORKS TO COMMUNICATE WITH THEIR VIEWERS...

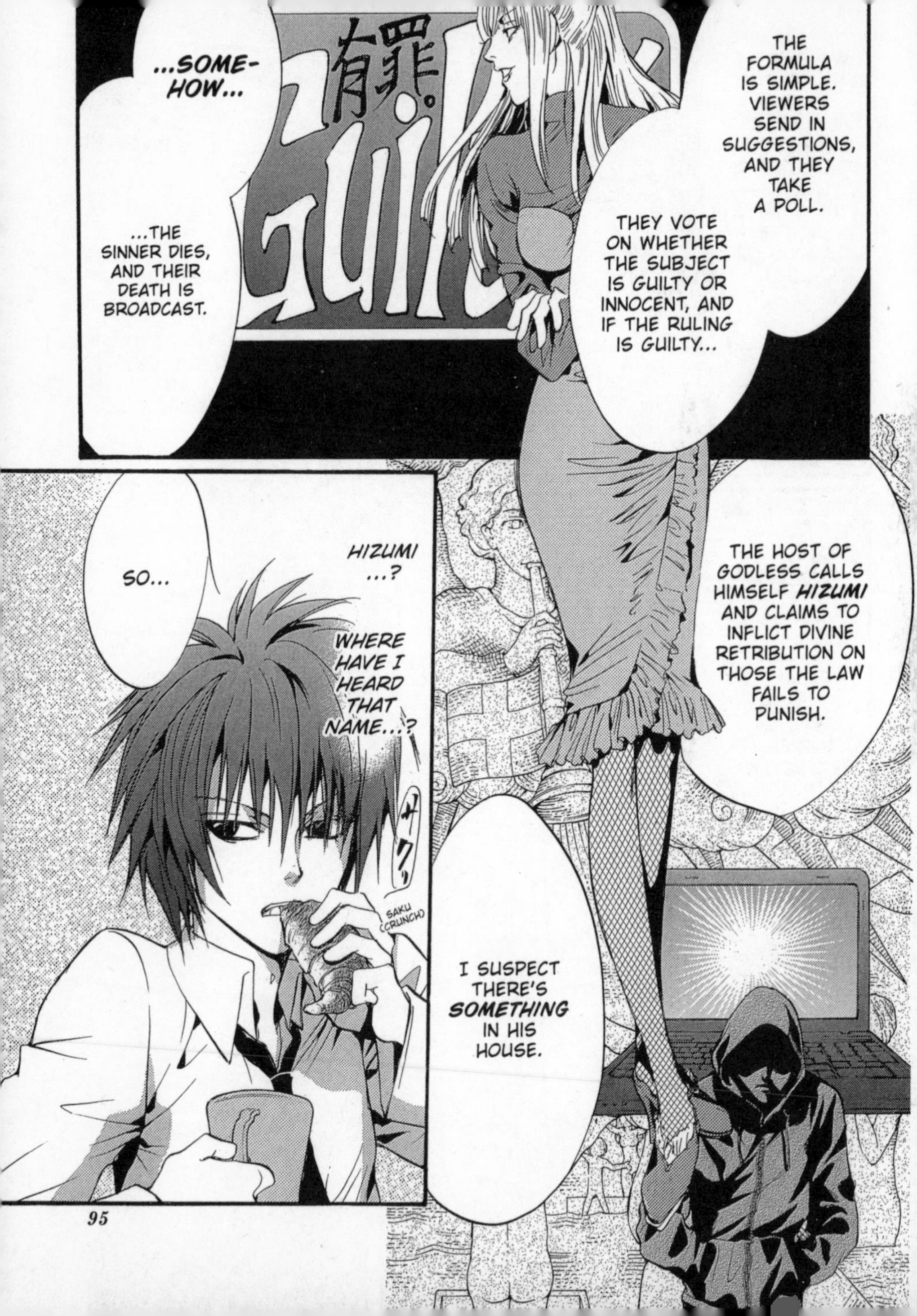
有罪。
THE FORMULA IS SIMPLE. VIEWERS SEND IN SUGGESTIONS, AND THEY TAKE A POLL.
THEY VOTE ON WHETHER THE SUBJECT IS GUILTY OR INNOCENT, AND IF THE RULING IS GUILTY...
...THE SINNER DIES, AND THEIR DEATH IS BROADCAST.
...SOME-HOW...
THE HOST OF GODLESS CALLS HIMSELF *HIZUMI* AND CLAIMS TO INFLICT DIVINE RETRIBUTION ON THOSE THE LAW FAILS TO PUNISH.
I SUSPECT THERE'S *SOMETHING* IN HIS HOUSE.
HIZUMI ...?
WHERE HAVE I HEARD THAT NAME...?
SO...
SAKU (CRUNCH)

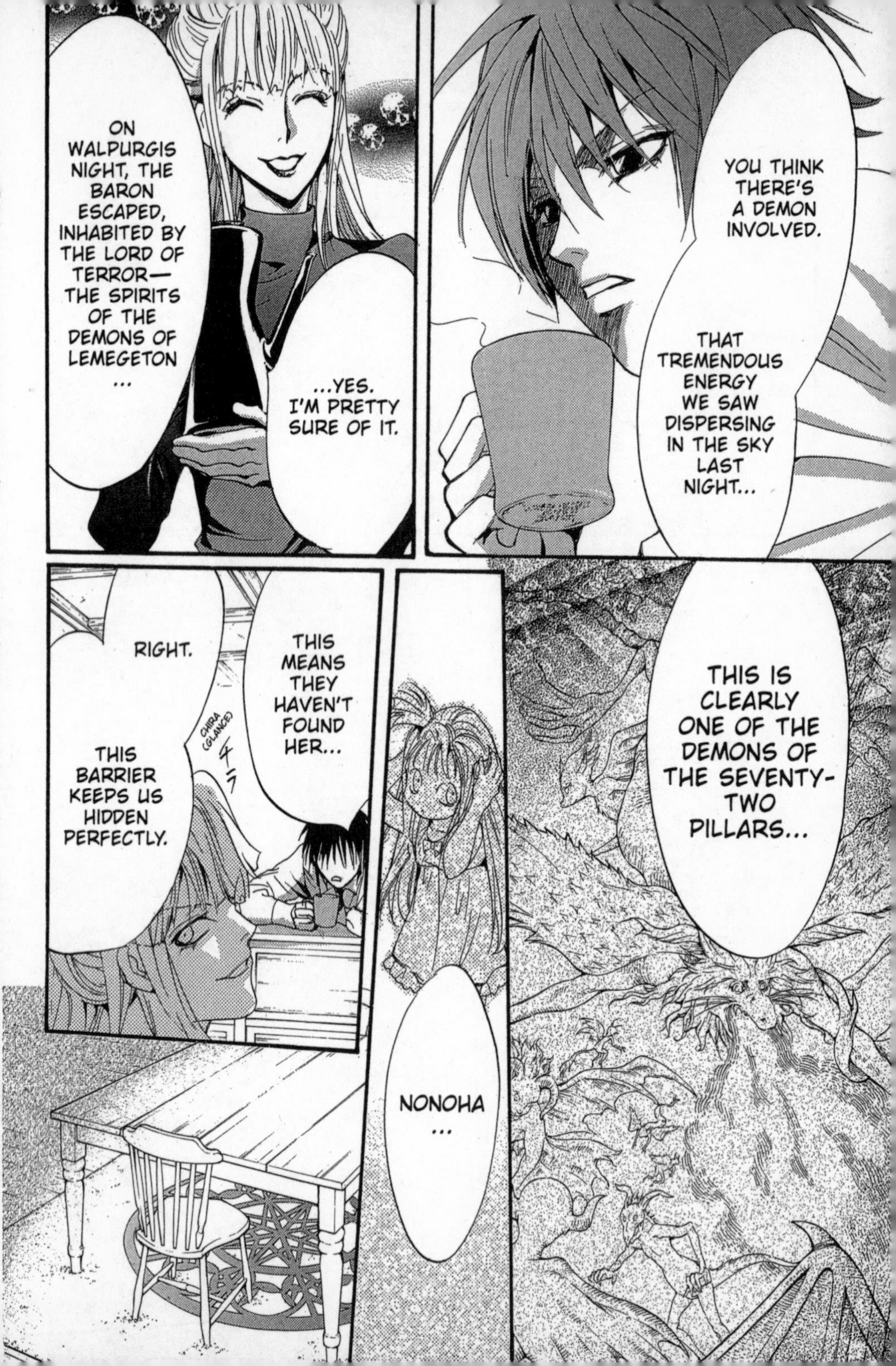
YOU THINK THERE'S A DEMON INVOLVED.
THAT TREMENDOUS ENERGY WE SAW DISPERSING IN THE SKY LAST NIGHT...
ON WALPURGIS NIGHT, THE BARON ESCAPED, INHABITED BY THE LORD OF TERROR—THE SPIRITS OF THE DEMONS OF LEMEGETON...
...YES. I'M PRETTY SURE OF IT.
THIS IS CLEARLY ONE OF THE DEMONS OF THE SEVENTY-TWO PILLARS...
NONOHA...
THIS MEANS THEY HAVEN'T FOUND HER...
RIGHT.
CHIRA (GLANCE)
THIS BARRIER KEEPS US HIDDEN PERFECTLY.

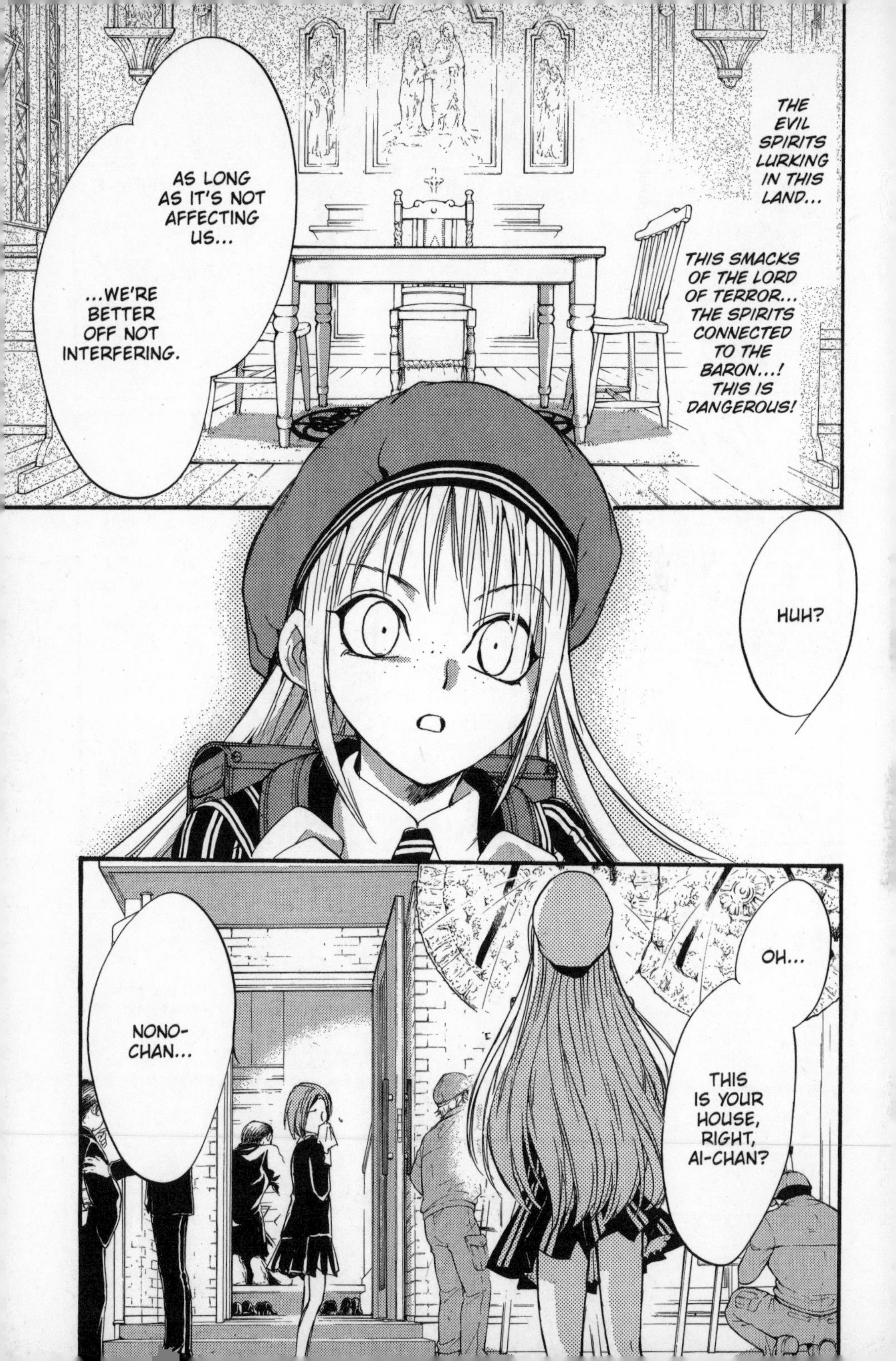
THE EVIL SPIRITS LURKING IN THIS LAND...
THIS SMACKS OF THE LORD OF TERROR... THE SPIRITS CONNECTED TO THE BARON...! THIS IS DANGEROUS!
AS LONG AS IT'S NOT AFFECTING US...
...WE'RE BETTER OFF NOT INTERFERING.
HUH?
OH...
THIS IS YOUR HOUSE, RIGHT, AI-CHAN?
NONO-CHAN...

MY OLDER SISTER DIED...

...IN AN ACCIDENT LAST NIGHT.

SO I WON'T BE GOING TO SCHOOL TODAY.

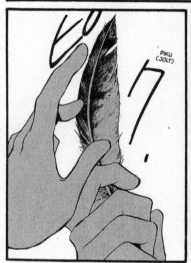

PIKU (JOLT)

A GROUP OF BAD KIDS SURROUNDED HER...AND A CONSTRUCTION SCAFFOLDING FELL ON HER. AND SHE...

OH NO... AI-CHAN...!!

OH...

THE PERSON WHO FOUND HER SAID MY SISTER WAS HOLDING THIS.

WHAT'S... THAT...?

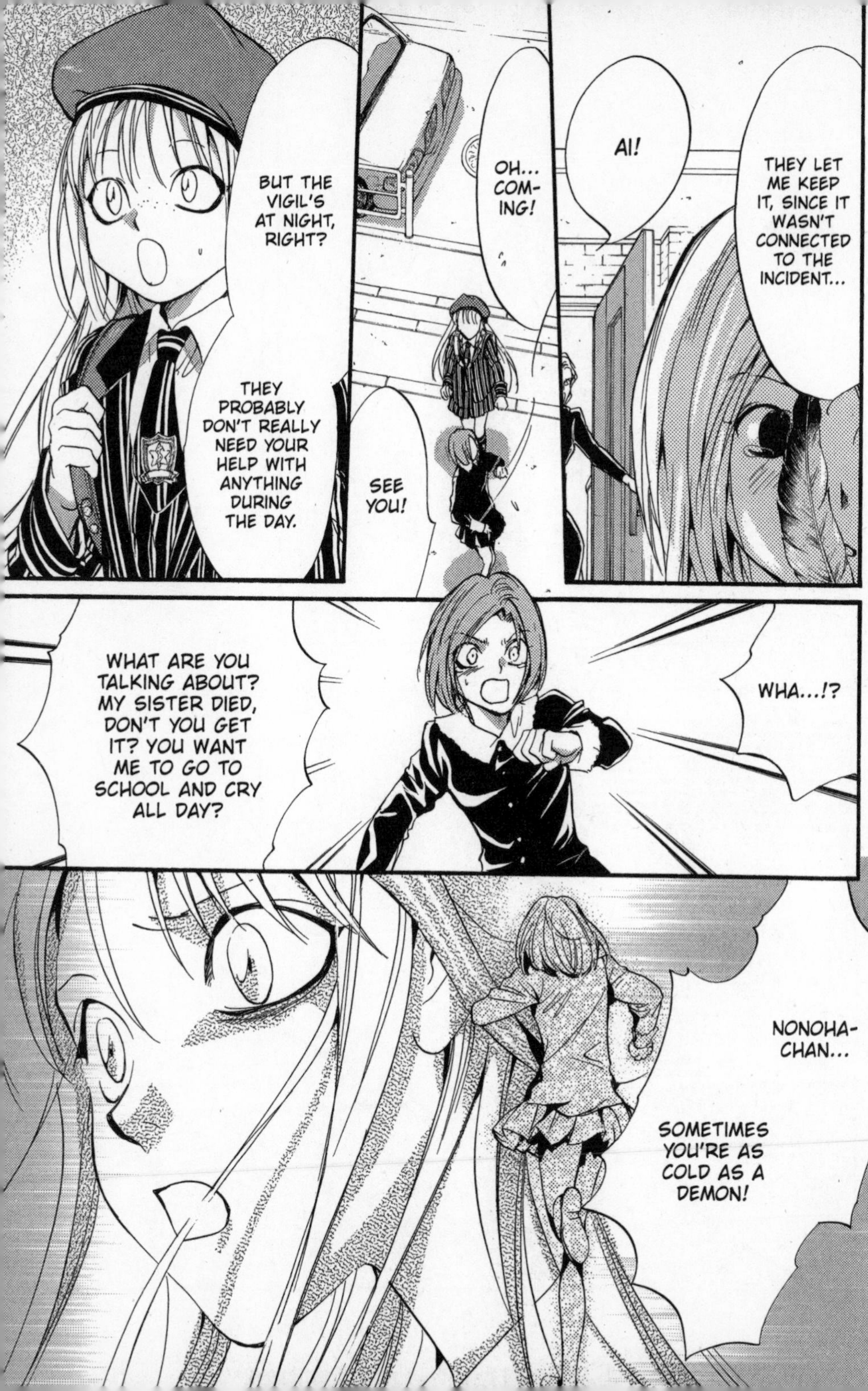
THEY LET ME KEEP IT, SINCE IT WASN'T CONNECTED TO THE INCIDENT...
AI!
OH... COMING!
SEE YOU!
BUT THE VIGIL'S AT NIGHT, RIGHT?
THEY PROBABLY DON'T REALLY NEED YOUR HELP WITH ANYTHING DURING THE DAY.
WHA...!?
WHAT ARE YOU TALKING ABOUT? MY SISTER DIED, DON'T YOU GET IT? YOU WANT ME TO GO TO SCHOOL AND CRY ALL DAY?
NONOHA-CHAN...
SOMETIMES YOU'RE AS COLD AS A DEMON!

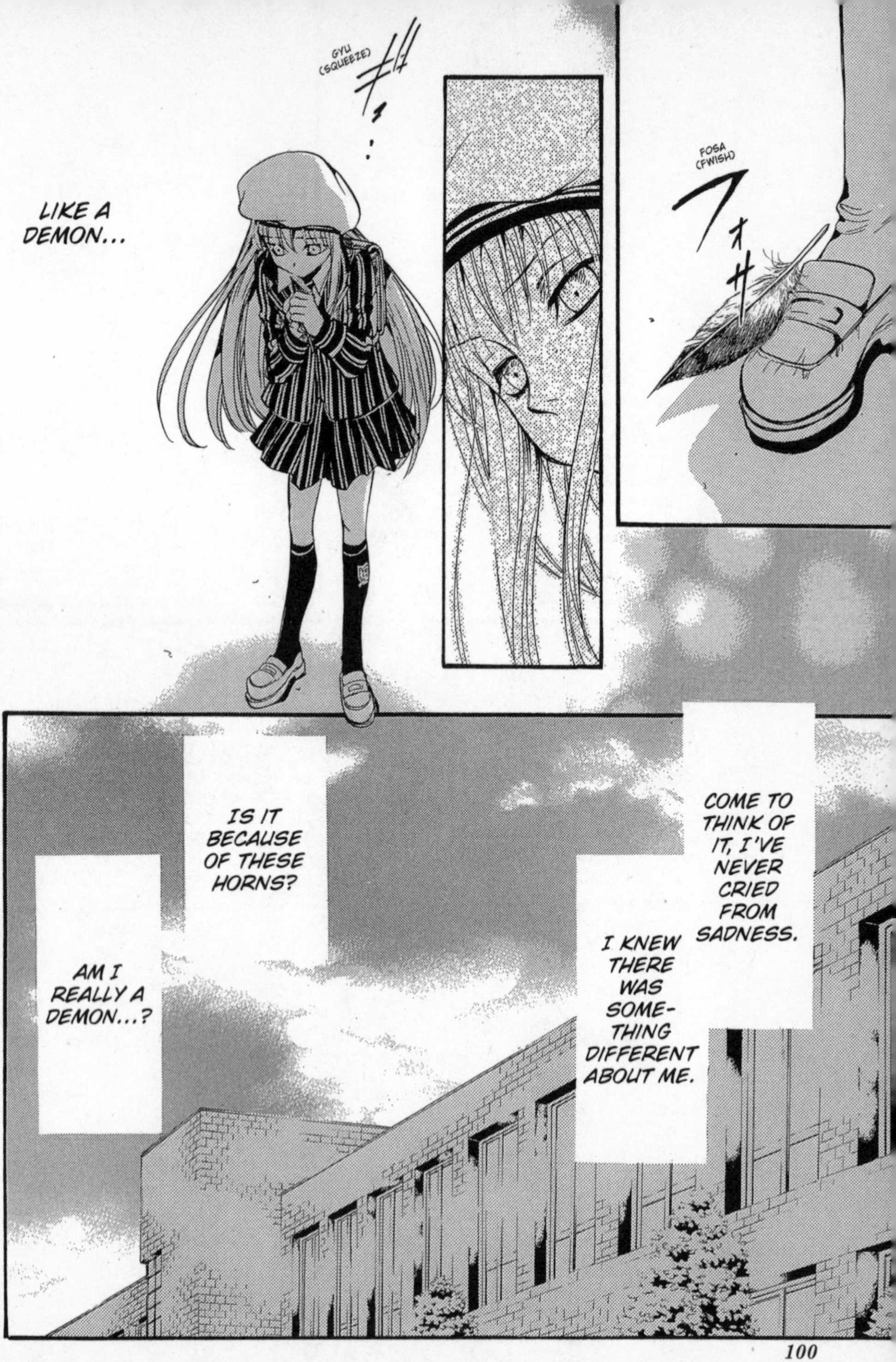
FOSA
(FWISH)
GYU
(SQUEEZE)
LIKE A DEMON...
COME TO THINK OF IT, I'VE NEVER CRIED FROM SADNESS.
I KNEW THERE WAS SOME-THING DIFFERENT ABOUT ME.
IS IT BECAUSE OF THESE HORNS?
AM I REALLY A DEMON...?

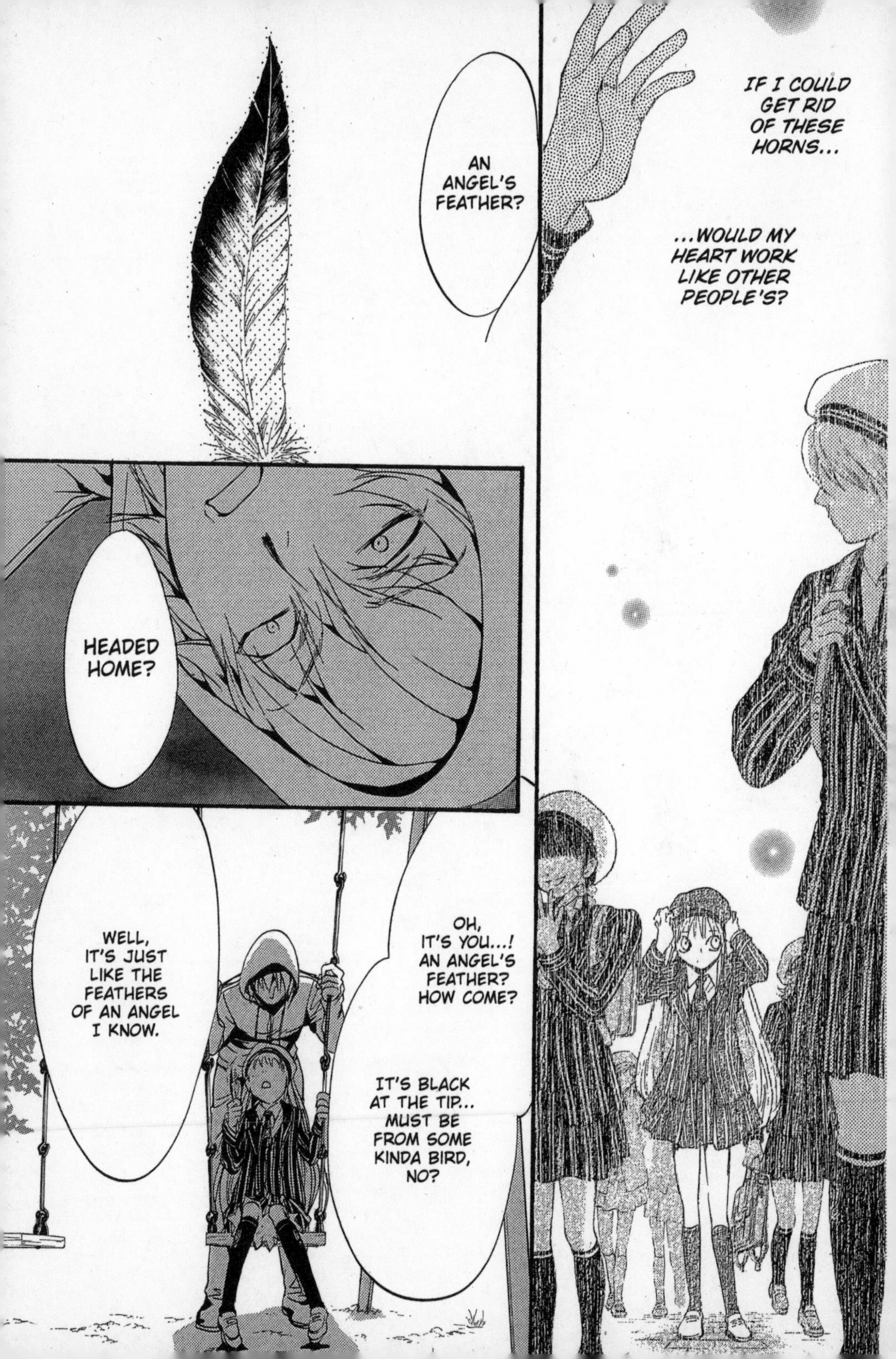
IF I COULD GET RID OF THESE HORNS...
...WOULD MY HEART WORK LIKE OTHER PEOPLE'S?
AN ANGEL'S FEATHER?
HEADED HOME?
OH, IT'S YOU...! AN ANGEL'S FEATHER? HOW COME?
IT'S BLACK AT THE TIP... MUST BE FROM SOME KINDA BIRD, NO?
WELL, IT'S JUST LIKE THE FEATHERS OF AN ANGEL I KNOW.

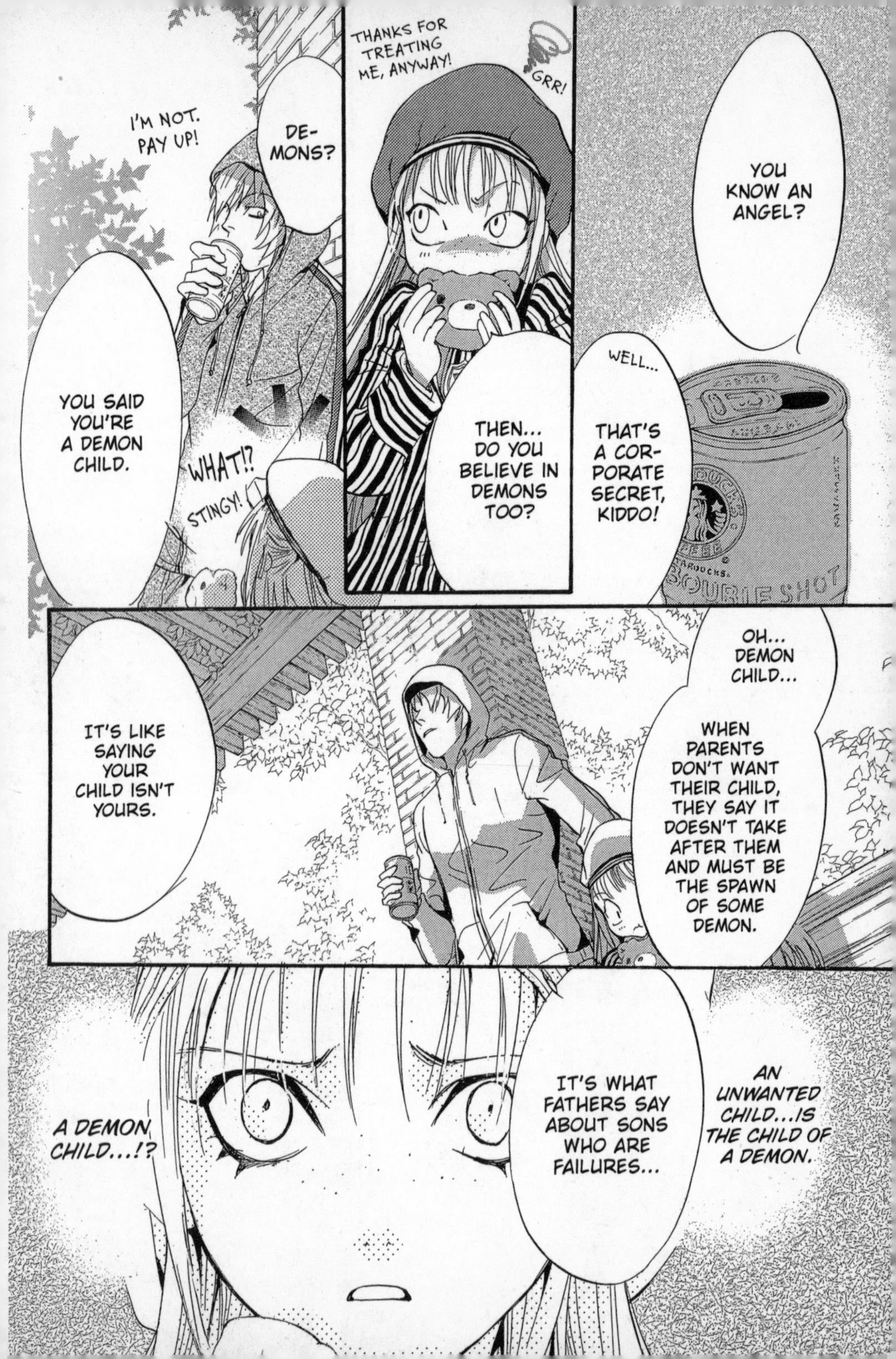
YOU KNOW AN ANGEL?
WELL...
THAT'S A CORPORATE SECRET, KIDDO!
GRR!
THANKS FOR TREATING ME, ANYWAY!
THEN... DO YOU BELIEVE IN DEMONS TOO?
DE-MONS?
I'M NOT. PAY UP!
YOU SAID YOU'RE A DEMON CHILD.
WHAT!?
STINGY!
OH... DEMON CHILD...
WHEN PARENTS DON'T WANT THEIR CHILD, THEY SAY IT DOESN'T TAKE AFTER THEM AND MUST BE THE SPAWN OF SOME DEMON.
IT'S LIKE SAYING YOUR CHILD ISN'T YOURS.
AN UNWANTED CHILD...IS THE CHILD OF A DEMON.
IT'S WHAT FATHERS SAY ABOUT SONS WHO ARE FAILURES...
A DEMON CHILD...!?

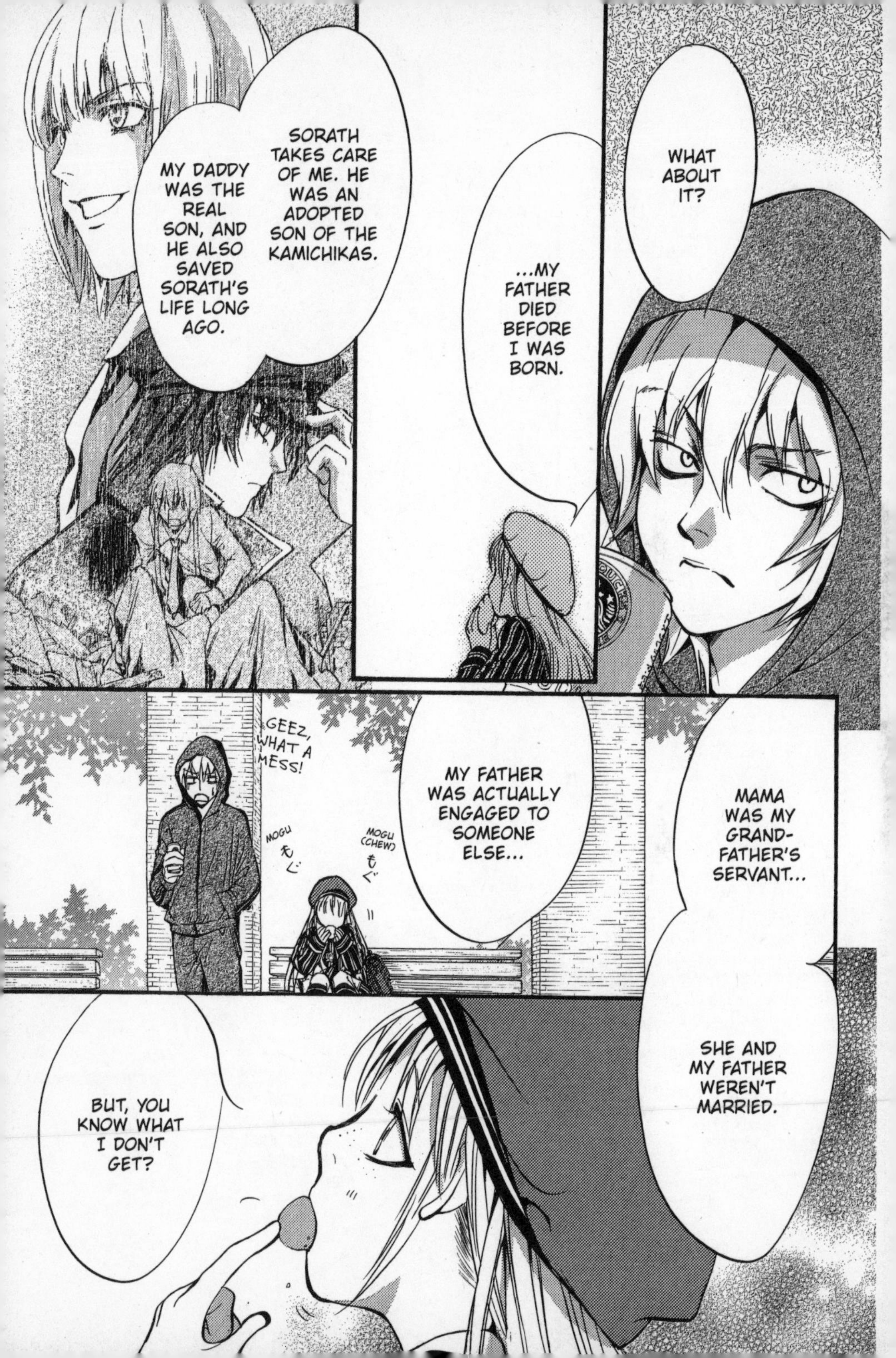
WHAT ABOUT IT?
...MY FATHER DIED BEFORE I WAS BORN.
SORATH TAKES CARE OF ME. HE WAS AN ADOPTED SON OF THE KAMICHIKAS.
MY DADDY WAS THE REAL SON, AND HE ALSO SAVED SORATH'S LIFE LONG AGO.
MAMA WAS MY GRAND-FATHER'S SERVANT...
SHE AND MY FATHER WEREN'T MARRIED.
MY FATHER WAS ACTUALLY ENGAGED TO SOMEONE ELSE...
MOGU (CHEW) もぐ
MOGU もぐ
GEEZ, WHAT A MESS!
BUT, YOU KNOW WHAT I DON'T GET?

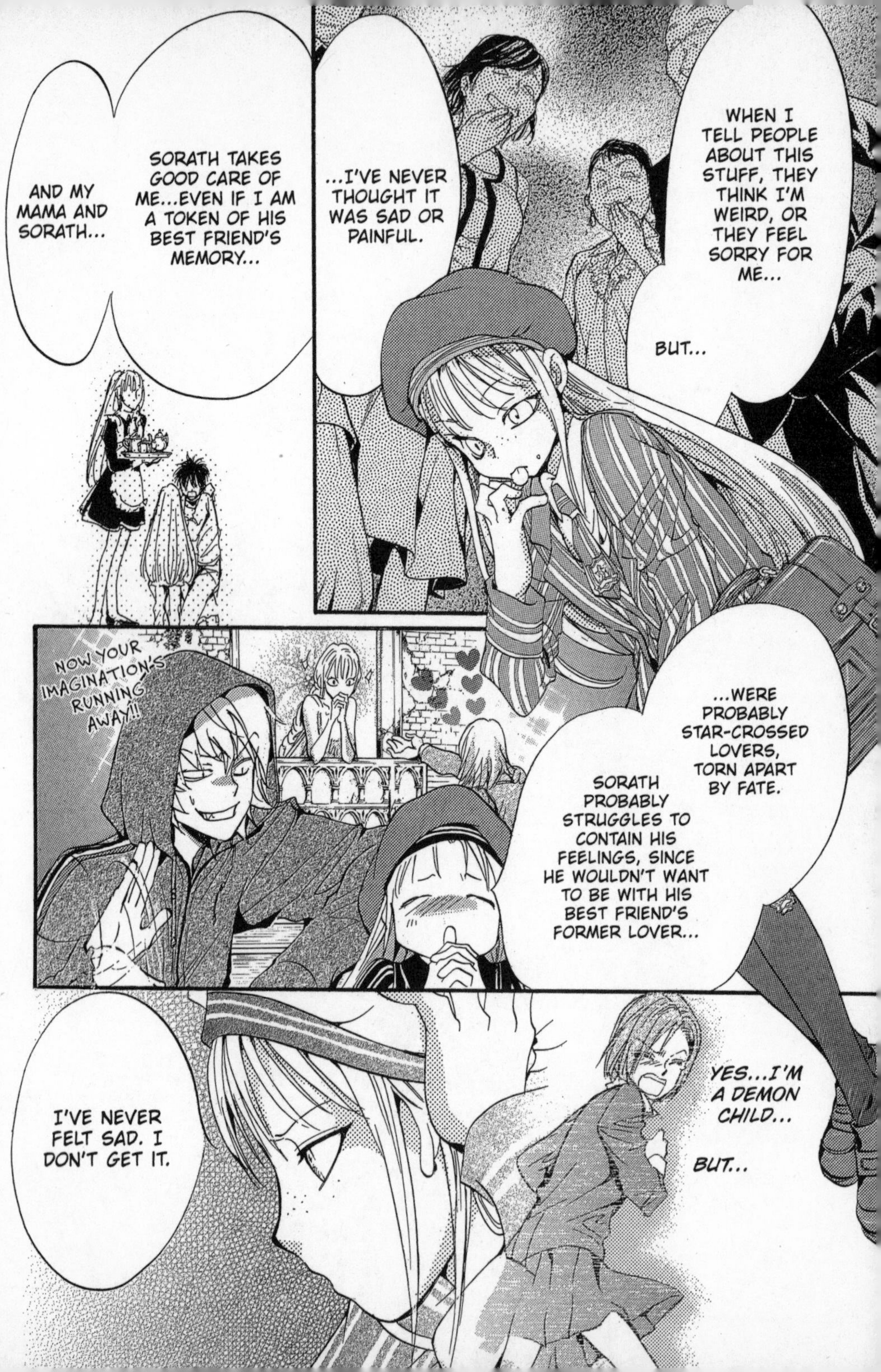
WHEN I TELL PEOPLE ABOUT THIS STUFF, THEY THINK I'M WEIRD, OR THEY FEEL SORRY FOR ME...
BUT...
...I'VE NEVER THOUGHT IT WAS SAD OR PAINFUL.
SORATH TAKES GOOD CARE OF ME...EVEN IF I AM A TOKEN OF HIS BEST FRIEND'S MEMORY...
AND MY MAMA AND SORATH...
...WERE PROBABLY STAR-CROSSED LOVERS, TORN APART BY FATE.
SORATH PROBABLY STRUGGLES TO CONTAIN HIS FEELINGS, SINCE HE WOULDN'T WANT TO BE WITH HIS BEST FRIEND'S FORMER LOVER...
NOW YOUR IMAGINATION'S RUNNING AWAY!!
YES...I'M A DEMON CHILD...
BUT...
I'VE NEVER FELT SAD. I DON'T GET IT.

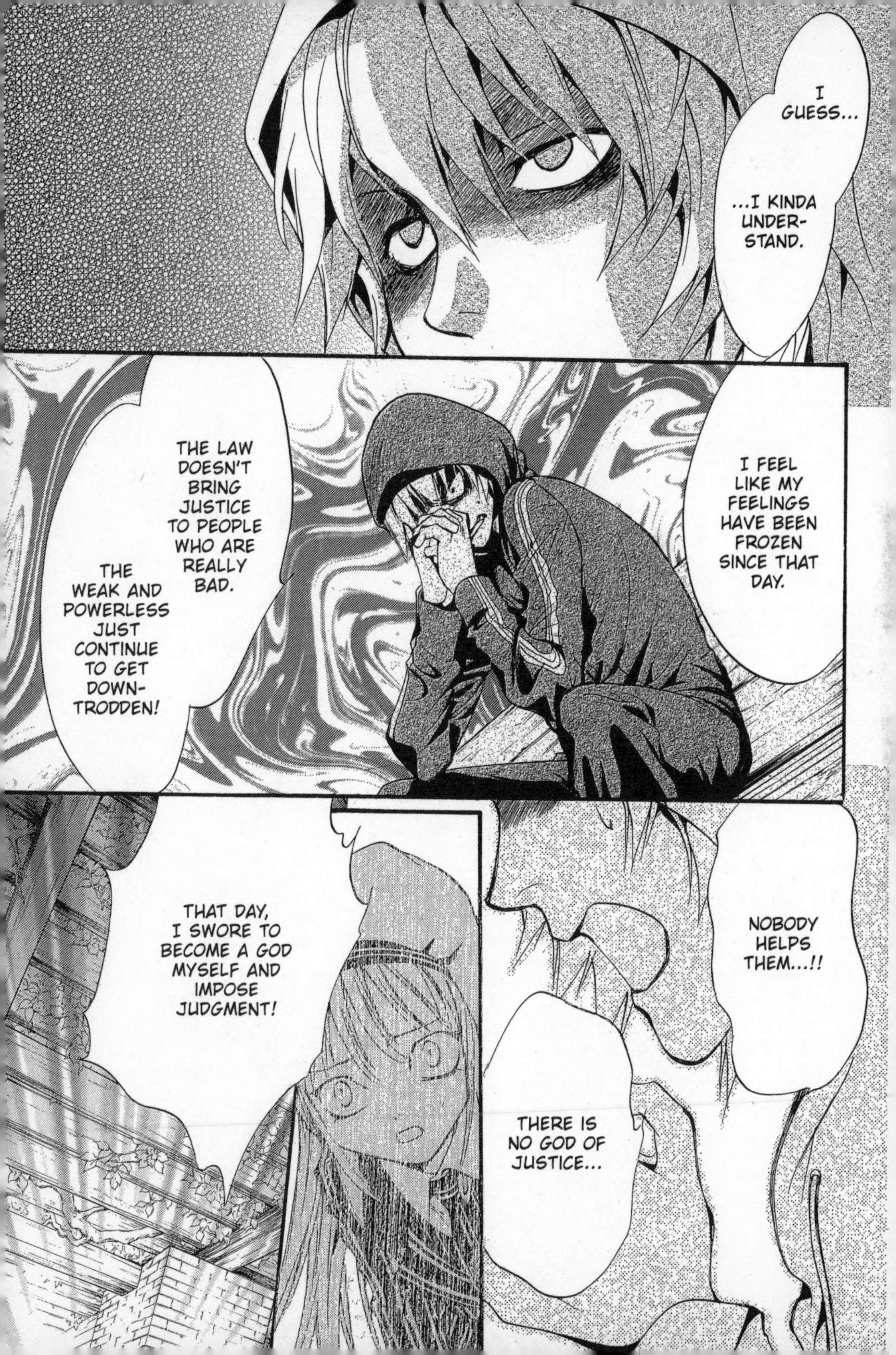

I GUESS...
...I KINDA UNDER-STAND.
I FEEL LIKE MY FEELINGS HAVE BEEN FROZEN SINCE THAT DAY.
THE LAW DOESN'T BRING JUSTICE TO PEOPLE WHO ARE REALLY BAD.
THE WEAK AND POWERLESS JUST CONTINUE TO GET DOWN-TRODDEN!
NOBODY HELPS THEM...!!
THERE IS NO GOD OF JUSTICE...
THAT DAY, I SWORE TO BECOME A GOD MYSELF AND IMPOSE JUDGMENT!

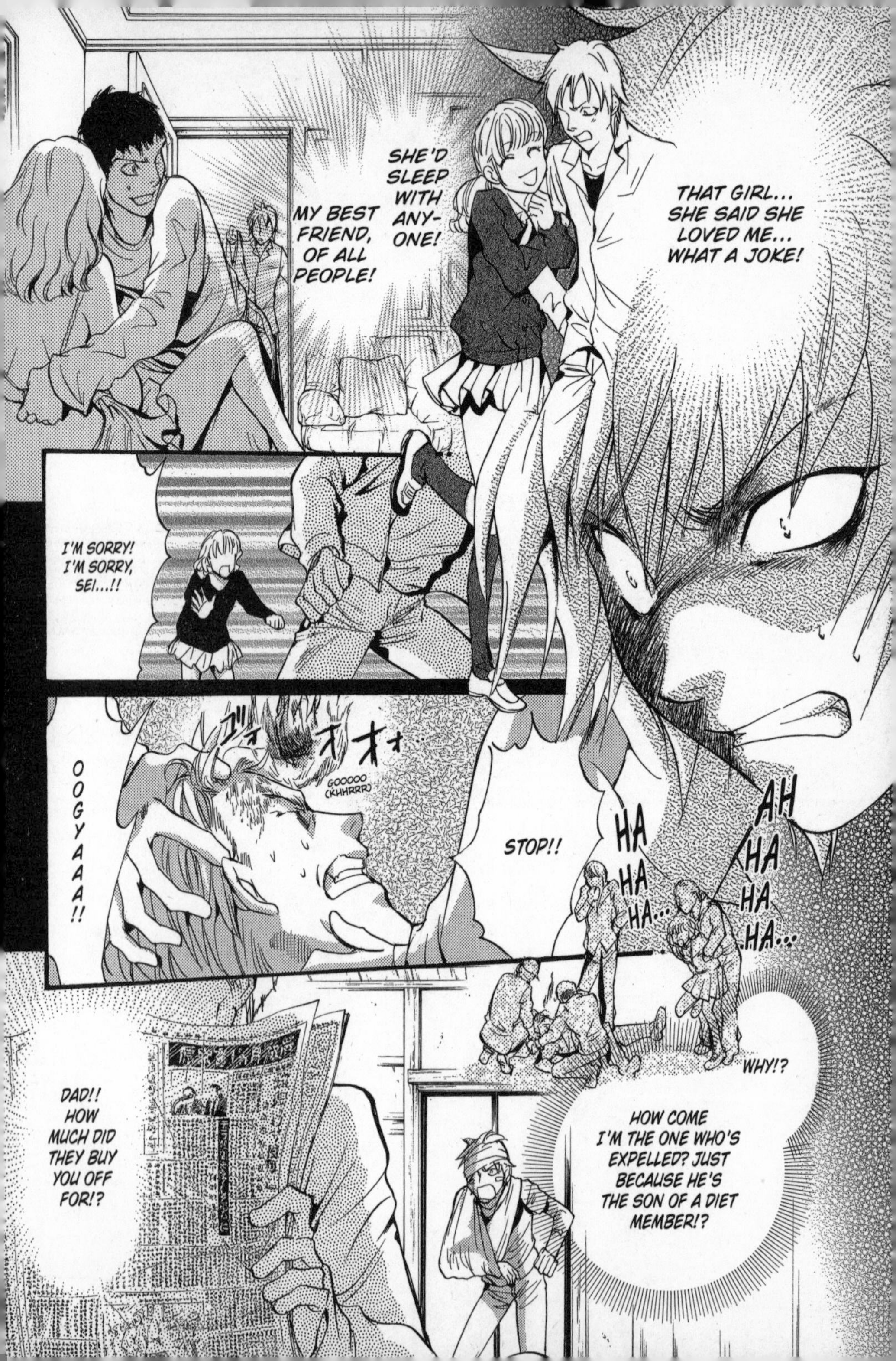
THAT GIRL... SHE SAID SHE LOVED ME... WHAT A JOKE!
SHE'D SLEEP WITH ANY-ONE!
MY BEST FRIEND, OF ALL PEOPLE!
I'M SORRY! I'M SORRY, SEI...!!
ゴォオオ
GOOOOO (KHHRRR)
OOGYAAAA!!
AH HA HA HA HA...
HA HA HA HA...
STOP!!
WHY!?
HOW COME I'M THE ONE WHO'S EXPELLED? JUST BECAUSE HE'S THE SON OF A DIET MEMBER!?
DAD!! HOW MUCH DID THEY BUY YOU OFF FOR!?

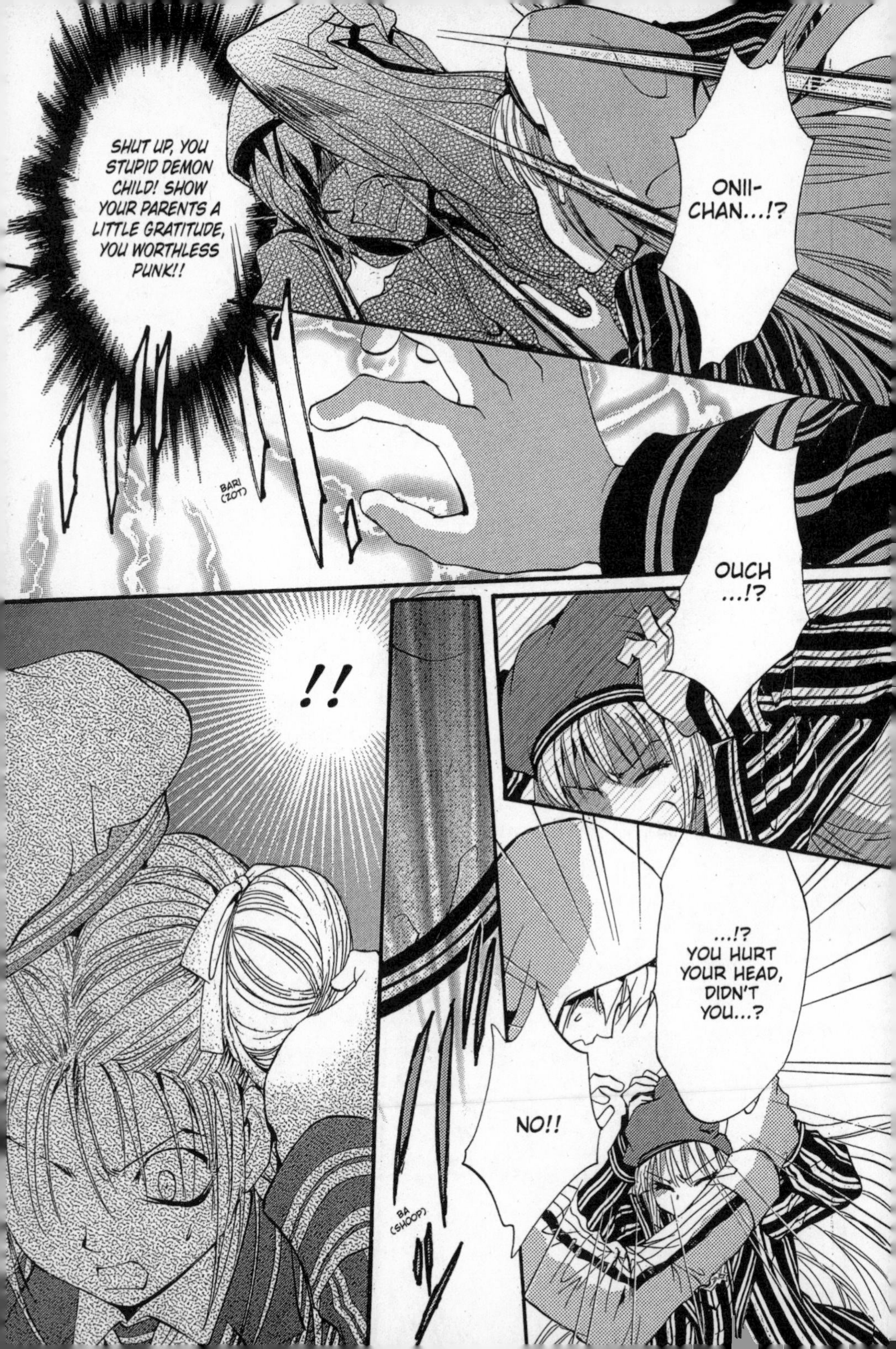

ONII-CHAN...!?
SHUT UP, YOU STUPID DEMON CHILD! SHOW YOUR PARENTS A LITTLE GRATITUDE, YOU WORTHLESS PUNK!!
BARI (ZOT)
OUCH ...!?
...!? YOU HURT YOUR HEAD, DIDN'T YOU...?
NO!!
BA (SHOOP)
!!

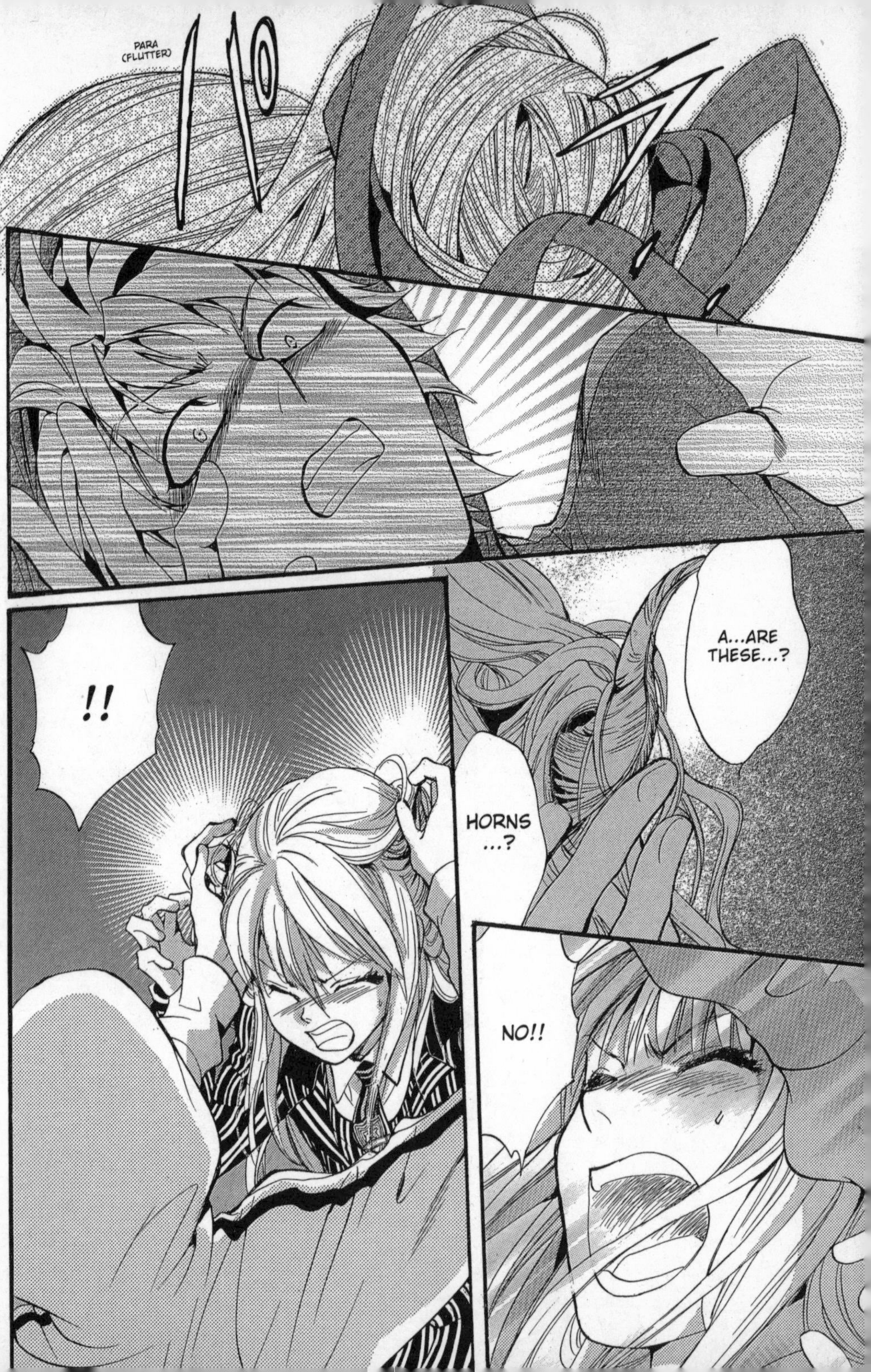
PARA (FLUTTER)
A...ARE THESE...?
HORNS ...?
NO!!
!!

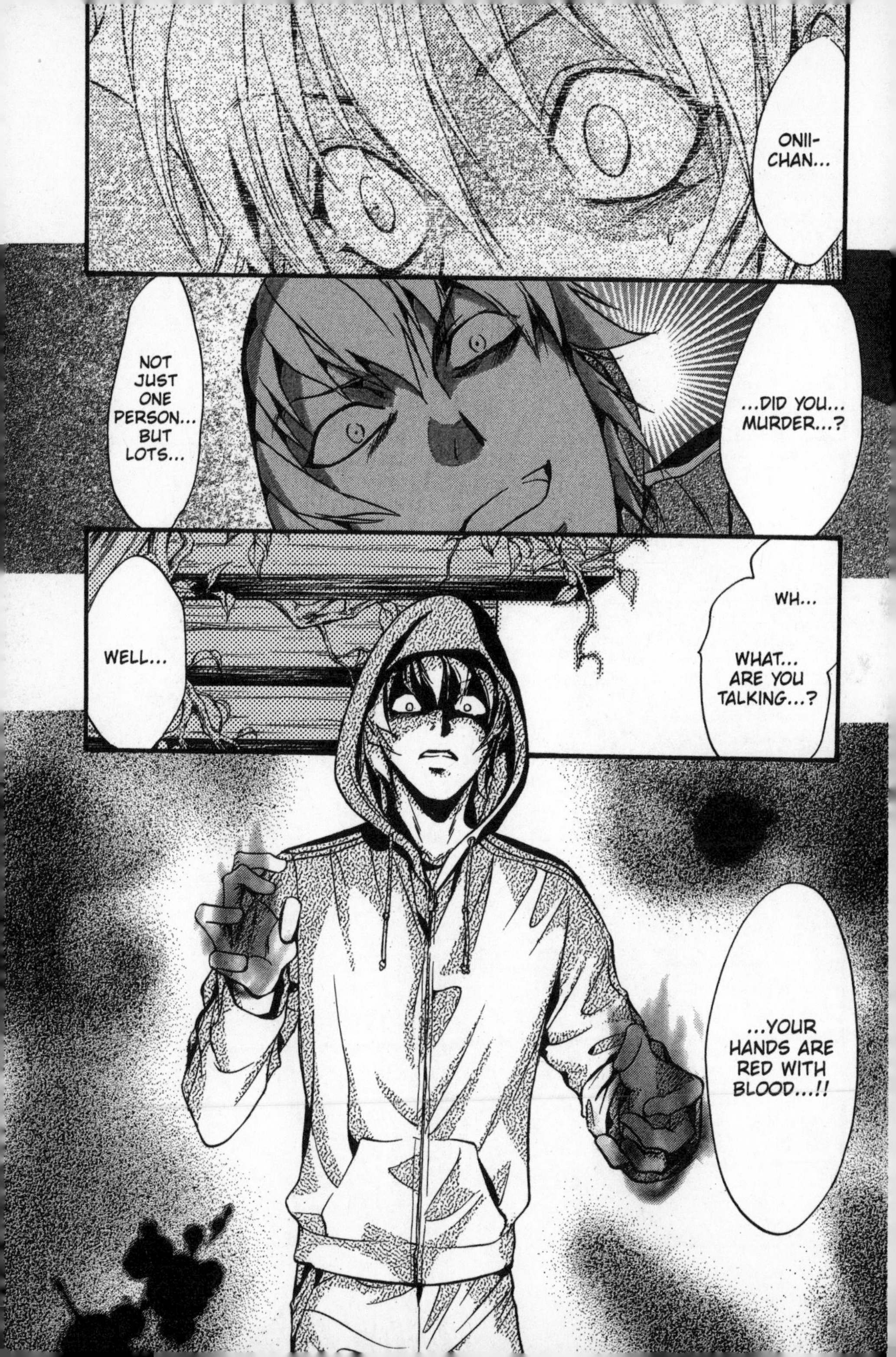
ONII-CHAN...
...DID YOU... MURDER...?
NOT JUST ONE PERSON... BUT LOTS...
WH...
WHAT... ARE YOU TALKING...?
WELL...
...YOUR HANDS ARE RED WITH BLOOD...!!

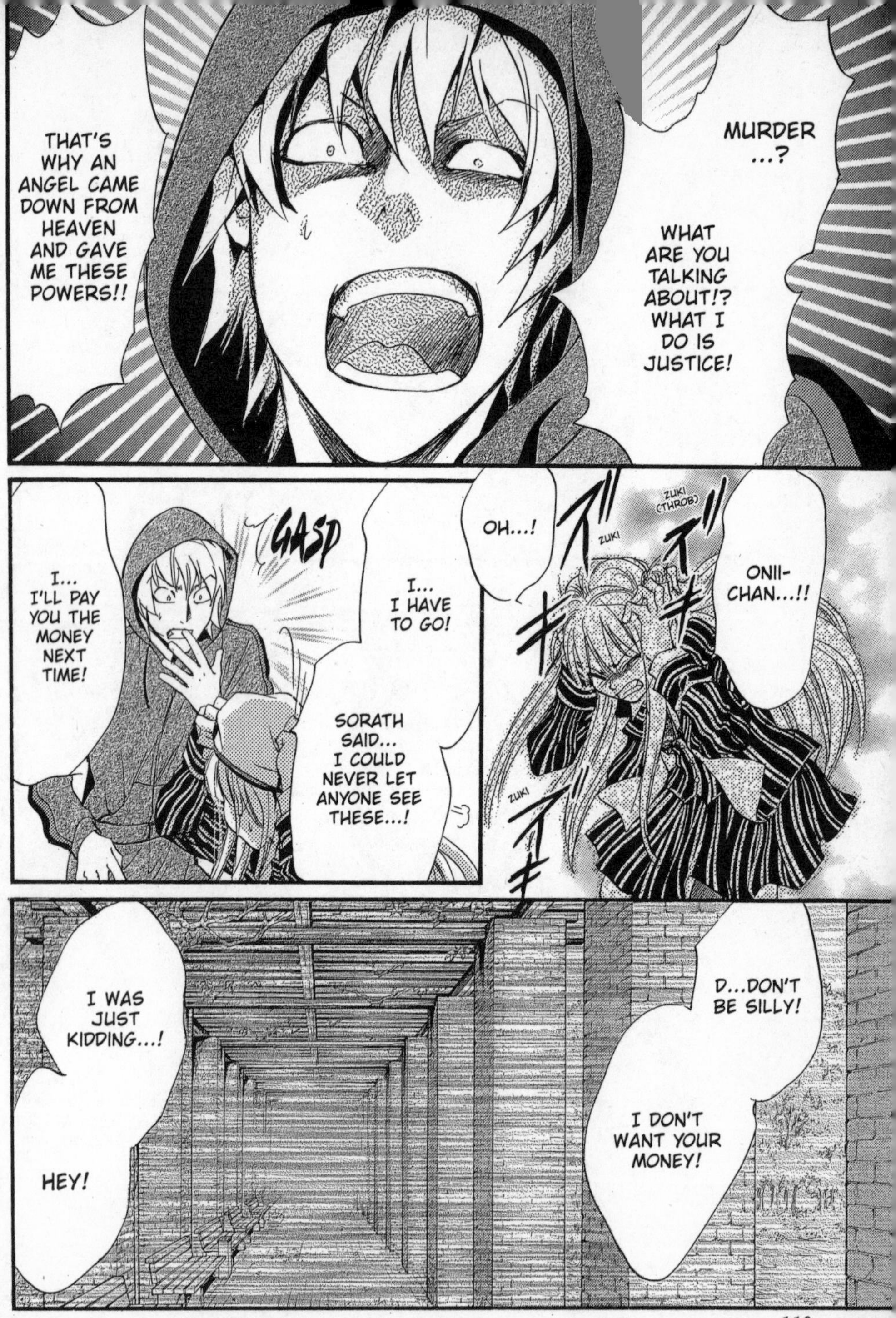
MURDER ...?
WHAT ARE YOU TALKING ABOUT!? WHAT I DO IS JUSTICE!
THAT'S WHY AN ANGEL CAME DOWN FROM HEAVEN AND GAVE ME THESE POWERS!!
ONII-CHAN...!!
ZUKI (THROB)
ZUKI
OH...!
ZUKI
SORATH SAID... I COULD NEVER LET ANYONE SEE THESE...!
I... I HAVE TO GO!
GASP
I... I'LL PAY YOU THE MONEY NEXT TIME!
D...DON'T BE SILLY!
I DON'T WANT YOUR MONEY!
I WAS JUST KIDDING...!
HEY!

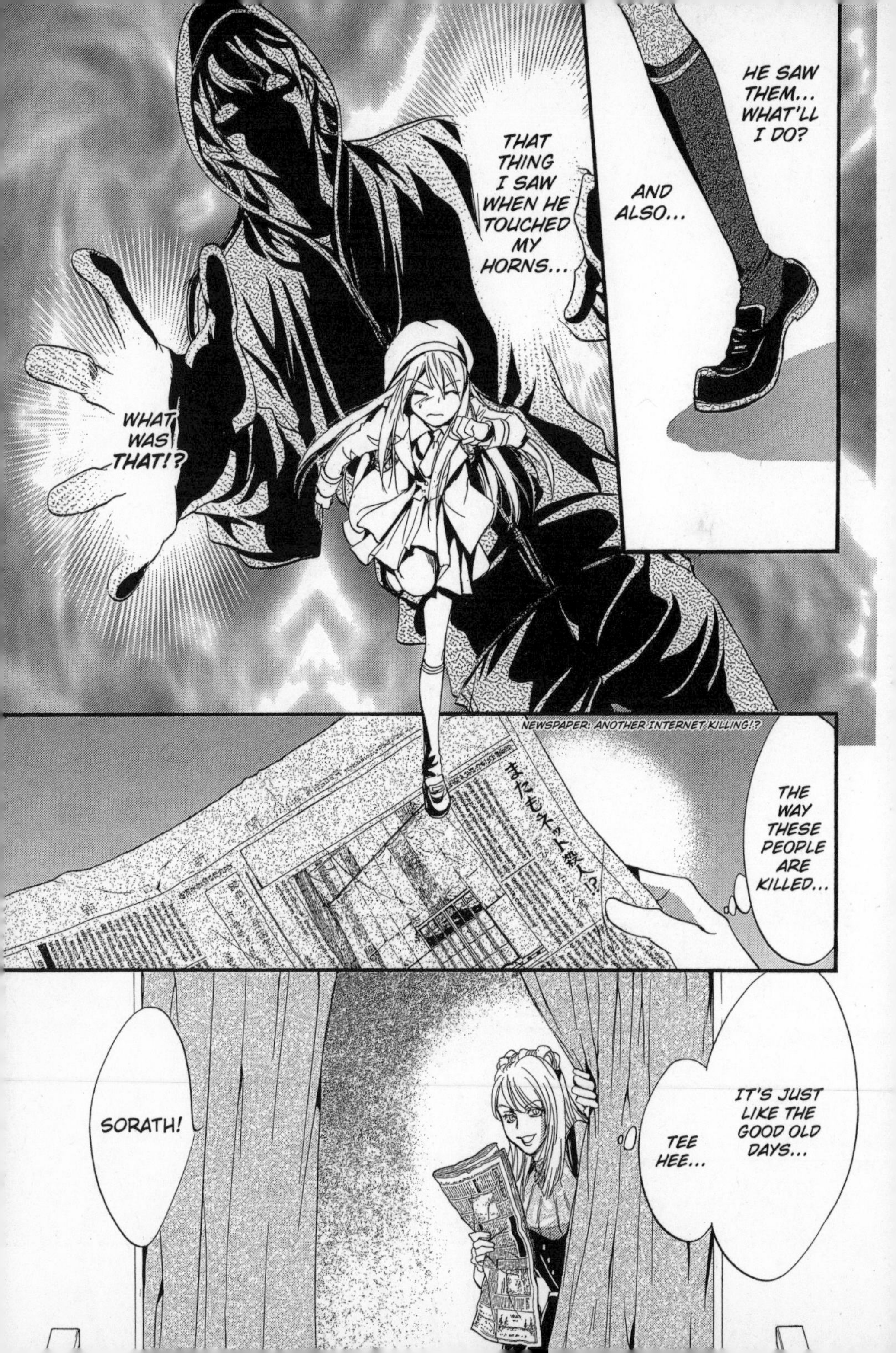

HE SAW THEM... WHAT'LL I DO?
AND ALSO...
THAT THING I SAW WHEN HE TOUCHED MY HORNS...
WHAT WAS THAT!?
NEWSPAPER: ANOTHER INTERNET KILLING!?
THE WAY THESE PEOPLE ARE KILLED...
IT'S JUST LIKE THE GOOD OLD DAYS...
TEE HEE...
SORATH!

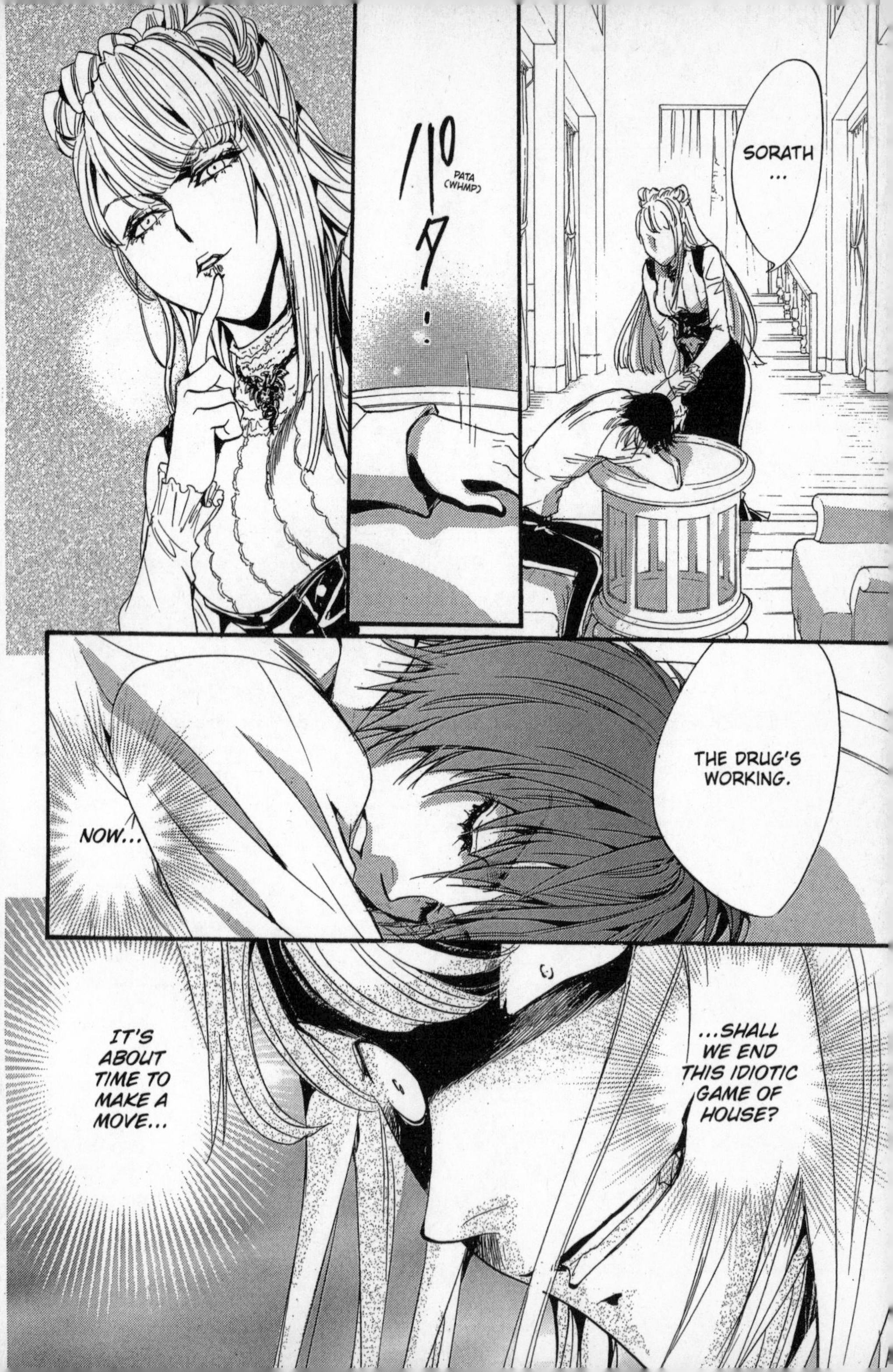
SORATH ...
PATA (WHMP)
THE DRUG'S WORKING.
NOW...
...SHALL WE END THIS IDIOTIC GAME OF HOUSE?
IT'S ABOUT TIME TO MAKE A MOVE...

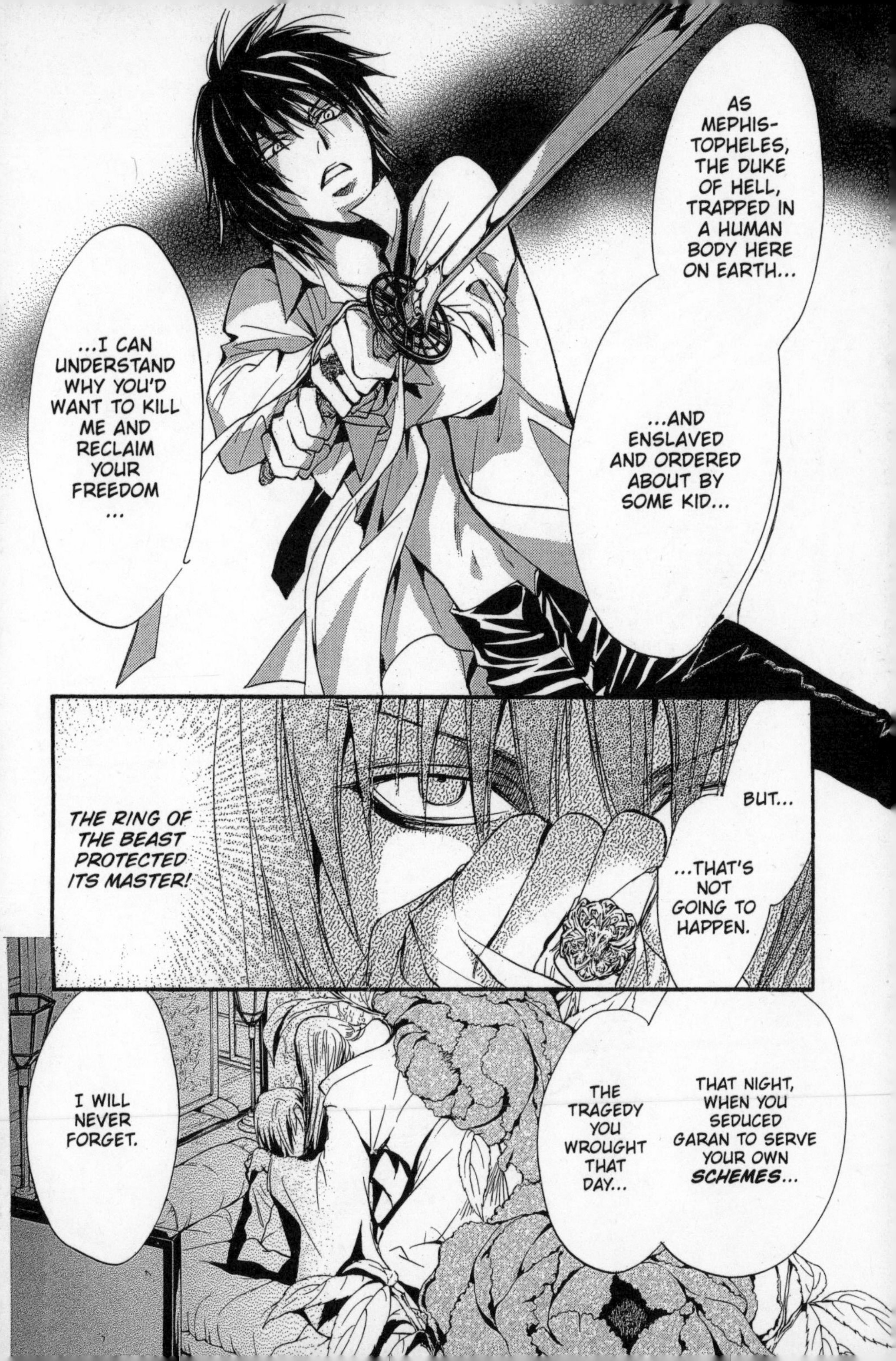
AS MEPHIS-TOPHELES, THE DUKE OF HELL, TRAPPED IN A HUMAN BODY HERE ON EARTH...
...AND ENSLAVED AND ORDERED ABOUT BY SOME KID...
...I CAN UNDERSTAND WHY YOU'D WANT TO KILL ME AND RECLAIM YOUR FREEDOM...
BUT...
...THAT'S NOT GOING TO HAPPEN.
THE RING OF THE BEAST PROTECTED ITS MASTER!
THAT NIGHT, WHEN YOU SEDUCED GARAN TO SERVE YOUR OWN ***SCHEMES***...
THE TRAGEDY YOU WROUGHT THAT DAY...
I WILL NEVER FORGET.

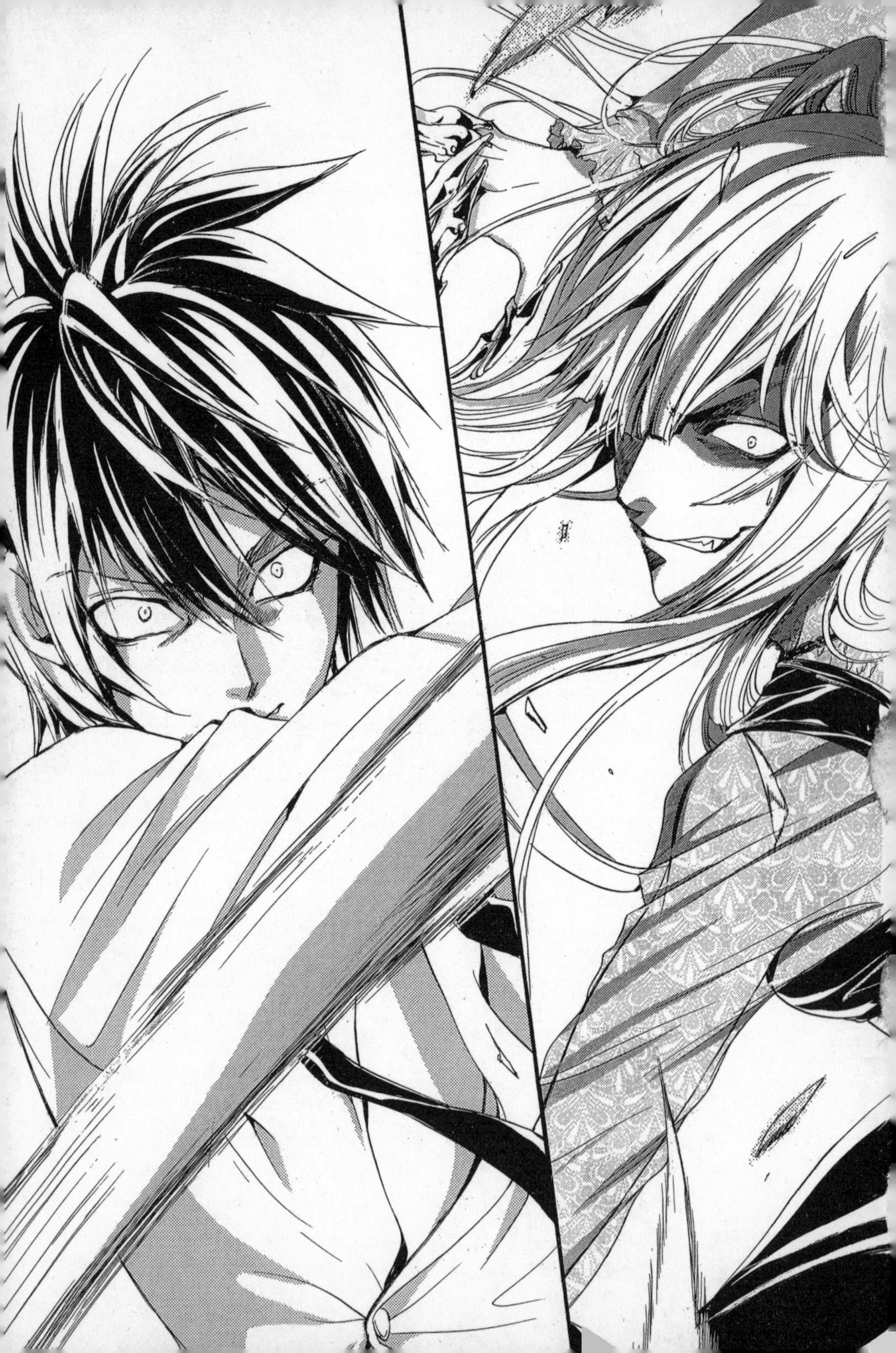

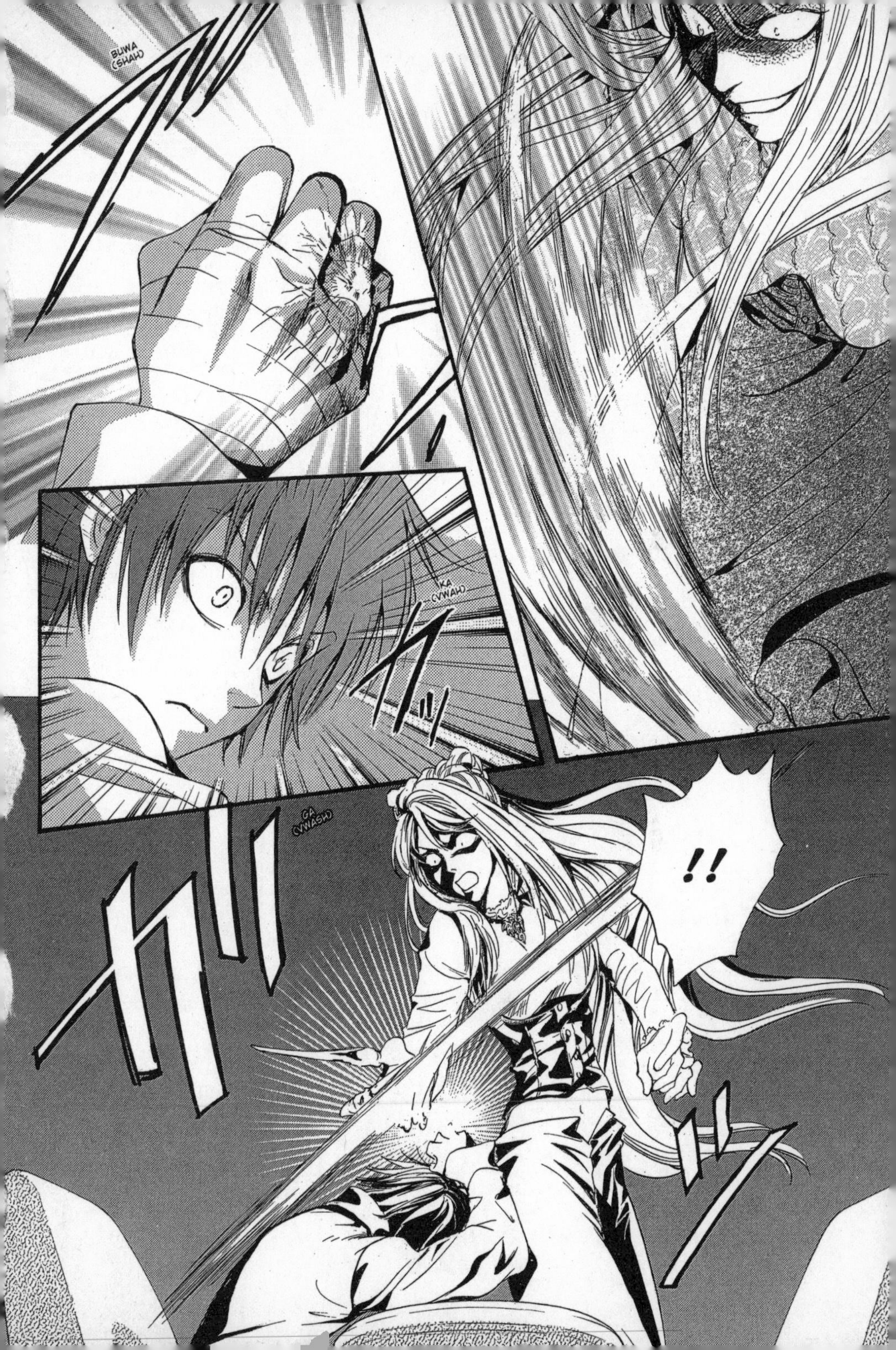
BUWA (SHAH)
KA (VWAH)
!!
GA (VWASH)

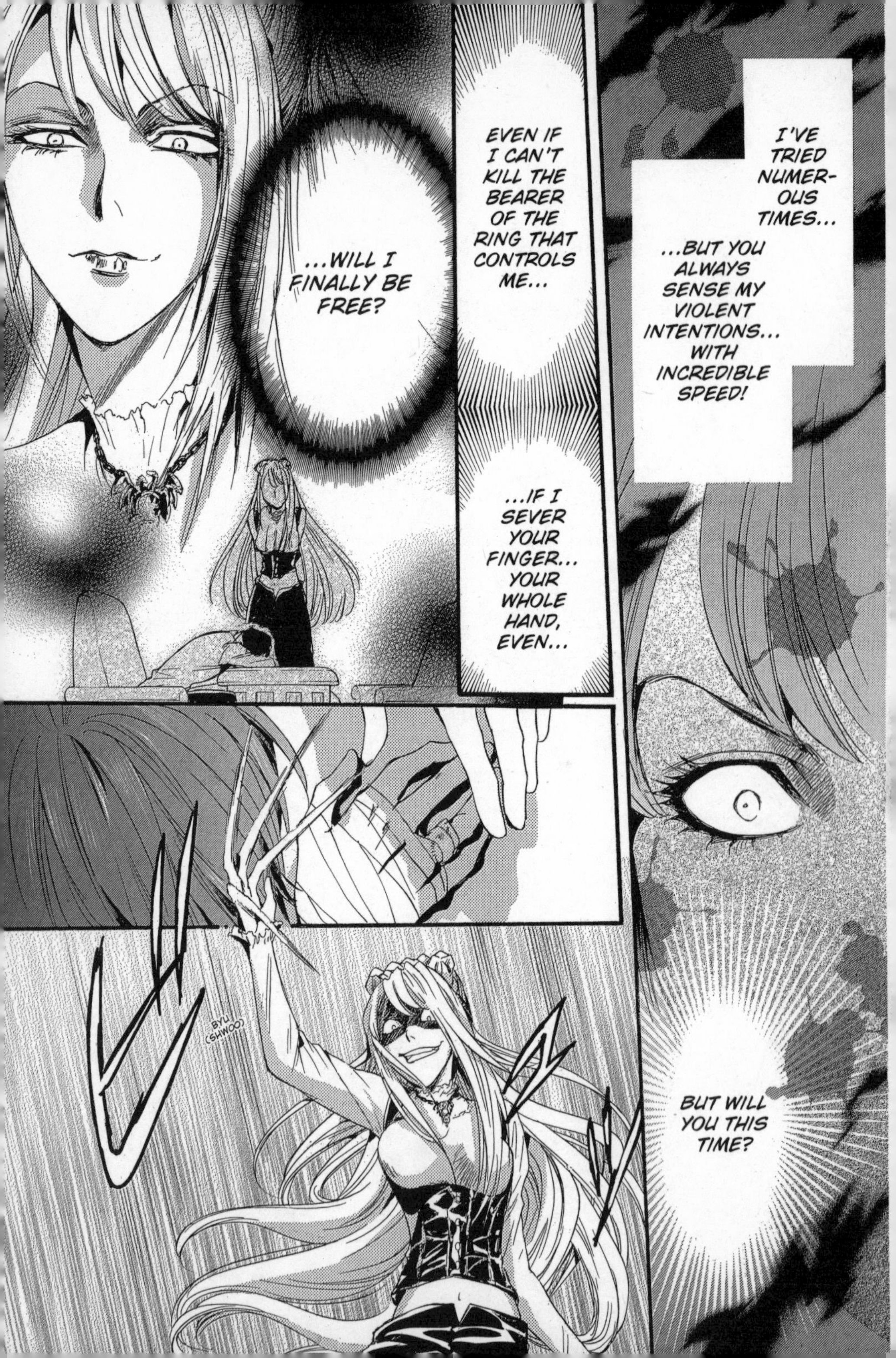
I'VE TRIED NUMEROUS TIMES...
...BUT YOU ALWAYS SENSE MY VIOLENT INTENTIONS... WITH INCREDIBLE SPEED!
BUT WILL YOU THIS TIME?
EVEN IF I CAN'T KILL THE BEARER OF THE RING THAT CONTROLS ME...
...IF I SEVER YOUR FINGER... YOUR WHOLE HAND, EVEN...
...WILL I FINALLY BE FREE?
BYU
(SHWOO)

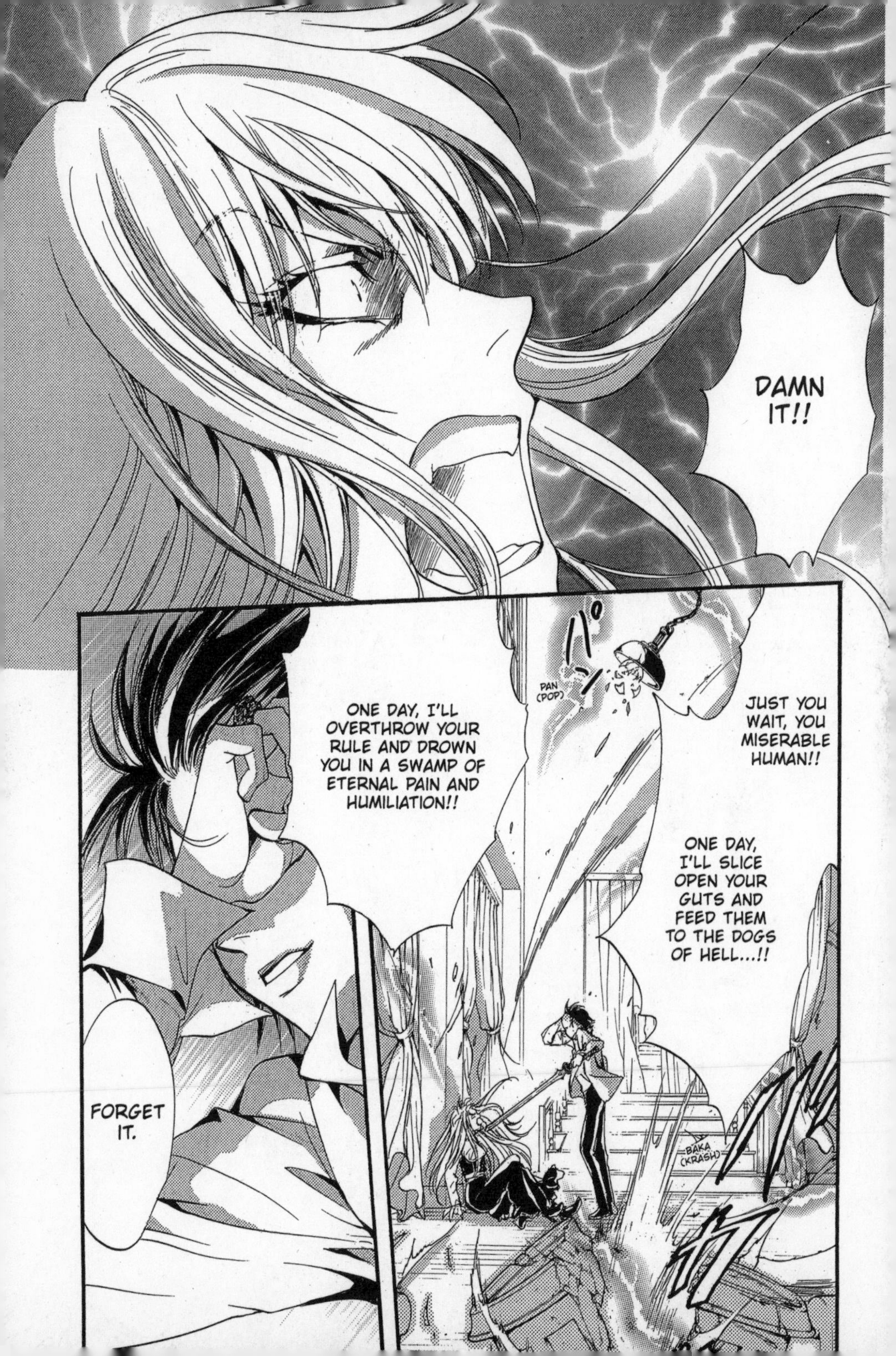
DAMN IT!!
PAN (POP)
JUST YOU WAIT, YOU MISERABLE HUMAN!!
ONE DAY, I'LL OVERTHROW YOUR RULE AND DROWN YOU IN A SWAMP OF ETERNAL PAIN AND HUMILIATION!!
ONE DAY, I'LL SLICE OPEN YOUR GUTS AND FEED THEM TO THE DOGS OF HELL...!!
BAKA (KRASH)
FORGET IT.

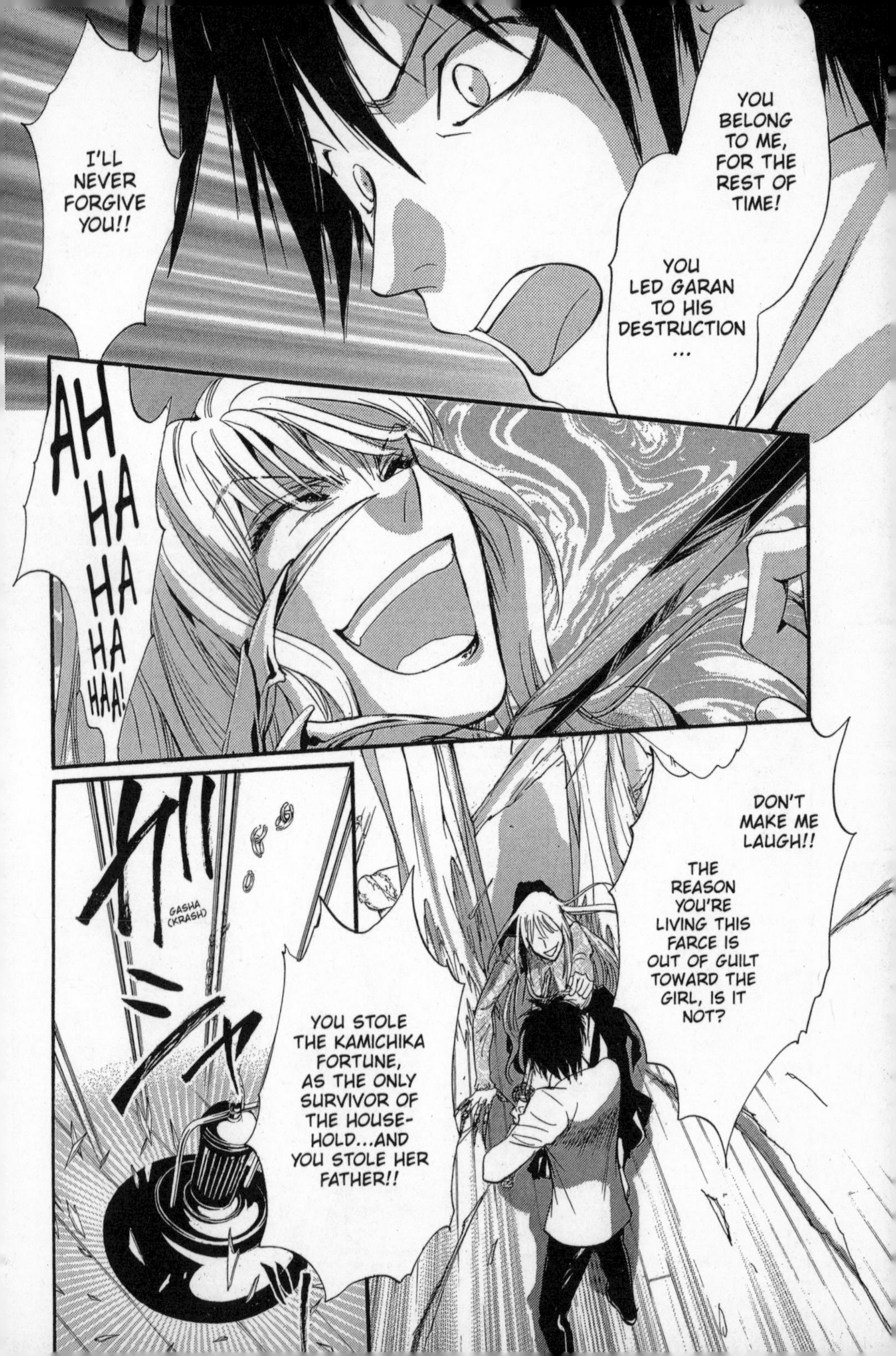
YOU BELONG TO ME, FOR THE REST OF TIME!
YOU LED GARAN TO HIS DESTRUCTION ...
I'LL NEVER FORGIVE YOU!!
AH HA HA HA HA HA HAA!
DON'T MAKE ME LAUGH!!
THE REASON YOU'RE LIVING THIS FARCE IS OUT OF GUILT TOWARD THE GIRL, IS IT NOT?
YOU STOLE THE KAMICHIKA FORTUNE, AS THE ONLY SURVIVOR OF THE HOUSE-HOLD...AND YOU STOLE HER FATHER!!
GASHA (KRASH)

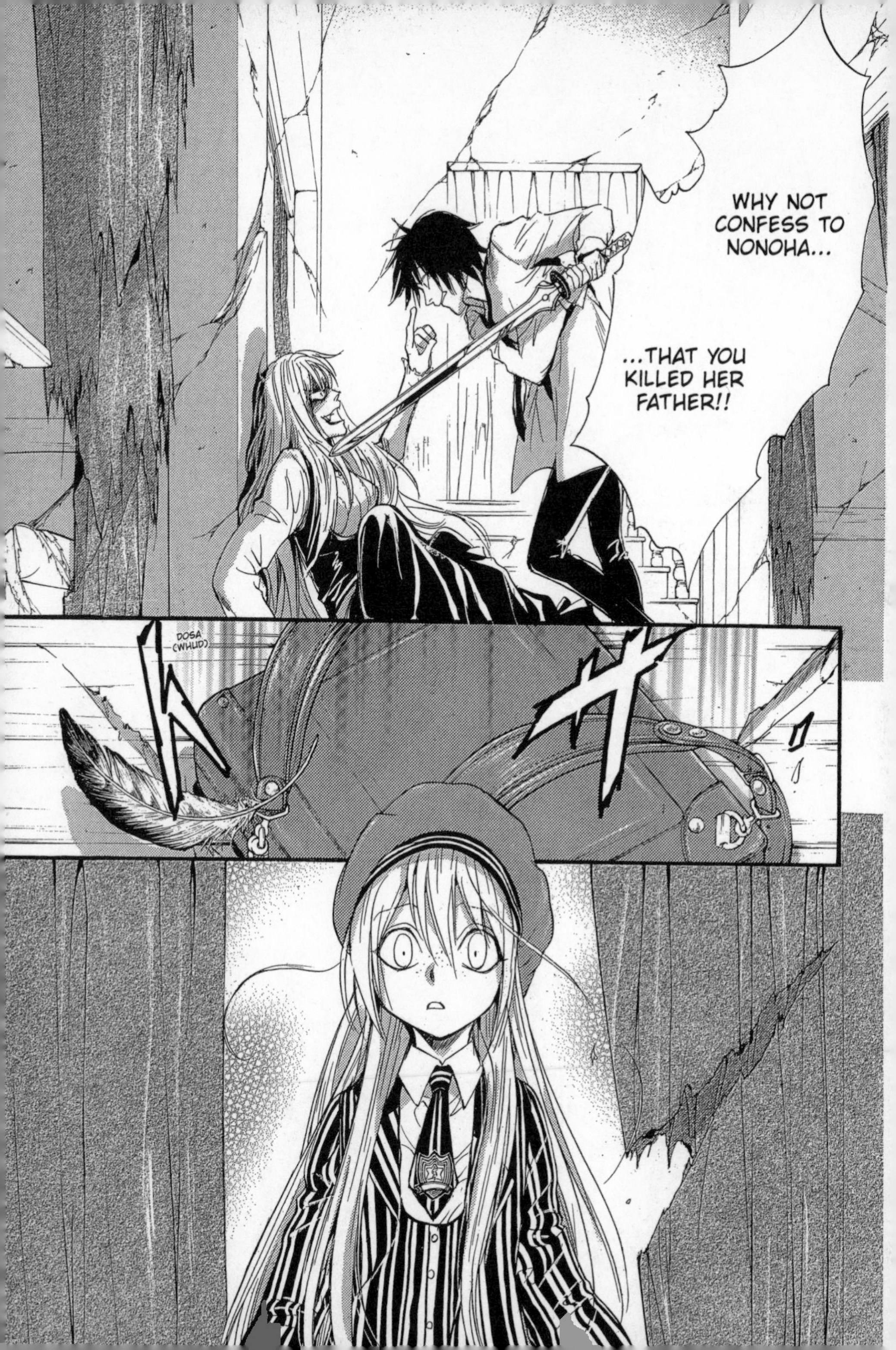
WHY NOT CONFESS TO NONOHA...
...THAT YOU KILLED HER FATHER!!
DOSA (WHUD)

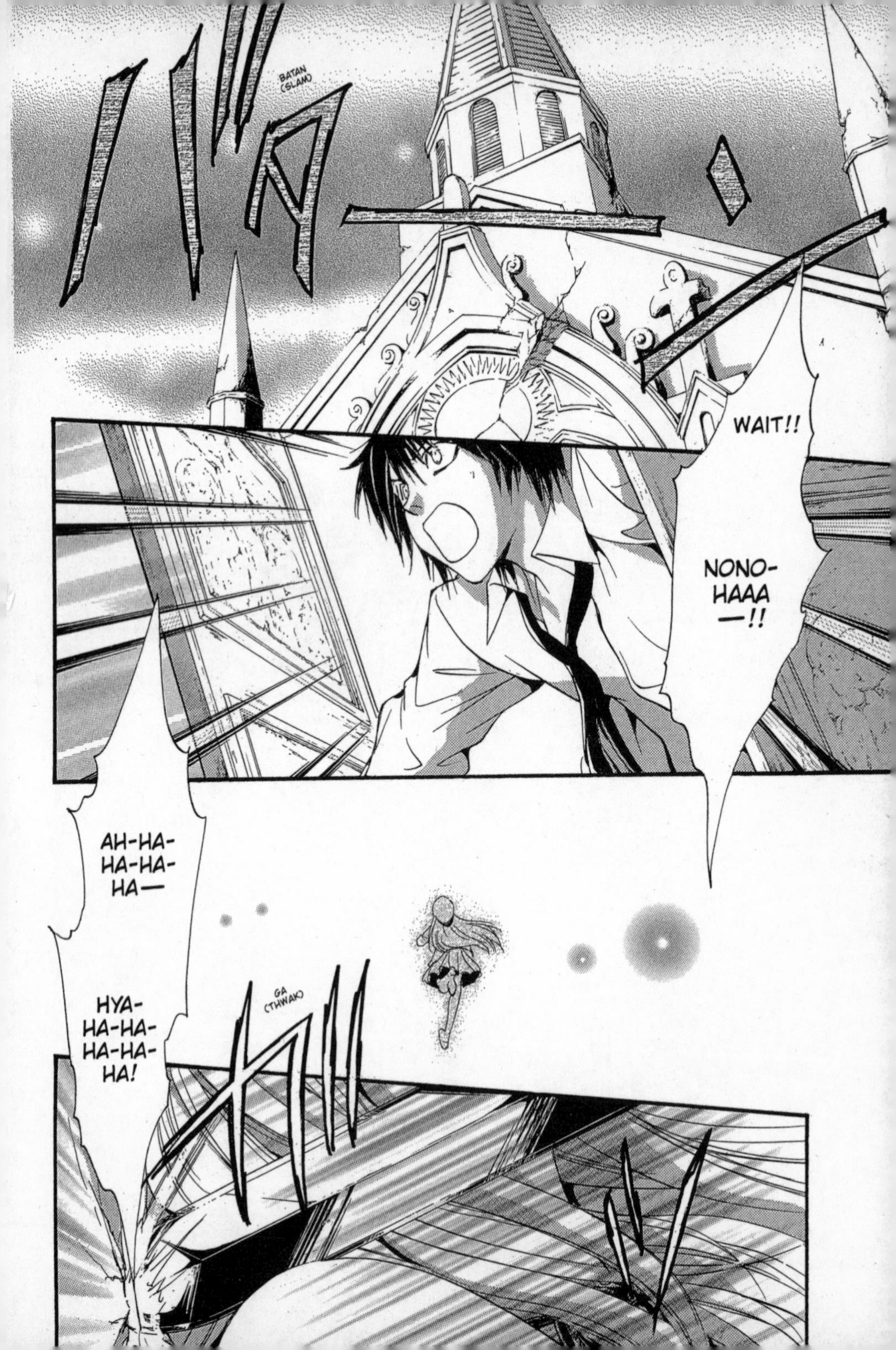
BATAN (GLAM)
WAIT!!
NONO-HAAA—!!
AH-HA-HA-HA-HA—
HYA-HA-HA-HA-HA-HA!
GA (THWAK)

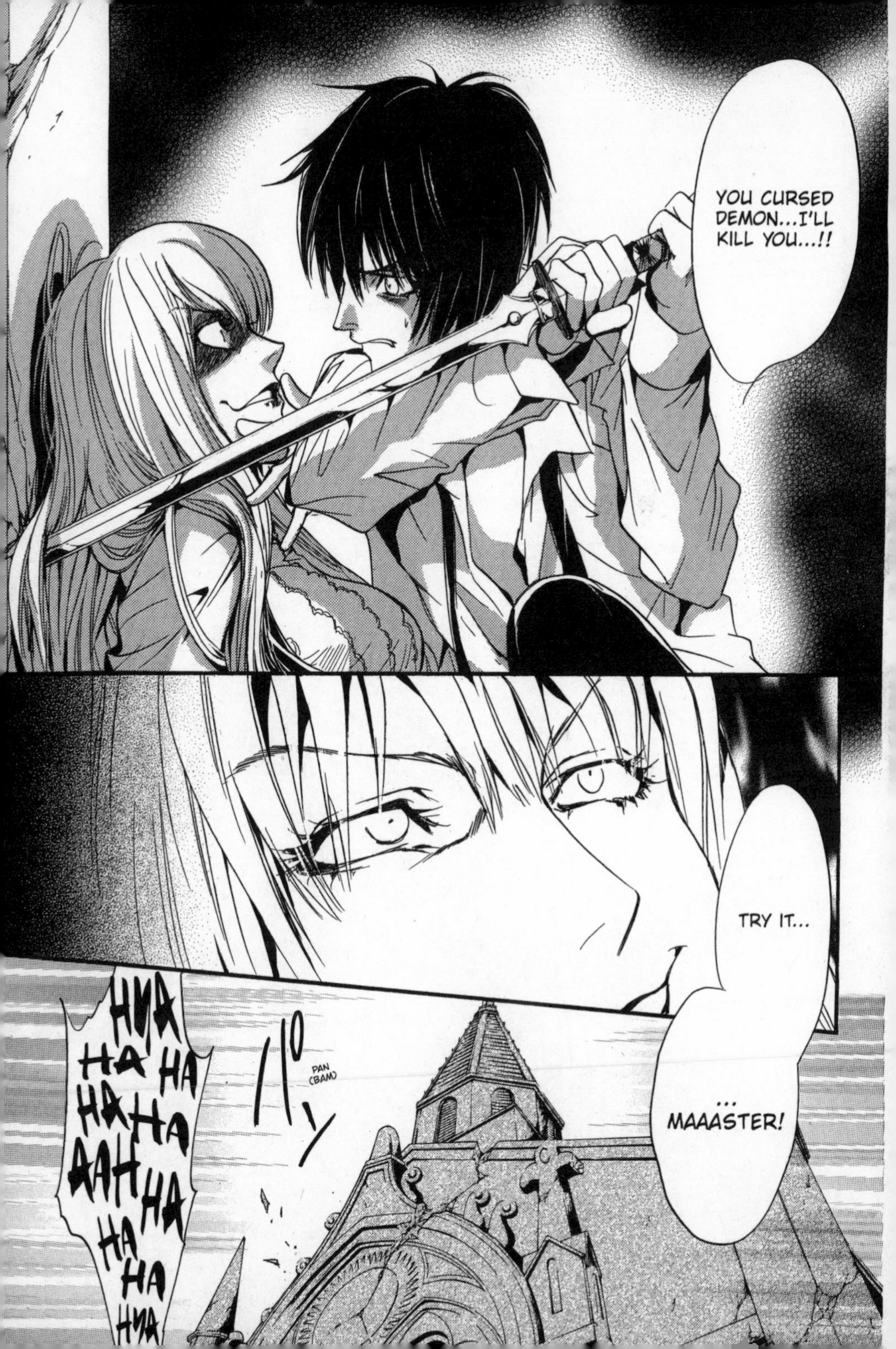
YOU CURSED DEMON...I'LL KILL YOU...!!
TRY IT...
...MAAASTER!
PAN (BAM)
HNA HA HA HA HA AAH HA HA HA HA HA HNA

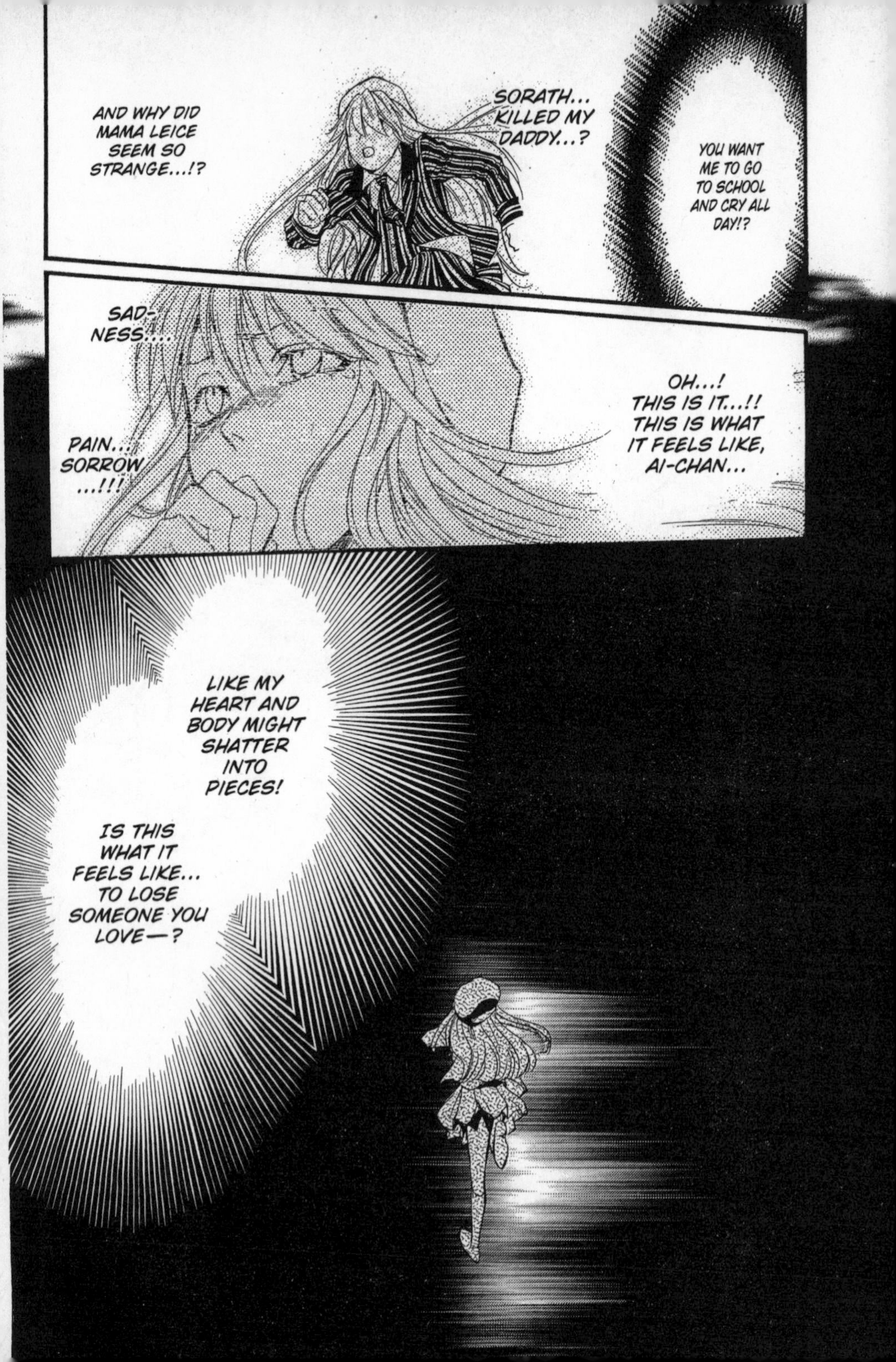
YOU WANT ME TO GO TO SCHOOL AND CRY ALL DAY!?
SORATH... KILLED MY DADDY...?
AND WHY DID MAMA LEICE SEEM SO STRANGE...!?
OH...! THIS IS IT...!! THIS IS WHAT IT FEELS LIKE, AI-CHAN...
SAD-NESS....
PAIN... SORROW ...!!!
LIKE MY HEART AND BODY MIGHT SHATTER INTO PIECES!
IS THIS WHAT IT FEELS LIKE... TO LOSE SOMEONE YOU LOVE—?

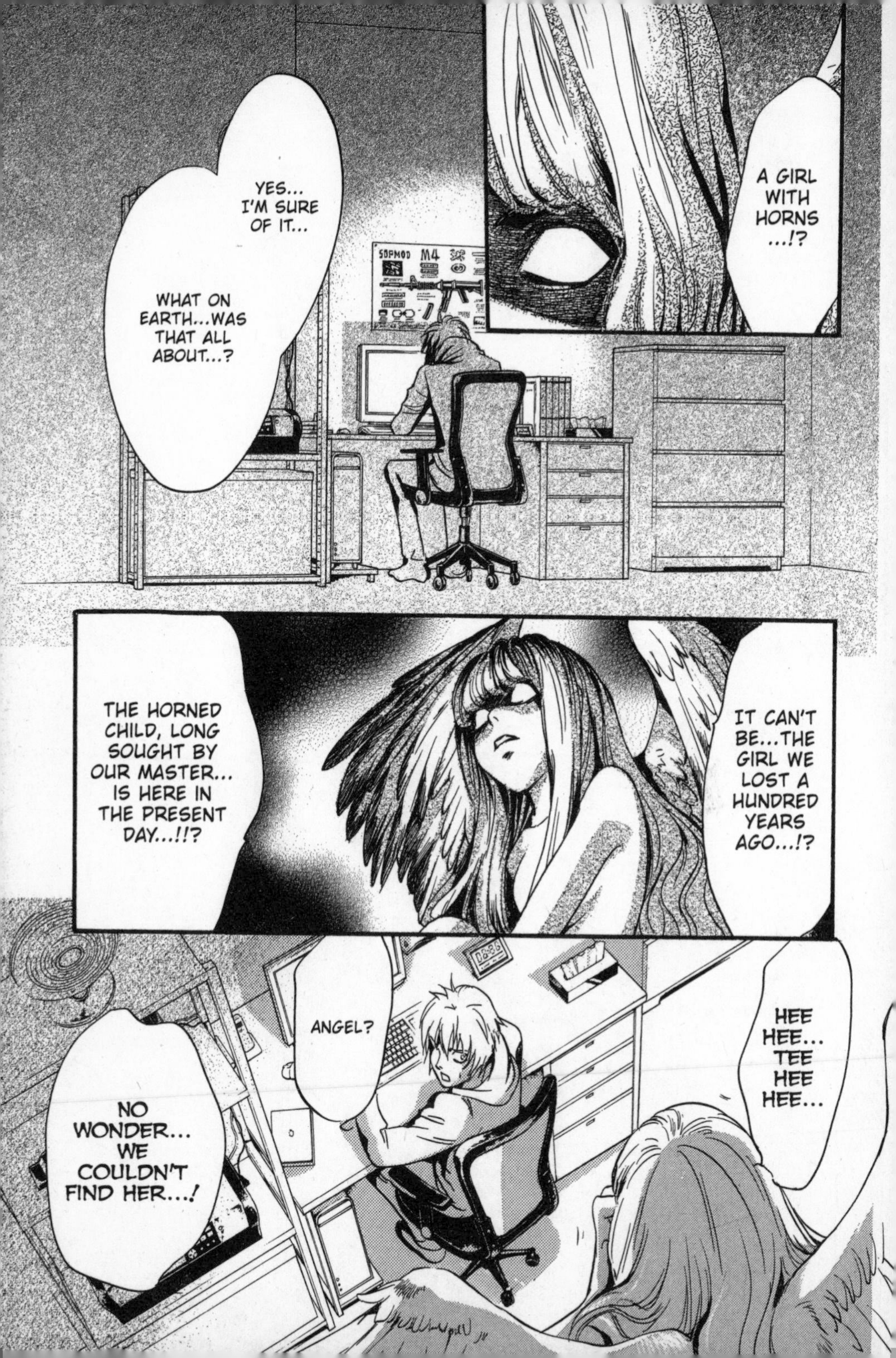
A GIRL WITH HORNS ...!?
YES... I'M SURE OF IT...
WHAT ON EARTH...WAS THAT ALL ABOUT...?
IT CAN'T BE...THE GIRL WE LOST A HUNDRED YEARS AGO...!?
THE HORNED CHILD, LONG SOUGHT BY OUR MASTER... IS HERE IN THE PRESENT DAY...!!?
HEE HEE... TEE HEE HEE...
ANGEL?
NO WONDER... WE COULDN'T FIND HER...!

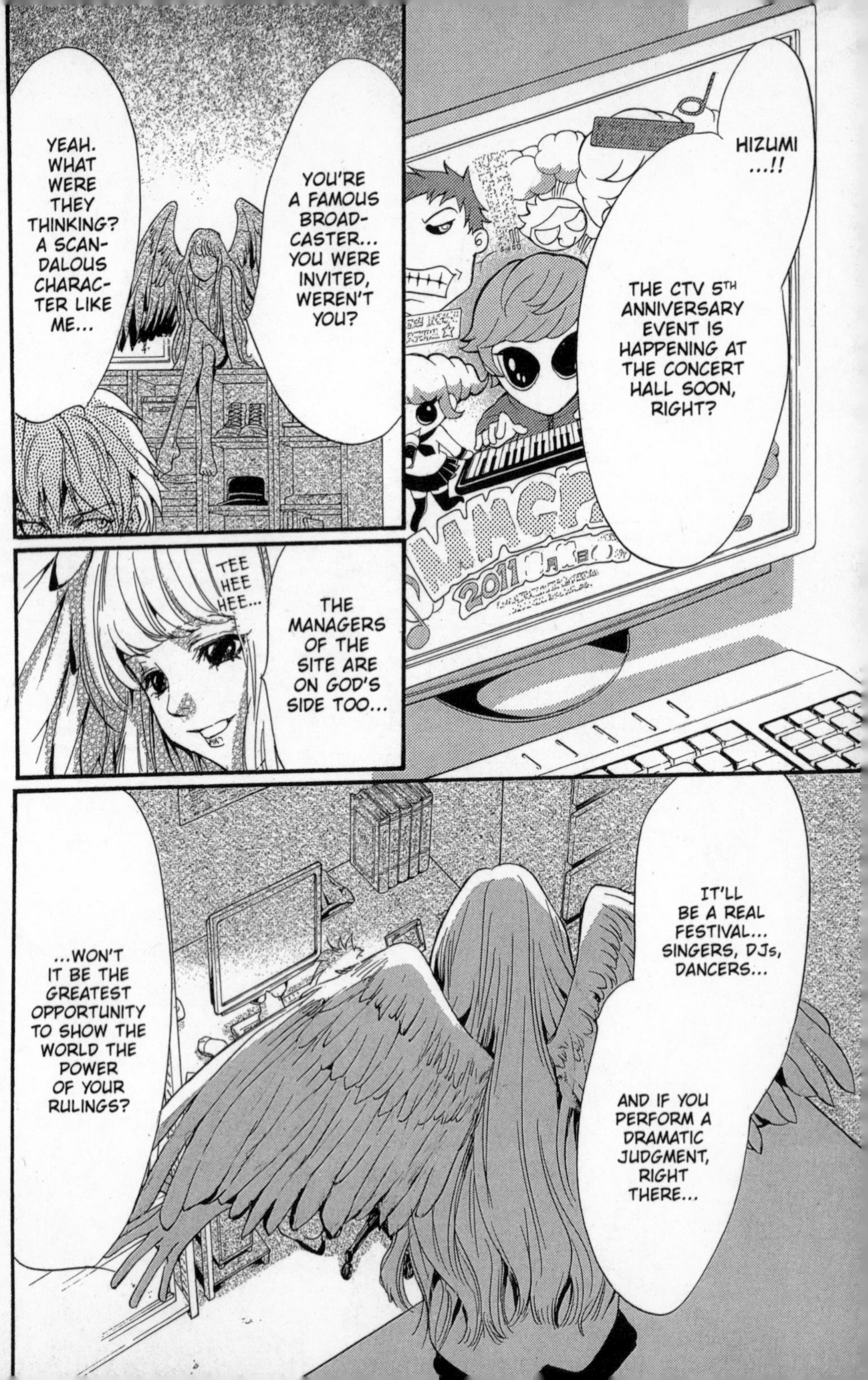
HIZUMI ...!!
THE CTV 5TH ANNIVERSARY EVENT IS HAPPENING AT THE CONCERT HALL SOON, RIGHT?
YOU'RE A FAMOUS BROAD-CASTER... YOU WERE INVITED, WEREN'T YOU?
YEAH. WHAT WERE THEY THINKING? A SCAN-DALOUS CHARAC-TER LIKE ME...
TEE HEE HEE...
THE MANAGERS OF THE SITE ARE ON GOD'S SIDE TOO...
IT'LL BE A REAL FESTIVAL... SINGERS, DJs, DANCERS...
AND IF YOU PERFORM A DRAMATIC JUDGMENT, RIGHT THERE...
...WON'T IT BE THE GREATEST OPPORTUNITY TO SHOW THE WORLD THE POWER OF YOUR RULINGS?

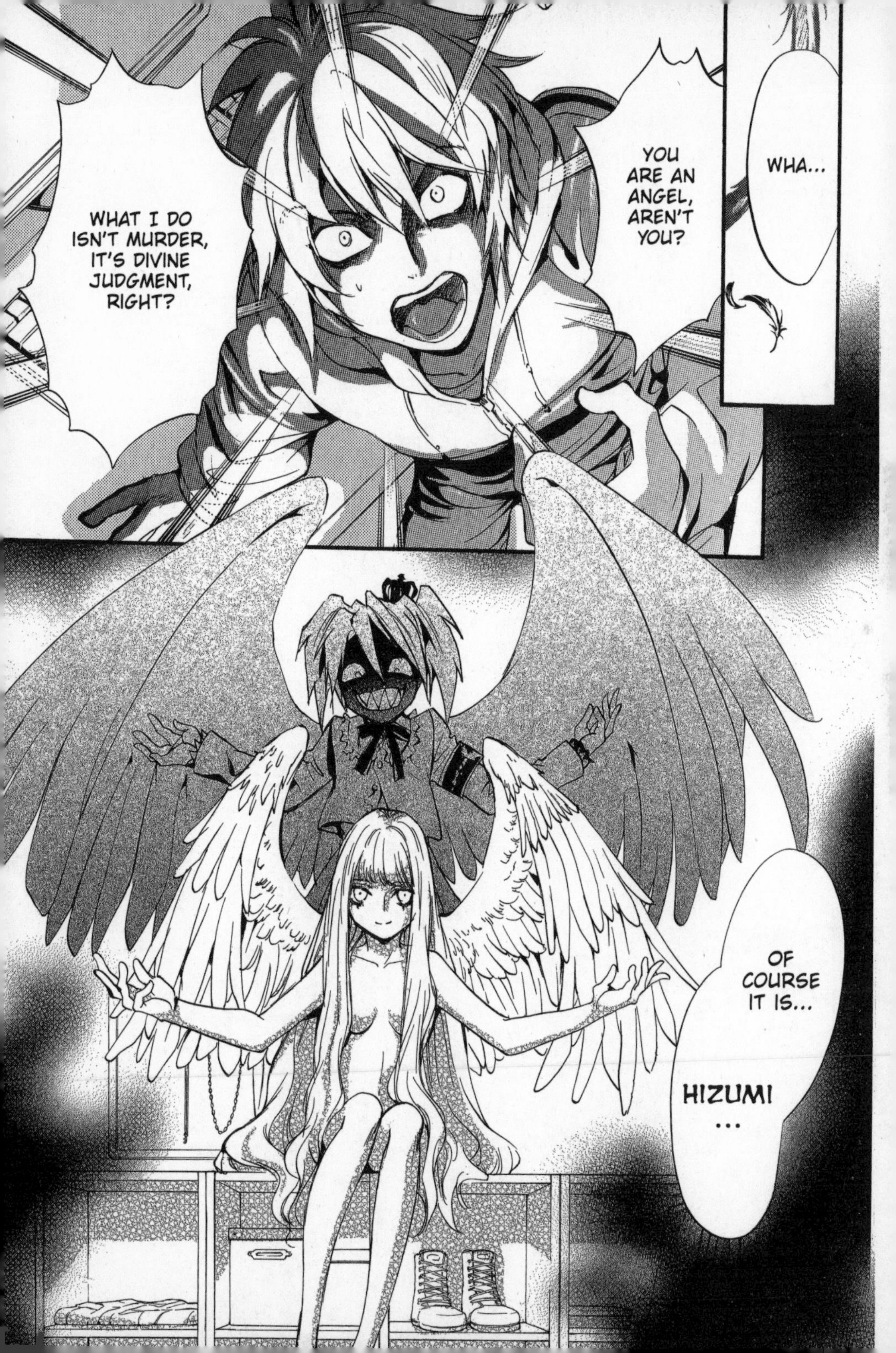
WHA...
YOU ARE AN ANGEL, AREN'T YOU?
WHAT I DO ISN'T MURDER, IT'S DIVINE JUDGMENT, RIGHT?
OF COURSE IT IS...
HIZUMI ...

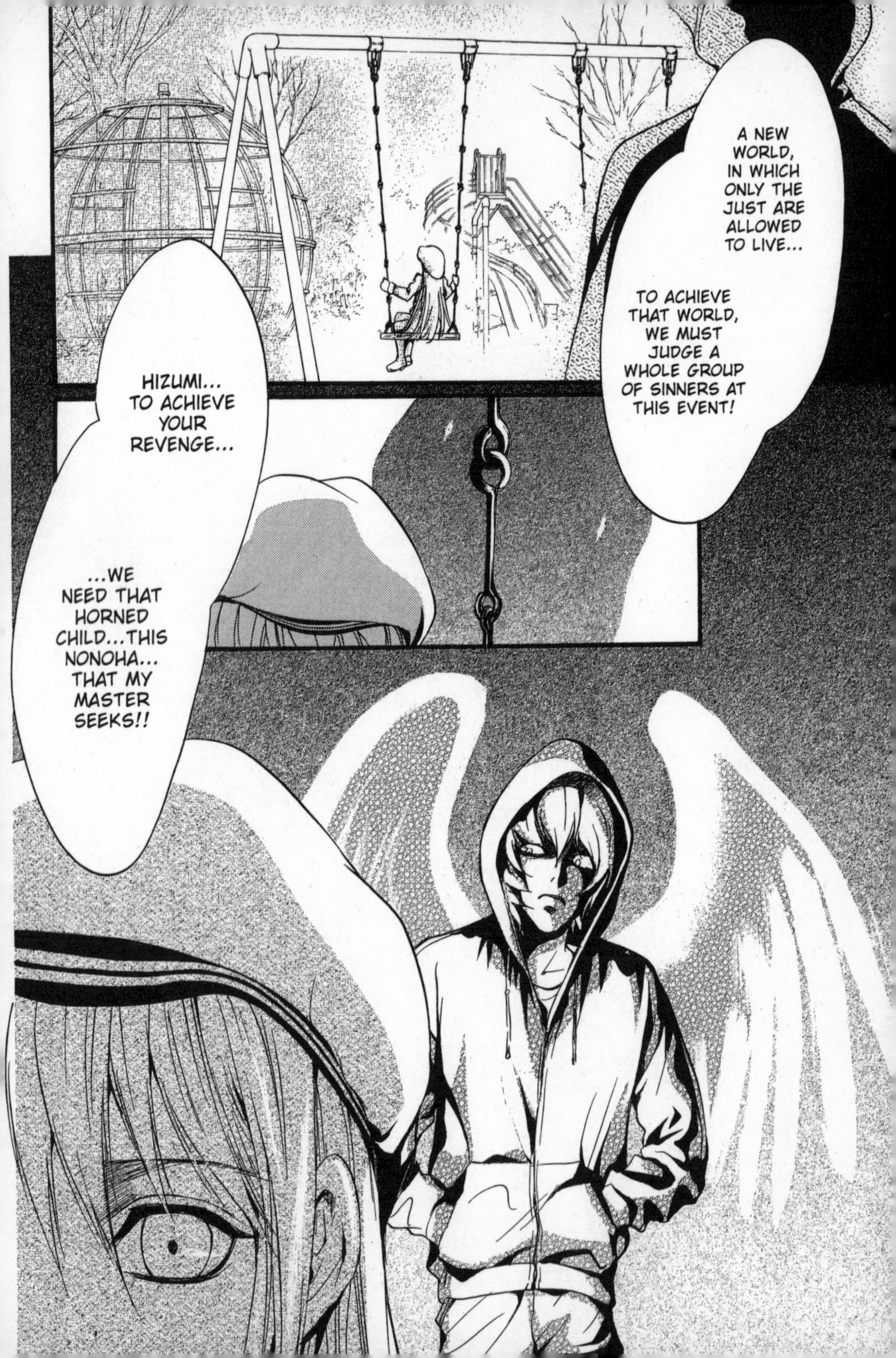
A NEW WORLD, IN WHICH ONLY THE JUST ARE ALLOWED TO LIVE...
TO ACHIEVE THAT WORLD, WE MUST JUDGE A WHOLE GROUP OF SINNERS AT THIS EVENT!
HIZUMI... TO ACHIEVE YOUR REVENGE...
...WE NEED THAT HORNED CHILD...THIS NONOHA... THAT MY MASTER SEEKS!!

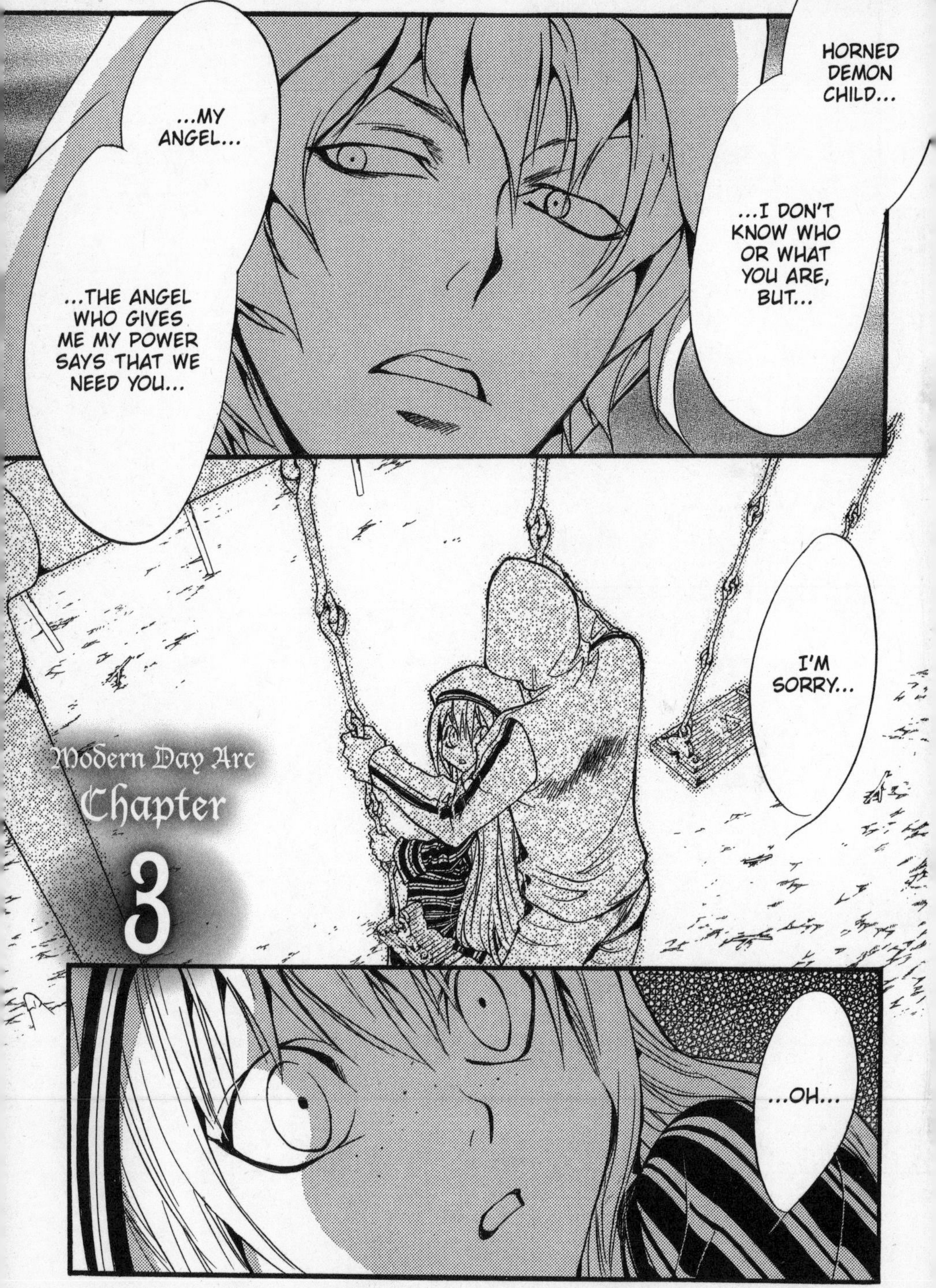
HORNED DEMON CHILD...
...I DON'T KNOW WHO OR WHAT YOU ARE, BUT...
...MY ANGEL...
...THE ANGEL WHO GIVES ME MY POWER SAYS THAT WE NEED YOU...
I'M SORRY...
Modern Day Arc
Chapter
3
...OH...

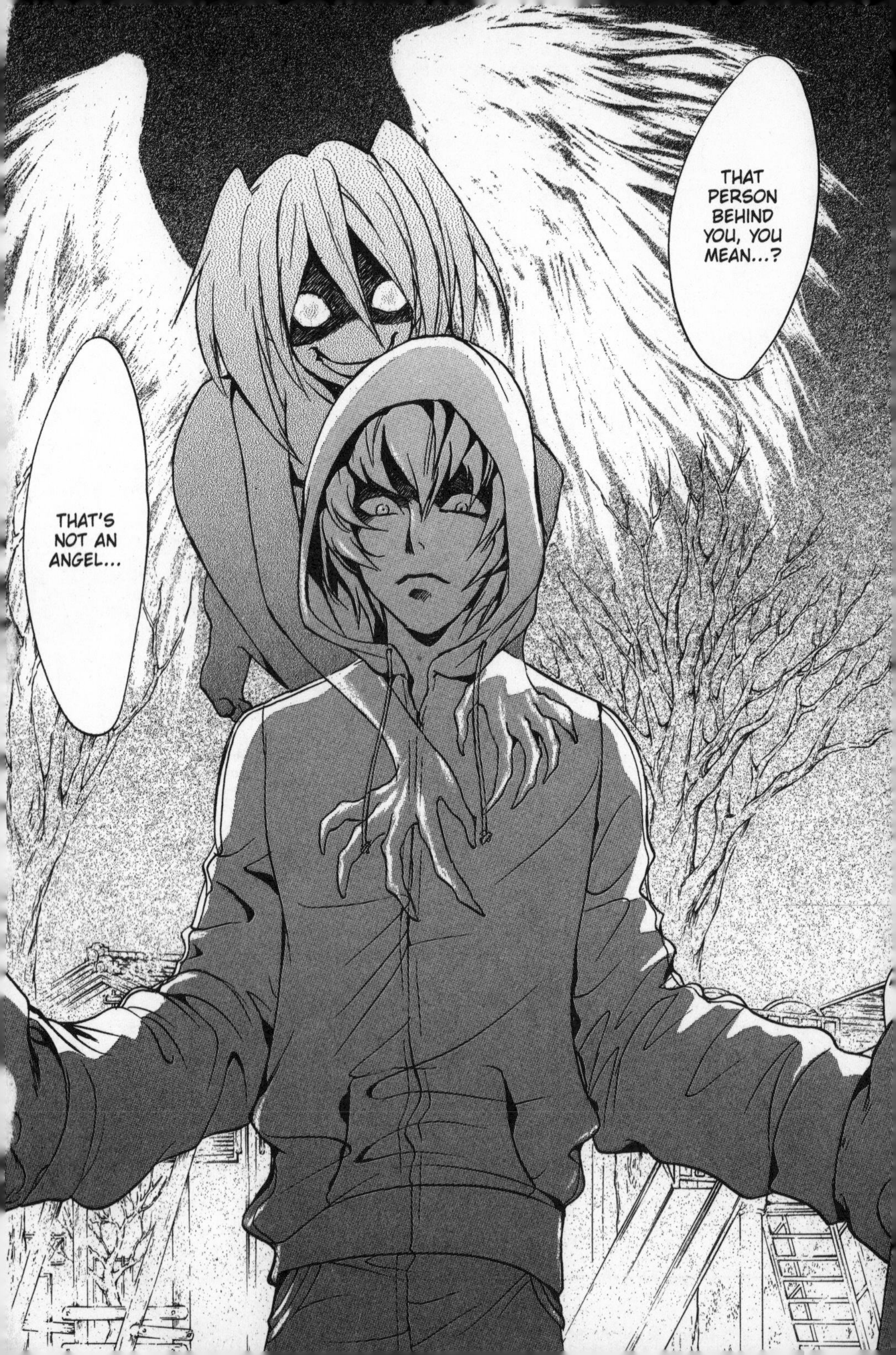
THAT PERSON BEHIND YOU, YOU MEAN...?
THAT'S NOT AN ANGEL...

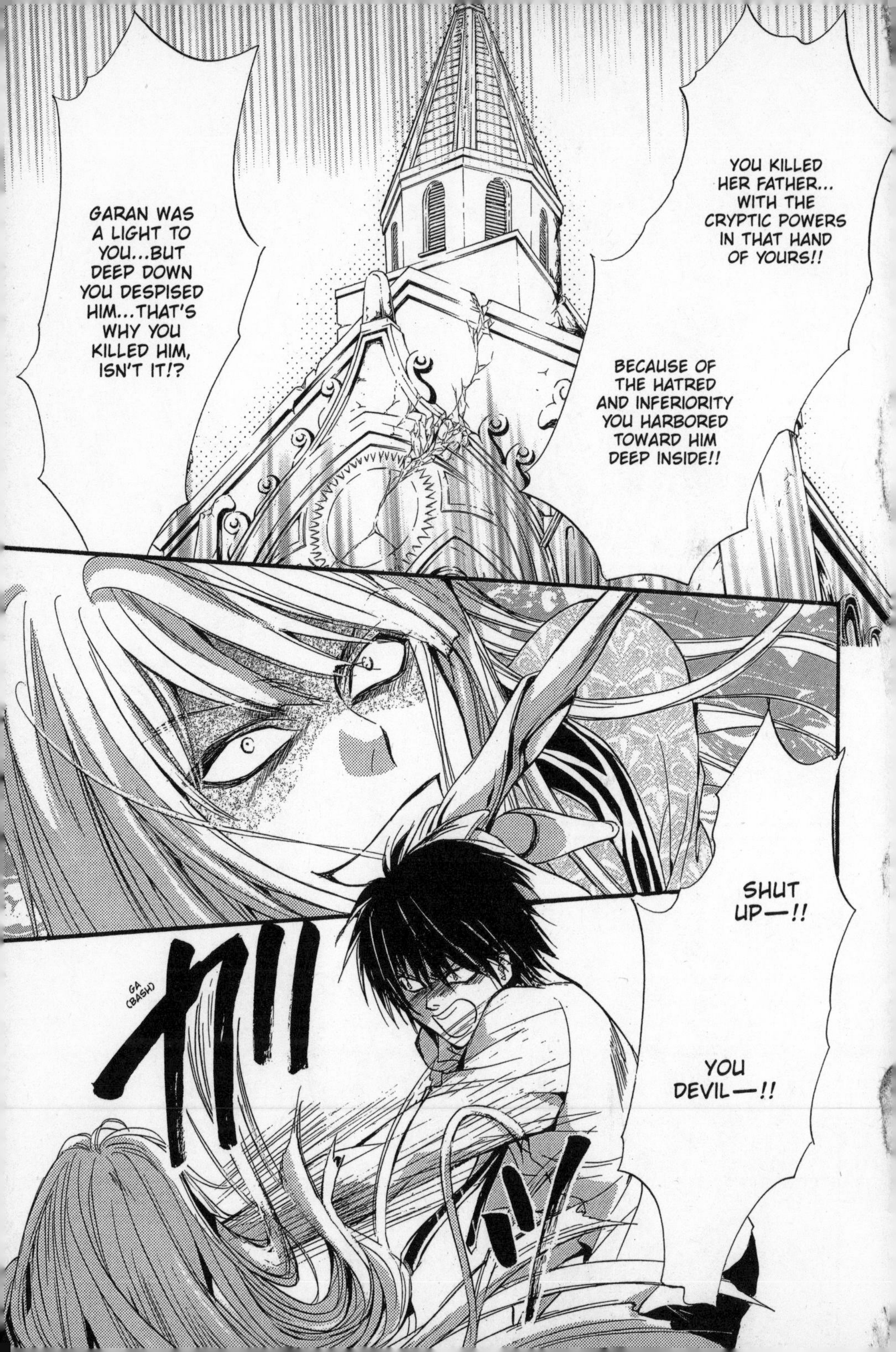
YOU KILLED HER FATHER... WITH THE CRYPTIC POWERS IN THAT HAND OF YOURS!!
BECAUSE OF THE HATRED AND INFERIORITY YOU HARBORED TOWARD HIM DEEP INSIDE!!
GARAN WAS A LIGHT TO YOU...BUT DEEP DOWN YOU DESPISED HIM...THAT'S WHY YOU KILLED HIM, ISN'T IT!?
SHUT UP—!!
YOU DEVIL—!!
GA (BASH)

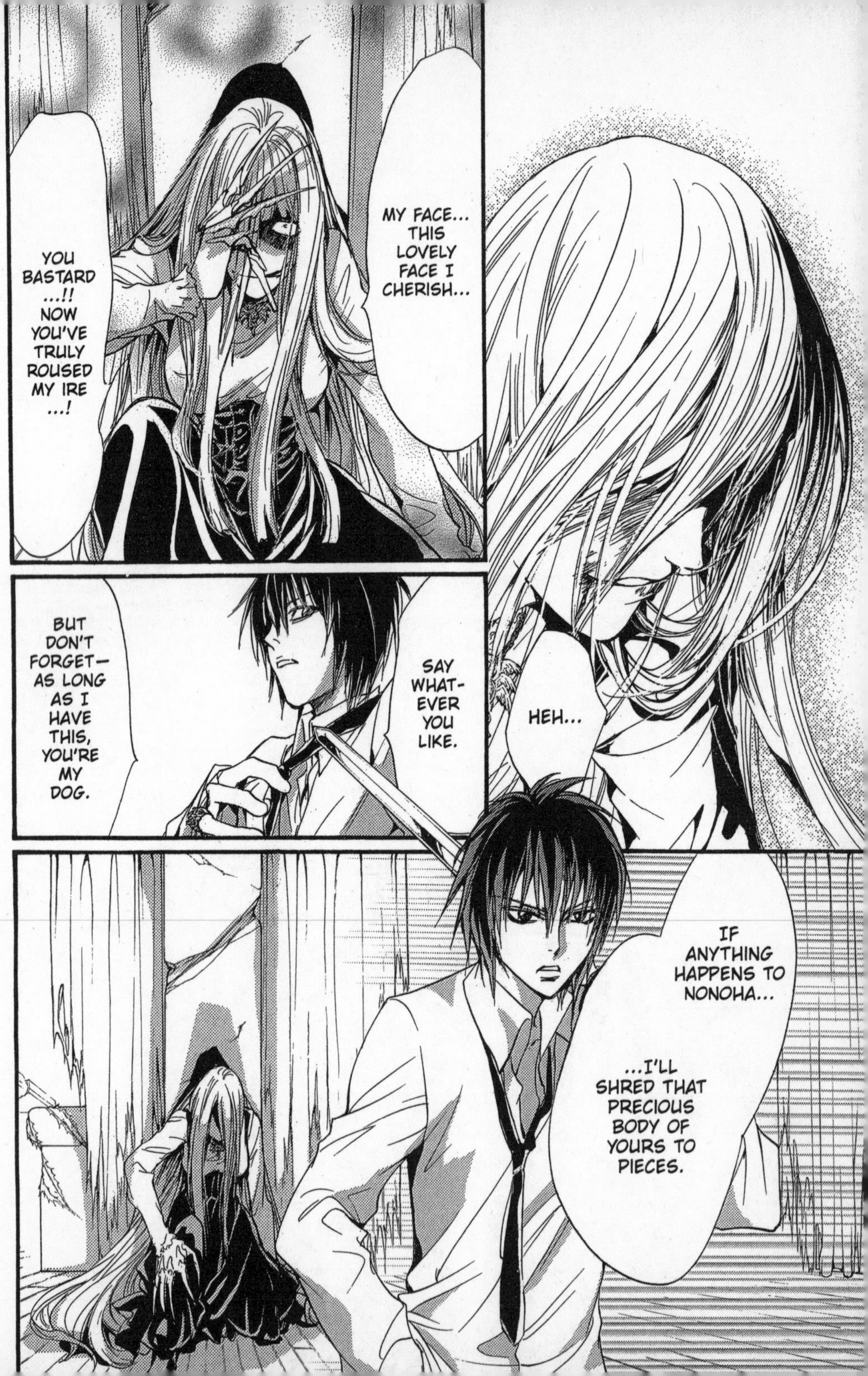
HEH...
MY FACE... THIS LOVELY FACE I CHERISH...
YOU BASTARD ...!! NOW YOU'VE TRULY ROUSED MY IRE ...!
SAY WHAT-EVER YOU LIKE.
BUT DON'T FORGET— AS LONG AS I HAVE THIS, YOU'RE MY DOG.
IF ANYTHING HAPPENS TO NONOHA...
...I'LL SHRED THAT PRECIOUS BODY OF YOURS TO PIECES.

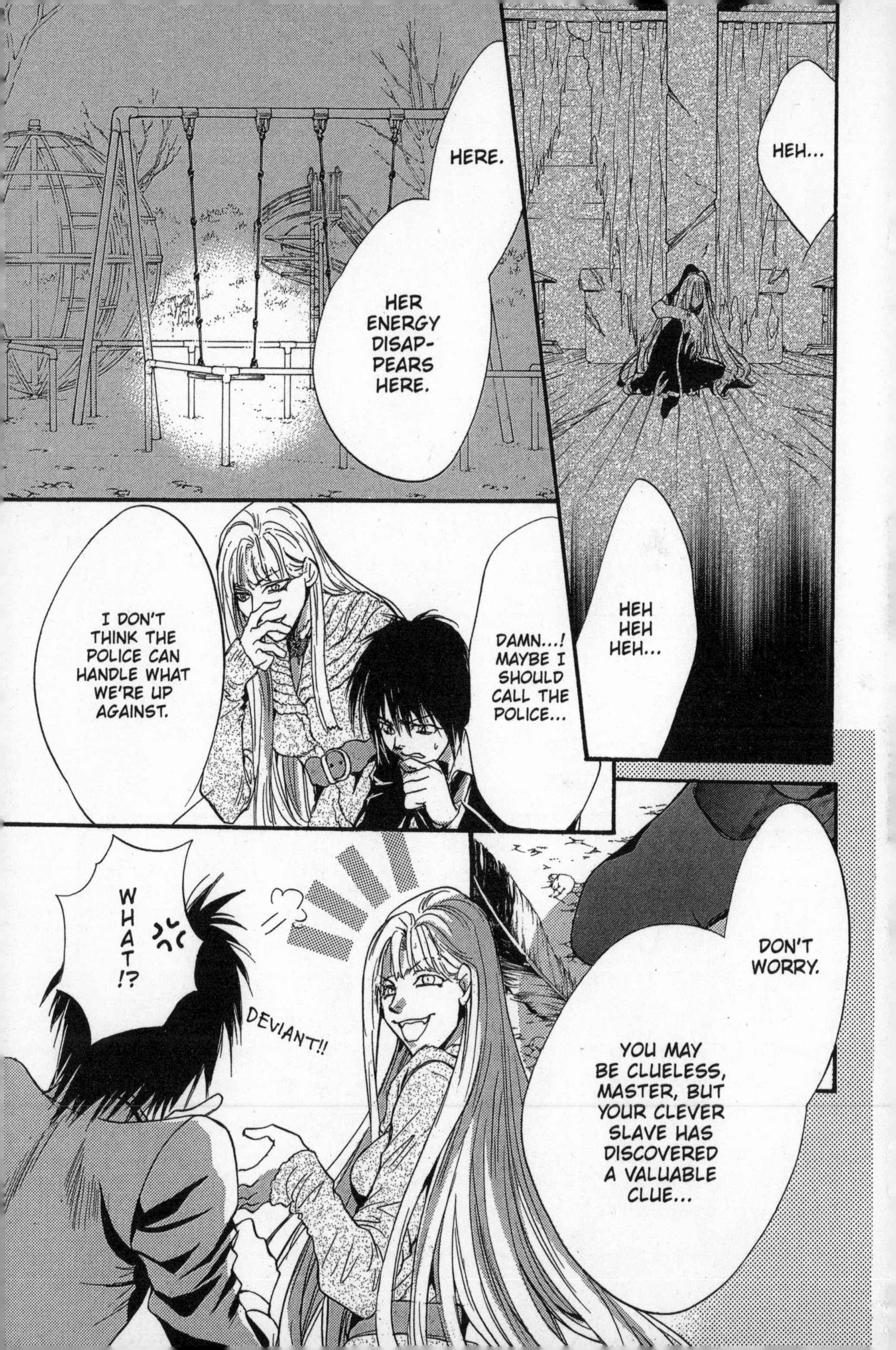
HEH...
HEH HEH HEH...
HERE.
HER ENERGY DISAP-PEARS HERE.
DAMN...! MAYBE I SHOULD CALL THE POLICE...
I DON'T THINK THE POLICE CAN HANDLE WHAT WE'RE UP AGAINST.
DON'T WORRY.
YOU MAY BE CLUELESS, MASTER, BUT YOUR CLEVER SLAVE HAS DISCOVERED A VALUABLE CLUE...
DEVIANT!!
WHAT!?

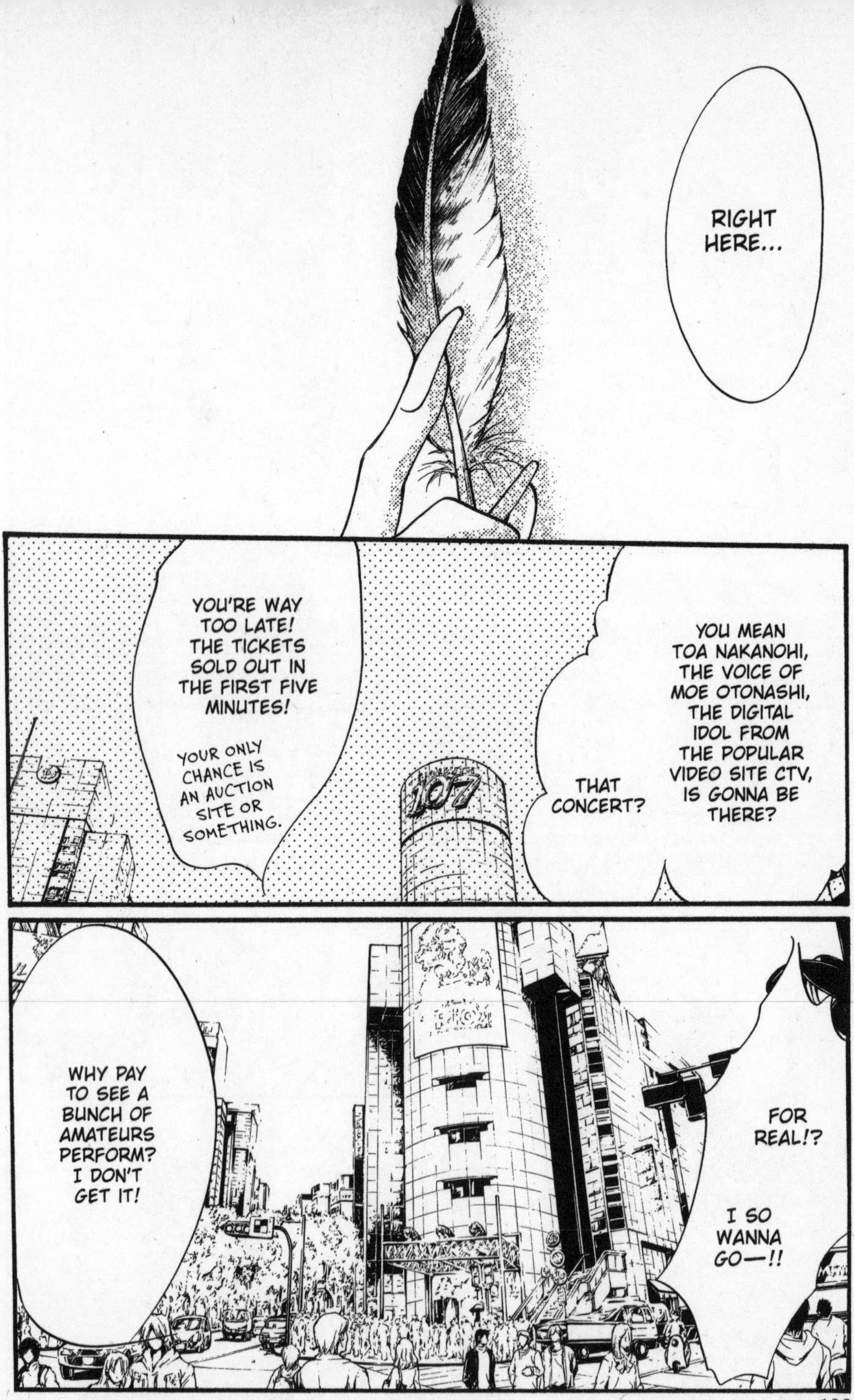
RIGHT HERE...
YOU MEAN TOA NAKANOHI, THE VOICE OF MOE OTONASHI, THE DIGITAL IDOL FROM THE POPULAR VIDEO SITE CTV, IS GONNA BE THERE?
THAT CONCERT?
YOU'RE WAY TOO LATE! THE TICKETS SOLD OUT IN THE FIRST FIVE MINUTES!
YOUR ONLY CHANCE IS AN AUCTION SITE OR SOMETHING.
FOR REAL!?
I SO WANNA GO—!!
WHY PAY TO SEE A BUNCH OF AMATEURS PERFORM? I DON'T GET IT!

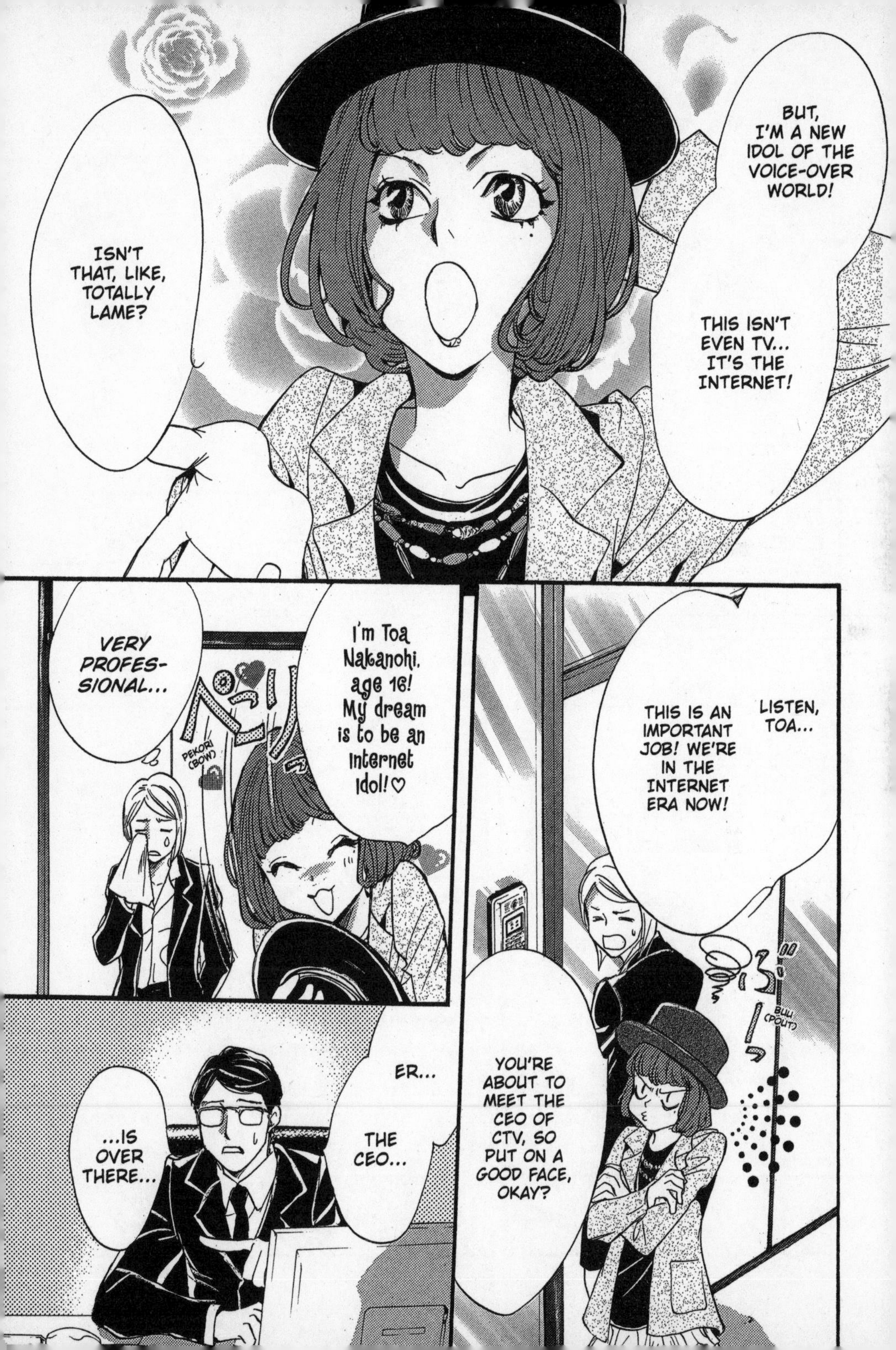
BUT, I'M A NEW IDOL OF THE VOICE-OVER WORLD!
THIS ISN'T EVEN TV... IT'S THE INTERNET!
ISN'T THAT, LIKE, TOTALLY LAME?
LISTEN, TOA...
THIS IS AN IMPORTANT JOB! WE'RE IN THE INTERNET ERA NOW!
BUU (POUT)
YOU'RE ABOUT TO MEET THE CEO OF CTV, SO PUT ON A GOOD FACE, OKAY?
I'm Toa Nakanohi, age 16! My dream is to be an internet idol!♡
PEKORI (BOW)
VERY PROFES-SIONAL...
ER...
THE CEO...
...IS OVER THERE...

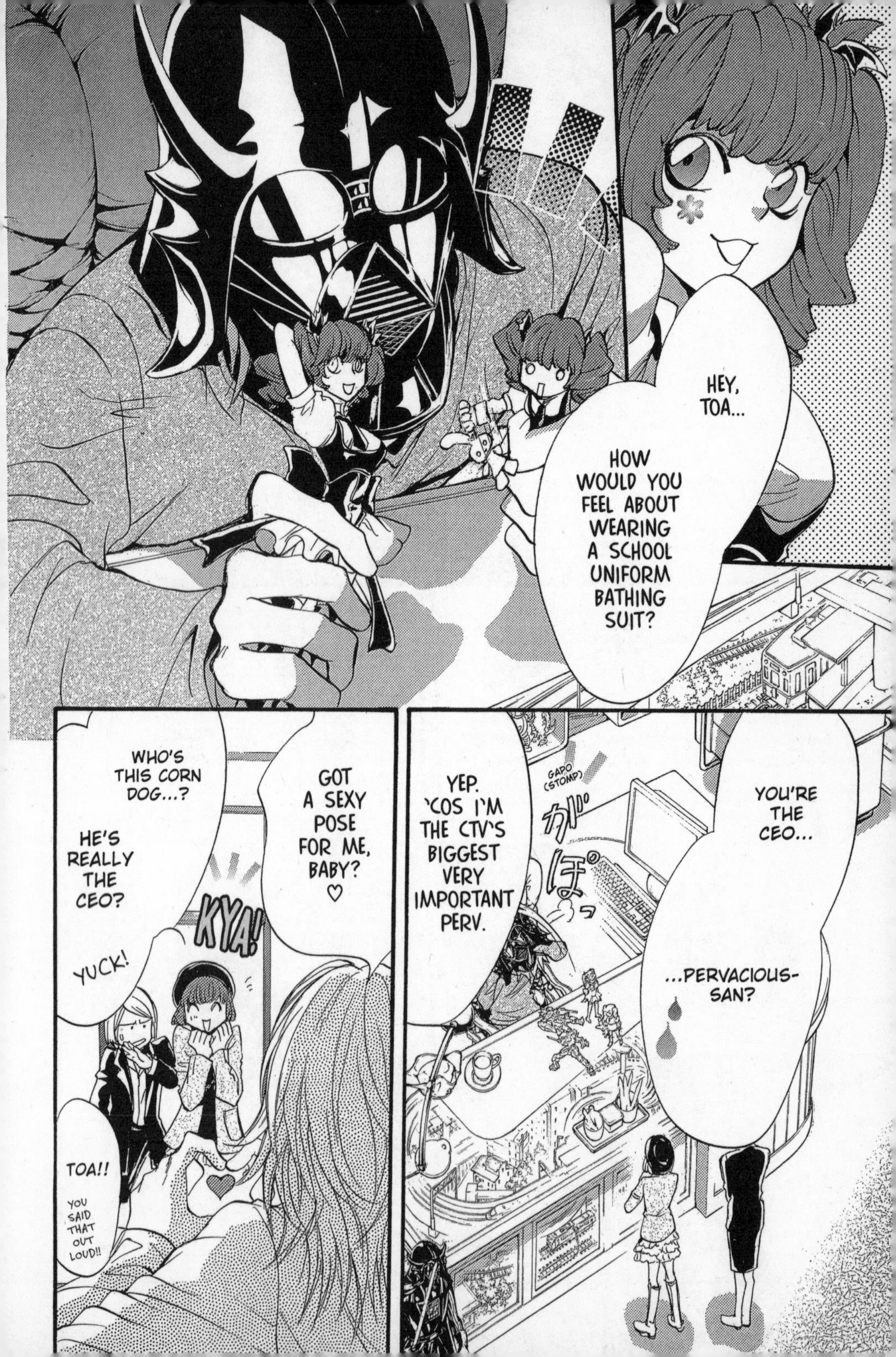
HEY, TOA...
HOW WOULD YOU FEEL ABOUT WEARING A SCHOOL UNIFORM BATHING SUIT?
YOU'RE THE CEO...
...PERVACIOUS-SAN?
GAPO (STOMP)
YEP. 'COS I'M THE CTV'S BIGGEST VERY IMPORTANT PERV.
GOT A SEXY POSE FOR ME, BABY? ♡
KYA!
WHO'S THIS CORN DOG...?
HE'S REALLY THE CEO?
YUCK!
TOA!!
YOU SAID THAT OUT LOUD!!

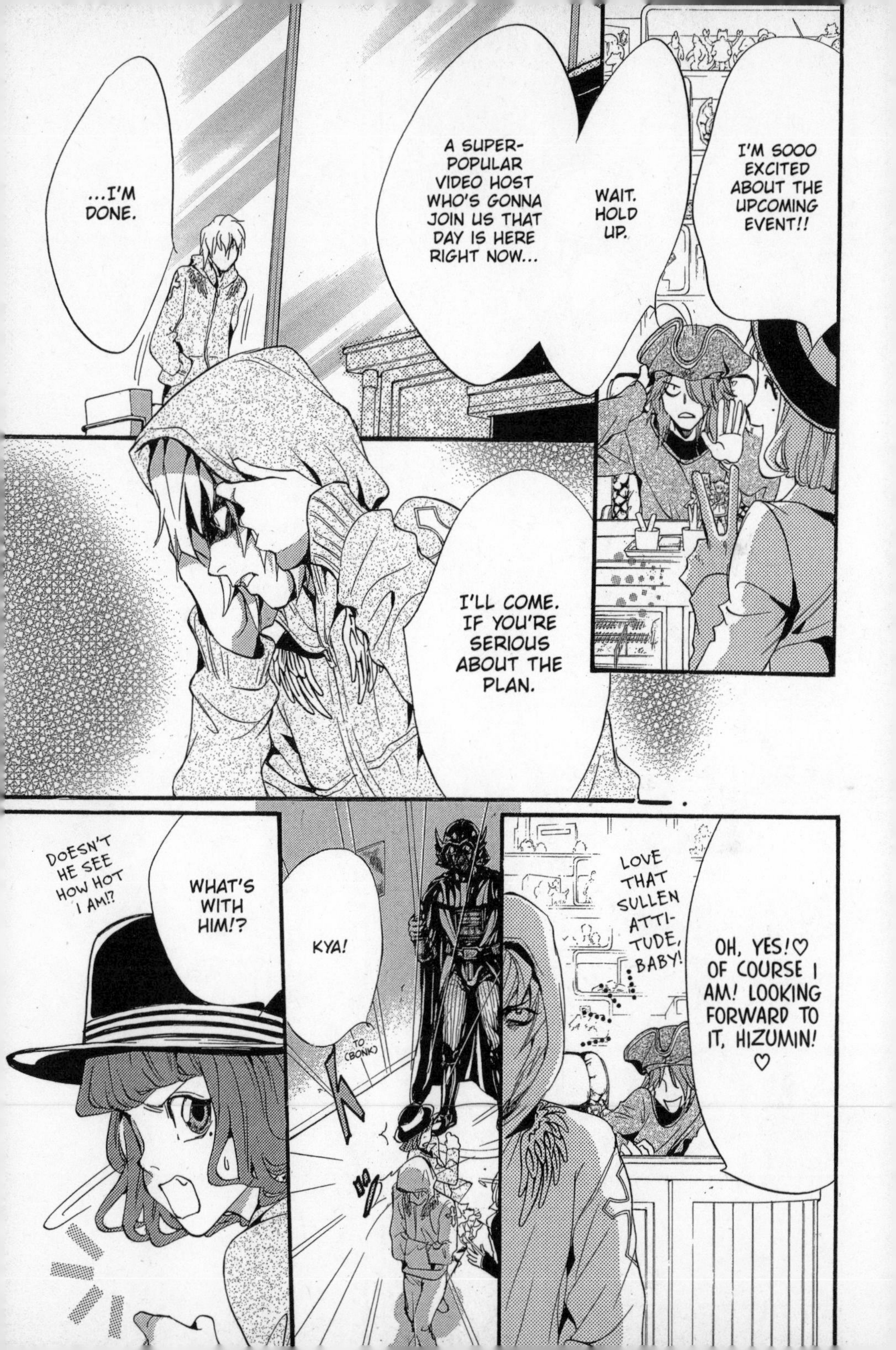
I'M SOOO EXCITED ABOUT THE UPCOMING EVENT!!
WAIT. HOLD UP.
A SUPER-POPULAR VIDEO HOST WHO'S GONNA JOIN US THAT DAY IS HERE RIGHT NOW...
...I'M DONE.
I'LL COME. IF YOU'RE SERIOUS ABOUT THE PLAN.
OH, YES!♡ OF COURSE I AM! LOOKING FORWARD TO IT, HIZUMIN! ♡
LOVE THAT SULLEN ATTITUDE, BABY!
KYA!
TO (BONK)
WHAT'S WITH HIM!?
DOESN'T HE SEE HOW HOT I AM!?

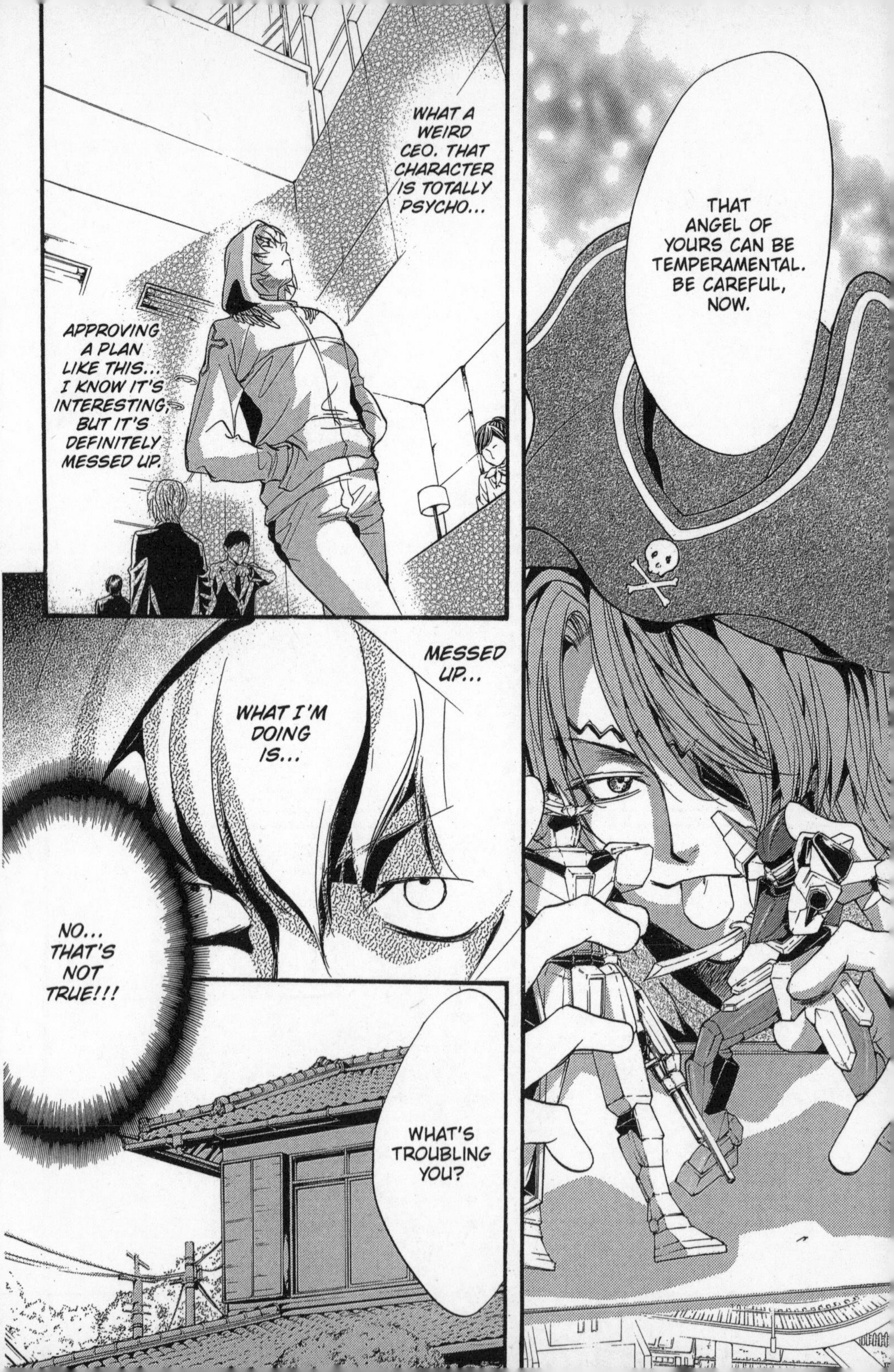
THAT ANGEL OF YOURS CAN BE TEMPERAMENTAL. BE CAREFUL, NOW.
WHAT A WEIRD CEO. THAT CHARACTER IS TOTALLY PSYCHO...
APPROVING A PLAN LIKE THIS... I KNOW IT'S INTERESTING, BUT IT'S DEFINITELY MESSED UP.
MESSED UP...
WHAT I'M DOING IS...
NO... THAT'S NOT TRUE!!!
WHAT'S TROUBLING YOU?

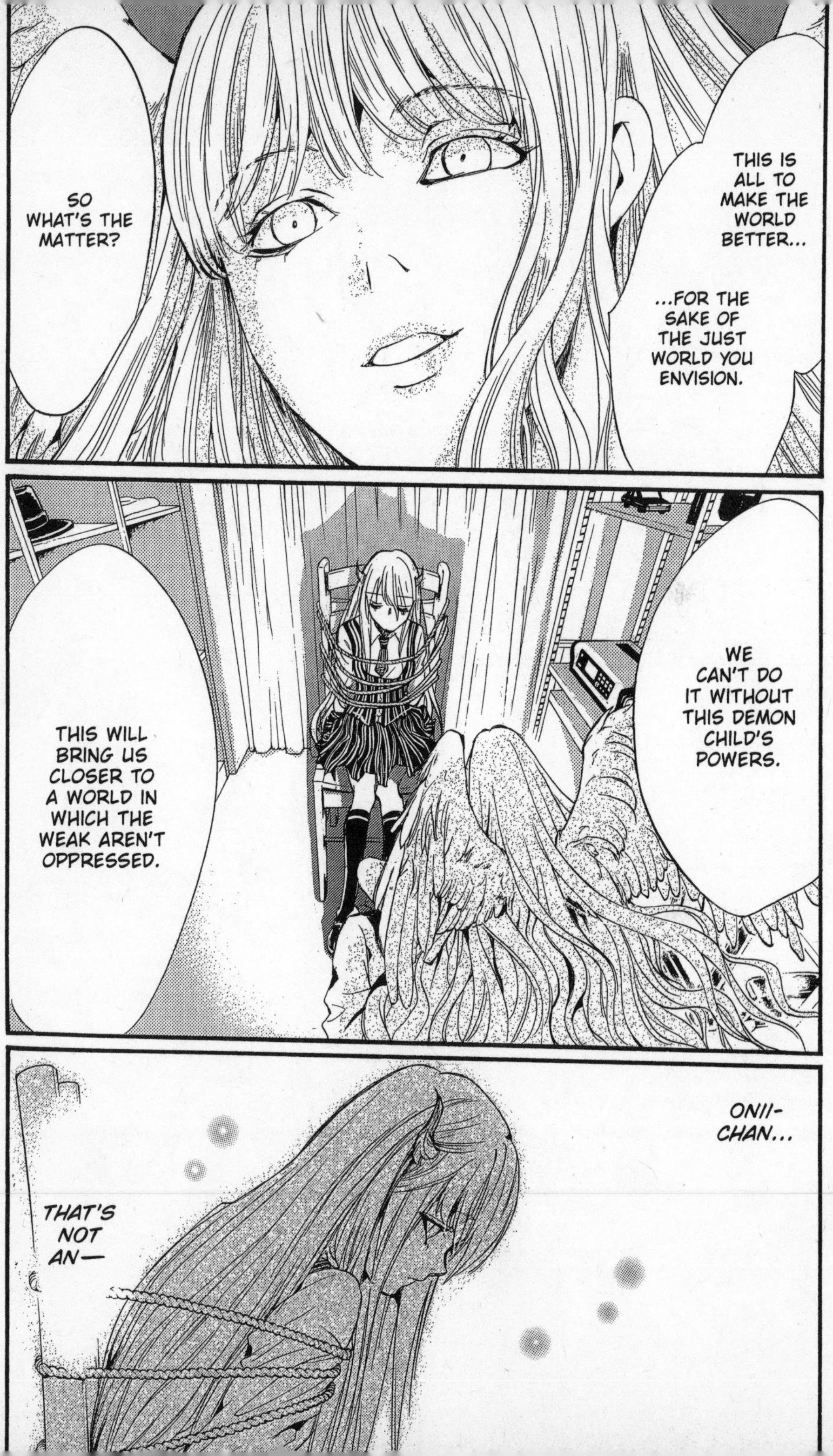
THIS IS ALL TO MAKE THE WORLD BETTER...
...FOR THE SAKE OF THE JUST WORLD YOU ENVISION.
SO WHAT'S THE MATTER?
WE CAN'T DO IT WITHOUT THIS DEMON CHILD'S POWERS.
THIS WILL BRING US CLOSER TO A WORLD IN WHICH THE WEAK AREN'T OPPRESSED.
ONII-CHAN...
THAT'S NOT AN—

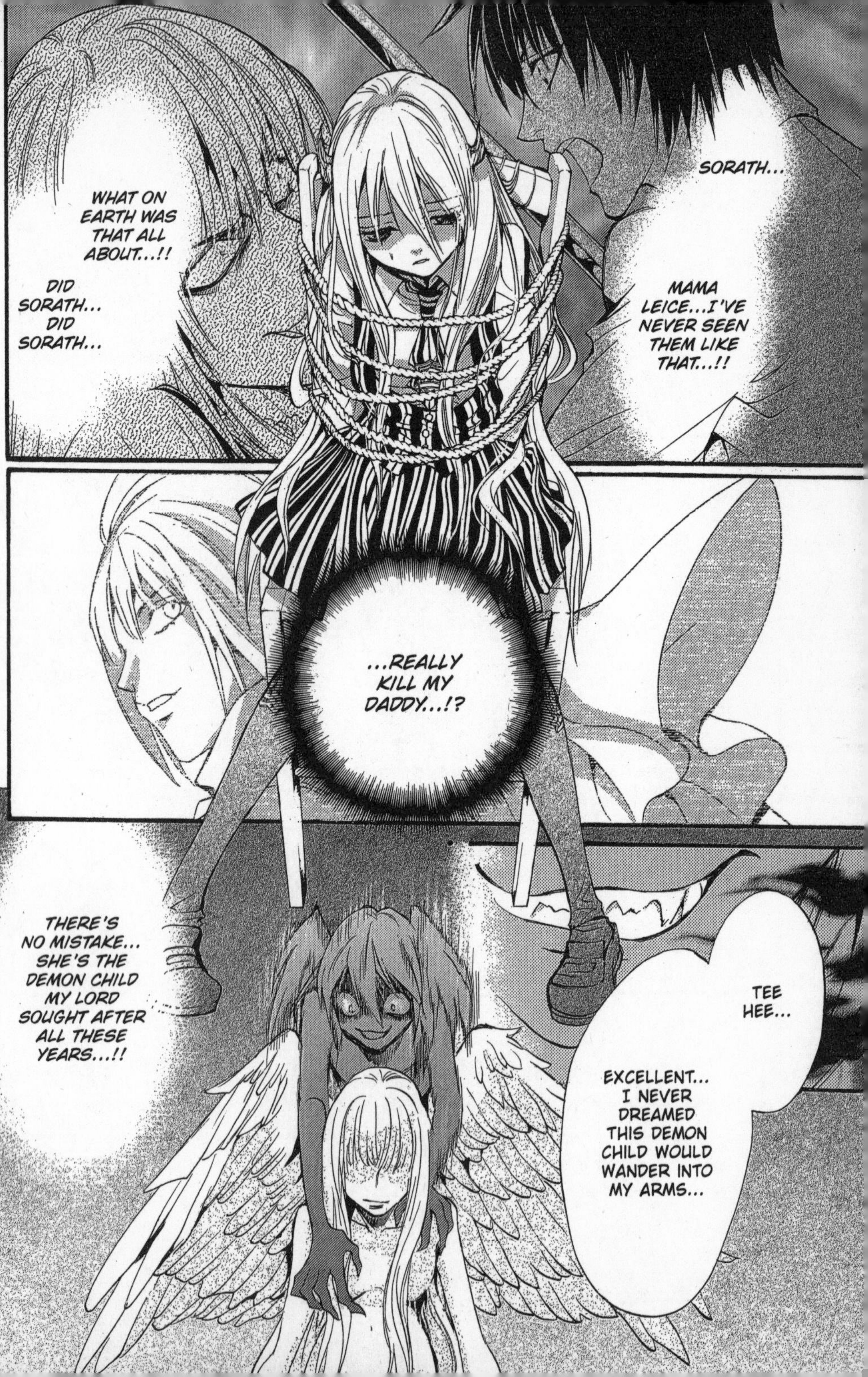
SORATH...
MAMA LEICE...I'VE NEVER SEEN THEM LIKE THAT...!!
WHAT ON EARTH WAS THAT ALL ABOUT...!!
DID SORATH... DID LORD SORATH...
...REALLY KILL MY DADDY...!?
TEE HEE...
EXCELLENT... I NEVER DREAMED THIS DEMON CHILD WOULD WANDER INTO MY ARMS...
THERE'S NO MISTAKE... SHE'S THE DEMON CHILD MY LORD SOUGHT AFTER ALL THESE YEARS...!!

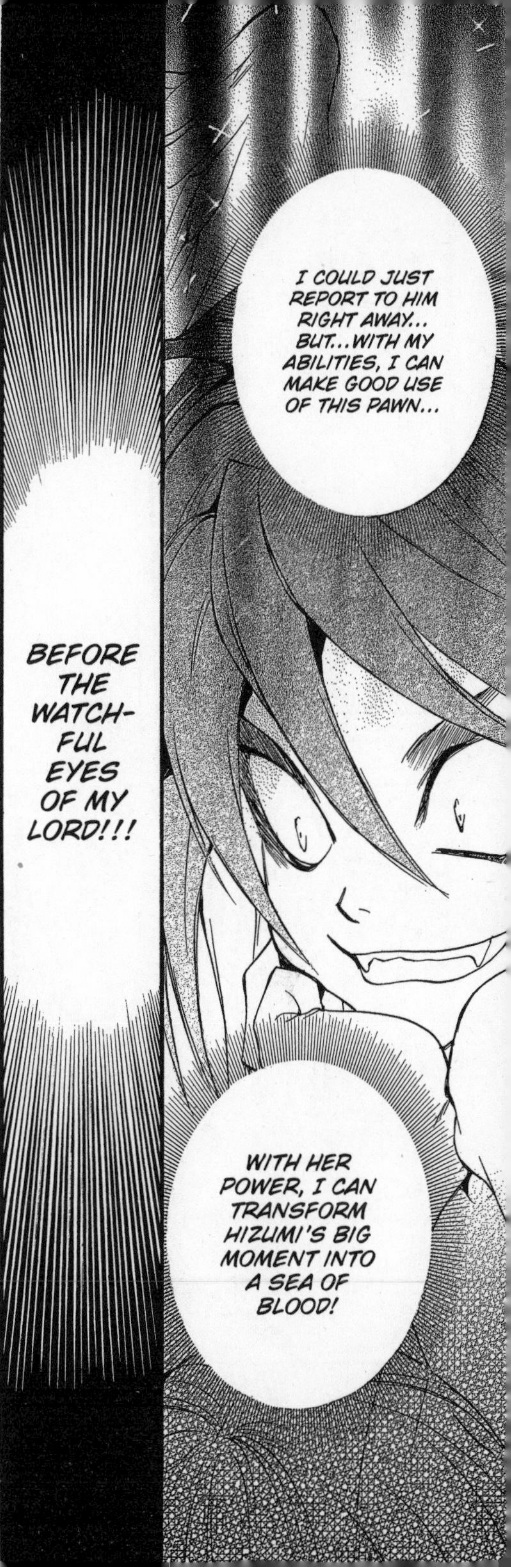
I COULD JUST REPORT TO HIM RIGHT AWAY... BUT...WITH MY ABILITIES, I CAN MAKE GOOD USE OF THIS PAWN...
WITH HER POWER, I CAN TRANSFORM HIZUMI'S BIG MOMENT INTO A SEA OF BLOOD!
BEFORE THE WATCH-FUL EYES OF MY LORD!!!

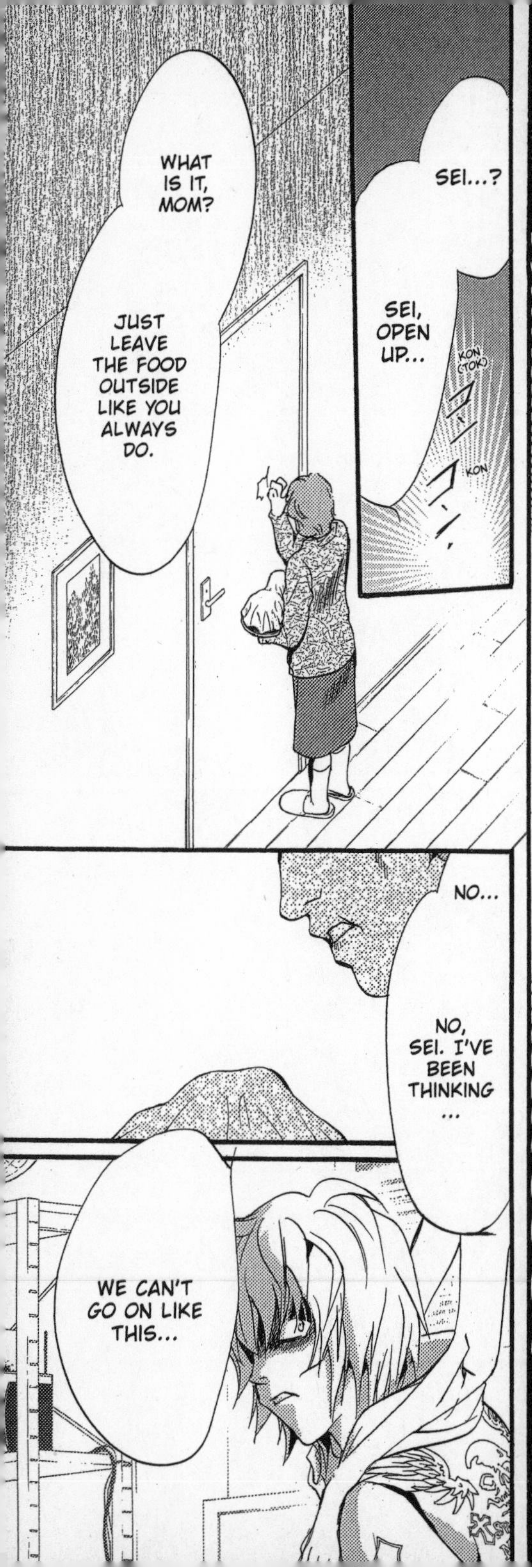
SEI...?
SEI, OPEN UP...
KON (TOK)
KON
WHAT IS IT, MOM?
JUST LEAVE THE FOOD OUTSIDE LIKE YOU ALWAYS DO.
NO...
NO, SEI. I'VE BEEN THINKING...
WE CAN'T GO ON LIKE THIS...

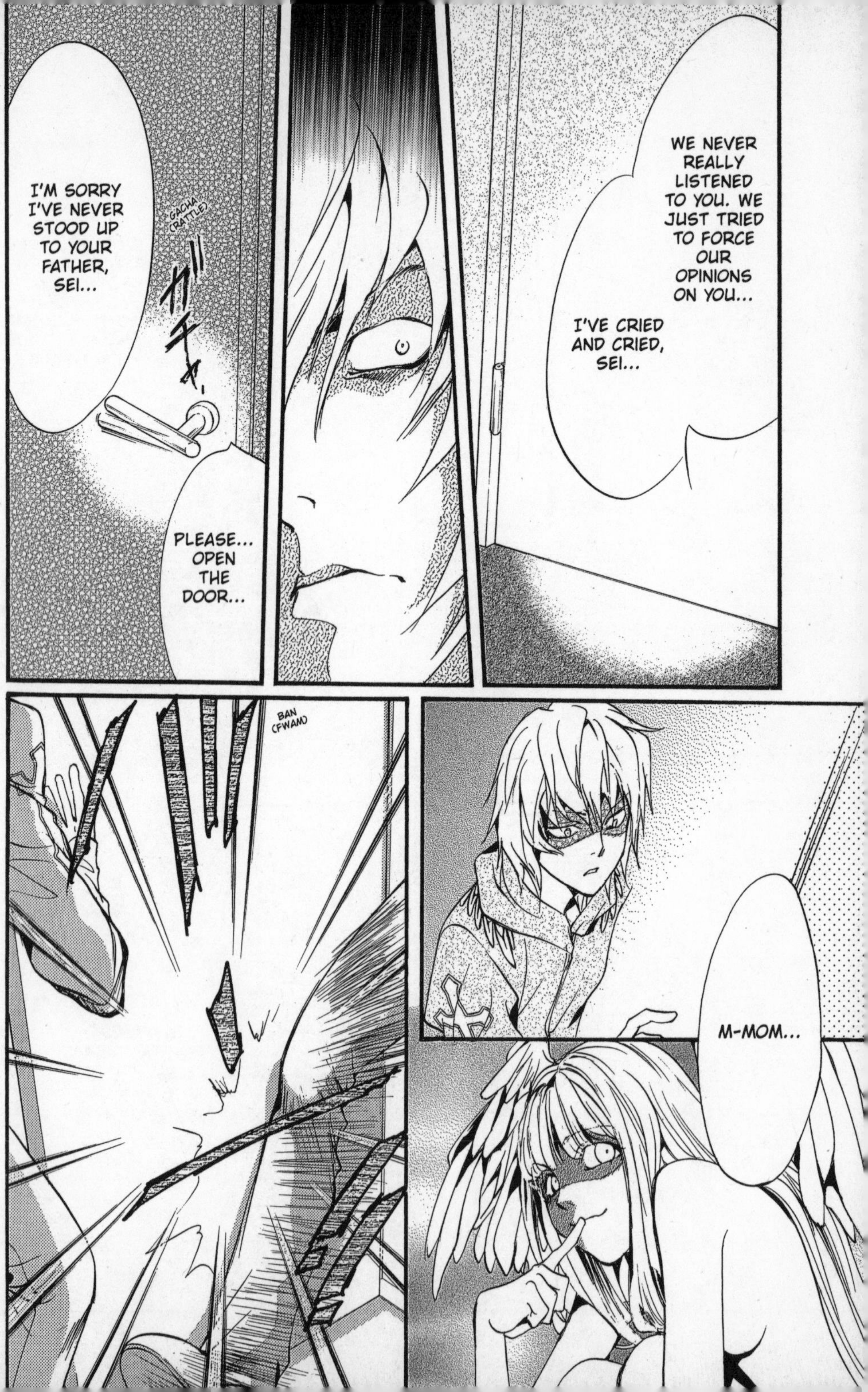
WE NEVER REALLY LISTENED TO YOU. WE JUST TRIED TO FORCE OUR OPINIONS ON YOU...
I'VE CRIED AND CRIED, SEI...
I'M SORRY I'VE NEVER STOOD UP TO YOUR FATHER, SEI...
GACHA (RATTLE)
PLEASE... OPEN THE DOOR...
M-MOM...
BAN (FWAM)

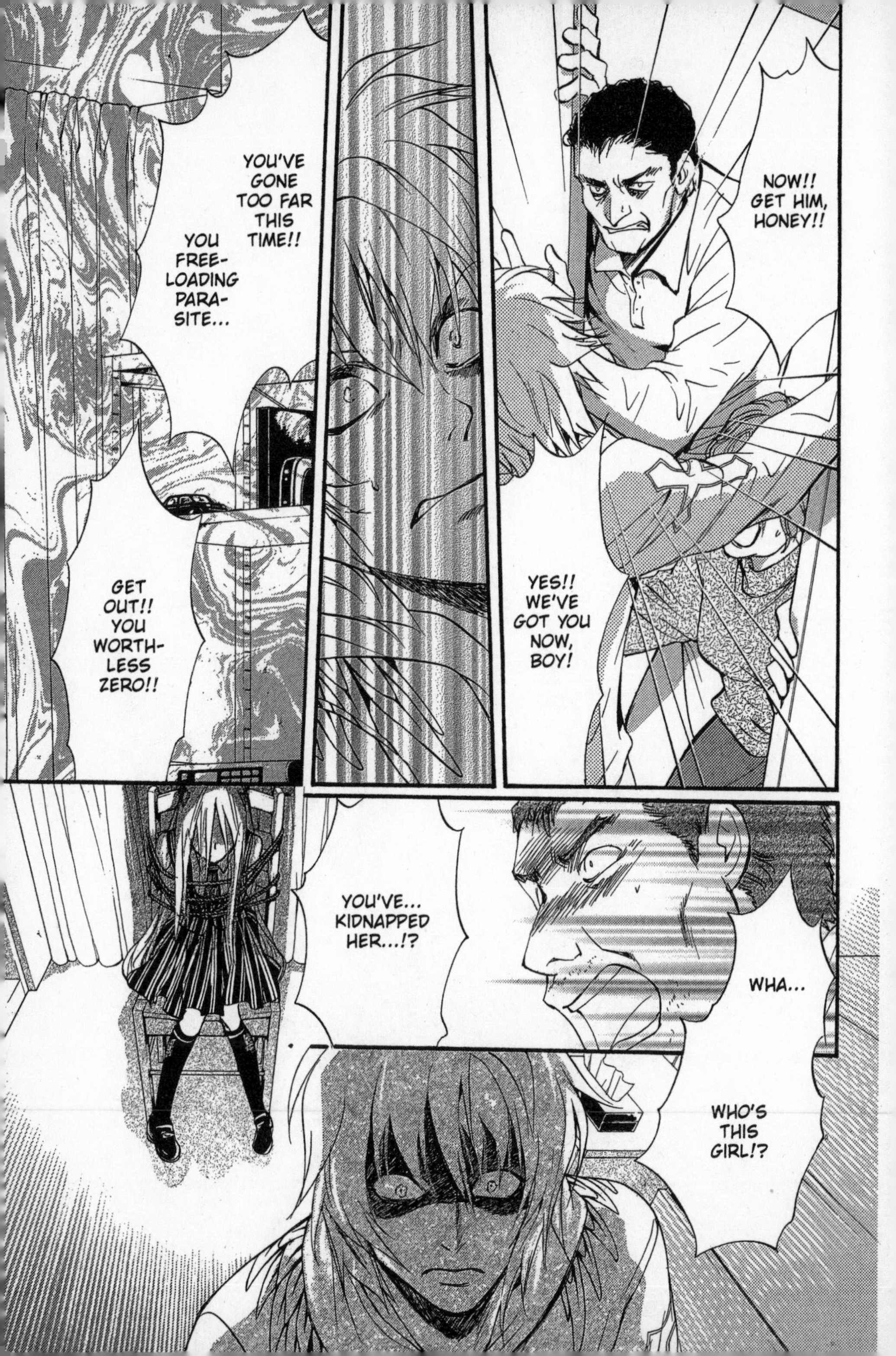
NOW!! GET HIM, HONEY!!
YES!! WE'VE GOT YOU NOW, BOY!
YOU'VE GONE TOO FAR THIS TIME!!
YOU FREE-LOADING PARA-SITE...
GET OUT!! YOU WORTH-LESS ZERO!!
WHA...
YOU'VE... KIDNAPPED HER...!?
WHO'S THIS GIRL!?

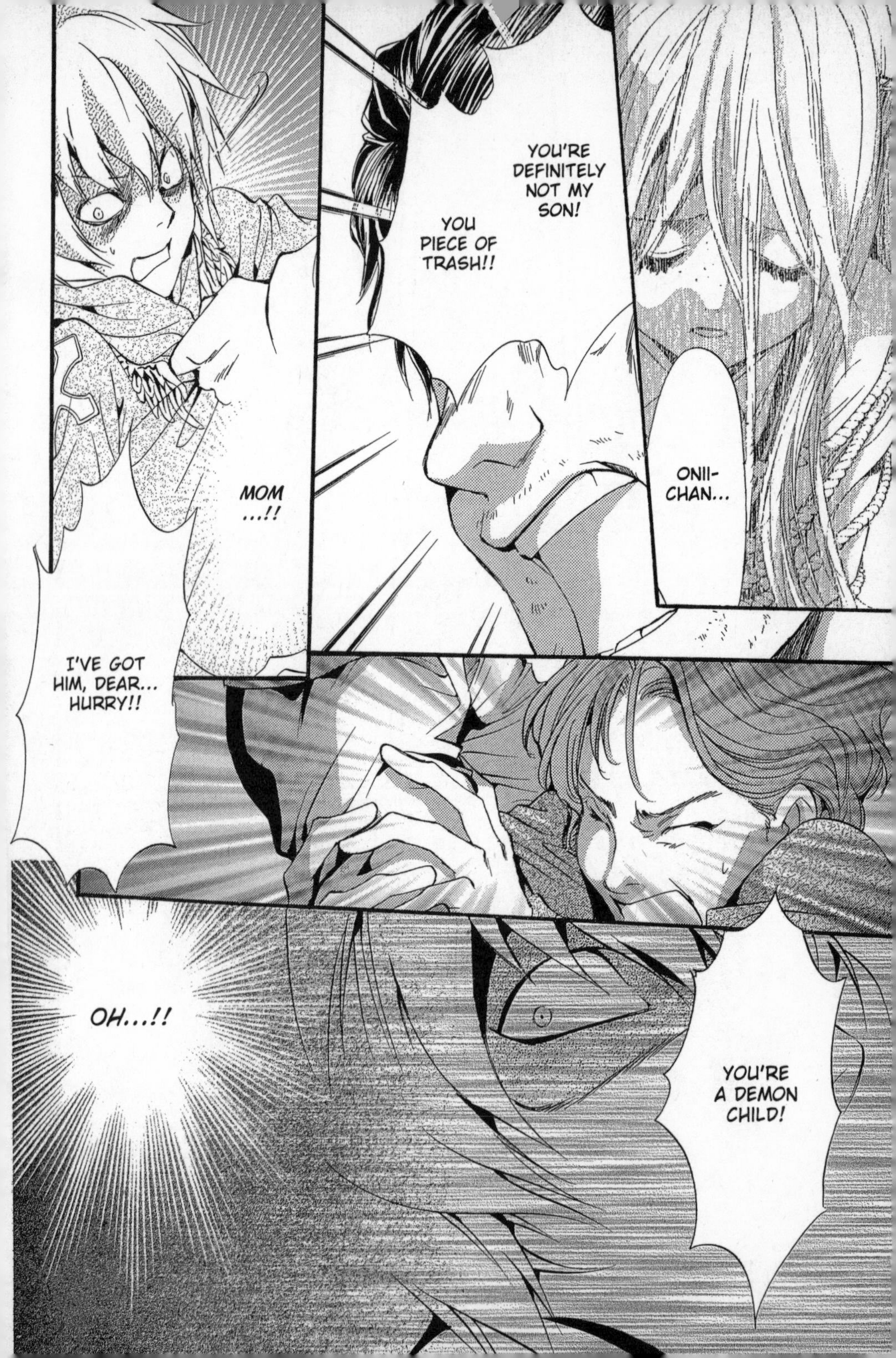
ONII-CHAN...
YOU'RE DEFINITELY NOT MY SON!
YOU PIECE OF TRASH!!
MOM ...!!
I'VE GOT HIM, DEAR... HURRY!!
YOU'RE A DEMON CHILD!
OH...!!

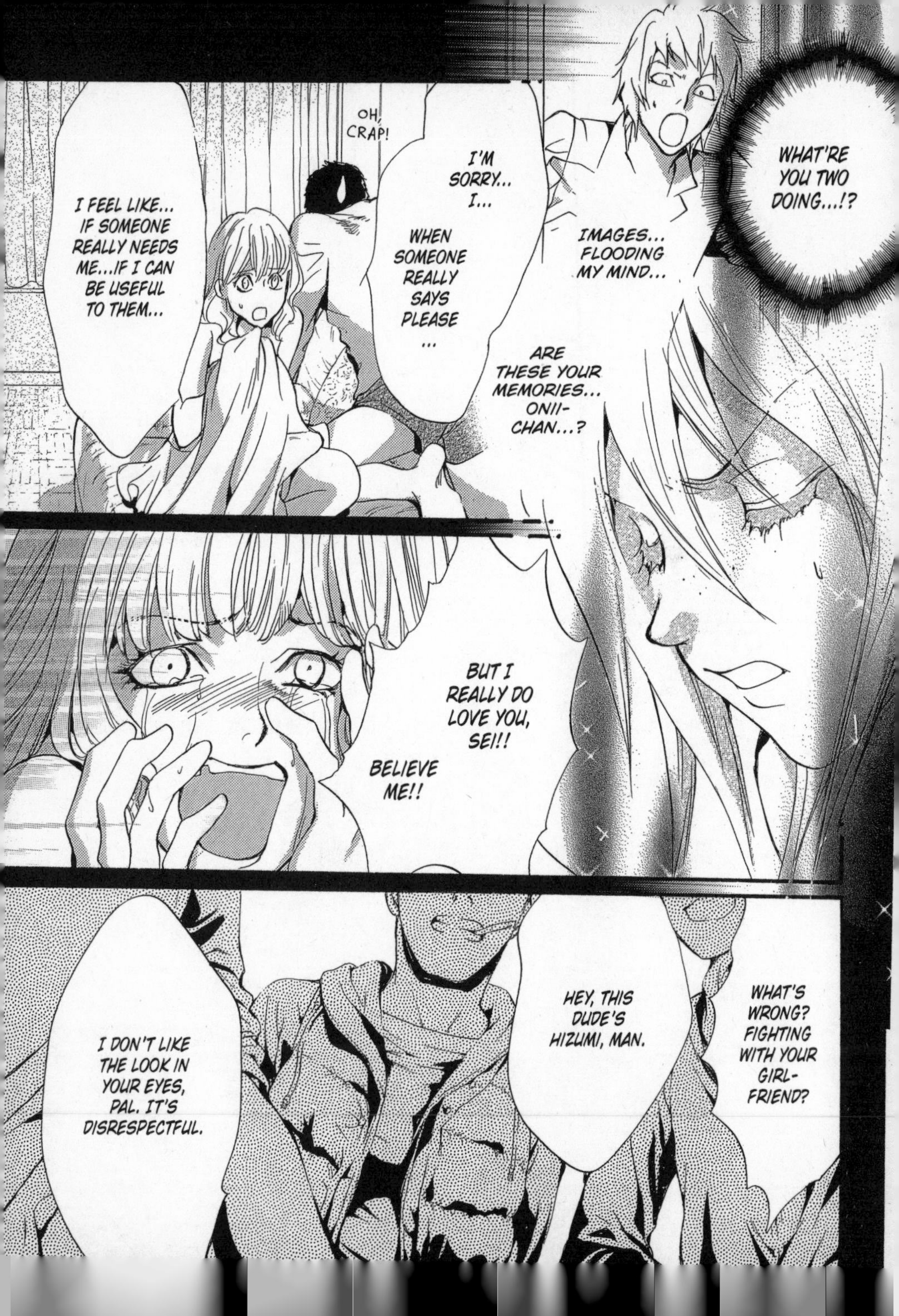
WHAT'RE YOU TWO DOING...!?
IMAGES... FLOODING MY MIND...
I'M SORRY... I...
WHEN SOMEONE REALLY SAYS PLEASE ...
OH, CRAP!
I FEEL LIKE... IF SOMEONE REALLY NEEDS ME...IF I CAN BE USEFUL TO THEM...
ARE THESE YOUR MEMORIES... ONII-CHAN...?
BUT I REALLY DO LOVE YOU, SEI!!
BELIEVE ME!!
WHAT'S WRONG? FIGHTING WITH YOUR GIRL-FRIEND?
HEY, THIS DUDE'S HIZUMI, MAN.
I DON'T LIKE THE LOOK IN YOUR EYES, PAL. IT'S DISRESPECTFUL.

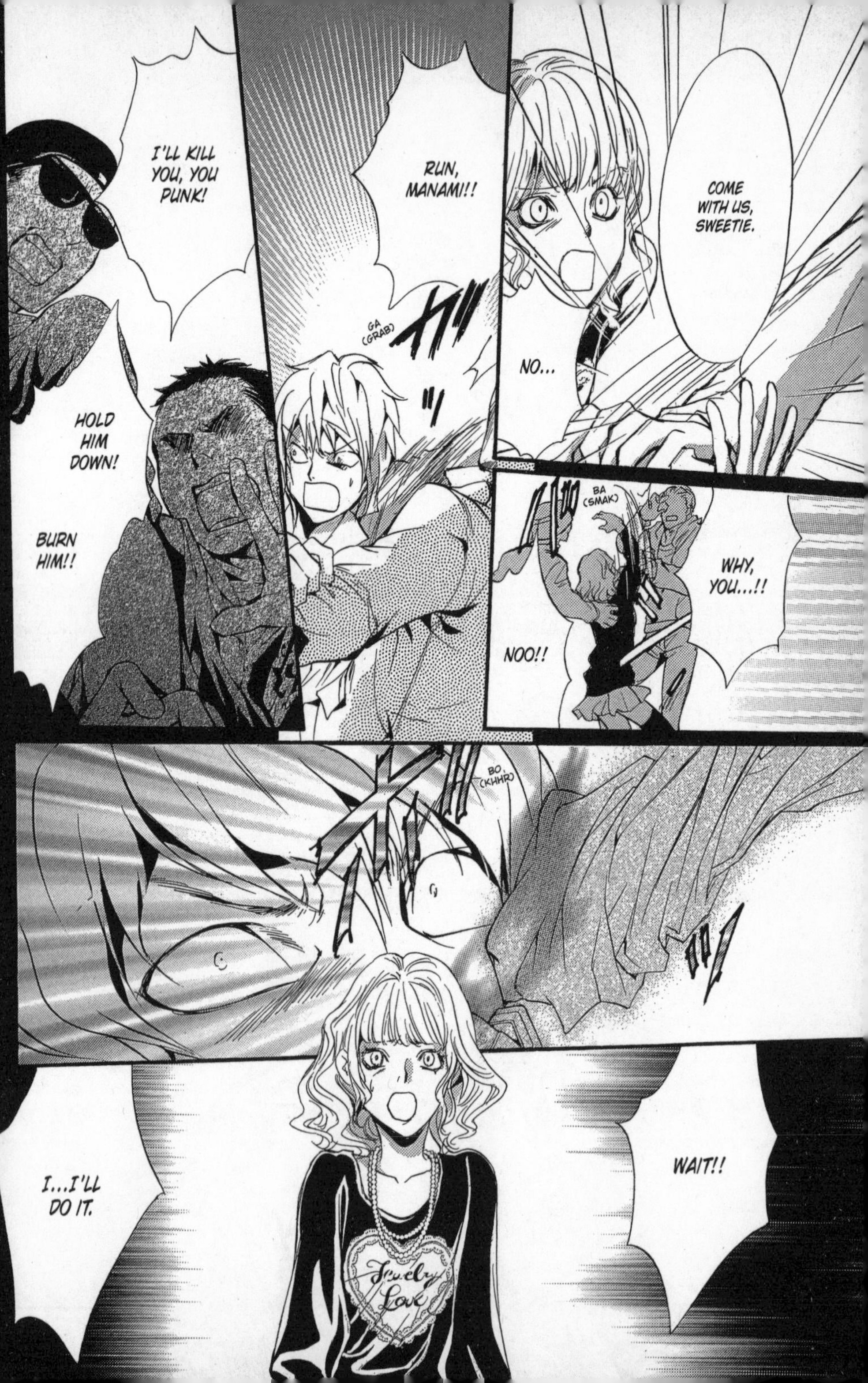
COME WITH US, SWEETIE.
NO...
WHY, YOU...!!
BA (SMAK)
NOO!!
RUN, MANAMI!!
GA (GRAB)
I'LL KILL YOU, YOU PUNK!
HOLD HIM DOWN!
BURN HIM!!
BO (KHHR)
WAIT!!
I...I'LL DO IT.

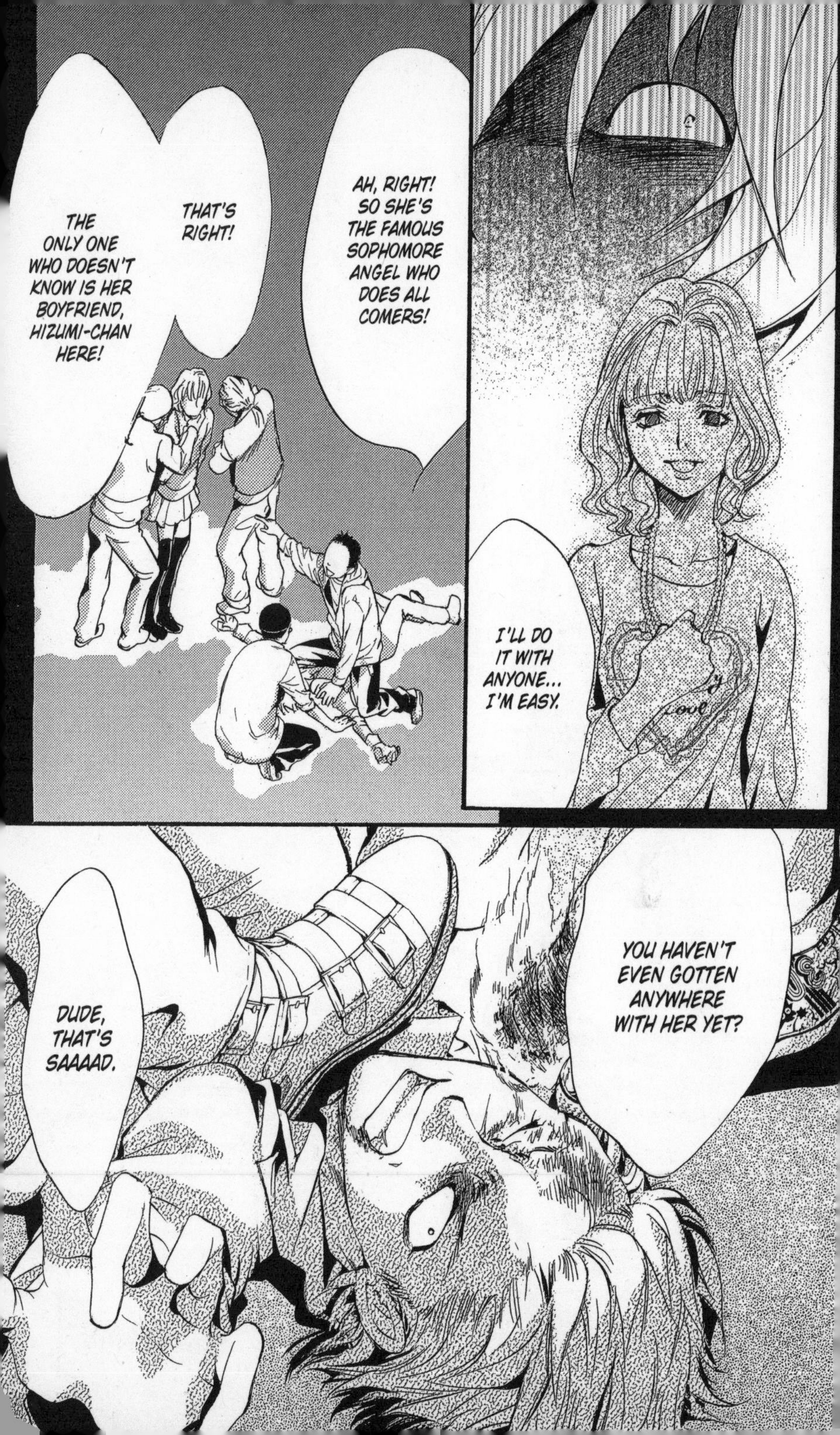
I'LL DO IT WITH ANYONE... I'M EASY.
AH, RIGHT! SO SHE'S THE FAMOUS SOPHOMORE ANGEL WHO DOES ALL COMERS!
THAT'S RIGHT!
THE ONLY ONE WHO DOESN'T KNOW IS HER BOYFRIEND, HIZUMI-CHAN HERE!
YOU HAVEN'T EVEN GOTTEN ANYWHERE WITH HER YET?
DUDE, THAT'S SAAAAD.

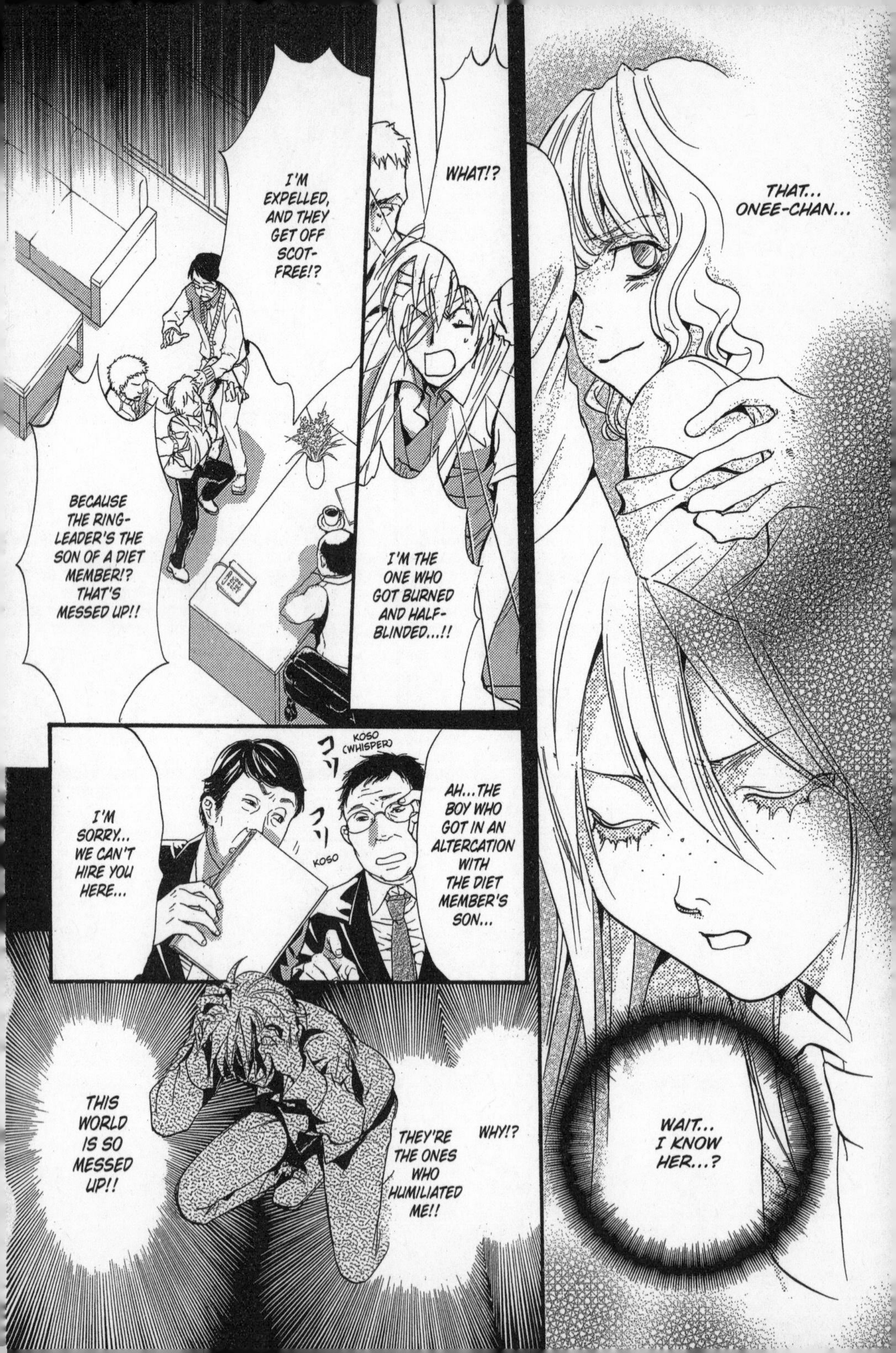

THAT... ONEE-CHAN...
WAIT... I KNOW HER...?
WHAT!?
I'M THE ONE WHO GOT BURNED AND HALF-BLINDED...!!
I'M EXPELLED, AND THEY GET OFF SCOT-FREE!?
BECAUSE THE RING-LEADER'S THE SON OF A DIET MEMBER!? THAT'S MESSED UP!!
AH...THE BOY WHO GOT IN AN ALTERCATION WITH THE DIET MEMBER'S SON...
コソ
KOSO (WHISPER)
コソ
KOSO
I'M SORRY... WE CAN'T HIRE YOU HERE...
WHY!?
THEY'RE THE ONES WHO HUMILIATED ME!!
THIS WORLD IS SO MESSED UP!!

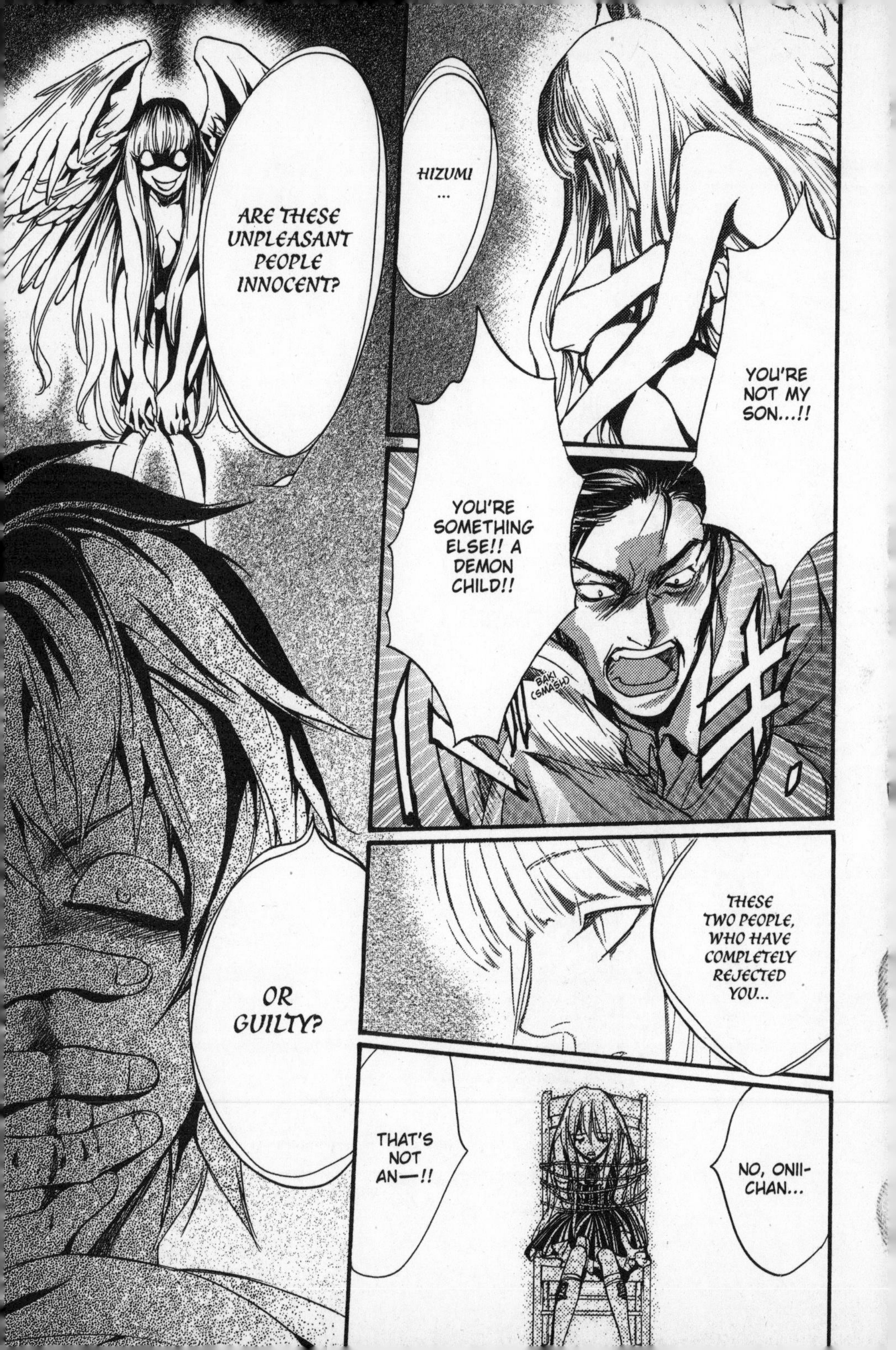
HIZUMI ...
YOU'RE NOT MY SON...!!
YOU'RE SOMETHING ELSE!! A DEMON CHILD!!
BAKI (SMASH)
THESE TWO PEOPLE, WHO HAVE COMPLETELY REJECTED YOU...
NO, ONII-CHAN...
THAT'S NOT AN—!!
ARE THESE UNPLEASANT PEOPLE INNOCENT?
OR GUILTY?

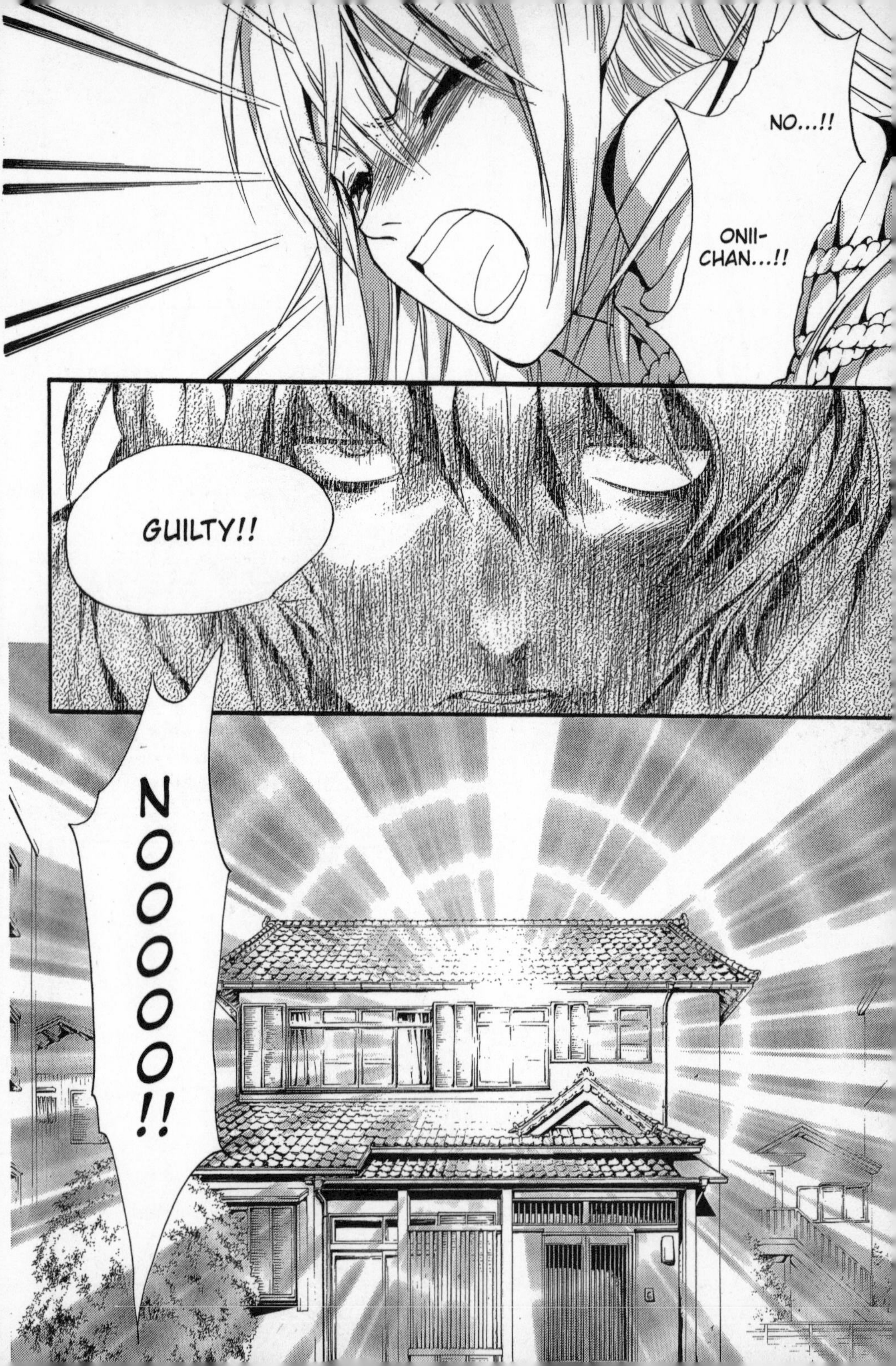
NO...!!
ONII-CHAN...!!
GUILTY!!
NOOOOOO!!

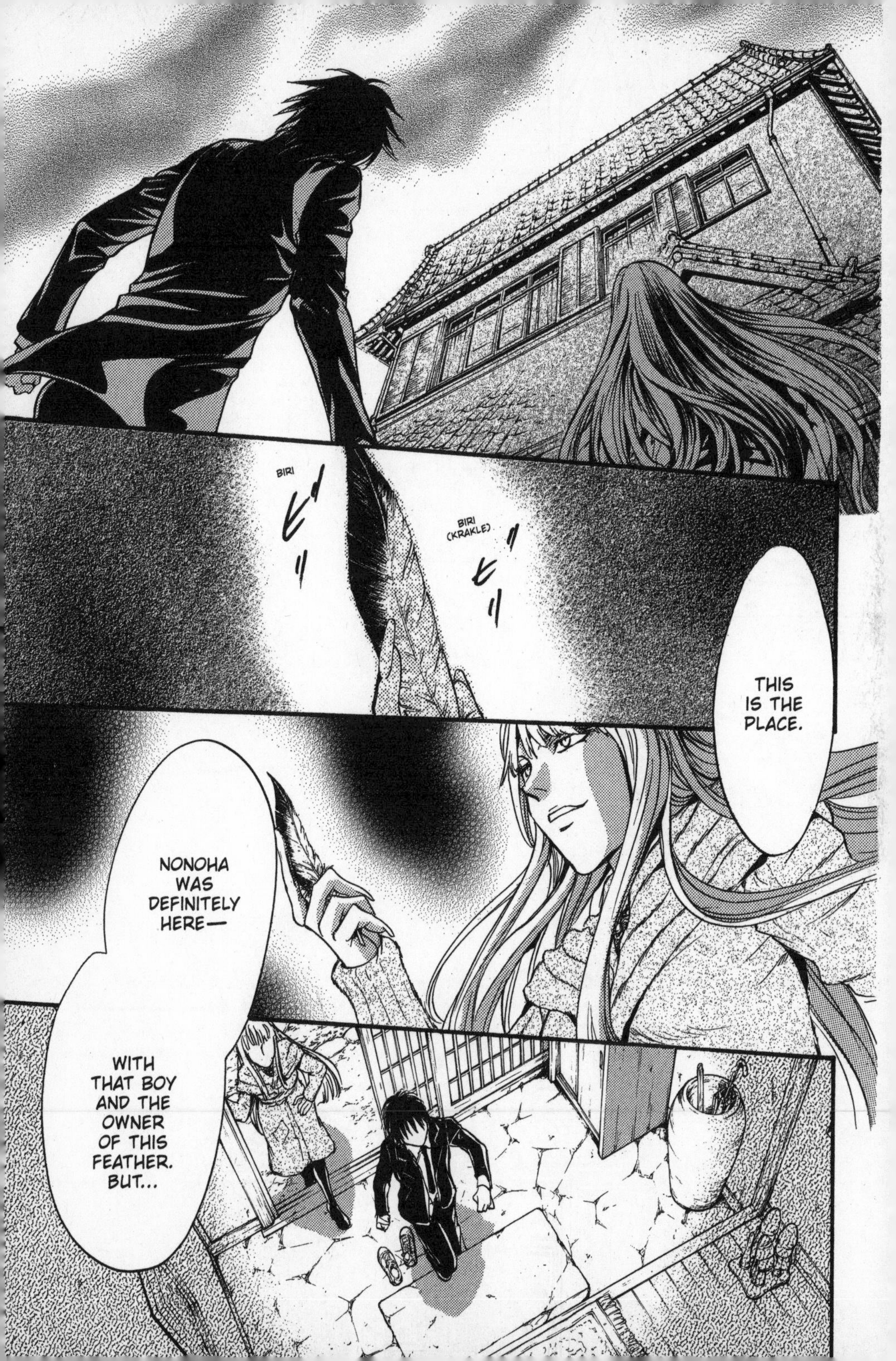
BIRI (KRAKLE)
BIRI
THIS IS THE PLACE.
NONOHA WAS DEFINITELY HERE—
WITH THAT BOY AND THE OWNER OF THIS FEATHER. BUT...

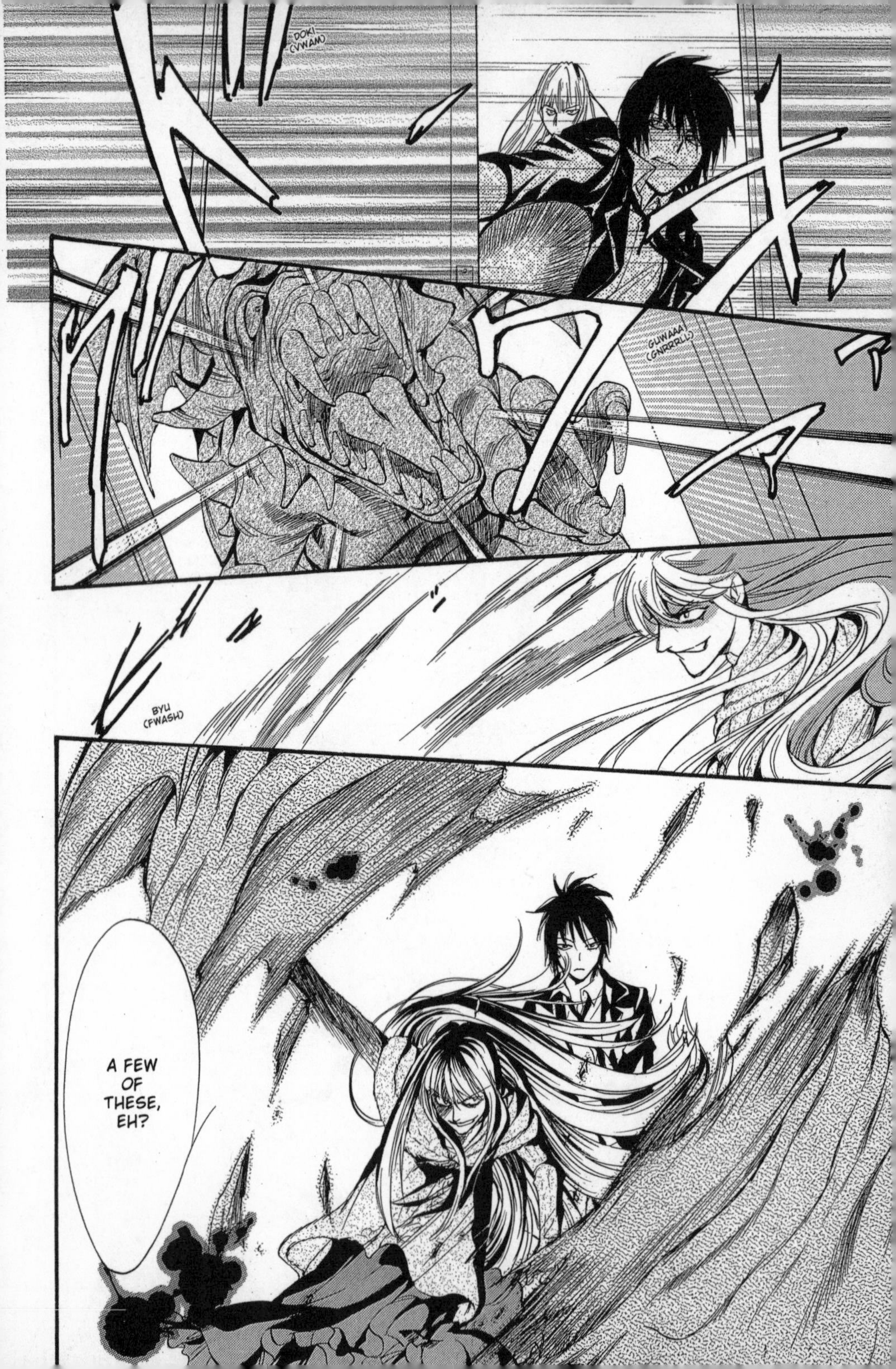
DOKI (VWAM)
GUWAAA (GNRRRLL)
BYU (FWASH)
A FEW OF THESE, EH?

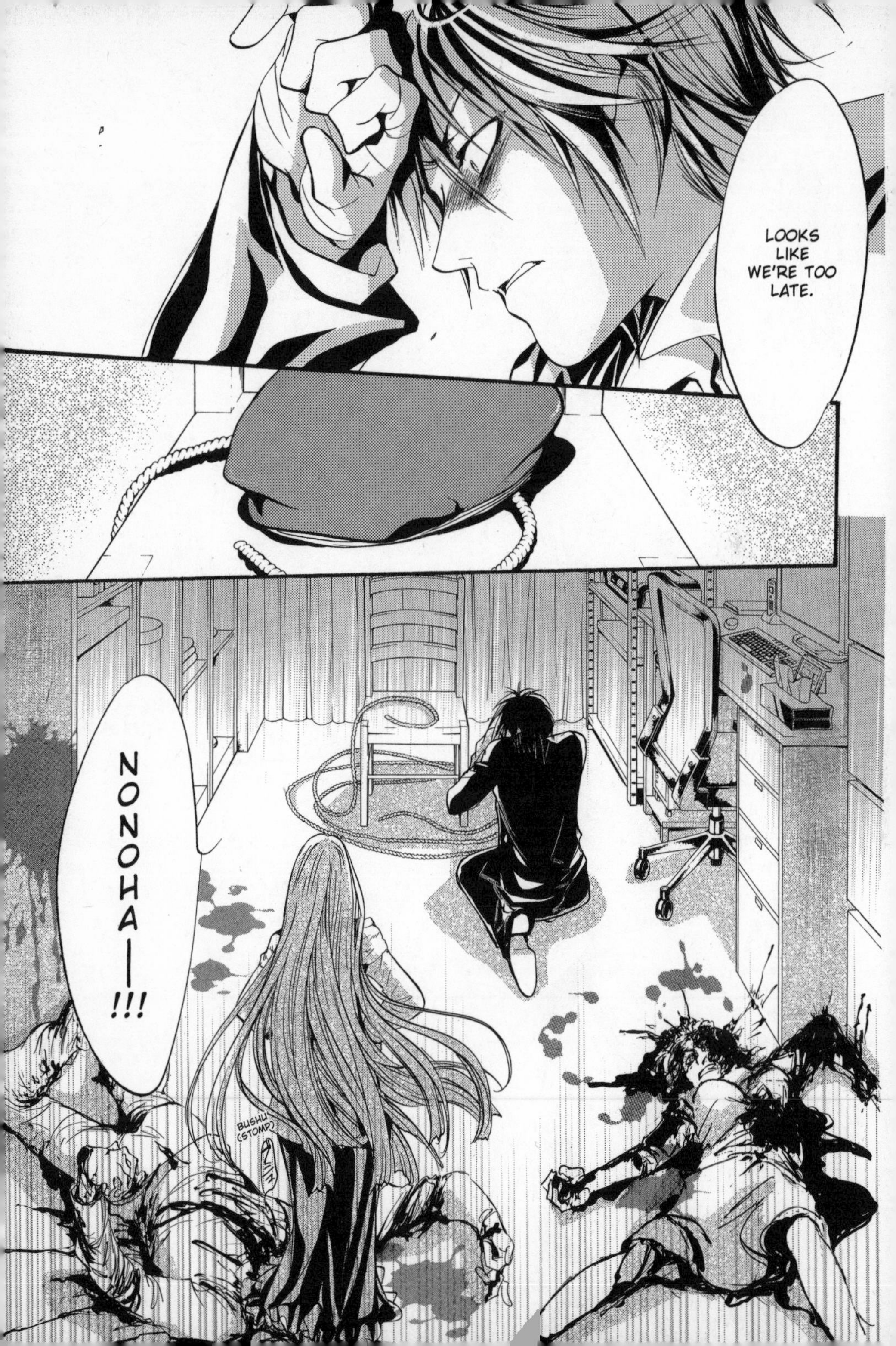
LOOKS LIKE WE'RE TOO LATE.
NONOHA—!!!
BUSHU (STOMP)

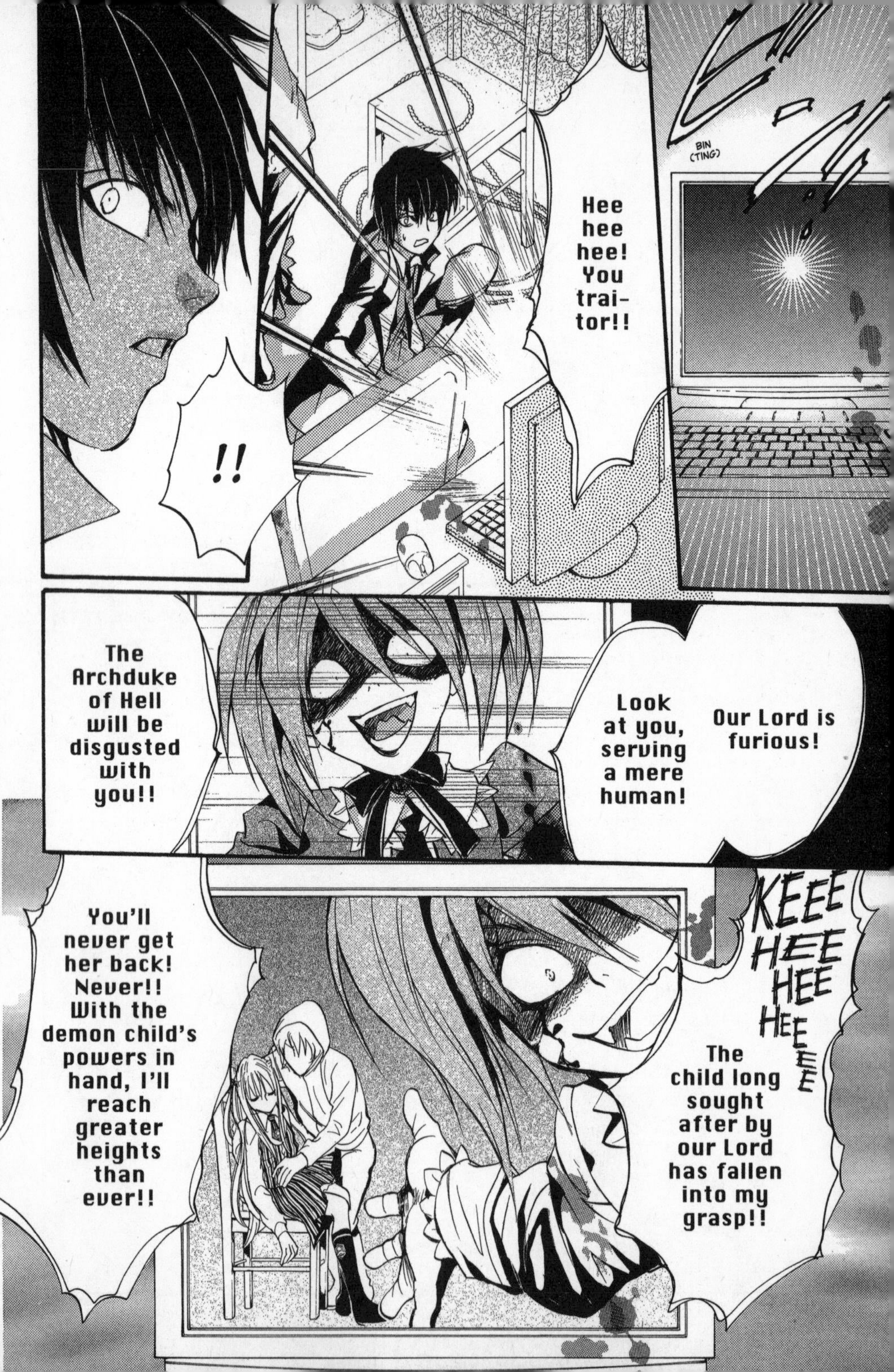
BIN (TING)
Hee hee hee! You trai- tor!!
!!
Our Lord is furious!
Look at you, serving a mere human!
The Archduke of Hell will be disgusted with you!!
KEEE HEE HEE HEEEEE
The child long sought after by our Lord has fallen into my grasp!!
You'll never get her back! Never!! With the demon child's powers in hand, I'll reach greater heights than ever!!

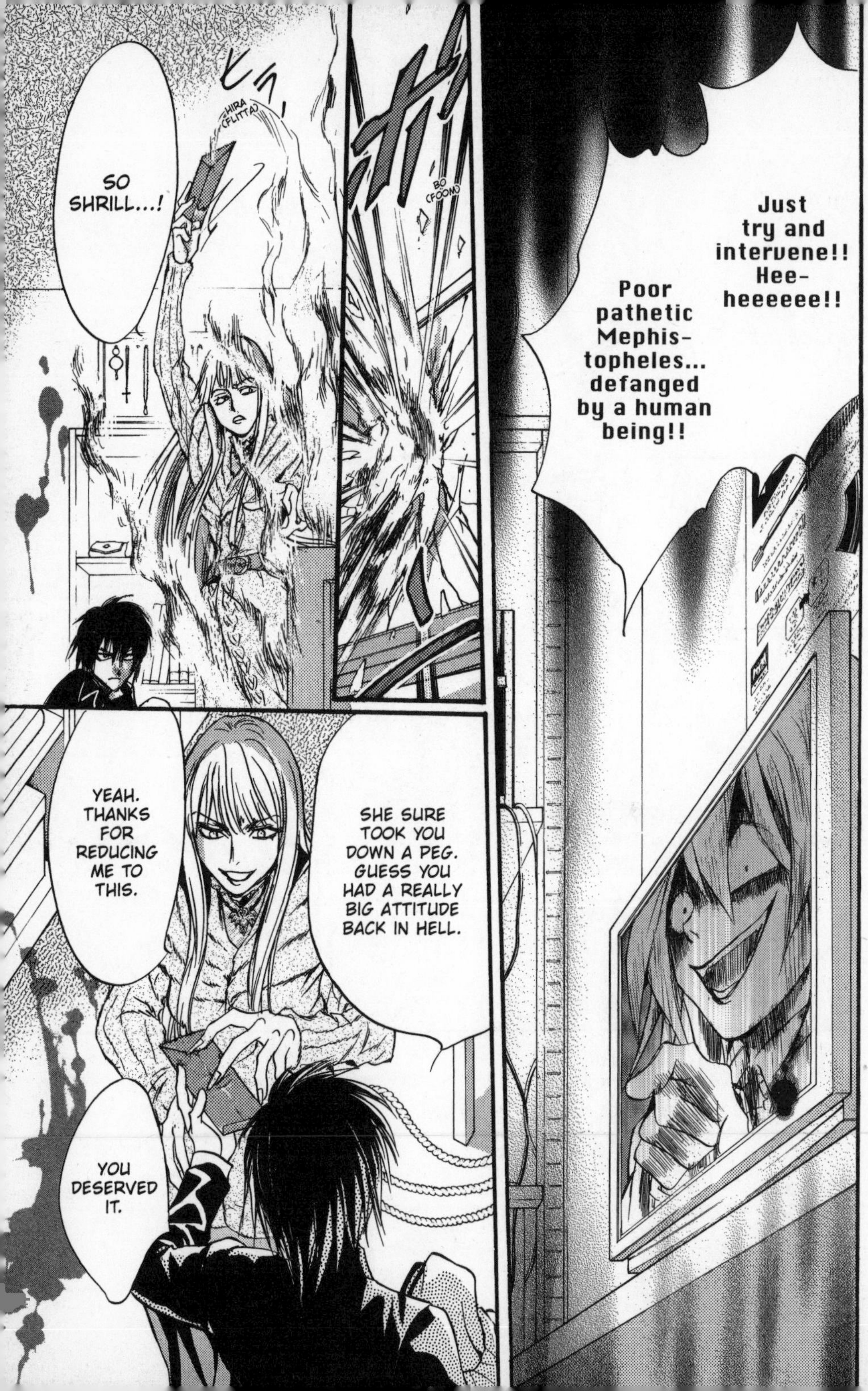
Just try and intervene!! Hee-heeeeee!!
Poor pathetic Mephistopheles... defanged by a human being!!
BO (FOOM)
HIRA (FLITTA)
SO SHRILL...!
SHE SURE TOOK YOU DOWN A PEG. GUESS YOU HAD A REALLY BIG ATTITUDE BACK IN HELL.
YEAH. THANKS FOR REDUCING ME TO THIS.
YOU DESERVED IT.

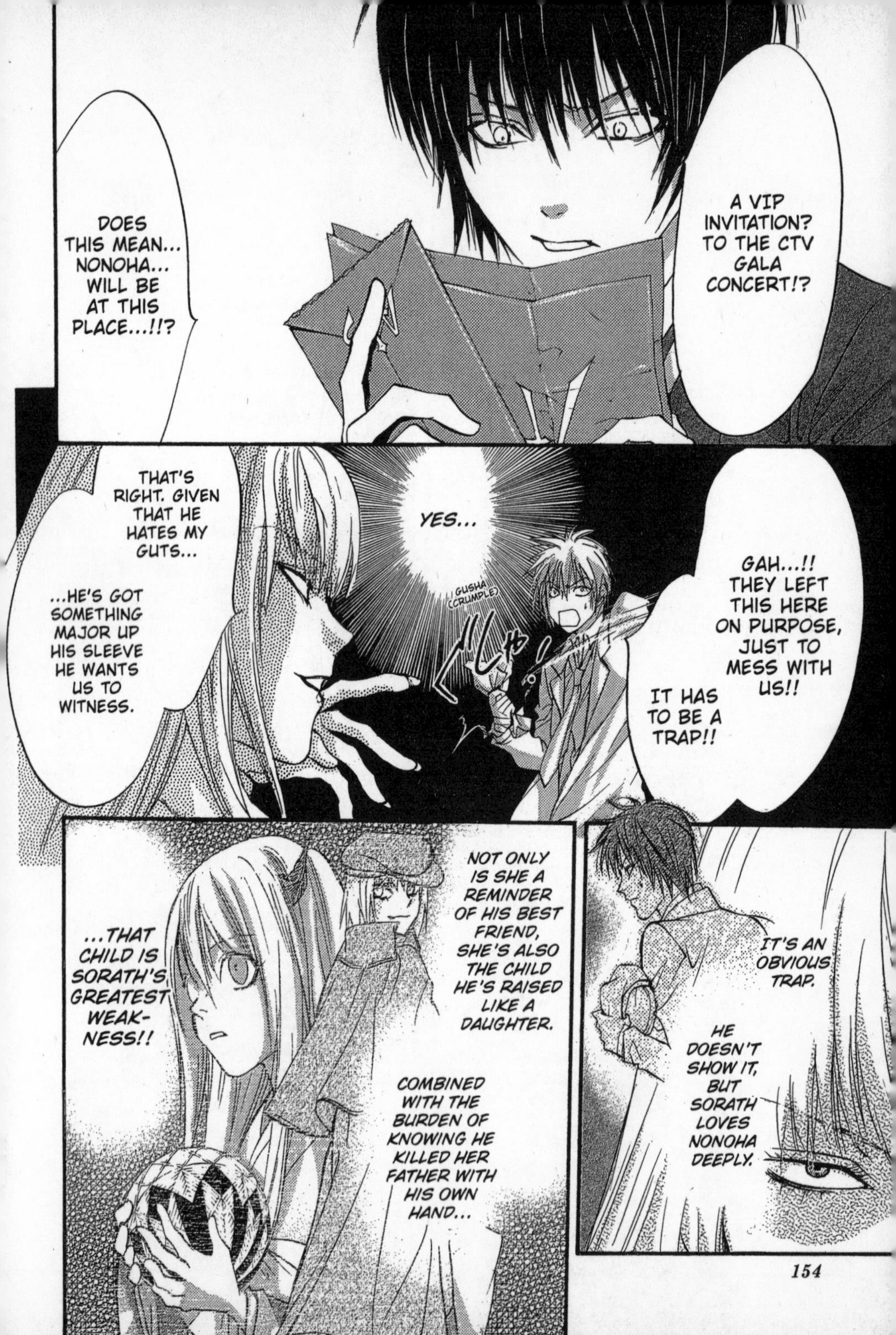
A VIP INVITATION? TO THE CTV GALA CONCERT!?
DOES THIS MEAN... NONOHA... WILL BE AT THIS PLACE...!!?
GAH...!! THEY LEFT THIS HERE ON PURPOSE, JUST TO MESS WITH US!!
IT HAS TO BE A TRAP!!
GUSHA (CRUMPLE)
YES...
THAT'S RIGHT. GIVEN THAT HE HATES MY GUTS...
...HE'S GOT SOMETHING MAJOR UP HIS SLEEVE HE WANTS US TO WITNESS.
IT'S AN OBVIOUS TRAP.
HE DOESN'T SHOW IT, BUT SORATH LOVES NONOHA DEEPLY.
NOT ONLY IS SHE A REMINDER OF HIS BEST FRIEND, SHE'S ALSO THE CHILD HE'S RAISED LIKE A DAUGHTER.
...THAT CHILD IS SORATH'S GREATEST WEAK-NESS!!
COMBINED WITH THE BURDEN OF KNOWING HE KILLED HER FATHER WITH HIS OWN HAND...

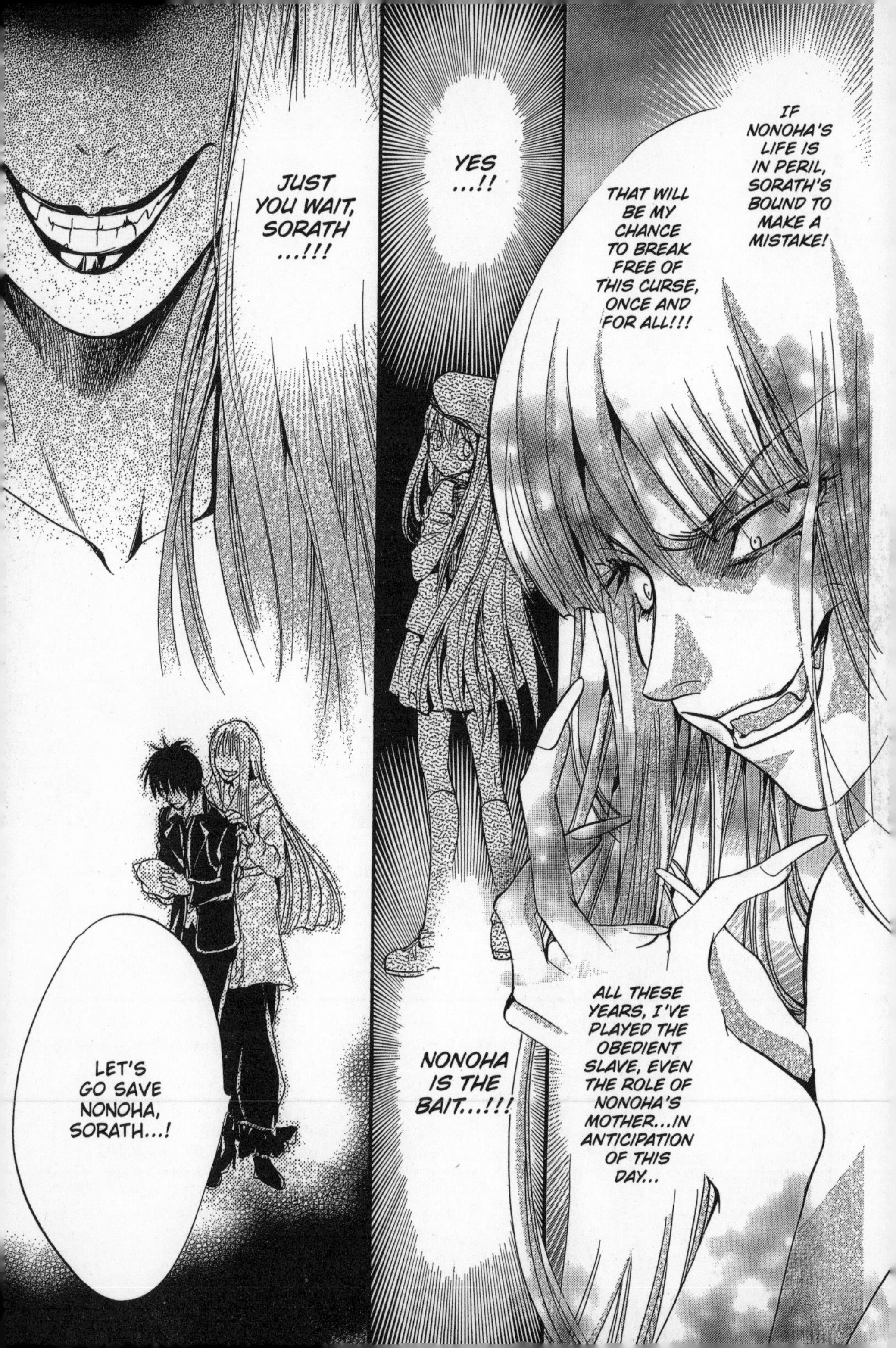
IF NONOHA'S LIFE IS IN PERIL, SORATH'S BOUND TO MAKE A MISTAKE!
THAT WILL BE MY CHANCE TO BREAK FREE OF THIS CURSE, ONCE AND FOR ALL!!!
ALL THESE YEARS, I'VE PLAYED THE OBEDIENT SLAVE, EVEN THE ROLE OF NONOHA'S MOTHER...IN ANTICIPATION OF THIS DAY...
NONOHA IS THE BAIT...!!!
YES ...!!
JUST YOU WAIT, SORATH ...!!!
LET'S GO SAVE NONOHA, SORATH...!

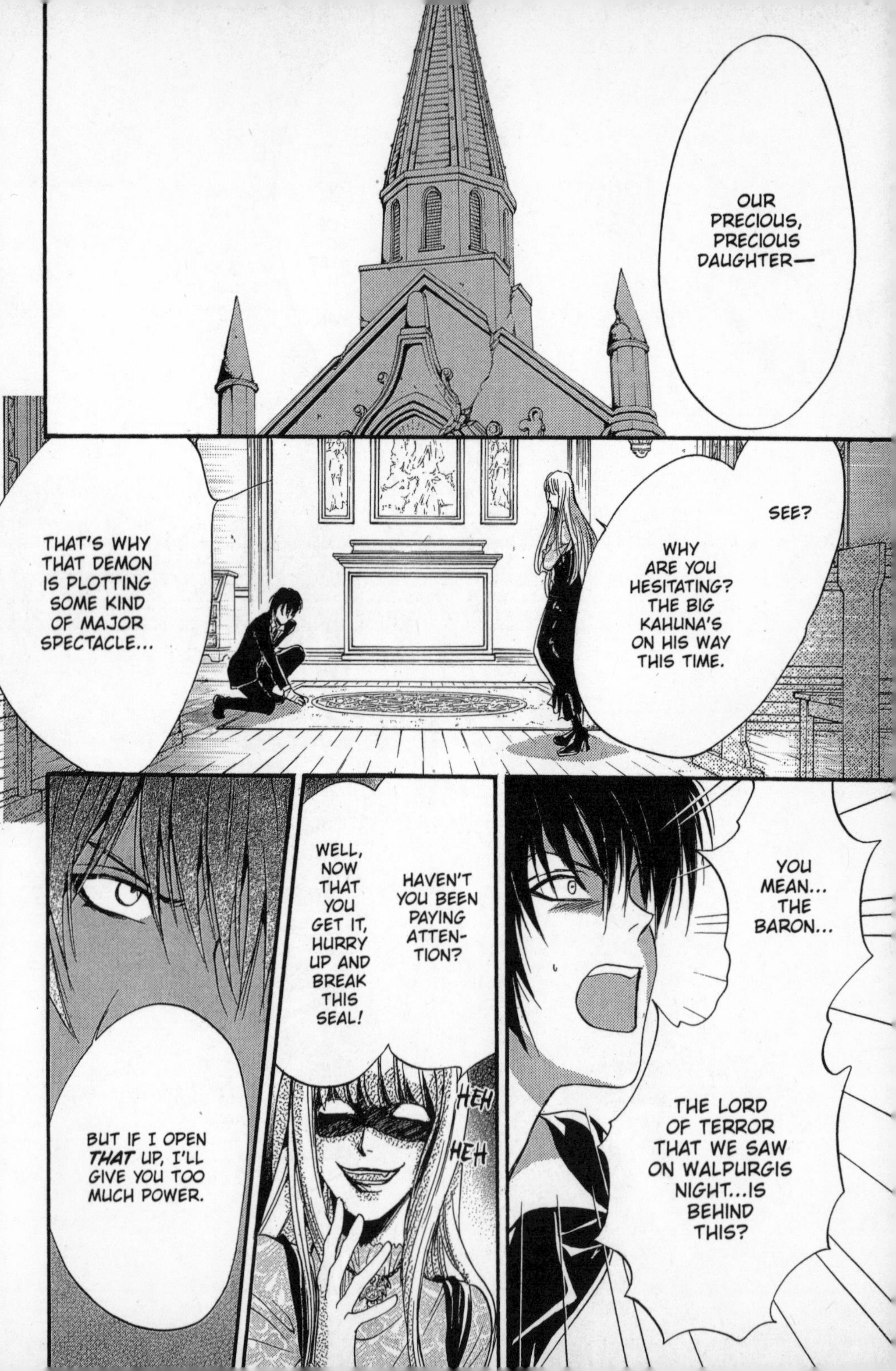
OUR PRECIOUS, PRECIOUS DAUGHTER—
SEE?
WHY ARE YOU HESITATING? THE BIG KAHUNA'S ON HIS WAY THIS TIME.
THAT'S WHY THAT DEMON IS PLOTTING SOME KIND OF MAJOR SPECTACLE...
YOU MEAN... THE BARON...
THE LORD OF TERROR THAT WE SAW ON WALPURGIS NIGHT...IS BEHIND THIS?
HAVEN'T YOU BEEN PAYING ATTENTION?
WELL, NOW THAT YOU GET IT, HURRY UP AND BREAK THIS SEAL!
HEH HEH
BUT IF I OPEN *THAT* UP, I'LL GIVE YOU TOO MUCH POWER.

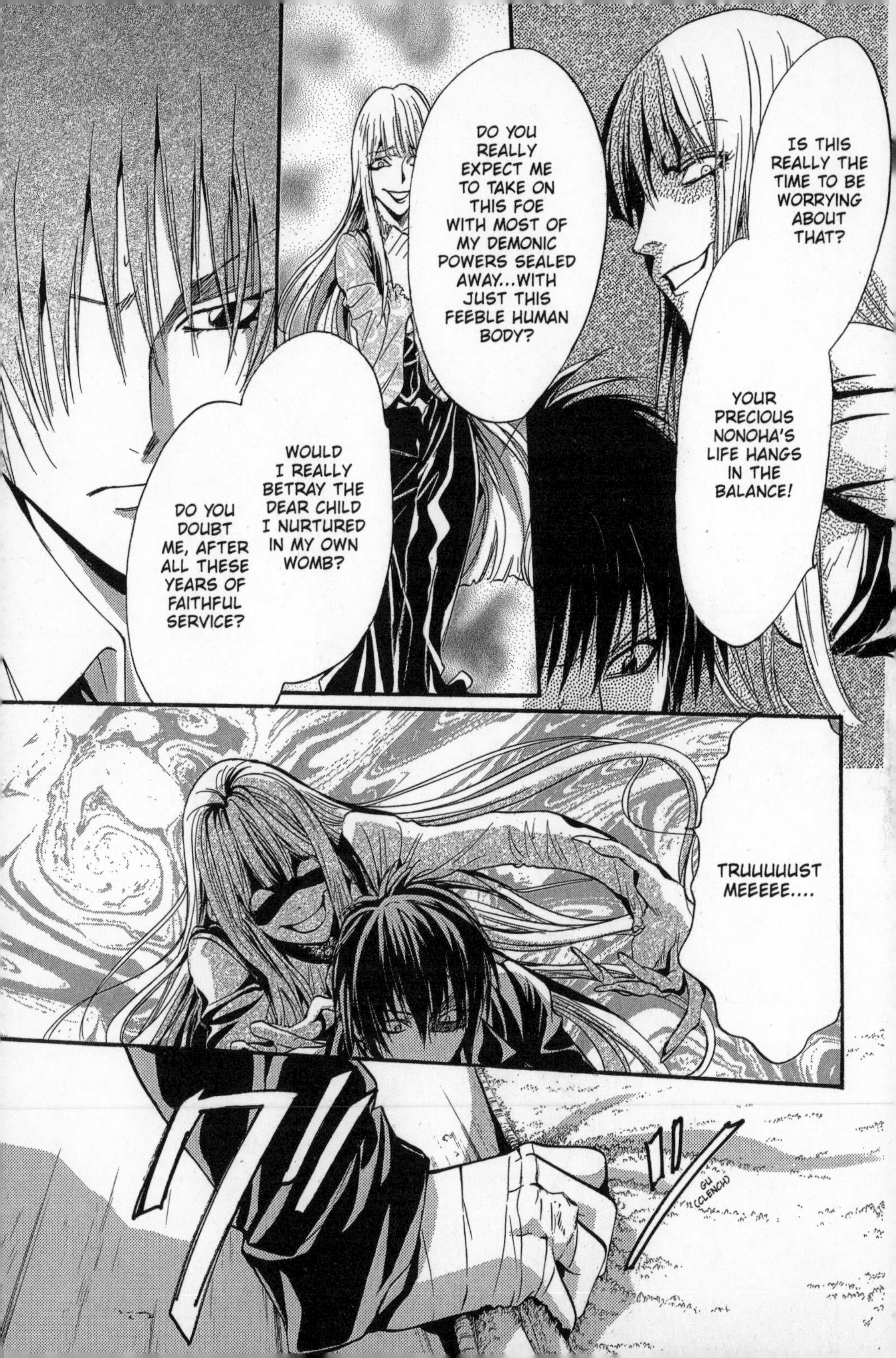
IS THIS REALLY THE TIME TO BE WORRYING ABOUT THAT?
YOUR PRECIOUS NONOHA'S LIFE HANGS IN THE BALANCE!
DO YOU REALLY EXPECT ME TO TAKE ON THIS FOE WITH MOST OF MY DEMONIC POWERS SEALED AWAY...WITH JUST THIS FEEBLE HUMAN BODY?
WOULD I REALLY BETRAY THE DEAR CHILD I NURTURED IN MY OWN WOMB?
DO YOU DOUBT ME, AFTER ALL THESE YEARS OF FAITHFUL SERVICE?
TRUUUUUST MEEEEE....
GU (CLENCH)

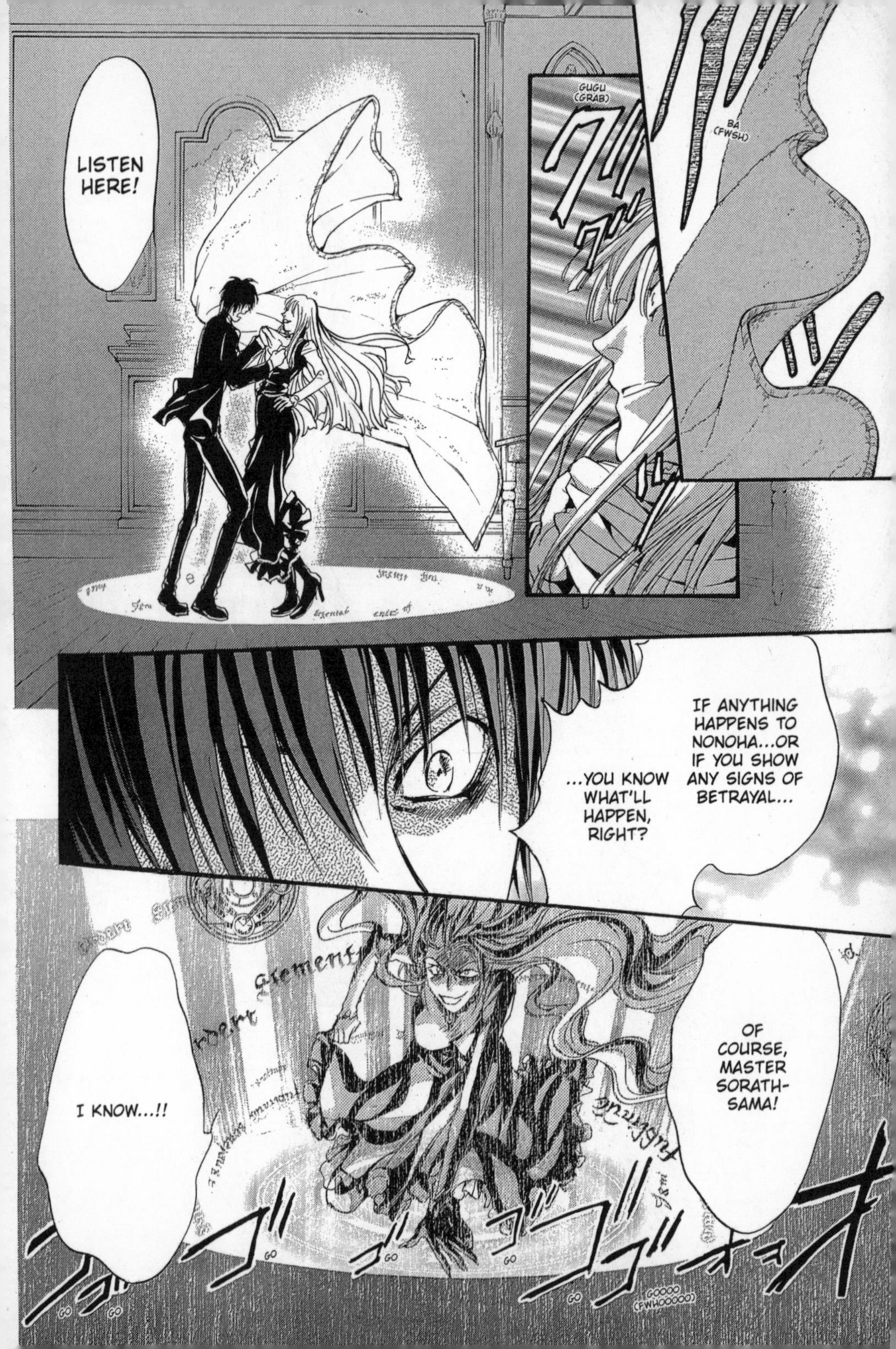
BA (FWSH)
GUGU (GRAB)
LISTEN HERE!
IF ANYTHING HAPPENS TO NONOHA...OR IF YOU SHOW ANY SIGNS OF BETRAYAL...
...YOU KNOW WHAT'LL HAPPEN, RIGHT?
OF COURSE, MASTER SORATH-SAMA!
I KNOW...!!
GOOOO (FWHOOOOO)
GO
GO
GO
GO
GO

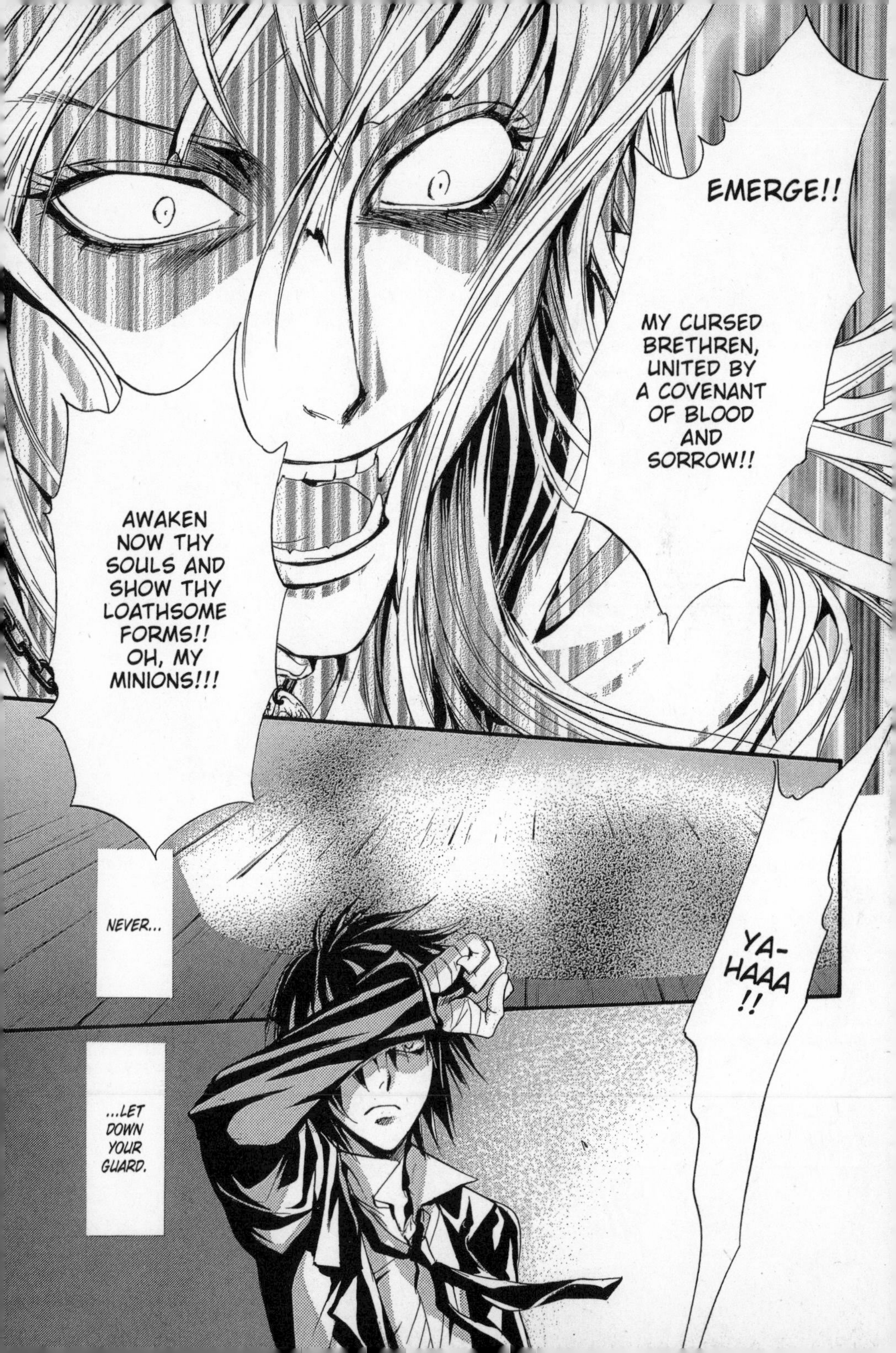
EMERGE!!
MY CURSED BRETHREN, UNITED BY A COVENANT OF BLOOD AND SORROW!!
AWAKEN NOW THY SOULS AND SHOW THY LOATHSOME FORMS!! OH, MY MINIONS!!!
YA-HAAA!!
NEVER...
...LET DOWN YOUR GUARD.

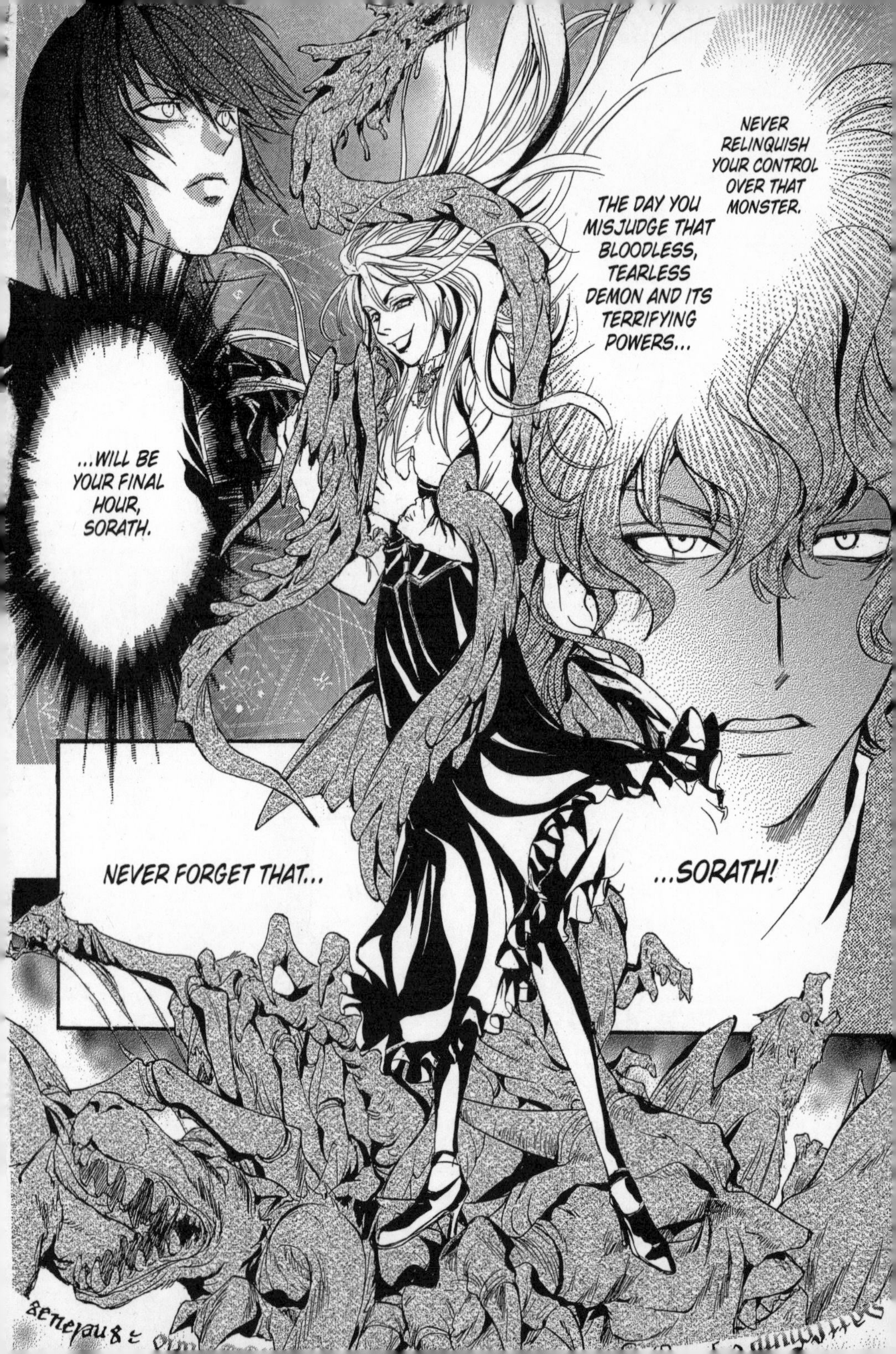
NEVER RELINQUISH YOUR CONTROL OVER THAT MONSTER.
THE DAY YOU MISJUDGE THAT BLOODLESS, TEARLESS DEMON AND ITS TERRIFYING POWERS...
...WILL BE YOUR FINAL HOUR, SORATH.
NEVER FORGET THAT... ...SORATH!

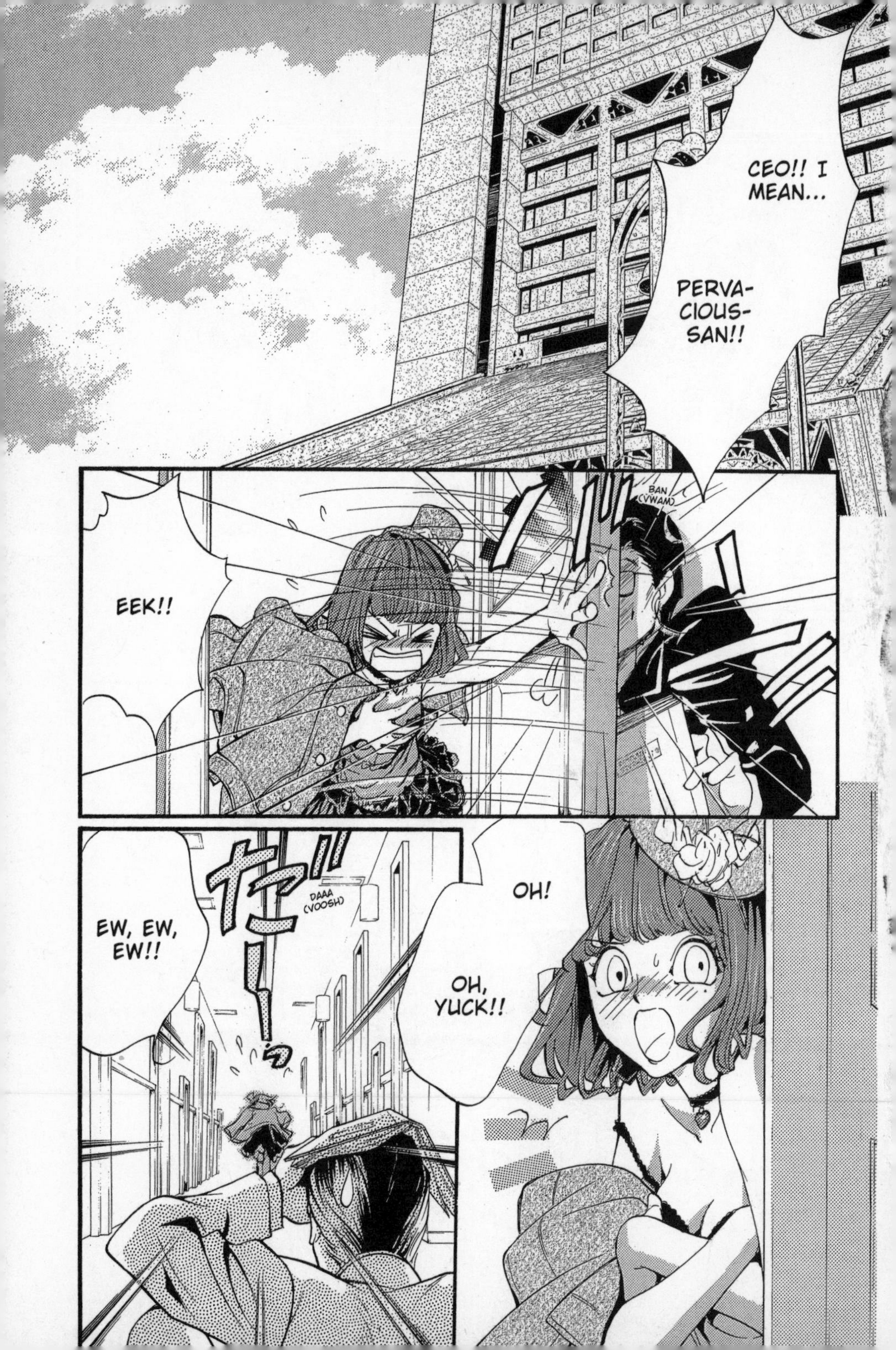
CEO!! I MEAN...
PERVACIOUS-SAN!!
BAN (VWAM)
EEK!!
OH!
OH, YUCK!!
DAAA (VOOSH)
EW, EW, EW!!

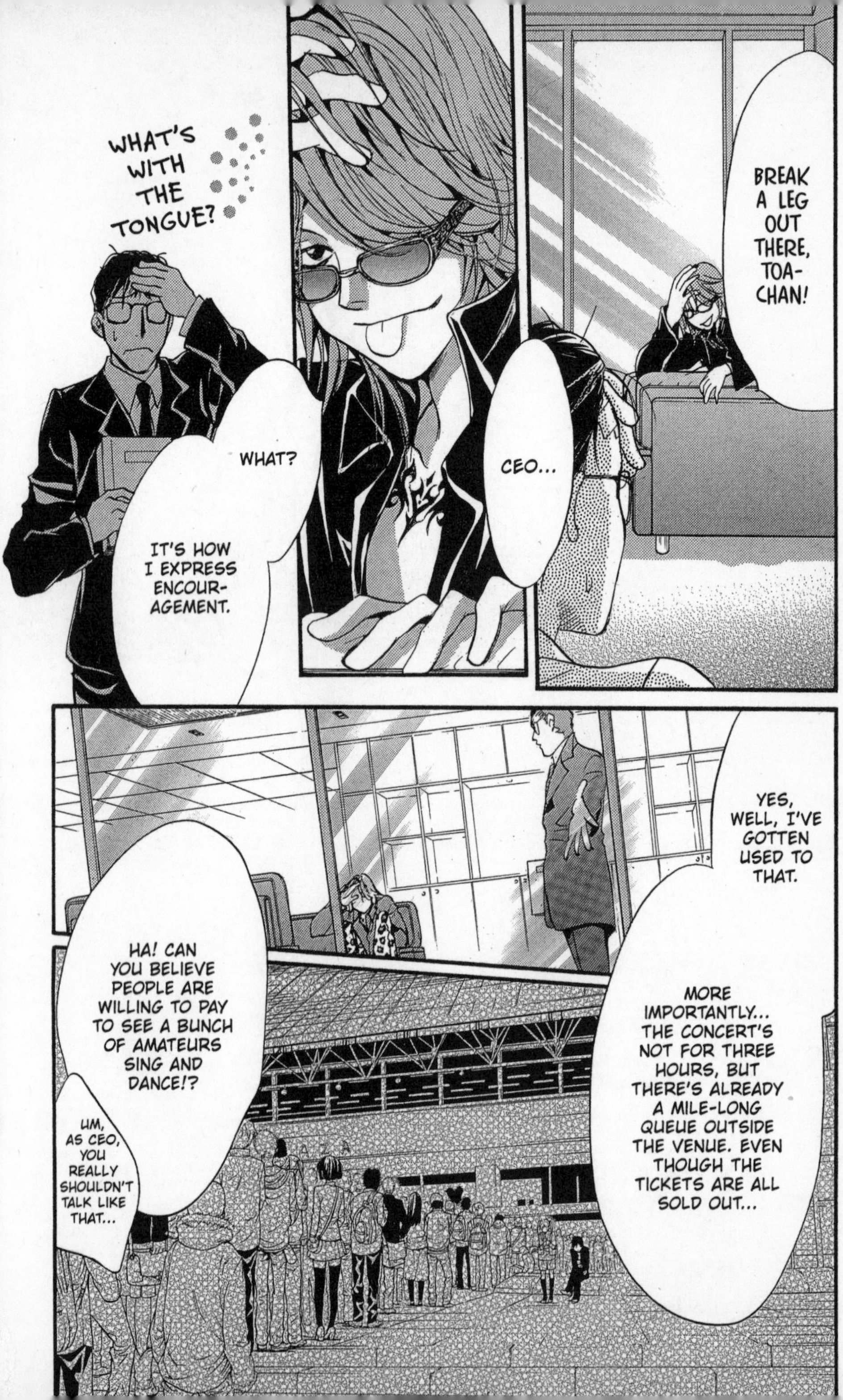
BREAK A LEG OUT THERE, TOA-CHAN!
CEO...
WHAT?
WHAT'S WITH THE TONGUE?
IT'S HOW I EXPRESS ENCOURAGEMENT.
YES, WELL, I'VE GOTTEN USED TO THAT.
MORE IMPORTANTLY... THE CONCERT'S NOT FOR THREE HOURS, BUT THERE'S ALREADY A MILE-LONG QUEUE OUTSIDE THE VENUE. EVEN THOUGH THE TICKETS ARE ALL SOLD OUT...
HA! CAN YOU BELIEVE PEOPLE ARE WILLING TO PAY TO SEE A BUNCH OF AMATEURS SING AND DANCE!?
UM, AS CEO, YOU REALLY SHOULDN'T TALK LIKE THAT...

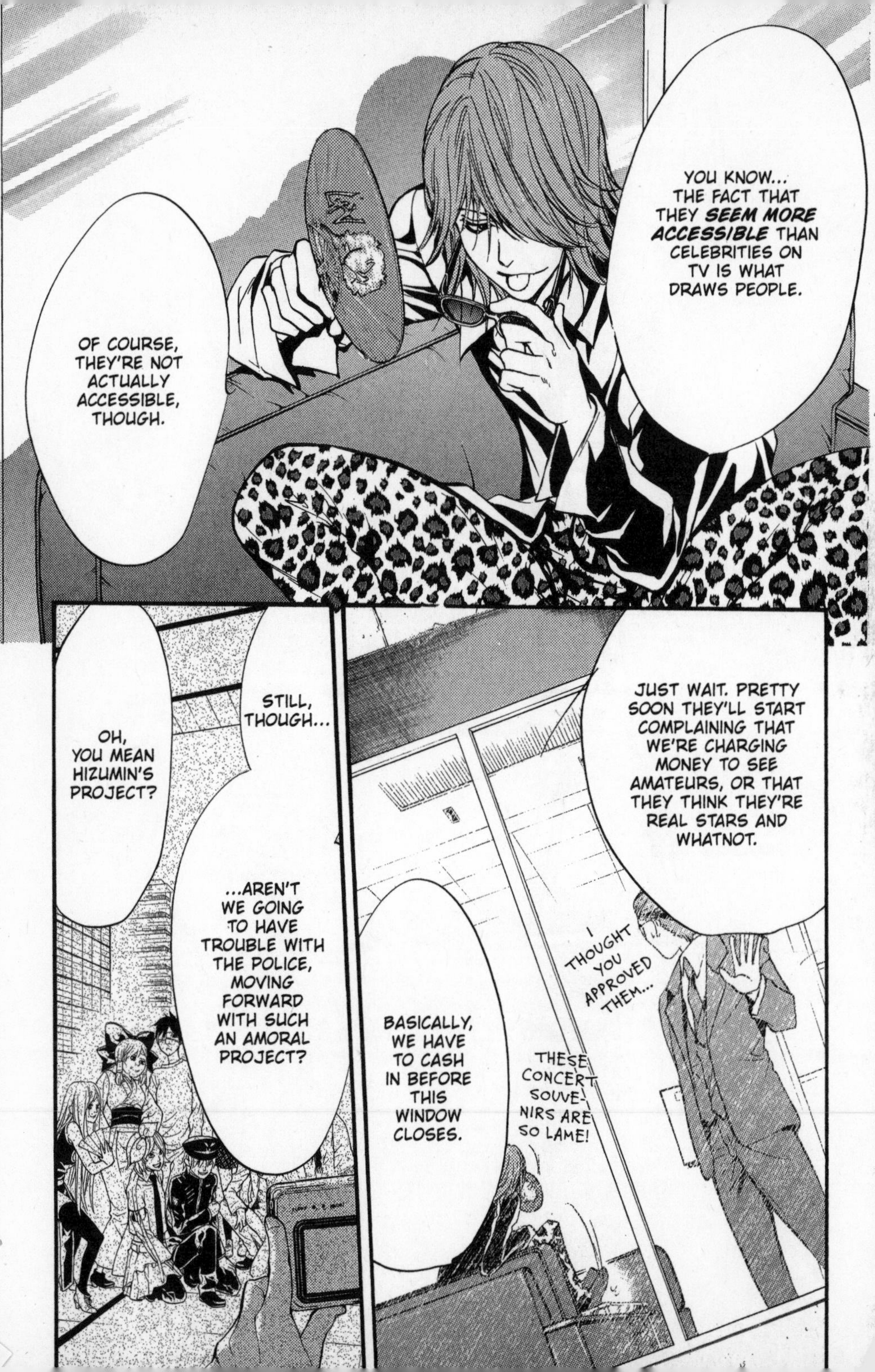
YOU KNOW... THE FACT THAT THEY ***SEEM MORE ACCESSIBLE*** THAN CELEBRITIES ON TV IS WHAT DRAWS PEOPLE.
OF COURSE, THEY'RE NOT ACTUALLY ACCESSIBLE, THOUGH.
JUST WAIT. PRETTY SOON THEY'LL START COMPLAINING THAT WE'RE CHARGING MONEY TO SEE AMATEURS, OR THAT THEY THINK THEY'RE REAL STARS AND WHATNOT.
I THOUGHT YOU APPROVED THEM...
BASICALLY, WE HAVE TO CASH IN BEFORE THIS WINDOW CLOSES.
THESE CONCERT SOUVE-NIRS ARE SO LAME!
STILL, THOUGH...
OH, YOU MEAN HIZUMIN'S PROJECT?
...AREN'T WE GOING TO HAVE TROUBLE WITH THE POLICE, MOVING FORWARD WITH SUCH AN AMORAL PROJECT?

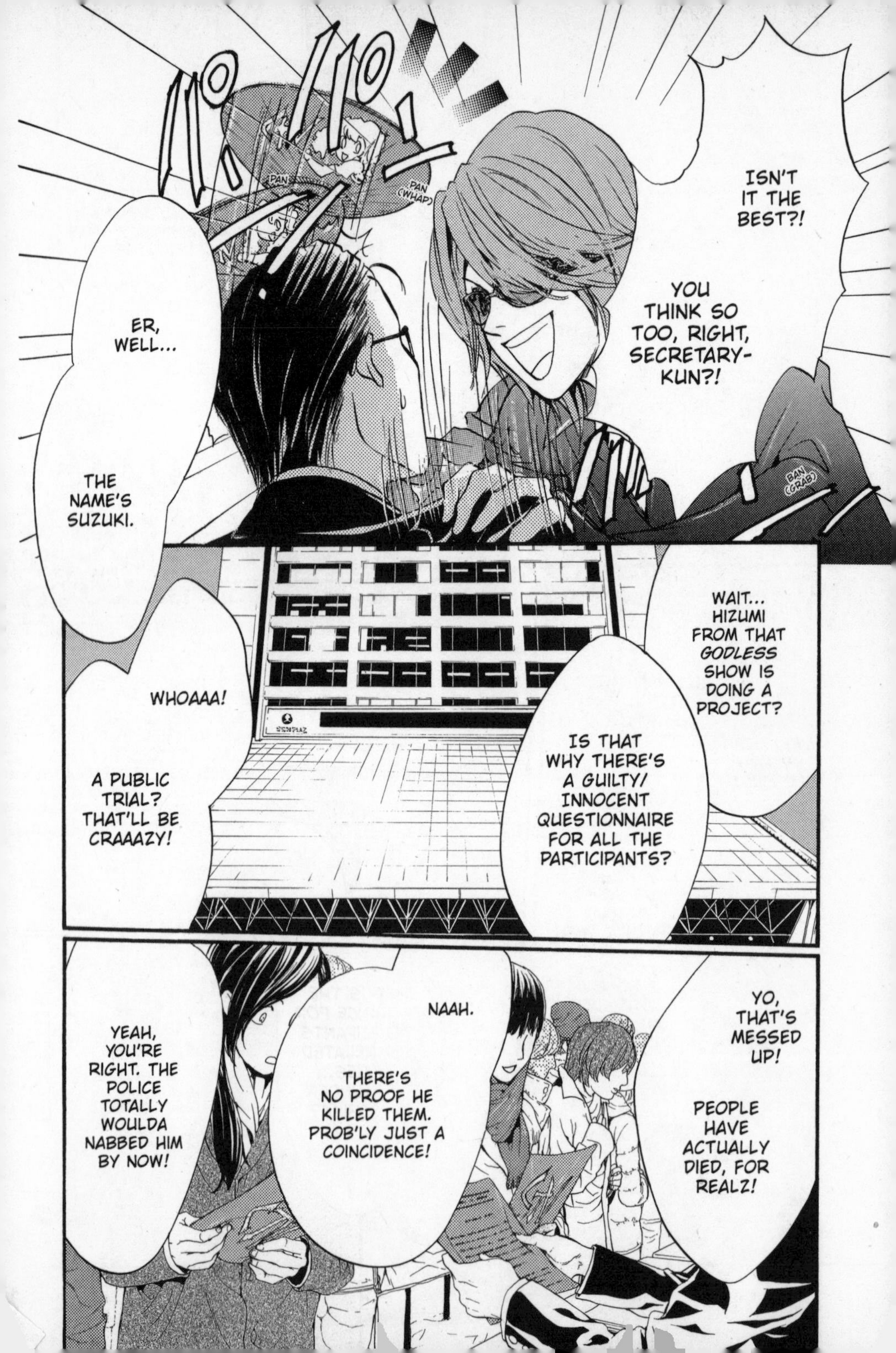
ISN'T IT THE BEST?!
YOU THINK SO TOO, RIGHT, SECRETARY-KUN?!
BAN (GRAB)
PAN (WHAP)
PAN
ER, WELL...
THE NAME'S SUZUKI.
WAIT... HIZUMI FROM THAT *GODLESS* SHOW IS DOING A PROJECT?
IS THAT WHY THERE'S A GUILTY/INNOCENT QUESTIONNAIRE FOR ALL THE PARTICIPANTS?
WHOAAA!
A PUBLIC TRIAL? THAT'LL BE CRAAAZY!
YO, THAT'S MESSED UP!
PEOPLE HAVE ACTUALLY DIED, FOR REALZ!
NAAH.
THERE'S NO PROOF HE KILLED THEM. PROB'LY JUST A COINCIDENCE!
YEAH, YOU'RE RIGHT. THE POLICE TOTALLY WOULDA NABBED HIM BY NOW!

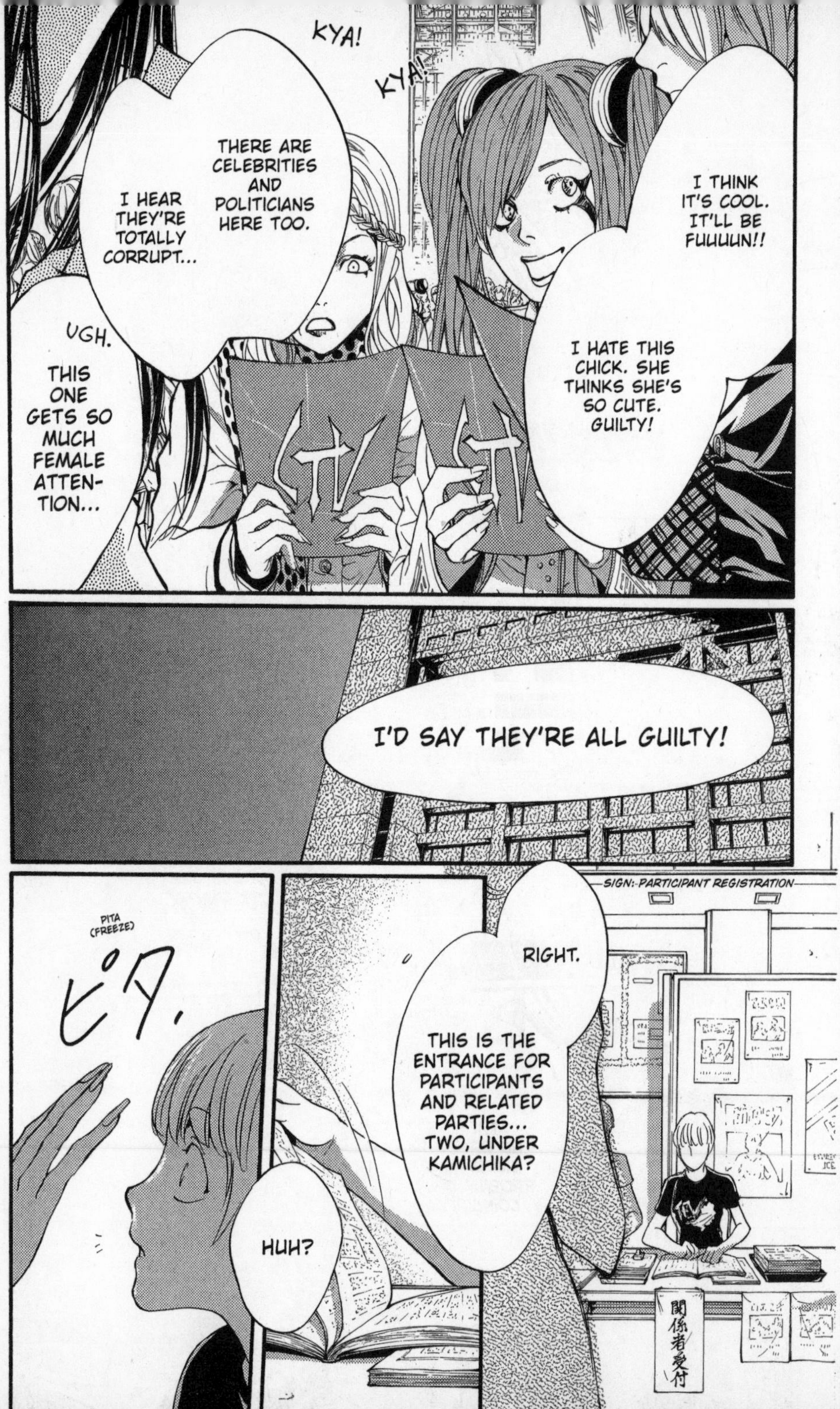
KYA!
KYA!
I THINK IT'S COOL. IT'LL BE FUUUUN!!
I HATE THIS CHICK. SHE THINKS SHE'S SO CUTE. GUILTY!
THERE ARE CELEBRITIES AND POLITICIANS HERE TOO.
I HEAR THEY'RE TOTALLY CORRUPT...
UGH.
THIS ONE GETS SO MUCH FEMALE ATTENTION...
I'D SAY THEY'RE ALL GUILTY!
SIGN: PARTICIPANT REGISTRATION
関係者受付
RIGHT.
THIS IS THE ENTRANCE FOR PARTICIPANTS AND RELATED PARTIES... TWO, UNDER KAMICHIKA?
HUH?
PITA (FREEZE)
ピタ.

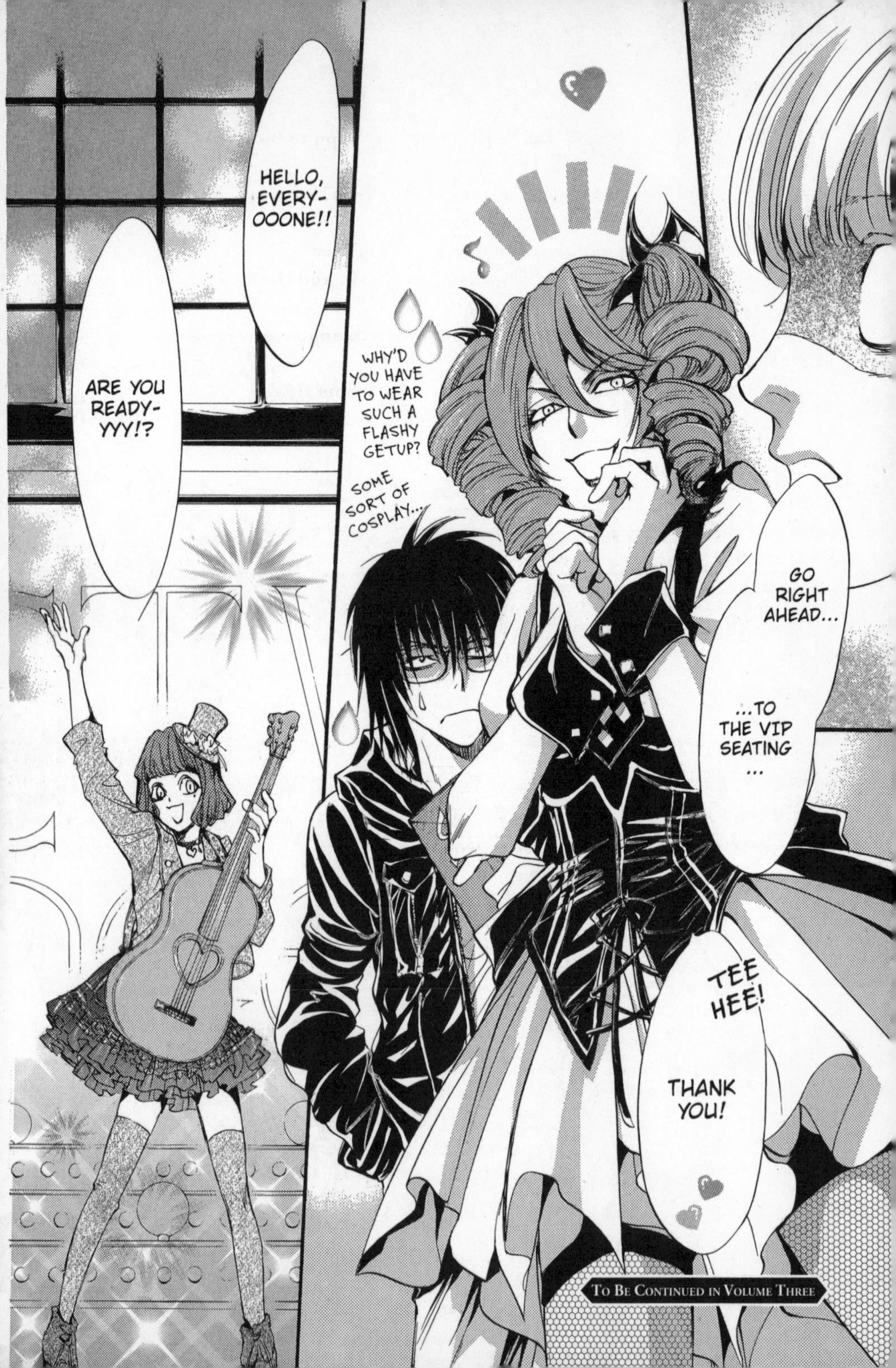
GO RIGHT AHEAD...
...TO THE VIP SEATING ...
TEE HEE!
THANK YOU!
WHY'D YOU HAVE TO WEAR SUCH A FLASHY GETUP?
SOME SORT OF COSPLAY...
HELLO, EVERY-OOONE!!
ARE YOU READY-YYY!?
TO BE CONTINUED IN VOLUME THREE

Afterword

A terrible tragedy has befallen Japan, but I'm happy to be here with all of you again.
I have no words to express my condolences towards those affected by the earthquake.
In Volume 2, our story enters a new Modern Day Arc.
Actually, the Taisho Era Arc was really Episode 0, and the true story starts now.
The video site in the story has nothing to do with any real video sites, just so you know.
I hope you enjoy the Modern Day Arc of *Demon from Afar*.

Kaori Yuki

Official site: UnDER GARDEN
http://www.yukikaori.jp
Twitter: @angelaid
(as of July 7, 2011)
(Japanese only)

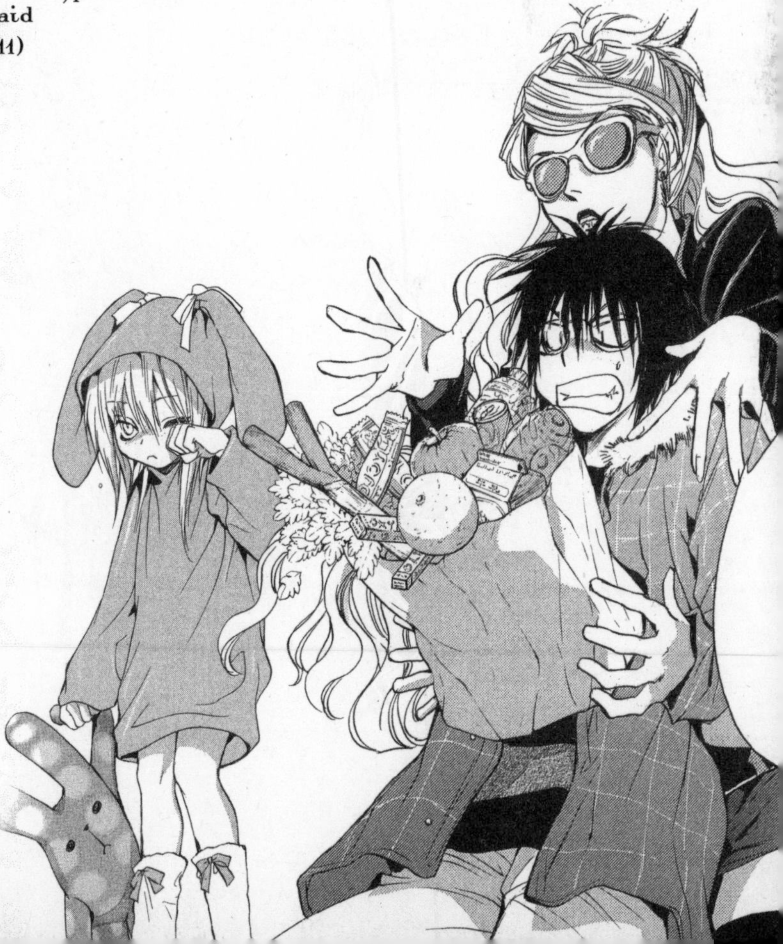

Translation Notes

COMMON HONORIFICS:

no honorific: Indicates familiarity or closeness; if used without permission or reason, addressing someone in this manner would constitute an insult.

-san: The Japanese equivalent of Mr./Mrs./Miss. If a situation calls for politeness, this is the fail-safe honorific.

-sama: Conveys great respect; may also indicate that the social status of the speaker is lower than that of the addressee.

-kun: Used most often when referring to boys, this indicates affection or familiarity. Occasionally used by older men among their peers, but it may also be used by anyone referring to a person of lower standing.

-chan: An affectionate honorific indicating familiarity used mostly in reference to girls; also used in reference to cute persons or animals of either gender.

onee: Japanese term for "older sister."

onii: Japanese term for "older brother."

PAGE 50
Hizumi: Translates to "warped" in Japanese.

PAGE 57
demon children: Changelings. Children who don't resemble their parents.

DEMON
FROM
AFAR

DEMON
FROM
AFAR

VOLUME
3

READ ON FOR A SNEAK PEAK
OF THE NEXT VOLUME,
ON SALE MAY 2015!

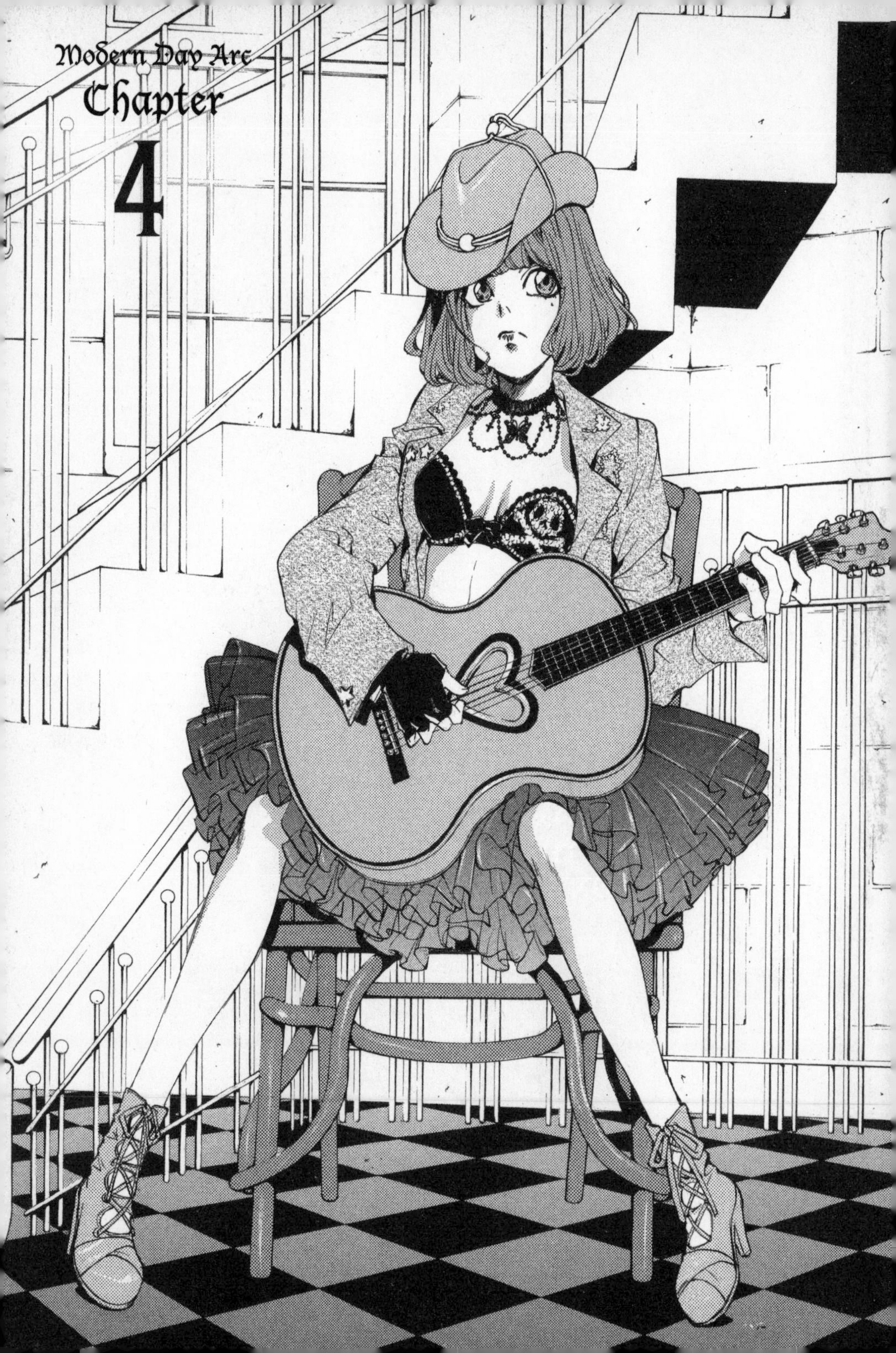
Modern Day Arc
Chapter
4

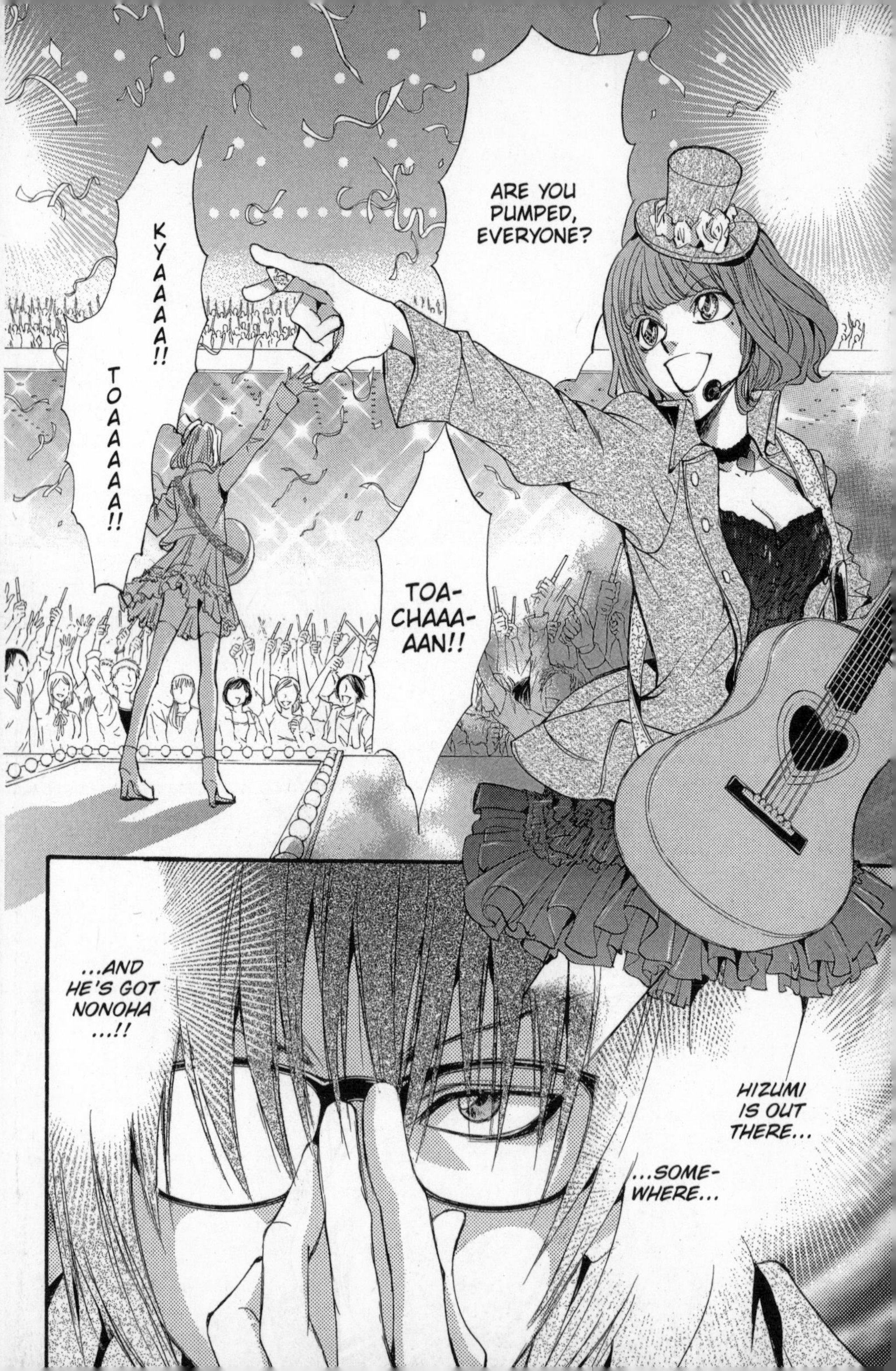
ARE YOU PUMPED, EVERYONE?
TOA-CHAAAA-AAN!!
KYAAAAA!!
TOAAAAAAA!!
HIZUMI IS OUT THERE...
...SOME-WHERE...
...AND HE'S GOT NONOHA ...!!

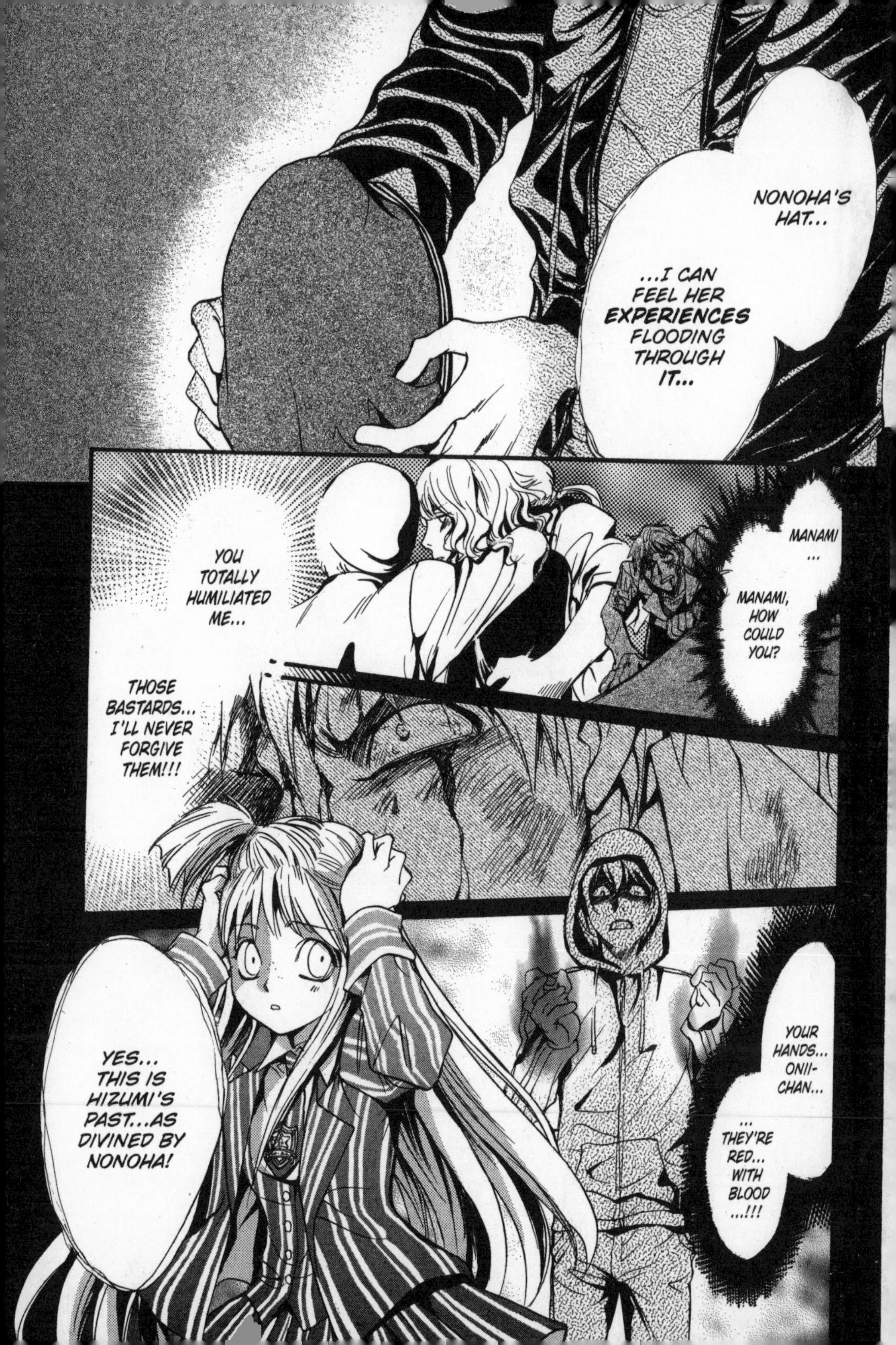
NONOHA'S HAT...
...I CAN FEEL HER EXPERIENCES FLOODING THROUGH IT...
MANAMI ...
MANAMI, HOW COULD YOU?
YOU TOTALLY HUMILIATED ME...
THOSE BASTARDS... I'LL NEVER FORGIVE THEM!!!
YOUR HANDS... ONII-CHAN...
... THEY'RE RED... WITH BLOOD ...!!!
YES... THIS IS HIZUMI'S PAST...AS DIVINED BY NONOHA!

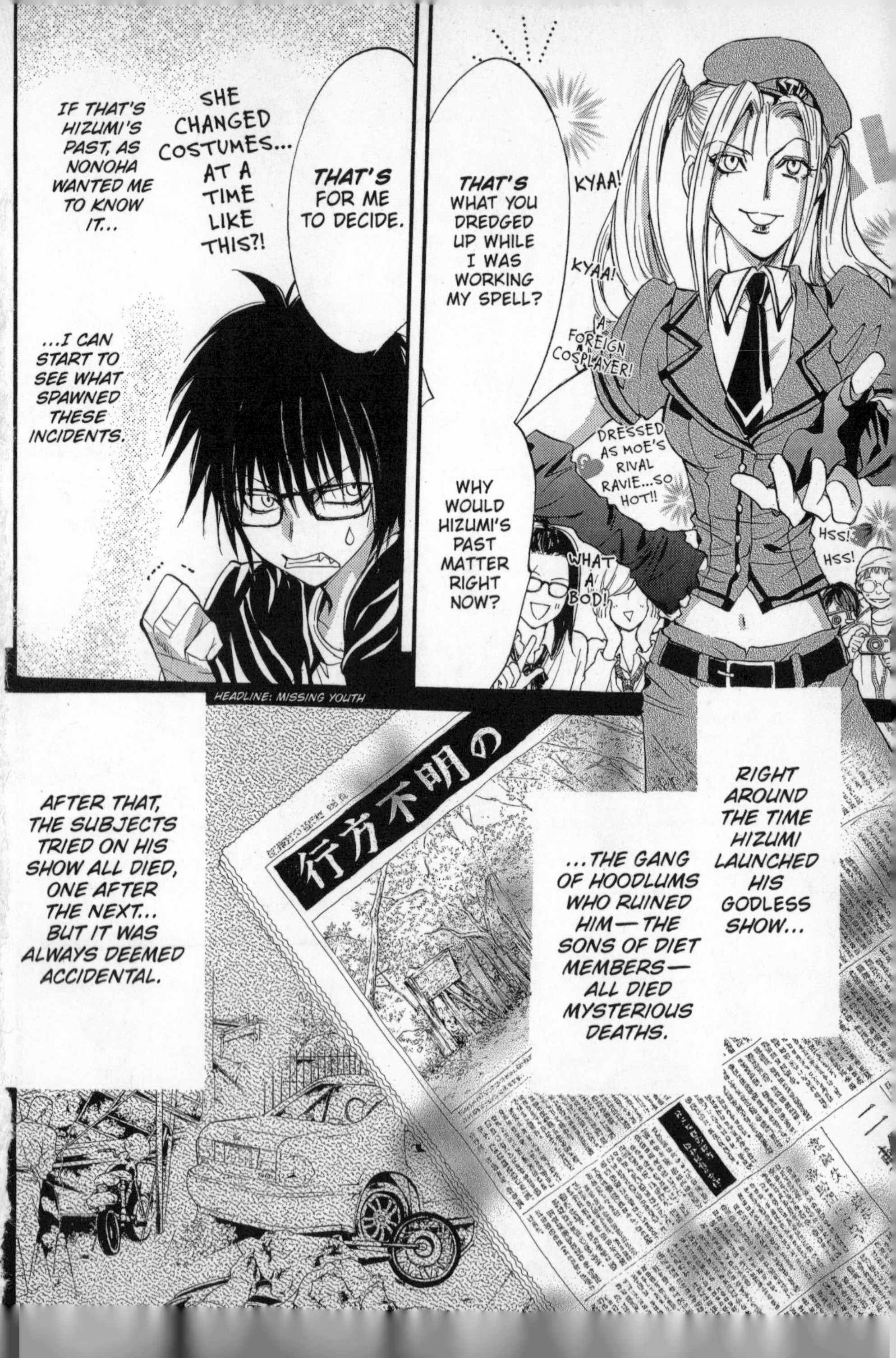
THAT'S WHAT YOU DREDGED UP WHILE I WAS WORKING MY SPELL?
KYAA!
KYAA!
A FOREIGN COSPLAYER!
DRESSED AS MOE'S RIVAL RAVIE...SO HOT!!
HSS! HSS!
WHY WOULD HIZUMI'S PAST MATTER RIGHT NOW?
WHAT A BOD!
THAT'S FOR ME TO DECIDE.
SHE CHANGED COSTUMES... AT A TIME LIKE THIS?!
IF THAT'S HIZUMI'S PAST, AS NONOHA WANTED ME TO KNOW IT...
...I CAN START TO SEE WHAT SPAWNED THESE INCIDENTS.
HEADLINE: MISSING YOUTH
行方不明の
RIGHT AROUND THE TIME HIZUMI LAUNCHED HIS GODLESS SHOW...
...THE GANG OF HOODLUMS WHO RUINED HIM—THE SONS OF DIET MEMBERS—ALL DIED MYSTERIOUS DEATHS.
AFTER THAT, THE SUBJECTS TRIED ON HIS SHOW ALL DIED, ONE AFTER THE NEXT... BUT IT WAS ALWAYS DEEMED ACCIDENTAL.

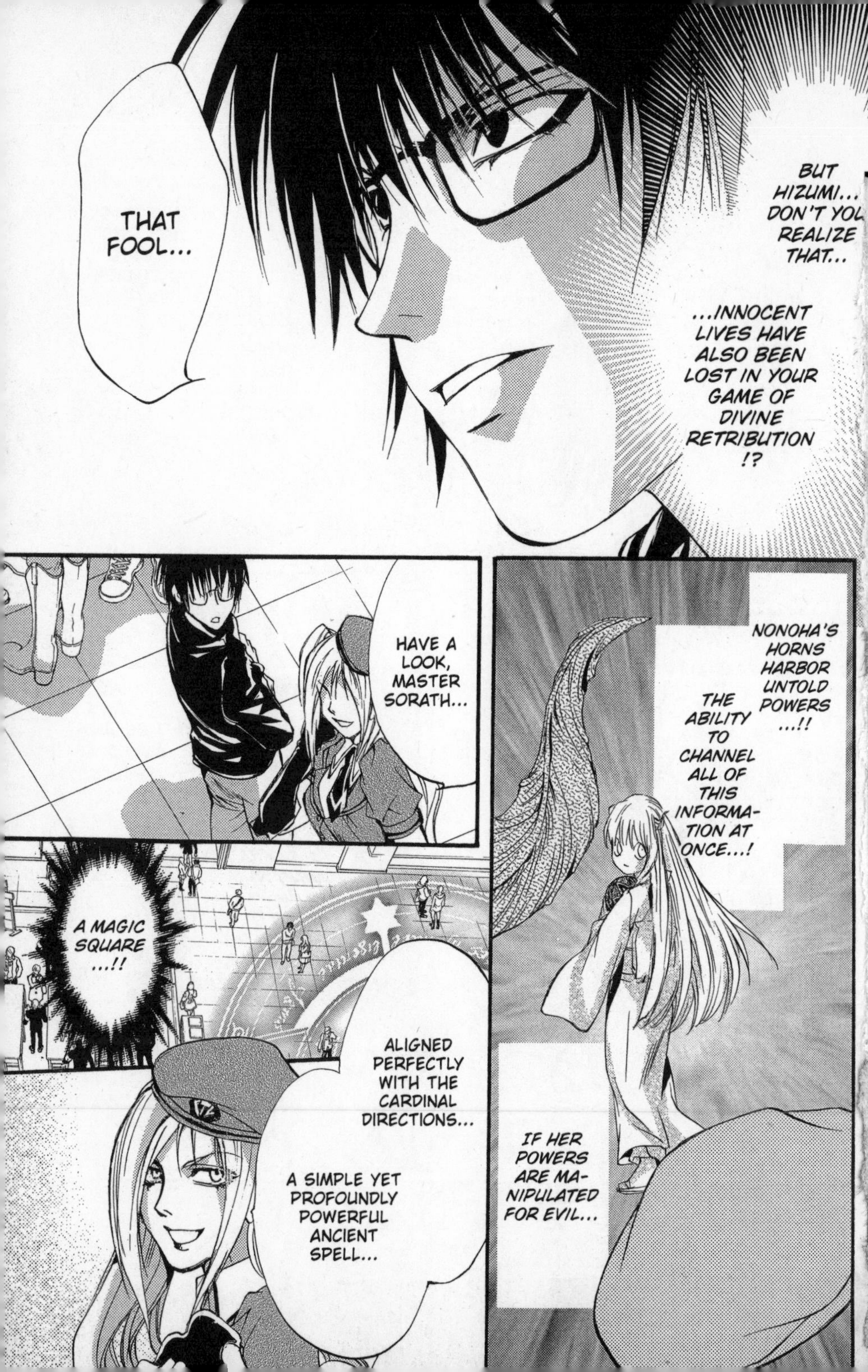

BUT HIZUMI... DON'T YOU REALIZE THAT...
...INNOCENT LIVES HAVE ALSO BEEN LOST IN YOUR GAME OF DIVINE RETRIBUTION !?
THAT FOOL...
NONOHA'S HORNS HARBOR UNTOLD POWERS ...!!
THE ABILITY TO CHANNEL ALL OF THIS INFORMATION AT ONCE...!
IF HER POWERS ARE MANIPULATED FOR EVIL...
HAVE A LOOK, MASTER SORATH...
A MAGIC SQUARE ...!!
ALIGNED PERFECTLY WITH THE CARDINAL DIRECTIONS...
A SIMPLE YET PROFOUNDLY POWERFUL ANCIENT SPELL...

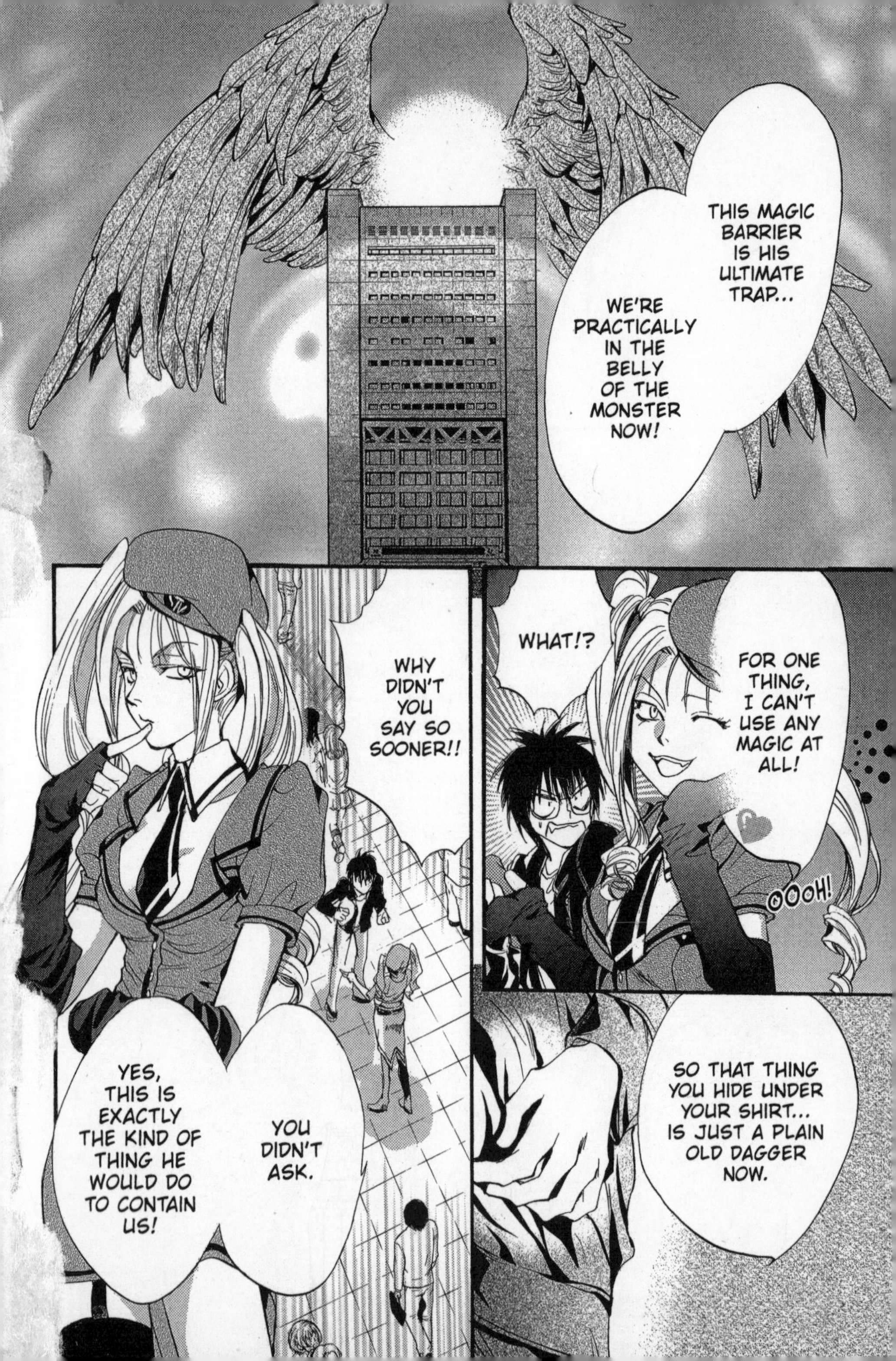
THIS MAGIC BARRIER IS HIS ULTIMATE TRAP...
WE'RE PRACTICALLY IN THE BELLY OF THE MONSTER NOW!
FOR ONE THING, I CAN'T USE ANY MAGIC AT ALL!
WHAT!?
OOOH!
SO THAT THING YOU HIDE UNDER YOUR SHIRT... IS JUST A PLAIN OLD DAGGER NOW.
WHY DIDN'T YOU SAY SO SOONER!!
YOU DIDN'T ASK.
YES, THIS IS EXACTLY THE KIND OF THING HE WOULD DO TO CONTAIN US!

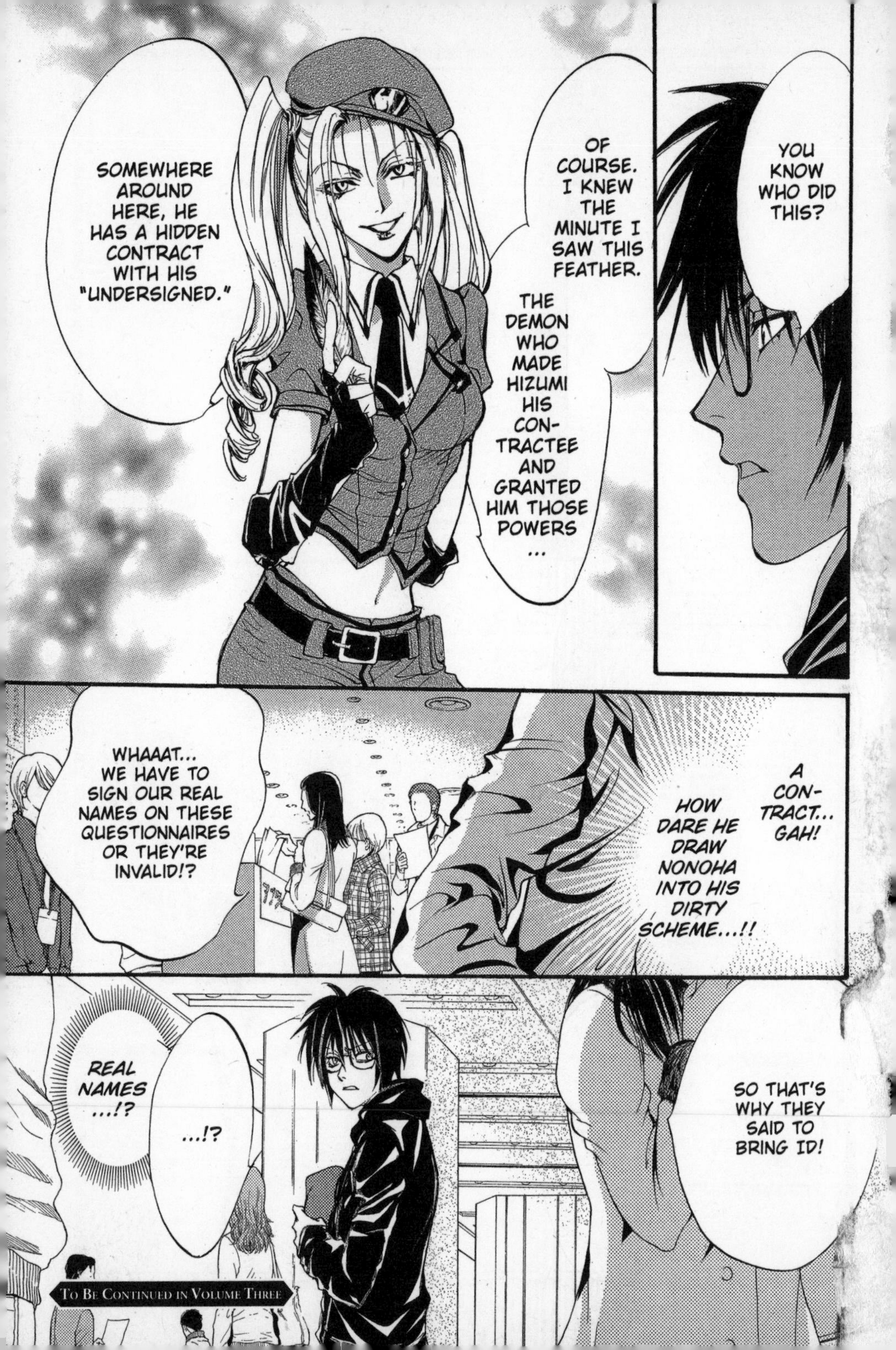
YOU KNOW WHO DID THIS?
OF COURSE. I KNEW THE MINUTE I SAW THIS FEATHER.
THE DEMON WHO MADE HIZUMI HIS CON-TRACTEE AND GRANTED HIM THOSE POWERS ...
SOMEWHERE AROUND HERE, HE HAS A HIDDEN CONTRACT WITH HIS "UNDERSIGNED."
A CON-TRACT... GAH!
HOW DARE HE DRAW NONOHA INTO HIS DIRTY SCHEME...!!
WHAAAT... WE HAVE TO SIGN OUR REAL NAMES ON THESE QUESTIONNAIRES OR THEY'RE INVALID!?
SO THAT'S WHY THEY SAID TO BRING ID!
...!?
REAL NAMES ...!?
To Be Continued in Volume Three

DEMON FROM AFAR 2

KAORI YUKI

Translation: Camellia Nieh   †   Lettering: Lys Blakeslee

IIKI NO KI
© 2011 Kaori Yuki. All rights reserved.
First published in Japan in 2011 by Kodansha Ltd., Tokyo. Publication rights for this English language edition arranged through Kodansha Ltd., Tokyo.

Translation © 2015 by Hachette Book Group, Inc.

Yen Press
Hachette Book Group
1290 Avenue of the Americas
New York, NY 10104

www.HachetteBookGroup.com
www.YenPress.com

Yen Press is an imprint of
Hachette Book Group, Inc.
The Yen Press name and logo are
trademarks of Hachette Book Group, Inc.

The publisher is not responsible for websites
(or their content) not owned by the publisher.

First Yen Press Edition: March 2015

ISBN: 978-0-316-38308-0

10 9 8 7 6 5 4 3 2 1

BVG

Printed in the United States of America

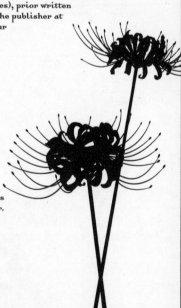